The Apotheosis of
Captain Cook

Captain James Cook, portrait by William Hodges

The Apotheosis of Captain Cook

*European Mythmaking
in the Pacific*

WITH A NEW AFTERWORD BY THE AUTHOR

Gananath Obeyesekere

PRINCETON UNIVERSITY PRESS

BISHOP MUSEUM PRESS

Copyright © 1992 by Princeton University Press
New preface and afterword copyright © 1997 by Princeton University Press
Published by Princeton University Press, 41 William Street,
Princeton, New Jersey 08540
In the United Kingdom: Princeton University Press, Chichester, West Sussex
In Hawai'i: Bishop Museum Press,
P.O. Box 19000-A, Honolulu, Hawai'i 96817

Library of Congress Cataloging-in-Publication Data

Obeyesekere, Gananath.
The apotheosis of Captain Cook : European mythmaking
in the Pacific / Gananath Obeyesekere
p.   cm.
Includes bibliographical references and index.
ISBN 0-691-05680-3 (Princeton University Press, cloth edition)
ISBN 0-691-05752-4 (Princeton University Press, paperback edition)
ISBN 0-930897-68-4 (Bishop Museum Press)
1. Hawaii—History—To 1893.   2. Hawaii—History—
To 1893—Historiography.   3. Cook, James, 1728–1779.   4. Polynesia—
Discovery and exploration.   5. Ethnology—Polynesia. I. Title.
DU626.O28   1992
996.9'02—dc20   91-42364

This book has been composed in Adobe Caslon

Princeton University Press books are printed on
acid-free paper, and meet the guidelines for permanence
and durability of the Committee on Production
Guidelines for Book Longevity of the
Council on Library Resources

First Princeton Paperback printing, 1994

http://pup.princeton.edu

Printed in the United States of America

3   5   7   9   10   8   6   4

A memorial for
Wijedasa

He shall break also the images of Beth-shē'-mĕsh,
that *is* in the land of Egypt; and the houses of the
Gods of the Egyptians he shall burn with fire.

Jeremiah 43:13

TABLE OF CONTENTS

CONTENTS

ILLUSTRATIONS

───────────────── ✣ ✣ ✣ ─────────────────

LIST OF ILLUSTRATIONS

PREFACE (1997)

——————————————— ❧❧ ———————————————

The Apotheosis of Captain Cook has had a remarkably controversial career. It was the subject of three published symposia, each containing criticisms from Pacific historians and ethnographers followed by my own responses.[1] It has been extensively reviewed in professional and popular journals. And recently, Marshall Sahlins has published his *How "Natives" Think: About Captain Cook, For Example,* a spirited and polemical counterattack on my criticisms of his work on Hawai'i. He is concerned primarily with the Hawai'ian end of the story rather than with my central theme of "European mythmaking in the Pacific." In this new edition, I have retorted with a detailed afterword that will make no sense unless the reader is familiar with Sahlins's book. The reader will also note that the afterword contains some material that has already been presented in the main text but recast and framed differently in order to meet Sahlins's criticisms. I think the issues that he and I raise are significant for the divergent ways in which we look at the human sciences. There is no final word on matters like this, but I am happy to have raised some serious methodological and ethical problems pertaining to the writing and construction of ethnography and the ways in which the native has been represented in our discipline. I ask the reader's patience if in the afterword I deal almost exclusively with Sahlins's work; my reactions to other critics have been dealt with in the symposia mentioned already, and these are easily available.

In general, I have found that literary critics and historians have been sympathetic to my work, but anthropologists have been harshly negative. This is not surprising because in the course of my book I am somewhat critical of my own discipline, though constructively, I hope. One Pacific ethnographer has suggested that I derived my idea of Cook's Kurtz persona after having seen the movie *Apocalypse Now,* a snide reference to my lack of education in English literature. (Ironically, I was trained in English literature before I became an anthropologist.) Another, writing in a professional journal, is surprised that *The New York Times* could have demeaned itself by reviewing such a bad book. Others have found that I have gratuitously attacked the great anthropological tradition that has emphasized "difference" and cultural relativism—which is quite true. Yet others have been upset because, like Sahlins, they have tended to idealize Cook. One can therefore expect Sahlins also to respond in a similar tone and manner in

How "Natives" Think. That work is stridently polemical and vituperative. I am dismayed that a leading thinker in our field has adopted this form of writing. I enjoyed the occasional good humor and puns, the rare *jouissance* in the text, which I can laugh at even though the jokes are at my expense. In general, it is difficult to respond to Sahlins's text without reacting to its style as well as its content. I have done both, though rather sparingly, and have put his words or phrases in quotation marks so that the reader will know that they constitute Sahlins's own language game turned on its head, as it were.

I have made only a few changes in the present edition, mostly correcting errors of fact which critics and friends have pointed out. I have also learned much from Sahlins's and others' criticisms, but I find it difficult to make serious changes in the body of my argument without recasting the whole book. For example, Sahlins and Valerio Valeri may well be right that I have minimized the important role of the Lono priests during Cook's visit and might have even skewed the genealogy of the other priest named Lono, alias Omiah. However, David Malo makes the point that the Lono priests were of an "inferior grade," whereas the priest Omiah whom Sahlins and Valeri have identified as a Lono priest, far from being of an inferior grade, was almost as sacred as the king himself.[2] Hence, settling issues of this sort are difficult and must await the work of future scholars. On the other hand, I am happy to acknowledge some of the criticisms pertaining to detail that Sahlins and others have pointed out. To give some examples: In the original edition I said that Sahlins interprets every single event during the Makahiki period as mythopraxis. This is my misreading of a footnote in his *Historical Metaphors,* and I have corrected it.[3] Sahlins also mentioned that the dismantling of the fence and images of the royal temple for firewood was not done by marines but ordinary sailors, and he is probably right, though the evidence is not unequivocal. Rob Borofsky points out that Cook did not "go round and round" the island of Hawai'i; he only went once.[4] Maybe he is right, though it matters little to the substance of my argument. Again, I did not adequately discriminate between Sahlins's use of the terms "stereotypic reproduction" and "mythopraxis," and I have now done so. Contrary to his denial, I still believe that Sahlins sees Hawai'ian history as "stereotypic reproduction" in such statements as the "capacity of Hawai'ian culture to reproduce itself as history" or "Hawai'ian culture would reproduce itself as history.[5]

I neither have the space nor the enthusiasm to respond to minor issues that Sahlins raises. It would take another book (and a tedious one) to deal with such issues and therefore I have deliberately ignored them, focusing instead on some of the more significant ones raised by him. As far as I am concerned, I want to close my argument with Sahlins with the afterword, at least for a while, and as far as the apotheosis of Cook is concerned.

Hawai'ian scholars and Polynesianists can take over from here. In the earlier edition, I had promised the reader a larger work that will include a psychoanalytic study of Cook, but I am afraid this work has to be postponed or abandoned. Instead, the controversy aroused by my book has provoked me to embark on another Cook book that deals with the representation of "cannibalism" in the wake of the discovery of Polynesia. This work will take up and further develop the methodological and theoretical issues raised here, though on a substantively different level. I have published several papers on this topic already and will give the reader a brief glimpse of this research in the afterword.[6]

In conclusion, I want to acknowledge the help of friends who have helped me with the revised edition and gave generously of their time and effort. Larry Rosen, John Charlot, and Ranjini Obeyesekere read the text in its entirety and made invaluable comments. I acknowledge with gratitude the help rendered by my friends and colleagues Jeanette Mageo, William Hamlin, Kerry Howe, Lisa Wynn, Julie Taylor, Jeannette Hoorn, Karen Peacock, and George Marcus. Finally, I must thank my patient editor, Mary Murrell, and Carol Zanca and Gail Vielbig in the anthropology department who assisted in this project in a multitude of ways.

NOTES

1. Gananath Obeyesekere, "Anthropology and the Cook Myth: A Response to Critics," *Social Analysis* (December 1993): 70–85; Valerio Valeri, review of *The Apotheosis of Captain Cook*, *Pacific Studies*, 17 (2) (1994): 103–55; Rob Borofsky, "Cook, Lono, Obeyesekere and Sahlins," *Current Anthropology* 38, no. 2 (April 1997): 255–82.
2. David Malo, *Hawai'ian Antiquities*, trans. Nathaniel B. Emerson (1898) (Honolulu: Bernice P. Bishop Museum, 1992), p. 159.
3. Marshall Sahlins, *Historical Metaphors and Mythical Realities: Structure in the Early History of the Sandwich Islands Kingdom* (Ann Arbor: University of Michigan Press, 1981), p. 74.
4. Borofsky, "Cook, Lono, Obeyesekere and Sahlins."
5. Sahlins, *Historical Metaphors*, pp. 12, 50.
6. "British Cannibals: Contemplation of an Event in the Death and Resurrection of James Cook, Explorer," in *Identities*, special issue, *Critical Inquiry* (June 1992), ed. Henry Louis Gates, Jr., and Anthony Appiah; "Cannibal Feasts in Nineteenth-Century Fiji: Seamens' Yarns and the Ethnographic Imagination," in *Cannibalism and the Colonial World*, Francis Barker, Peter Hulme, and Margeret Iverson, eds. (Cambridge: Cambridge University Press, forthcoming).

PREFACE

This book deals with an important episode in both European and Polynesian cultural history and imagination, namely, the apotheosis and later transfiguration of the famous European explorer Captain James Cook. I have worked intensively on the logs and journals pertaining to Cook's voyages. These are my primary resource. I also have had to deal with the Hawaiian past. Not being a Polynesianist, I am conscious of treading uncertain ground. In part I am ashamed to confess that I have not visited any of the places in Polynesia that Cook so meticulously mapped. Only belatedly, after writing the first draft of this book, did I visit the place where Cook first landed in Hawai'i, Kealakekua Bay, and also the site of the temple (*heiau*) where he was ceremonially received as a god. There is no particular design to this avoidance, only a lack of time combined with academic impecuniousness.

In the course of working on this project, I have been in debt to various friends, colleagues, and institutions. The National Humanities Center invited me to be a Mellon Foundation Fellow for the year 1989–90. I thank the Mellon Foundation and the Center for providing me the time and facilities to write up this material, and my own University for generously advancing my sabbatical. At the center itself, I benefited from the intellectual stimulation of "fellow fellows" and that of Robert Connor, the center's director, whenever we met at lunch. The research was facilitated by the fantastic efficiency of the library staff and other staff people. I especially thank Karen Carroll and Linda Morgan, who typed endless versions of my Cook material and Kent Mullikin, who was a quiet, unobtrusive presence ministering to our academic needs.

The writing of this book required archival research in London. This was made possible by a Distinguished Visitor Fellowship at the London School of Economics offered by the Suntory-Toyota International Centre for Economics and Related Disciplines (STICERD). I must thank my friends at the L.S.E. for this wonderful opportunity and Ioan Lewis and Maurice Bloch for their generous hospitality and intellectual stimulation. Jonathan Parry and Chris Fuller not only read drafts of some important chapters but also, along with Margaret Parry, Penny Logan, Jonathan and Julia Spencer, Liz Nissan and Jock Stirrat, and James and Judy Brow, conspired to make our stay particularly memorable. Charles Hallisey was good enough to recheck archival material for me after I had left London.

My wife, Ranjini, was both a critical reader and a calming presence at every stage of writing this book.

Ethnography is a peculiar enterprise. You can speak of people with some amount of authority only if you have done fieldwork in that area. Historians and other scholars do not confront this problem, for it is assumed that the societies they study can be known through primary and secondary sources. I think our ethnographic self-arrogation is an illusion, for as far as Polynesia is concerned, there is no way one could become an ethnographer of a past that barely exists today. Much of that past is in fact enshrined in the texts of Cook's last voyage and must therefore be imaginatively "re-ethnographized." These texts must naturally be supplemented with whatever we can glean from texts collected by later Hawaiian scholars. Both sources must be treated with a great deal of critical reserve. For myself I have primarily relied on the ships' journals that I quote in extenso. I have retained the flavor of the originals and have made no changes in the texts, except to spell out certain abbreviations such as "&" and Capt.

This book is also about Hawai'i during the historical period of Cook's arrival. It must therefore contend with Hawaiian history and ethnography, which I studied to the best of my ability by immersing myself in Polynesian and Hawaiian ethnohistorical sources. These sources were all new to me and must be so for most of my readers. I therefore quote my sources in detail; I also on occasion repeat an important event or interpretation. This is a heuristic device to restore the reader's attention and a stylistic device to emphasize a different aspect of that event or its interpretation. I do not treat all texts the same way; I am suspicious of some and treat others more seriously. I try to disentangle fantasy, gossip, and hearsay from more reliable eyewitness accounts. Consequently the reader might well disagree with the stand I have taken regarding a particular text.

I finished the first draft of this book in the middle of January 1991. While the draft went to press, I made a most important pilgrimage to Hawai'i to check my version against that of scholars of Hawaiian history and culture. I thank Geoff White of the East-West Center who graciously handled this part of the project by arranging meetings, coordinating two lectures I gave, and introducing me to the marvelous Pacific and Hawaiian collection at the University of Hawai'i. I thank Karen Peacock, Pacific curator, for her unfailing courtesy and helpfulness. Rob Borofsky not only gave me the benefit of his expertise but also drove me around to savor the spectacular beauty of Oahu. Borofsky and White introduced me to the most recent work on Polynesian ethnography; the benefits of that reading will appear in my later work on Cook. I also thank Mark Jurgensmeyer, a fellow South Asianist, for his help in establishing contact

with Hawaiian historians Haunani Kay Trask and Lilikalā Kameʻelei-
hiwa; additional thanks go to Jeanette Mageo for her stimulating company and for introducing me to Samoan ethnography.

In Princeton itself I had the benefit of a critical reading of the manuscript by my colleagues Jim Boon and Joan Dayan, a fellow at the Shelby
Cullom Davis Center for Historical Studies. And Greg Dening in distant Melbourne also read the whole work and made numerous suggestions for its improvement, while Diane Eells and Lynne Withey helped
me locate some obscure references. Margaret Case of the Princeton University Press, always a good adviser, cast a critical eye on the manuscript
and made suggestions for the reorganization of the original draft. Col-
leen Fee typed several versions from my handwritten scrawls, while
Pauline Caulk, patient and meticulous as ever, typed and virtually edited
the final typescript. Marta Steele was a superb copy editor whose efforts
improved the final version of this book. As recently as last July (1991), I
made another visit to Hawaiʻi. I thank Lee Swenson and Vijaya Nagara-
jan for arranging this trip and for introducing me to the Hawaiian political activists Collette Machado and Emmett Aluli. On this trip I visited
the Huntington Library, and Susan Naulty helped me by locating the
texts of that important work *Omai, or a Trip round the World*.

I owe an enduring intellectual debt to John Charlot, whose knowledge
of Hawaiian history and culture is probably unparalleled. I was a total
stranger to him, and yet at short notice he spent several days reading my
manuscript and then spent hours with me clarifying details of Hawaiian
ethnography, thus helping me to eliminate blunders. It is impossible to
acknowledge this debt in any detail because it applies to too many places.
I found it fascinating that Charlot, a meticulous cultural historian with
an eye for detail, and I, an inveterate interpretive anthropologist, could
agree on the general lines of interpretation spelled out in this book pertaining to the events following Cook's arrival in Hawaiʻi, his apotheosis,
death, and subsequent "return." The reason is, I think, that both of us, in
our different ways, feel that ethnography is an empirical discipline that
cannot afford to turn its back on *evidence*. Ethnographic interpretation
cannot flout evidence, even though one might argue that evidence is
opaque and subject to multiple interpretations. There are places where
Charlot and I part company, for where the evidence is lacking, skimpy,
unclear, or even false (false evidence being a part of life), I think it necessary to affirm Hocart's dictum that "imagination must always keep ahead
of proof as an advanced detachment to spy out the land."[1]

The writing of this book has been exciting yet emotionally difficult for
me. The reader will soon realize that this book and my continuing work
on the Cook voyages pertain to "terror," and it is no accident that the
book was written in a context of terror. The culture of terror in turn can-

not be divorced from the larger culture of violence that overwhelms us today. It is manifest in our everyday lives in a multiplicity of forms: in the everyday horror stories of besieged cities, in the fantasyland of cinema and television, in the "moral economy" of weapons manufacture and trade, and in the wars, small and large, that such economies must inevitably foster. Although I was horrified to watch on recent television a huge picture of the patriot missile displayed by its maker with a placard underneath it saying, "Protecting the Innocent," I am even more appalled at the public acceptance of the culture of violence and the seeming suspension of the public conscience. In my own mind, however, I cannot disentangle the global culture of violence from the culture of terror in my own native land, Sri Lanka. In this space of twenty-four thousand square miles of spectacularly beautiful country, rich in traditions of radical non-violence, there have emerged, over the last ten years, forms of fearful violence that have psychically overwhelmed the physical space of that island. The terror over there is practiced by a variety of political groups, right and left, Sinhala and Tamil, Buddhist and Hindu, all of whom kill brutally yet with a devastating rationality. There are no good or bad guys in the deadly game of contemporary political violence; those who champion the cause of the oppressed can be as brutal as their oppressors.

Traditional social science, I believe, simply bypasses the terror in explaining it. No theory of nationalism, for example, can explain how "They" could cut off the heads of a dozen or so students and plant them in a row at the fountain near the entrance of the University at Peradeniya where I once taught; or butcher men, women, and children in border villages; or smash the faces of victims to deface any human feature; or gun down people praying at a shrine. . . . The litany of death by terror seems to have no end. And those who get killed are often bystanders or those who, like my friend Wijedasa, simply could not reveal to men carrying guns the whereabouts of someone they love.

Whenever I would come to Sri Lanka, it was Wijedasa who drove me around in his taxi. I got to know him well over the years. I see this tall, gentle, dignified man often in my mind's eye in his white sarong and shirt in the taxi stand near his old beat-up car that he had bought after slaving for many years in the Middle East. Then one day They came there to get his son, who They said was a terrorist. I remember Wijedasa once telling me that he was fearful for his son's safety and had sent him to live with relatives in a far-off place. He would not tell Them where his son was; on the second visit he still refused and They took him away. The general scenario is simple enough: A person is taken to the beach, shot, and then dumped into the ocean; or burnt with others in a pyre of heaped-up tires; or simply left lying around as a lesson to others. I do not know what happened to Wijedasa's son; his wife and daughter fled in fear and, I am told, one of them went back to that dreadful haven, the Middle East, to find money to support the other.

I do not know what good a memorial of this sort does. It does not help banish his apparition from my mind, nor does it help mitigate the terror. I suppose it is enough if some of us are moved to an awareness that the thousands who have been killed all over the world are people like Wijedasa, ordinary people, whose families haven't even been given a chance to mourn. And perhaps a memorial to Wijedasa might serve as an encouragement to those who, back home, record such events, refusing to keep silent.

The Apotheosis of
Captain Cook

I

---〰〰---

Captain Cook and the European Imagination

When the great navigator and "discoverer" of Polynesia James Cook landed on the shores of Hawai'i on Sunday, 17 January 1779, during the festival of Makahiki, he was greeted as the returning god Lono. This is fact; and it is incorporated into practically every history of Hawai'i and into every biography, novel, or account of this redoubtable man. Kuykendall, one of the foremost scholars of Hawaiian history, states this fact in a succinct and sober statement:

> To the Hawaiians, Captain Cook was the god Lono. As soon as he went on shore, accompanied by some of his officers, he was taken in hand by priests and made the central figure of an elaborate ceremony in the heiau [temple] of Hikiau, by which the priests meant to acknowledge him as the incarnation of Lono; up to the last day of his life he was treated by the natives with a respect amounting to adoration.[1]

I question this "fact," which I show was created in the European imagination of the eighteenth century and after and was based on antecedent "myth models" pertaining to the redoubtable explorer cum civilizer who is a god to the "natives." To put it bluntly, I doubt that the natives created their European god; the Europeans created him for them. This "European god" is a myth of conquest, imperialism, and civilization—a triad that cannot be easily separated. This book therefore is not another biography of Cook; it subverts biography by blurring the distinction between biography, hagiography, and myth.

The Cook biography has a fine contemporary retelling in the works of J. C. Beaglehole and Lynne Withey.[2] For many Europeans, Australians, and New Zealanders, Cook is part of their heritage. He appears in children's stories and in classroom histories as a new type of explorer who was, according to Beaglehole, a great navigator, a decent human being, the man who described Polynesia and its peoples, a man with "a real feeling for human rights and decencies"[3] (see Figure 1). In regard to the latter achieve-

PART ONE

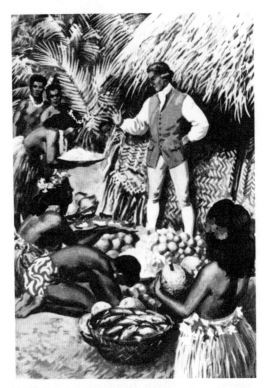

Figure 1. "They believed him to be the god of their tribe, by name Orono," illustration from a children's storybook (L. Peach, *The Story of Captain Cook*)

ment, he is a kind of ancestor of us anthropologists. A foremost ethnographer of Polynesia, Douglas Oliver, pays homage to James Cook thus: "So skillful was he in his relations with most islanders that among many Polynesians his name ('Toote') was remembered and respected for generations."[4] R. A. Skelton further elaborates on Cook's success as one of the first ethnographers:

> The same qualities of sympathy and recognition of the right of men to be different characterize Cook's dealings with native peoples. His combination of friendliness and firmness, his success in communication on equal terms, his eager interests in the island societies of Polynesia, in the way in which their people organized their lives, in their manners and customs, and in the reasons for them—all these factors assured the safety of his expeditions. More than this: Cook was able to bring back a priceless record of a way of life that the other Europeans were to destroy.[5]

And a contemporary scholar, in an insightful book on the cultural construction of the Australian landscape as a way of colonizing it, makes a rather dubious distinction between the "Explorer," the true open-minded scientist without any faddish preconceptions, and the "Discoverer" who stereotypes the world according to his scientific prejudices. Cook was a true explorer, we are told, especially as he mapped and labeled the coast of New South Wales.[6]

There are good reasons for this view of Cook. The voyages that he led heralded a shift in the goals of discovery from conquest, plunder, and imperial appropriation to scientific exploration devoid of any explicit agenda for conquest or for the exploitation and terrorization of native peoples. The very first such voyage to the South Seas, in 1768, was sponsored by the Royal Society, the nation's premier scientific organization. The ship *Endeavour* and the crew were provided by the Admiralty, and George III, who was interested in both science and discovery, granted the society the sum of £4,000. The man in command of the ship was Lieutenant James Cook, born in 1728 in a Yorkshire village where his father was a day laborer. The major goal of the voyage was to observe the transit of Venus from some location in the South Seas. Wallis's discovery and violent pacification of Tahiti in 1767 made this island a natural choice for observing the transit. Wallis had failed in his attempt to find a southern continent, which many believed existed. To search for this continent was one of the subsidiary goals of the voyage.

The ship *Endeavour* set sail from Plymouth on 25 August 1768, bound for Tahiti. The details of these voyages are not my concern in this book. It is, however, important to emphasize the scientific aspects of the voyage. The ship was, in a sense, a floating laboratory. The major scientific figure was Sir Joseph Banks who, accompanied by Dr. Solander, a student of the great Linnaeus, was primarily interested in botanical collections and taxonomies. Banks also took with him Sydney Parkinson, the ship's artist skilled in drawing botanical subjects, especially flowers and fruits; and Alexander Buchan, more interested in human forms and landscapes. Charles Green was on board as the Admiralty astronomer. When the ship reached Tahiti on 13 April 1769, eight months after leaving England, Banks effectively switched roles from botanist to ethnographer.

The transit was observed on 19 July, but this scientific achievement was easily superseded by others, especially in the areas of ethnography, botany, and zoology.[7] Cook himself systematically surveyed Tahiti and the other "Society Islands," Huahine, Ra'iatea, and Taha'a. In this first voyage, Cook also began his apprenticeship as an ethnographer, a role he developed more fully in the second and third voyages.

Cook left these islands in the middle of August and then sailed southward toward New Zealand, discovered by the Dutchman Abel Tasman in

1642. New Zealand was first sighted on 6 October 1769. Queen Charlotte Sound became Cook's base there, from which he began the systematic mapping of the New Zealand coast and then the coast of New South Wales. His first contact with Maoris in a canoe was sudden and left several Maoris dead. It is worth noting Cook's own conscience-stricken record of this event:

> I am aware that most humane men who have not experienced things of this nature will cencure my conduct in fireing upon the people in this boat nor do I my self think that the reason I had for seizing upon her will att all justify me, and had I thought they would have made the least resistance I would not have come near them, but as they did I was not to stand still and suffer either myself or those that were with me to be knocked on the head.[8]

The latter part of the statement exemplifies the attitude of Cook toward natives: Any resistance cannot be tolerated. By the third voyage the Maoris had fully accepted the reality of English power. There was virtually no resistance, and social relations between Maori and English went on in splendid harmony (or so it seemed).

The long voyage home was completed on 12 July 1771 when the ship anchored in the Downs outside the Thames. Cook's care for the health of the crew had been such that not one person had died of illness on the voyage to Tahiti, though the crew was decimated on the return trip in Batavia, owing to malaria and other tropical diseases. In fact, health on board ship was satisfactorily maintained through all three voyages. The press made the voyage famous, but it was considered Banks's voyage, not Cook's. Cook's voyage was the second one, mooted soon after his return by the same sponsors, to explore the South Seas further and especially to prove or disprove the existence of a southern continent, already rendered dubious by the first voyage. Two new ships built at Whitby were bought for the second voyage: the *Resolution* under Cook's command and the *Adventure* under Captain Furneaux's. Banks, dissatisfied with the accommodations provided him, withdrew in a fit of pique and his place was taken by the distinguished German philosopher and naturalist Johann Reinhold Forster and his talented eighteen-year-old son, George, ably assisted later by a young Swedish naturalist, Anders Sparrman, whom they picked up at the Cape of Good Hope. William Wales was the astronomer, and the famous William Hodges was the artist on board. Forster became effectively an ethnographer, as had Banks previously, and wrote one of the first books that not only dealt with the lifeways of primitive peoples but also attempted to formulate the principles of social structure in these societies.[9] Beaglehole and Withey give a detailed account of this voyage, which extended the scope of Cook's discovery of Polynesia by including the Tongan group, other little-known places like Easter Island, and especially the Melanesian group named by him the New Hebrides and New Caledonia. One of the remarkable events on this voyage is that in New Zealand the two ships parted company and a group of sailors from the *Adventure* who were attempting to collect fresh greens from Grass Cove in Queen Charlotte Sound were set upon by Maoris, killed, and then eaten—ample enough proof of the Maoris' famed anthropophagous propensities. I show elsewhere that cannibalism is as much a European fantasy as it is a Maori practice. Both were exacerbated during the long and tense relationship between Maoris and whites beginning with Cook's voyages.[10]

The second trip took three years to complete. It made Cook a famous man, one of the greatest navigators of all time, who exemplified the new spirit of discovery that can peaceably conjoin science, exploration, and discovery—a true representative of the Enlightenment. But less than a year after his return, he was asked to head a third expedition. This time he was to search for the Northwest Passage, a navigable waterway people believed crossed North America from east to west, which would shorten the distance enormously for trade between Europe and China. It was on this trip up north that Cook discovered Hawai'i, whose natives supposedly thought he was their own benevolent god Lono coming from beyond the skies in time for their annual festival and ritual complex, the Makahiki.

I have drawn the material for my analyses of this "event" literally and metaphorically from other people's footnotes. In the literal sense, I found Beaglehole's extensive notes in his superb edition of Cook's voyages fascinating and indispensable. I pursued many of them to their archival sources and, influenced by the insights of modern critical practice, I have brought these footnotes to the surface and made them central to my interpretive strategy, revealing a Cook different from the dominant vision of the humane persona of the Enlightenment. Admittedly this other Cook—unreasoning, irrational, and violent—clearly emerges only in the third voyage, the voyage that resulted in his apotheosis in Hawai'i and his death on that sad island. And that is what I want to understand. Many scholars, looking at the Hawaiian sojourn in isolation from the rest of the voyage, have focused entirely on the Hawaiian mythicization of James Cook as their long-awaited god Lono. But my questioning of this orthodoxy has led me to focus on the *relation* between the foreigners and the Hawaiians as indispensable for understanding what went on in Hawai'i during those fateful weeks and after; and this includes the myth of the apotheosis itself. A major thrust of this work has to do with the genesis of this myth and various refractions of it that emerged as a consequence of the relationship between Hawaiians and Europeans. And that cannot be understood in isolation from the larger relations between Polynesians and Cook and his crew in this last voyage.[11]

It might seem to the reader that my vision of Cook is as one-sided and biased as the ones I have rejected. This is true; but it is the violent and irrational aspect of Cook's character that I think is necessary to make sense of the crucial events in Hawai'i that culminated in this death. Furthermore, this aspect of Cook's character was so prominent as to overwhelm the more balanced persona of his earlier voyages. It cannot be put into footnotes; for the most part it *is* the face of James Cook.

Myth Models

Readers will be curious as to how I, a Sri Lankan native and an anthropologist working in an American university, became interested in Cook. It is, in fact, precisely out of these existential predicaments that my interest in Cook developed and flowered. The apotheosis of James Cook is the subject of the recent work of Marshall Sahlins, one of the most creative thinkers in our field.[12] He employs it to demonstrate and further develop a structural theory of history. I am not unsympathetic to that theory; it is the illustrative example that provoked my ire.

When Sahlins expounded his thesis at one of the Gauss Seminars at Princeton University in 1983, I was completely taken aback at his assertion that when Cook arrived in Hawai'i the natives believed that he was their god Lono and called him Lono. Why so? Naturally my mind went back to my Sri Lankan and South Asian experience. I could not think of any parallel example in the long history of contact between foreigners and Sri Lankans or, for that matter, Indians. It is not unusual for Sri Lankans (and other people) to deify *dead* ancestors and heroes, but I could not think of one Sri Lankan or South Asian example of a postmortem deification of a European, let alone a *premortem* one. (The only example that floated into my mind was that of Esmiss Esmoor, a famous Hindu goddess, the deified spirit of Mrs. Moore in E. M. Forster's *A Passage to India*!) This in turn led me to reflect, as Sahlins lectured on, that the apotheosis of a great navigator was not unprecedented in the European record of voyages, because Columbus and Cortés were also (supposedly) deified in the same manner. Could it be that the myth of Lono was a European construction, attributing to the native the belief that the European was a god? And was it influenced by the prior myths of Columbus and especially Cortés? An even wilder thought: Is it possible that Cortés's apotheosis itself was primarily a European invention based on prior "myth models" in Europe's antecedent history? Or one invented de novo by them? Or was it at the very least created out of the interaction between conquistadors and Aztecs?

On the other hand, it would not surprise me if Europeans were treated very much like native *chiefs*, especially after resistance to imperial rule was effectively broken. Let me quote an experience of Leonard Woolf at the time he was a British civil servant in Kandy, Sri Lanka, in 1907:

> I arrived here after dark in a slight thunderstorm after riding 24 miles, but the headmen and villagers met me in procession ½ mile from the village and brought me in with tom-toms and dancers. Then I had to stand in the rain outside for ten minutes while each member of the crowd came and prostrated himself or herself and touched the ground with his forehead.[13]

If we did not know enough of Sri Lankan culture, we might say that Leonard Woolf was treated as a god, as Cook was in Hawai'i. The paucity of data might even make things look worse (or better), for gods are indeed treated in this way—and so are kings and chiefs on ceremonial occasions. What further historical investigation can easily reveal, however, is that this could occur only after the conquest and after the suppression of a major rebellion in 1848. From that point on, the British took over the role of local chiefs.

Contrast Woolf's experience with that of Robert Andrews, a British ambassador to the court of the independent Kandyan Kingdom in 1796, where similar rituals were performed, but *in reverse*:

> The Sovereign of Candia arrived in all his glory seated on a throne of solid Gold richly studded with precious Stones of various Colors and Crown of Mossy Gold adorned his brows enriched with valuable and shining Gems the product of his native Sovereignty the moment he blazed upon our sight Lieutenant Kingston and myself (with the salver on my head) were directed to kneel while the Native Courtiers who attended Us prostrated themselves on the ground.[14]

Andrews was lucky that he had only to kneel; previous Dutch ambassadors had had to fall prostrate before the king. Shifts in ceremonial are historically conditioned and can be rendered intelligible in varying contexts of unequal power relationships. The historical conditions in Hawai'i were not parallel to those in Sri Lanka, but I think the Hawaiian ceremonials of prostration before Cook-Lono must also be seen in terms of the power politics of that period.

The South Asian data made me skeptical about the thesis of Cook's apotheosis. I therefore tried to familiarize myself with whatever information I could gather on Cook. During the few months following Sahlins's talk, I read Beaglehole's biography and enough of Cook's own journals to present a seminar before my colleagues at Princeton University questioning the myth of Lono and also, to my surprise, being able to question the humanist image of James Cook himself. During my sabbatical year (1989–90) at the National Humanities Center in North Carolina, I began to read more intensively and write up my material, not on the apotheosis per se, but on James Cook himself. My fascination with this man resulted in a shift in emphasis: I was now much more interested in Cook and the voyages of discovery than the specific event—his apotheosis—that drew me to these materials in the first place. My argument with Sahlins began to sound far too parochial.

But the more I read and wrote about Cook and his times, the more the goal of completing that book seemed to elude me. I doubt I can finish the book for a couple of years yet. Consequently the old argument with Sahlins seemed attractive once again, being more manageable. This project on the apotheosis of Cook can acquaint the reader, in a preliminary sort of way, with the ingredients that the larger Cook-book might contain. I do not try here to present an explicit analysis of Cook's character. I describe instead the trail of violence, beginning with his stay in Tonga in April 1777, that led Cook to his death in Hawai'i on 14 February 1779.

One of my basic assumptions is that mythmaking, which scholars assume to be primarily an activity of non-Western societies, is equally prolific in European thought. A myth, in the loose conventional view of the term, is most often a sacred story about gods and founding ancestors or stories about ancestral heroes (legends). According to the first definition, there are not many myths in European thought. There are, however, plenty of myths about ancestral heroes, among whom Cook might fit easily. But I think that both notions of myth have to be stretched to understand mythmaking in Western culture. Myths in the classic sense of sacred stories may be out of fashion, but "myth models" are not. I use "myth model" in two ways: First, an important or paradigmatic myth may serve as a model for other kinds of myth construction. Second and more importantly, a "myth model" refers to an underlying set of ideas (a myth structure or cluster of mythemes) employed in a variety of narrative forms. These idea-sets are "structures of the long run" that get attached to larger narrative forms such as fiction, history, or biography. Historical conditions obviously play a role in resuscitating a myth model buried in a tradition; and political and social conditions may either foster a particular myth model, rendering it dominant, or help in the invention of a new myth model based on older ones no longer apposite to the times. Thus one can have myth models surfacing in a variety of contexts, supplementing actual myths of ancestral heroes that are also being created. These latter myths are not sacred stories in the literal sense, but they have a similar power and are exactly isomorphic with stories (legends) about ancestors. Thus the various myths about Cook—for example, the "humanist" one—express the idea of the explorer apposite to the civilization's perception of itself and contrast with former myths, such as that of a Cortés, a Pizarro, or a Drake, that are no longer relevant to a more liberal, "enlightened" age. The lived person is totally subsumed in the myth and in fact is irrelevant, except in footnotes.

Myth models are much more elusive than the more easily identifiable genre of myths or legends. In the societies that anthropologists traditionally study, myth models are also used in the construction of actual myths. Thus in Buddhism the myth of the Buddha's life provides a myth model—of the Prince living in luxury and then, satiated with hedonism, renouncing the world—that appears as the basis for other myths or segments thereof. Myth models in this sense are *not* necessarily hidden or unconscious infrastructures in Lévi-Strauss's sense as, for example, his idea that Oedipus's swollen foot represents "autochthonous origins."[15] Myth models can, and often do, appear as surface structures; they exist on the level of content; they often embody a narrative theme. Todorov says that in Western civilization logos has conquered mythos; I contend that mythos still reigns there under the banner of logos.[16]

Let me demonstrate this idea of myth models in relation to my proposed larger work on Cook: In spite of my interest in psychoanalytic theory, I feel it is futile to analyze Cook the man explicitly in these terms, because we know little of his childhood or of his relation with his parents and with his own spouse and children. I have therefore adopted another strategy, psychological if you will, that might help me to talk about Cook the man, insofar as we know about him from the available texts. I suggest that one of the most enduring ideas in Western culture is that of the redoubtable person coming from Europe to a savage land, a harbinger of civilization who remains immune to savage ways, maintaining his integrity and identity. I shall give it a label and call it the "Prospero" syndrome or myth model. Then there is its opposite: the civilizer who loses his identity and goes native and becomes the very savage he despises. I call this the "Kurtz" syndrome, once again from its most famous embodiment. These myth models are, in Geertz's felicitous phrase, models of and for reality.[17] They are constructed out of real-life experiences and then, in turn, influence consciously or unconsciously both art (narrative) and lived existence. Hence the relevance of the ambiguous word *model*. Insofar as these myth models appear in fiction (theater or the novel), we tend to treat them as inventions of the author. They are, however, models circulating in a variety of ways in Western culture and consciousness—and also employed in fictional narratives, lending these narratives a mythic power.

In my analysis of Cook, I hope to use the Prospero and Kurtz models as a device to talk about Cook's complex persona. During the third voyage, Cook's Kurtz persona seems to take over. Acting for the most part on an unconscious level, the civilizer in effect takes on the characteristics of the savage—characteristics imputed to the savage by the civilizer's culture. The

Africans of Conrad's narrative exist only in Marlow's European imagination. We know that the idea of the savage constructed by the civilizer can easily be seen as the hived-off part of the civilizer's own being, his shadow side as it were, foisted on the savage. *The Apotheosis of Captain Cook* in effect deals with Cook's Kurtz persona. However, because the Prospero persona barely appears in the third voyage, let me deal with it briefly in this introduction.

Cook's Prospero persona is as intrinsic to him as is the Kurtz. The first two voyages exhibit this well. True to the model, Cook is the civilizer, bringing a new vision of the world to the savage lands of the South Seas. This aspect of the civilizer's persona is expressed in a variety of powerful symbolic sequences pertaining to fertility and order. His ship is loaded with domestic animals and English garden plants and is self-consciously recognized as a Noah's ark. When Cook lands in a new land, he not only takes it over on behalf of the Crown in a series of ceremonial acts but wherever he goes he plants English gardens. The act is primarily symbolic, supplanting the disorderly way of savage peoples with ordered landscapes on the English model. Pairs of domestic animals are carefully set loose, away from the depredations of unthinking savages, to *domesticate* a savage land. These symbolic acts of domestication (see Figures 9 and 10) are also acts of appropriation parallel to the symbolic taking over of the country by the ceremonial planting of the English flag. Cook is very self-conscious about these performances and everywhere asserts that the fructification of the new land will help not only the natives but also other European sailors and settlers who might touch these shores. Other navigators performed these symbolic acts of the civilizer before Cook did, but Cook is passionately committed to them, and I shall show in the later work that they can be related, in a psychoanalytic sense, to Cook's own complex sexuality.

Parallel with these symbolic performances are the scientific activities of the voyage. To highlight a few: The systematic charting and mapping of the coast is not only a major scientific activity but is also simultaneously a symbolic activity whereby the alien land is mapped out, identified, and systematically renamed with familiar English names. Paul Carter has noted parallel acts for New South Wales.[18] The larger the land and the sparser its population, the more easily it can be overpowered with toponymy. The most systematic example is New Zealand: Virtually every place named by Cook has an English name, thereby making familiar an unfamiliar landscape. These landscapes and other exotic objects are painted by the ship's artists and familiarized in the new travel books and museum exhibitions, as are the botanical and zoological classifications of the alien landscape. In this early period, the presence of the natives' savage culture is pejoratively mapped: Cannibal Cove, Murderers Bay, Kidnappers Cape. I think it no accident that the most systematically colonized countries are also the ones systematically relabeled: New Zealand, Australia, Tasmania.

Implicit in the thrust of civilization is a dark side that parallels the Kurtz persona of the civilizer. Both are facets of the same enterprise. They constitute what one might call the "paradox of civilization"—ipso facto the paradox of imperialism—however benevolent that civilization conceives itself to be.

In the very first voyage of the *Endeavour*, Lord Morton, president of the Royal Society, gave Cook instructions on proper civilized behavior. In his "Hints offered to the consideration of Captain Cooke, Mr. Banks, Dr. Solander, and the other Gentlemen who go upon the Expedition on Board the *Endeavour*," he urged them thus: "To exercise the utmost patience and forebearance with respect to the Natives of the several lands where the ship may touch. To check the petulance of the Sailors and restrain the wanton use of Fire Arms. To have it still in view that shedding the blood of these people is a crime of the highest nature." He added that these people are the "legal possessors of the several Regions they inhabit" and therefore justified in attempting to "repel intruders, whom they may apprehend are come to disturb them in the quiet possession of their country."[19] This humane vision of peaceful exploration contradicts the secret instructions of the Admiralty that require the alien lands to be appropriated on behalf of the Crown, thereby *dispossessing* the rights of native peoples—hence, the paradox of civilization that parallels the contradictions in the very being of the civilizer himself.

The clearest example of this paradox comes from the second voyage, when Cook's ships, badly in need of provisions, anchored at the tiny Polynesian island of Niue in June 1774. When Cook's officers were "erecting the English colours as usual on these occasions," the natives attacked them with stones and darts.[20] Cook tried to parley with them, but because this had little effect, he shot at one assailant. Fortunately the gun did not fire. Wales, the astronomer, called this "an Inhospitable and Savage Isle." And the name that Cook gave it? Savage Island: "because of the conduct and aspect [physical appearance] of these Islanders."[21] The manifestation of "resistance" on the interpersonal level is labeled as "insolence," a key word in the ship's lexicon.

The paradox of civilization, or the "imperialist paradox," is not something that I have discovered from reading these texts. It was noted by such contemporaries as Hawkesworth, who saw its inevitability and justified its necessity:

> The regret with which I have recorded the destruction of poor naked savages, by our firearms, in the course of these expeditions, when they endeavoured to repress the invaders of their country ...

13

this however appears to be an evil which, if discoveries of new countries are attempted cannot be avoided, resistance will always be made, and if those who resist are not overpowered, the attempt must be relinquished.[22]

The civilizational paradox set the stage for many forms of resistance among native populations even when they had been "pacified." But this structural dimension of violence is not all. It goes hand in hand with a more deadly, more elusive, personal violence. Fanny Burney was probably right when she thought Cook was "the most moderate, humane and gentle circumnavigator that ever went out upon discoveries."[23] I have no doubt that Cook presented himself in this way to his contemporaries. But out there, as a sea captain, in the lonely and seemingly limitless Pacific, did he retain that same persona? There the niceties of civilized living do not operate. The life forms on board ship and in remote atolls where Europeans met Polynesians were insulated physically, socially, and psychically from the world of civilized living and the rules that governed the dinner table at the Burneys'. Like other insulated arenas, the conditions of shipboard life and contact with natives brought to the surface the dark and hidden side of one's own being. Cook was the "gentle navigator" at home; he was a despot on board ship, as Trevenen noted.[24] Dening says that there were many more beatings on Cook's voyages than on the famed *Bounty*.[25] In other words, the arenas carved out in the Pacific were also spaces for acting out sex and violence.

The problem of Polynesian sexuality is far too complicated for me to deal with in this work. The question of Cook's relation to the violence that was endemic to a ship's lifeways is more directly relevant to our theme. Reinhold Forster has argued that on the first two voyages the presence of scientists acted as a brake on violence toward Polynesians. Banks, owing to his class background, was for the most part outside and above the hierarchies on board ship. The Forsters did not get along well with Cook, who did not have the same control over them as he had over his own crew. Indeed, during an altercation Forster made it clear that because he was appointed by George III himself he was not bound to follow the Captain's command.[26] It is therefore possible that Cook himself effectively saw to it that there were no professional scientists on the third voyage. According to Forster, Lieutenant King told him that when he visited Cook prior to sailing and asked him why there were no professional scientists as in previous voyages, Cook expostulated, "Curse the scientists and all science into the bargain."[27] Forster then insightfully noted, rather pompously to be sure, that the previous voyages had distinguished scientists on board who, as the representatives of the civil society, acted as a buffer between Cook and the world of Polynesians.

On his first voyage Cook was accompanied by Banks and Solander, who were the representatives of science and art (*emollit mores nec finit esse feros*); and on the second voyage I and my son accompanied him and were his daily companions at table and elsewhere. He therefore of necessity acquired through our presence a greater respect and reverence for his own character and good name. Our mode of thought, our principles, and our habits had their effect on him in the course of time through having them constantly before his notice, and these restrained him from practising cruelties upon the harmless South-Sea-Islanders.[28]

I think there is some truth to this assertion, though contrary to Forster it can be shown that Cook's propensities to violence always existed and were expressed in a variety of ways in the earlier voyages, though on a much lesser scale of intensity. These failings were, in fact, noted by Forster himself in his recently published journals edited by Michael Hoare.[29]

Improvisation, Rationality, and Savage Thought

Myth models, I suggested, can appear in a variety of narrative forms. They can also appear in our own scholarly research. Implicit in both Prospero and Kurtz is a commonplace assumption of the savage mind that is given to prelogical or mystical thought and in turn is fundamentally opposed to the logical and rational ways of thinking of modern man. I do not object to mythic thought per se but to the assumption of a lack of rational reflection implicit in the premise of prelogical, mystic, or mythic thought. Furthermore, prelogicality and mysticality are, in the Western myth model, associated with "feeling," and feeling is opposed to thought. Thus, if natives think mystically, prelogically, or like children, they must, it is assumed, lack mature ratiocinative abilities. This is not the invention of Lévy-Bruhl;[30] it existed prior to his work and continues to influence contemporary social thought. Even those who explicitly try to counter the idea of a savage mind end up, as Lévi-Strauss does, with categorical distinctions not too far removed from the older models. Lévi-Strauss's savage logic, though not confined to savages, is a "science of the concrete" rooted in *bricolage*, the shallow experimental skill of the European artisan. Then there is the categorical opposition he makes between cold and hot societies: "the former seeking, by the institutions they give themselves, to annul the possible effect of historical factors on their equilibrium and continuity in a quasi-automatic fashion; the latter resolutely internalizing the historical process and making it the moving power of their development."[31] And how can one ignore Freud's preposterous idea that natives think like children? This is not something that emerges from the logic of psychoanalytic theory but from Freud's European inheritance of the prelogical savage.[32] The idea of the prelogical or childlike native, or one who lives in a "cold" society, or given to unreflective traditional thought, or governed by a rigid cosmic or mythic world picture, is the social scientists' myth of the Other. Whatever form the myth takes, it must explicitly or implicitly postulate a radical disjunction between Western self and society and those of the preindustrial world. By contrast I want to render fuzzy these binary distinctions without falling victim to the idea that because human beings are biologically a single species, thought processes everywhere must accurately reflect that commonality irrespective of the supervention of culture. I am sympathetic to theories that can deal with similarity and difference constituted on the basis of a common human neurobiological nature.

Let me briefly examine the human scientist's myth of the Other and the dilemmas it involves by a brief critique of one of the most provocative books of our time, Todorov's *The Conquest of America*, the immediate intellectual precursor of Sahlins's own work.[33] Todorov, in contrast to Sahlins, is informed by a deep ethical concern, namely, his sympathy for the Aztecs and his unequivocal condemnation of the brutality of the conquest. The success of this book depends to a large extent on Todorov's style: a lucid, simple prose disturbingly juxtaposed with Spanish accounts of the simple and stark brutality of the conquistadors. For the latter the Aztecs are the radical Other: savage or animal-like or heathen, they can be exterminated with impunity. In Todorov's *Conquest* the mastermind is not Columbus but Cortés, an exemplar of modernity who could manipulate signs in a pragmatic, rational manner so as to overwhelm the traditional, cosmologically bound Aztecs. Hence Todorov's question: "Did the Spaniards defeat the Indians by means of signs?"[34]

Todorov himself provides an affirmative answer. Aztec culture, he says, was "overdetermined" by signs. If Freud's idea of overdetermination placed emphasis on multiple meanings and motivations and a semantic and syntactic looseness, this is not the case with Todorov's. "Their [Aztec and Mayan] verbal education favors paradigm over syntagm, code over context, conformity-to-order over efficacity-of-the-moment, the past over the present. Now, the Spanish invasion creates a radically new, entirely unprecedented situation, in which the act of improvisation matters more than that of ritual."[35] The implication is clear that ritual is hostile to improvisation. Behind Todorov's radical antitheses lies another crucial distinction pertaining to self and society. In the cosmologically and ritually constricting world of the Aztecs, there are no *individuals* as such. The person "is merely the constitutive element of that other totality, the collectivity."[36] Todorov could have as easily used "dividual," that wonderful neologism employed by McKim Marriott to describe those other Indians, the Hindus.[37] If in Todorov's scheme signs (culture) and persons are bound together in this manner, it should not surprise us if there is little room for motivation, agency, or the significance of the subject in the molding of society and consciousness.

Todorov seems unaware of the peculiar bind in which he is caught. He quotes extensively from Spanish texts that describe the brutalization of the Indians, but these are the very texts that represent the Indians' stereotypic Otherness. The modern scholar accepts the accuracy of these older accounts of the Indian because they fit his theory of signs which tells us that the Indians are bound by signs; consequently they can be easily subjugated by the Spanish who have mastery over signs. Todorov does not recognize that *his* representation of the Aztec is a by-product of sixteenth-century Spanish representations, mediated, however, by his theory of signs. In effect, the difference between the two is one of ethical orientation and not one of divergent representation. Todorov's vision of the Other is a continuation of a major Spanish (and European) myth model dealing with the savage mind. Nevertheless, it is possible to show from Todorov's own rendering of Spanish histories that the Aztecs were as capable of spontaneity and improvisation as the Spaniards were capable of being dupes of their improvisational understanding of Aztec culture and mentality.

For Todorov the Aztecs are "dividuals"; hence, when people are selected as sacrificial victims, they simply accept their fate. But does resignation to the inevitability of death imply the power of society over the individual? Must someone protest and shout out to the world the unfairness of his existential fate in order to assert his individuality? In fact, in the very next sentence, Todorov gives an example of "tearful [Aztec] soldiers saddened by the death of their comrades"; this suggests that they were *not* entirely dominated by a ritualistic, dividualized, fatalistic world.[38] Moreover, the ritualism of the Aztecs may not be as constricting and ordered as Todorov imagines: "The religious rites are in themselves so numerous and so complex that they mobilize a veritable army of functionaries."[39] It is doubtful whether these rituals could have been invented, perpetuated, and changed without creative improvisation. And finally, consider Todorov's summary of Bernal Diaz's description of a human sacrifice: "In order to discourage the intruders, the Aztec warriors inform them [the Spaniards] that they will be sacrificed and eaten, by themselves or by wild beasts; and when on one occasion prisoners were taken, matters are so arranged so as to sacrifice them under the eyes of Cortes' soldiers."[40] And here is Bernal Diaz's own characterization of this event: "Then they ate their flesh with a sauce of peppers and tomatoes. They sacrificed all our men in this way, eating their legs/arms, offering their hearts and blood to their idols, as I have said, and throwing their trunks and entrails to the lions and tigers and serpents and snakes that they kept in their wild-beast houses."[41] If Todorov and Bernal Diaz are right, here is an excellent example of Aztecs manipulating a human sacrifice for political purposes, utilizing a conventional sign system to frighten the Spaniards, and no doubt succeeding.

Now let me consider one of Todorov's examples of Cortés's improvisational skills that was also designed to scare the Aztecs and demoralize them: "At first the Indians are not sure that the Spaniards' horses are mortal beings; in order to sustain this uncertainty, Cortes has the animal corpses buried during the night after the battle."[42] Todorov and his Spanish writers think alike; both assume that Cortés's tactic proves his strategic mastery of signs such that his "conquest of improvisation leads to that of the kingdom."[43] But were the Indians naive enough to believe that Spanish horses did not belong to the broad mortal class of the quadrupeds in their own midst? And did not the Aztecs see Spanish horses wounded, bleeding, and falling down, if not dead? And how did the Spaniards manage to bury their dead horses and then cover up the evidence of burial without Indians detecting them? One could as easily argue that Cortés erroneously interpreted Indian beliefs on the basis of European misconceptions of the savage mind, in which case Cortés thinks (and Todorov thinks) that he (Cortés) was a master of signs when in fact he was performing foolish scenarios. I am not suggesting that Cortés was not a clever strategist. He was; but he was also a victim of a sign system based on European conceptions of the Other. Similarly, from Todorov's own account, the Aztecs also appear to have been both victims and masters of their sign systems, but not in the European style. Admittedly their society was a hieratic one, but it did not exclude improvisation. Because their style of improvisation and rationality was so different from that of the Spanish, it could easily elude the documentation of early chroniclers.[44]

Anthropologists nowadays will for the most part affirm that members of preliterate societies can and do act rationally in terms of their own cultural values. This is true of Aztecs and Polynesians alike. What I question, however, is the logical status of that imputed rationality. Insofar as it leaves little room for reflection and flexibility, it is not all that far removed from prior notions of prelogicality. Thus, Todorov's preliterates cannot manipulate signs to their advantage; their thought processes are inflexible; they cannot rationally weigh alternative or multiple courses of action. Todorov's error is to conceptualize preliterate culture on the model of *langue* rather than *parole* and then to exempt European culture from this model. It is well known that structuralism from Saussure to Lévi-Strauss must postulate a synchronic world ordered into an interconnected semiotic system. Thus language, in the Saussurean conception, is viewed as a purely arbitrary system of signs in which *parole* or speech is subsidiary to *langue*, the formal dimension of language. *Parole* is the world's messiness that the semiotic order shuns. If one, following Lévi-Strauss, extends this idea to culture, then culture too, as in Todorov, becomes a system of signs that orders experience.[45] The logical consequence of the adoption of this prejudicial position is the perpetuation of the older myth model of savage mentality. What Todorov says of Columbus is also true of Todorov: "Columbus has discovered America but not the Americans."[46]

There are many ways to counter this narrow view of "prelogical mentality." Following thinkers like Bakhtin, one must give greater prominence to *parole* in the field of culture. This "turn" is itself sufficient to free us from the view of the inflexibility of cosmological thought. Improvisation need not be alien to cosmological thought: It can be intrinsic to its invention, practice, and performance. Once one assumes that cultural beliefs are multiple and not in reality organized into a single systemic order of signs, then one can be liberated from the view that "everything happens as if [for Aztecs and other preliterates] signs automatically and necessarily proceed from the world they designate"[47] and do not therefore possess manipulative flexibility. However, it is not necessary to assume that manipulative flexibility is cross-culturally uniform; some societies obviously provide greater leeway than others do.

In this book I focus primarily on an area of cognitive life where manipulative flexibility is readily evident. Following Max Weber, I emphasize "practical rationality," namely, the process whereby human beings reflectively assess the implications of a problem in terms of practical criteria.[48] For example, if I fall seriously ill in Sri Lanka, I might decide to consult a shaman or an M.D., or my astrologer or a seer; or I might go see an Ayurvedic physician, or simply do nothing and blame my karma, or say it is my karma and then perversely perform some of the foregoing alternatives, or say there's a new type of medicine in a neighboring country, so why not give it a try. Underlying these alternatives and the judgments I make is a form of reasoning I have labeled "practical" or "pragmatic rationality."

It is hard to imagine how people could conduct their economic lives without such "practical rationality."[49] So it is with warfare, in which there is a variety of strategies to surprise or overcome an enemy and situational judgments are required by every good commander in choosing the best of the various culturally defined strategies. Inventiveness and change are also probable components in such situations. The strategies are culture-bound; but some are more bound than others. In much of Polynesia, human sacrifice was considered absolutely essential to warfare, and anthropologists have speculated, rightly, on its enormous cosmological significance. Yet in spite of its deep-structural embeddedness, Kamehameha of Hawai'i simply let it go moribund during his arduous campaign of interisland consolidation, because he probably believed that human sacrifice was not suitable for his conception of the state. By contrast, modern anthropologists insist on foisting on the actors of the past a sort of invariant means-goals nexus and an assumption of the inflexibility of cosmological thought. If Kamehameha were an anthropologist, he would continue to practice human sacrifices.

The Weberian idea of a pragmatic rationality has a utilitarian quality about it. I want to divest it of its utilitarian aura and expand it to include reflective decision making by a calculation or weighing of the issues involved in any problematic situation. Although practical decision making is also intrinsic to common sense, it is the reflective element that distinguishes practical rationality from common sense. Geertz perceptively shows that the famous Azande witchcraft explanations might well be "mystical," but they are also used to protect Azande commonsense assumptions regarding their world.[50] "Men plug the dikes of their most needed beliefs with whatever mud they can find."[51] Furthermore, Geertz recognizes that whereas there is a taken-for-granted quality ("naturalness") to common sense, "practical rationality," as I use it, is a much more reasoned and reflective way of thinking.

The distinction between common sense and practical rationality is, however, easily blurred. It is indeed the case that common sense has a taken-for-granted quality. But what happens when commonsense assumptions are violated? People might well begin to plug the dikes of their much-needed beliefs, but in a variety of ways. Their actions might result in irrational behavior; but they could just as easily practice reflective reasoning and argumentation and make judgments based on a careful weighing of the issues involved. For example, the normal beliefs of the Hawaiians were that their god Lono "arrives" at the Makahiki festival as an invisible presence when he is invited by priests. Furthermore, he is represented iconically in various ways in temple images. When James Cook arrived during the festival in two large ships with a large number of people who neither looked Polynesian nor spoke the native language, the Hawaiians, it is said, thought he was the god Lono. By contrast, I argue in this book that Cook's arrival would *violate* Hawaiian commonsense expectations, though it could be consonant with European assumptions regarding native perceptions of white "civilizers." The violation of normal expectations could produce "problems of meaning" that in turn might result in a variety of arguments pertaining to the new arrivals. This would, I think, include judgments based on a rational weighing of the issues involved. It is this ability to make reasoned judgments that I call "practical rationality"; and although it exists in the field of utility, it is not coterminous with utility. Furthermore, practical rationality is not concerned with the rationality of *belief*, which is the way rationality has been framed in recent debates.[52] I refer to a mode of thinking, not to a mode of thought. This mode of thinking can operate in greater or lesser measure in a variety of spheres; for example, in magic, medicine, or spirit possession. The deliberation over issues entails, on the purely individual level, an argument with oneself on the pros and cons relating to a particular problem. When practical rationality involves more than one person, as it often does, it is invariably associated with argument, debate, and contentious discourse resulting in a formation of judgments, whether consensually validated or not.

The notion of practical rationality sketched above, I believe, links us as human beings to our common biological nature and to perceptual and cognitive mechanisms that are products thereof. These perceptual and cognitive mechanisms are also not "culture free;" but neither is culture free from them. The fact that my universe is a culturally constituted behavioral environment does not mean I am bound to it in a way that renders discrimination impossible. The idea of practical rationality provides me with a bit of space where I can talk of Polynesians who are like me in some sense. Such spaces, though not easy to create, are necessary if one is to talk of the other culture in human terms.

The assumption of a lack of discrimination in cosmologically bound natives is endemic to Polynesian ethnography. Thus, when Cook arrived in Hawai'i, some anthropologists thought that for Hawaiians he was the god Lono arrived in person; others, like Kuykendall, the author of my opening quotation, thought that he was a kind of *avatar* of Lono, not metaphorically, but literally. Other anthropologists are not sure but believe that insofar as Hawaiian chiefs were considered "divinities" Cook's divinity was perfectly consonant with native thought. But real-life natives, I think, make a variety of *discriminations* about the nature of divinity. In South Asia, the king is considered an embodiment of Śiva; yet, as a native, I know that this form of Śiva is different from someone like Sai Baba, who claims he is the *avatar* of Śiva; or from the possessed person I consult who becomes a vehicle of that god; or from Śiva worshipped in his phallic representation (*lingam*) in my temple; or from Śiva ornately dressed in full regalia when the priest opens the curtains of the temple; or from my friend whose name is Śiva, whom I meet in the cafeteria; and so on. But the anthropologist's version of the native cannot make these discriminations regarding the varying refractions of the essence of the one god. Thus, for Marshall Sahlins, there is not all that much difference between King Kalani'opu'u of Hawai'i, who is the embodiment of the god Kū, and the god Kū who is worshiped in the temple and brings success in war. We (we assume) can make these discriminations but we should not be ethnocentric and foolishly assume natives can. I think the reverse is true: The native can make all sorts of subtle discriminations in his field of beliefs; the outsider-anthropologist practicing a form of reverse discrimination cannot. Needless to say, my reified "anthropologist" is the one who has reified the whole idea of a symbolic or cosmological order that exists superorganically outside the consciousnesses of human beings.

II

————————— ❧❧ —————————

The Third Coming: A Flashback to the South Seas

Cook arrived in England on 29 July 1775 after over three years of exploration and scientific discovery. He was justly proud that he lost only four men during this second voyage, and only one by disease. He was a truly famous person, yet plain and unpretentious. Boswell, who had dinner with him, wrote: "It was curious to see Cook, a grave steady man, and his wife, a decent plump Englishwoman, and think he was preparing to sail round the world."[1] The apt characterization "a grave, steady man" is consonant with the "humanism" that practically every writer has associated with him. He seems more like the conventional, duty-bound unheroic captains in Conrad, not Kurtz. This is correct; yet Freud has warned us to be suspicious of those who are too moral, too upright and inflexible in their principles. Who would have expected Cook, even in his first voyage, to be a bit of a crook?

> We may feel disconcerted ourselves, reading through the ship's muster-books, to find rising out of the Pacific Ocean as it were, in April 1769 a James Cook who becomes Hicks's servant, and then in September 1769 a Nathaniel Cook, A.B. In May 1771 the first becomes the servant of Clerke, on his promotion to third lieutenant, and the second becomes the carpenter's servant. Who were these two persons thus listed, without details of origin or age? They were the sons of Lieutenant James Cook, aged six years and five years respectively, and were then comfortably at home at 7 Assembly Row. Their names were on the ship's books 'earning time' so that, if they should enter the navy, they could sit their lieutenant's examination in the shortest period practically possible, irrespective of the letter of the regulations.[2]

Beaglehole calls this "chicanery," though an accepted custom in the navy. Nevertheless it is "in flagrant defiance of an act of parliament which threatened the penalty of permanent dismissal from the service."[3]

One can forgive Cook for this minor lapse when it is remembered that we are not dealing with a modern society. It has been shown that Italians, and other Third World peoples, are much possessed by what one could aptly call "moral familism" (call it "amoral familism" if you will), that is, conditions wherein familial ethics prevail over impersonal bureaucratic rules.[4] It is somewhat anomalous to see this in Cook, the uptight Conradian captain, devoted to duty and to the Navy's bureaucratic procedures. Yet before we cast a stone at Cook, let us ask ourselves, what upright citizen hasn't fudged his income tax returns? Cook was no crook; indubitably, as he embarked on his great voyages of discovery, he was the great civilizer, a Prospero of the Enlightenment.

Yet Prospero also has his shadow side. He beats Caliban into abject submission; he terrifies Ariel, that free spirit, and bids him do his magic work under threat of imprisonment. He is lonely, isolated, a stern and moral man. Nevertheless, the shadow side of Prospero's persona does not engulf him in a heart of darkness as it did Conrad's Kurtz. The tempest subsides; Prospero is restored to his kingdom and his daughter gets married to a young prince. Not so with Cook; a stern and lonely man, he had lived in august detachment on the island of his own inner isolation—his ship, aptly named the *Resolution*. He had no Miranda. He was now forty-seven; he had married at age thirty-four a woman thirteen years his junior. He saw her only intermittently, never for more than a year at a stretch. He had a harvest of sons; but the joys of domesticity were denied to him, for he had hardly spent any time with them.[5] After his long and strenuous second voyage, it seemed that for him too the tempest would subside; he too could reap the rewards of a life well lived in the service of his nation. He lectured at the Royal Society. He was made a post captain with a sinecure at the Greenwich Hospital that ensured freedom from financial worry. He was busy working at his journals, cooperating with his editor the Rev. John Douglas, canon of Windsor, to ensure that the style and contents "might be unexceptionable to the nicest readers." "In short," he told Douglas, "my desire is that nothing indecent may appear in the whole book, and you cannot oblige me more than by pointing out whatever may appear to you as such."[6] Unlike his narrative of the first voyage, which was easily outshone by Banks's, Cook wrote the shipboard narratives of his second voyage with an eye to an increasingly eager reading public. He was no litterateur, but his journals had a down-to-earth quality, and the descriptions of places, practices, and events are superbly detailed, if not evocative of the forms of life of Pacific Islanders. Reinhold Forster might have been a serious competitor, but in a series of admiralty intrigues his journals were silenced, only to appear as a book without official imprimatur, without Hodges's paintings, and written in the guise of his son's name.[7]

One of the great scientific achievements of Cook's second voyage was to disprove once and for all the existence of a southern continent, a Terra

Australis, that had occupied the minds and fantasies of the best European scientists for a long time. Yet other fantasies remained. It was believed that the Northwest Passage could eliminate the long voyage between England and China now undertaken via the Cape of Good Hope. Though several attempts were made, leading to important explorations and discoveries, the quest was virtually abandoned by the mid-seventeenth century. But in George III's time the issue was taken up once again, and even though a great deal of skepticism was expressed, it won enough support to warrant at least another expedition. With the revolt of the American colonies, British trade and imperial interests now seemed focused in the East, and a passage through the north of North America, from the Atlantic to the Pacific, seemed inviting. There *is* a Northwest Passage. That we know. (We now know that it is not navigable.) The fantasy of a Northwest Passage was compounded by a piece of knowledge that many took for granted: Seawater does not freeze; icebergs have been driven into the sea from freshwater rivers; hence in the proper season, the passage from the Pacific to the Atlantic would be entirely navigable. And who would be fit to undertake such a formidable enterprise if not the redoubtable navigator, James Cook?

I think one can agree with Beaglehole that his friends in the Admiralty "knew him well enough to entrap him, a willing prisoner."[8] Cook, it should be remembered, personally asked for the sinecure at Greenwich Hospital. Yet it did not occur to Lord Sandwich "that it was his duty, as head of the navy, to impose a period of rest on Cook. . . . His faculties had simply been stretched to the uttermost for a long period."[9] On the second voyage Cook was, on the basis of his experience of the first, skeptical about the existence of a southern continent, and he had enough energy and will to prove or disprove its existence. In any case the excitement of the earlier voyages was that of discovery, or charting new places and appropriating them for the Crown and expanding the knowledge of world geography, geology, botany, and ethnography. There was no such mission on the third voyage. There was a promise of a handsome financial reward for discovering the passage, but it was doubtful that Cook believed in its existence.[10] He was back with his wife and young family; yet before he could even settle down he was to leave for a long, uncertain voyage, perhaps more out of a sense of duty than conviction or will.

The third voyage had a subsidiary goal, to return Mai, the Tahitian, who had been brought to England by Furneaux and soon become a favorite in London high society, a competitor with Ahutoru whom Bouganville had brought to Paris earlier (who was on Marion du Fresne's expedition of 1772, returning to Tahiti, when he died en route). Mai carried with him a lot of goods, including a variety of deadly weapons and ammunition, and a coat of mail generously provided by George III presumably to protect his protégé from the slings and spears of jealous fellow countrymen. George III, a patron of all these voyages, impressed by Cook's vision of refurbishing Polynesian gardens with English domestic animals and plants, gave a bull with two cows and their calves to add to the already plentiful existent stock on board. For Europeans Tahiti was an Arcadia; it was therefore apt that Lord Bessborough should send a peacock and a peahen to that island, to reproduce in the avian world the beauty of the physical surroundings and the sensual charms of its people. "Sweet red wine" was perhaps purchased en route, according to previous custom; there were no apes.[11]

The ships, however, were not suited to carry such a precious cargo. Cook's own famous ship the *Resolution*, with 112 on board, was repaired and nicely refurbished for the occasion; the new ship the *Discovery*, with seventy on the crew, was in the charge of Captain Clerke, who had sailed with Cook on the earlier voyages (and was to die of TB in the desolate cold of the north after Cook's own death). The navy contractors who repaired the *Resolution* did such a shoddy job that it sprang a major leak before it even left the English Channel. Both ships gave the navigators endless trouble.

Cook left Plymouth on 13 July 1776 and Clerke, who had trouble with debtors (the "Israelites"), left three weeks later but arrived at the Cape of Good Hope at almost the same time as Cook did on 10 November.[12] Cook lost several of his domestic animals to human predators here, but "added two young bulls, two Heifers, two young stone Horses, two Mares, two Rams, several Ewes and Goats and some Rabbits and Poultry, all of them intended for New Zealand, Otaheite [Tahiti] and the neighbouring islands, or any other place we might meet, where there was a prospect that the leaving of some of them might prove usefull to posterity."[13] No wonder then that several journalists, Cook included, thought of their ship as a Noah's ark. Unhappily, en route to New Zealand on one of the Kerguelen islands, properly named the island of Desolation, two bulls, a heifer, two rams, and many of the goats died. "With now only the bull and the bull calf left, hopes of changing the cannibal diet of New Zealanders were fading," says Beaglehole.[14] From there the voyage proceeded to what is now Tasmania, where eight natives met them "without shewing the least mark of fear and with the greatest confidence imaginable."[15] These Tasmanian people barely exist, having been largely wiped out by disease and white hunters not too long afterward. "I tooke the two Pigs a boar and a Sow, and carried them about a mile within the woods at the head of the bay and left them by the side of a fresh Water brook."[16] Note that Cook himself performs this piece of symbolic action almost in loving fashion. He would have added others, but apparently the Tasmanians initially tried to grab and carry off the pigs for their supper, and Cook wasn't willing to take too many chances with the increasingly scarce cattle, sheep, and goats.

One of Cook's tasks was to reconstruct the events that led to the massacre of Captain Furneaux's men at Grass Cove. Mai was on that trip and now encouraged Cook to punish those responsible. Cook gathered information on that tragedy, but he refused to take revenge even though he thought he identified the group and their leader, Kahura. Many, especially Mai, solicited Kahura's death, but Kahura, instead of running away, permitted the ship's artist, Webber, to paint his portrait. Cook admired his aplomb: "I must confess I admired his courage and was not a little pleased at the confidence he put in me."[17] This is vintage Cook, as it were. The "cannibal chief" yields to Cook, puts his faith in him, and Cook forgives him. But like the father and disciplinarian that he was, he warned them all: "I should think no more of it as it was sometime sence and done when I was not there, but if ever they made a Second attempt of that kind, they might rest assured of feeling the weight of my resentment."[18] The phrase "done when I was not there" is especially significant. For the authoritarian persona, the world can be an extension of his own being: If the massacre had happened to his own crew, when he was there, the consequences would have been different. The natives were like children. They were to be warned and forgiven for the first time, but no second lapse would be tolerated. A stern schoolmaster, a stern father of the people, a stern commander—but forgiving. For their part the Maoris had learned the lessons of the first two trips: There was little thieving, and Cook had no provocation to shoot. The women were also beginning to be controlled, with the better ones carefully guarded and the crew given "the mere refuse and outcastes among them."[19] Trade was established and well regularized, but the effects on those who possessed British goods were not all that beneficial—foreboding of the destructive intertribal trade wars of the nineteenth century: "No longer before our Arrival the Inhabitants of Charlotte's Sound had been taken unawares and fifty of them destroyed by the people of Admiralty Bay."[20] On 27 February 1777 the two ships, caulked and repaired, sailed Tahiti bound from Cape Palliser, with two Maori boys on board as servants for Mai, weeping and singing doleful songs for several days afterward.

Twenty days later James King reported an event (unrecorded by Cook himself) that suggests the first crack in Cook's composure on this trip: "The Ship's Company put to ⅔ Allowance of salt provisions . . . owing to some appearance of general disobedience among the people; many complaints had been made to the Captain of inferior Officers and particularly others having their victuals stolen but no offender could be found; the Captain to put a stop to these thefts told the people that if they would not themselves try to find out the thieves, he would whenever meat was stolen, for the next day put them on ⅔ Allowance. . . ."[21] Naturally people protested at being punished for no fault of their own and refused to eat the two-thirds allowance. Cook thought this "a very mutinous proceeding" and because honest people should try to find out the source of the theft, he would "not only put them at ⅔ Allowance the day after, but that it should continue, and that they also should be deprived of having their raw meat etc."[22] This harsh treatment of hard workers suggests that Cook had temporarily lost his grasp of shipboard life, a herald of what was to follow: more floggings for misconduct, desertions, and "mutinous" behavior than in any of the previous voyages. The particular event also gives us a hint about the psychological aspects of the relation between Cook and ordinary seamen: He was a stern father, and the psychology of food giving and withdrawal expressed this nicely. Bad conduct leads to withdrawal of food (love), and good conduct is often rewarded with extra food, and especially grog, the mixture of brandy and water, indispensable for ordinary seamen. Excessive harshness from the father does not lead to open rebellion; the sons perversely refuse to eat food.

Cook's plan was to sail to Tahiti and from there up north to the Arctic. Consequently, he headed northeast from New Zealand on a new route through a group of Polynesian islands (now named after him) and thence to Tonga, named the Friendly Islands, where he stayed for about two and a half months. From there the voyage proceeded to the Tahitian islands, and then came the serendipitous discovery of another Serendib, Hawai'i. In this work I shall focus only on a narrow theme, namely Cook's increasing propensity for violence and his erratic, often irrational, behavior. These characterological traits were always there; but in this last voyage they seem to have engulfed Cook in a heart of darkness from which there was no escape. My brief survey of the Kurtz persona in Cook is to show that the events that led to his death in Hawai'i were by no means unique but presaged in Tonga and Tahiti.

It was in early May 1778 when they anchored in Nomuka, one of the Tongan islands. People crowded on board, and chiefs cleared the decks with violence such that "blood gushed out of both mouth and nostrils" of one man.[23] Cook was appalled. But the fact is that according to Tongan culture these people in their eagerness to visit the ship unwittingly violated the Tongan norms regarding deference behavior before chiefs. Ordinary seamen could be whipped for parallel infractions. But the English, like other European explorers, simply could not see any parallelism whatever. Their criticisms applied to Polynesian commensal rules also. On 8 May, Cook invited Finau, a powerful chief, and others to dinner, and noted as he did on previous occasions, that not only were women excluded but the principle of exclusion applied to chiefs also, such that "none but Tapah [Kepa] was allowed to sit at table with him."[24] In fact, similar rules existed on board ship: Ordinary seamen were totally excluded from the officer's table; and the officers' privilege of eating with the captain was highly restricted and regulated according to time, place, and circumstance. Both were hierarchical societies, but the English were as incapable of critical reflection about their own hierarchies as the Polynesians were regarding theirs. Both, however, could be critical of each other, in their own different ways.

Polynesian violence might well have triggered Cook's own. "Theft" of course was the provocation, and, says Cook, "even some of the Chiefs did not think this profession beneath them."[25] When a chief in Finau's own entourage stole a "bolt belonging to the spun yarn wench," Cook ordered "a dozen lashes and make him pay a hog for his liberty, after this we were not troubled with thieves of rank."[26] The flogging of chiefs before their own people is an extraordinary action for Cook, and Anderson, the ships' surgeon, generally uncritical of Cook, noted:

> I am far from thinking there was any injustice in punishing this man for the theft as it cannot be determined what might be the consequence if such practices had been permitted but that he should be confin'd in a painfull posture for some hours after or a ransom demanded after proper punishment for the crime had been inflicted I believe will scarcely be found consonant with the principles of justice or humanity upon the strictest scrutiny.[27]

But Anderson's scruples were not shared by Captain Clerke, considered to be a man of high spirits, who enjoyed playing pranks and practical jokes, a veritable "wag and lusty extrovert."[28] Cook says Clerke "hit upon a method which had some effect, this was by shaving their heads for though it is not a very uncommon thing to see both men and women with their heads shaved, yet its being done on this occasion was looked upon as a mark of infamy and marked out the man."[29] Both actions reveal a crucial shift in Cook's strategy toward the Polynesians: A chief is being whipped on board and treated as if he were in a class with common seamen, and commoners were given the treatment accorded to prisoners in British jails of that period. The punishments continued: Kepa was a "friend" who, like Finau, was extremely helpful to the crew. Yet when Kepa's son was caught attempting to steal Clerke's cat, he was put in irons.[30] From the point of view of shipboard norms, these were perfectly acceptable punishments.

A week later, having "exhausted the island of all most everything it produced," Cook left for another Tongan island, Lifuka.[31] Cook thought that the Tongans loved the British because they were being treated so well. But we know from Mariner that before Cook left Nomuka a group of chiefs planned to kill him and his officers, probably the very morning (20 May) when a series of wonderful displays were planned to entertain the English. Beaglehole thinks that the Tongans were planning to steal the ships and their goods; but it is equally plausible that the planned murder of Cook and his officers was in retaliation for the public humiliation of chiefs. The plan did not succeed because Finau opted out of it at the last moment.[32]

The punishments imposed on these islanders indicated a fundamental implicit premise of all these voyages: Polynesians were in some manner being brought in line with the judicial norms prevalent on British ships. They expressed an important political reality on the formal level of inter-personal relations: the Polynesians, including their chiefs, were subordinate to the commanders' authority, be it Cook's or Cortés's. The Enlightenment did not produce a change in this basic norm, even though the manner of its implementation might have changed. Ordinary Polynesians were on a par with the crew; chiefs were not, but they were clearly below the officers. There was, however, one important qualitative difference regarding the punishments imposed on Polynesians: The admiralty rules clearly stipulated that no crew member could be given more than twelve lashes per day, though this might have been violated in practice occasionally. This rule obviously did not apply to Polynesians during this third voyage. Cook himself rarely mentions these punishments but Bayly, the astronomer, gives a clear picture of the procedures employed. Stolen objects, he says, were gotten back by applying to the chiefs. "But whenever we catch a Thief he is punished with a severe flogging and if he is a man of Property Captain Cook obliges them to ransom him with Hoggs and Fruit, and in some instances may be said to have been guilty of great cruelty."[33]

Though these punishments were rarely mentioned by Cook in his own journal, glimpses from the logs of some officers show that such punishments were becoming common and conventionalized. Edgar, the *Discovery's* Master, noted the following instances for two weeks in June:

13 June: Punished one of the Indians with 3 dozen lashes on shore for theft.

14 June: At ten in the Morning punish'd one of the Indians with 2 dozen lashes for theft and turned him out of the ship. At ½ past two in the afternoon punished one of the Indians with 36 lashes for Theft.

17 June: At ½ past 1 in the Afternoon punish'd an Indian with 4 dozen lashes and turned him out of the Ship.

23 June: At Noon Captain Cooke shot an Indian in the side with small shot as he was escaping from the ships he having committed theft.

24 June: At three in the Afternoon Captain Clerke punish'd an Indian Chief with 5 dozen lashes for having stolen one tumbler and two Wine glasses during the time he was at Dinner with him.

28 June: About 10 in the Morning those of the old Offenders who had ston'd our Centinels and Wood Cutters were taken prisoners. Cap-

tain Cooke punish'd one with 3 dozen lashes, another with 4 dozen
and the third with 6 dozen lashes. . . . After this a strange punishment was inflicted on the Man which received Six dozen as Captain
Cooke said that he might be known hereafter, as well as to deter the
rest from theft or using us ill when on Shore—this was by scoring
both his arms with a common knife by one of our Seamen, Longitu-
dinally and transversely, into the Bone.[34]

To put the last case differently: Cook ordered a cross to be cut on both
shoulders (arms), penetrating to the bone, of a man who had suffered already from seventy-two lashes, six times the limit prescribed by the admiralty for ordinary crew members. This Polynesian, who we are told belonged to a group who had stoned the woodcutters and sentinels, wore the
cross literally as a punishment for theft. The major journals hardly refer to
events of this sort, but it appears that ordinary Tongans were resisting the
British presence in their own fashion. We know from the previous voyages
that the ship's crew often cut down trees for firewood or other purposes
without permission, and it is likely that the woodcutters were stoned for
this reason.[35] But Edgar's entry for 20 June suggests that the discontent
was more widespread: "During the latter part of our Stay at Amsterdam
[Tonga], some of the lower class of Indians become very troublesome, particularly to the Centinels and wood Cutters, in the Evenings . . . "[36]

These acts of routinized violence were occasionally met with ritualized
lamentations by the women. When a man stole a pewter basin and was
caught red-handed, Cook observed: "On this occasion three old Women
who were in the Canoe made loud lamentations over the man and beat
their breasts and faces in a most violent manner, and all of this was done
without sheding a teer."[37]

This was 18 June. On this very day Cook, fearful that his domestic animals would also be stolen, decided to distribute them. "With this View the
next evening I assembled all the Chiefs before our house where the Cattle
was" and distributed them in the following manner: To Paulaho, a young
English bull and a cow; to Maealiuaki (who apparently had no interest in
this business) a cape ram and two ewes; to Finau, a horse and a mare.[38] The
animals were nicely coupled to breed and fertilize this Tongan island. The
chiefs were given instructions on their various uses and told "they were not
to kill any till they became very numerous, and lastly, they and their Children were to remember that they had come from the Men of Britane."[39]
We must remember that King George himself had donated some animals,
and it is as if these domestic animals carried his royal imprimatur. Cook
was acting an imperial role when he summoned the great men of the nation
and dispensed his largesse.

This imperiousness was much more clearly evident in the events of the next morning, when, in spite of his generosity, Cook found that "one of our Kids and two Turkey-cocks" were missing. I shall not examine here the symbolic import of these libidinous creatures for Cook, but for now note that his reaction was partly overdetermined by his role as civilizer, taming savage lands with animals domesticated in England, and, in this case in addition, carrying the imprimatur of his sovereign. Cook found the king and other important chiefs drinking kava. He put guards around them and "they were not to stir" till the animals and everything else were returned. The chiefs calmly continued to drink their kava. People began gathering restlessly outside, but Cook says, "I told their chiefs to give orders that no more should appear which they did and their orders were obeyed."[40] He then ordered them on board and "kept them there till near 4 o'Clock," when the animals were returned. Cook was effectively taking chiefs hostage; the latter, like the Tahitian chiefs, were learning to handle Cook, waiting for his rage to subside while they drank kava. Ordinary people, fearful of their chiefs' safety, were more hostilely disposed. On the European side, Samwell explicitly justified Cook's conduct, but Gilbert, a naive seventeen-year-old midshipman, did not, although he also idealized Cook but found his behavior incomprehensible and "rather unbecoming of an European."[41] For apparently, according to Gilbert, Cook used to fire with ball or small shot "as they were swimming or paddling to the shore and suffering the people [sailors] (as he rowed after them) to beat them with the oars, and stick the boat hook into them where ever they could hit them."[42] Strange behaviors, unrecorded by any of the major journal writers, unnoticed by most biographers.

Cook's attitude to native chiefs is very complex. They must be held subordinate to him, and perhaps even to the British crown. Yet both here and in his previous voyages, Cook enjoyed the company of "great men," entertaining them on board ship and being reciprocally feted by them. For the first time, however, he noted his admiration for the ceremonies of prostration practiced by Polynesians before their chiefs. The "decorum observed in the presence of their great men, particularly the Kings . . . is truly admirable."[43] Cook had no familiarity with European courtly styles, yet he says that the Tongan etiquette was far superior to those of Europe. It is in relation to Tongan "etiquette" that Cook's empathy surfaced. If we untangle the sources of this, both cultural and personal, it seems that Cook was in the first place self-conscious of his role as the representative of George III. He was acting out the ambassadorial role with the royalty of another nation. It was not formal role-playing; the role had personal meaning to him. Cook was a son of a day laborer and an entirely self-made man. He was totally alienated from those of his own original class background, the denizens of the ship's lower depths. He was also alienated from the gentlemen upstairs privileged in education, manners, and upbringing. His aloofness, if not the despotism noted by both crew and officers, was related to this alienation. He was caught in the middle of a sharply differentiated class system on board ship. He had practically no friends or confidants there. With the native chiefs, however, he could eat and drink, and his needs for company and sociability were expressed in his relationship with chiefs. Here was an area of life carved out in remote islands where he could act the ambassadorial role in his own style, far from the conventional diplomatic style of the nobility and gentlemen of the courts of Europe, about which he knew little. The decorum of the Tongan nobility which Cook so admired had nothing in common with that of civilized European nations, though he thought it did. In fraternizing with the Polynesian chiefs, Cook was expressing his appreciation for something his own ship lacked: Though crew and officers obeyed him implicitly, as the Tongans did their chiefs, the Tongans' ceremonialization of their subservience and humility "in the presence of their great men" greatly impressed Cook.

Sociability and decorum drew Cook into the kava circle of Tongan chiefly life. It was on the second voyage that Cook and his officers became acquainted with kava. They were repelled by the way it was brewed, but Cook was impressed by the sociability it fostered.[44] Cook was invited to a kava circle by Paulaho, the "king," on 7 June, only four days after landing in Nomuka. Soon Cook was fully ensconced in the kava circle, so that Lieutenant Williamson noted on 17 July that "Captain Cook often drank of it, holding it as an argument that seamen should eat and drink everything that came in their way."[45] Beaglehole is probably correct when he says that by the end of his Tongan stay Cook was "drinking endless kava."[46]

Cook was ready to sail to Tahiti on 6 July when a slight change of winds forced a postponement of a few days. This gave him an opportunity to see the 'inasi ceremony, held on this occasion for the coming of age of the son of Paulaho, the "king" or Tu'i Tonga. Cook admitted to barely understanding complex religious rites, but he described the ceremony well. For present purposes, what is striking is Cook's role in it. He and Mai were permitted to witness the ceremony from a special enclosure after Cook had stripped himself to the waist, let his hair fall down, and taken off his hat. Right through the long and complex proceedings, Cook ignored the restrictions imposed on him, boldly violating tabus and walking on consecrated ground. Two or three people were appointed to watch over him, but he evaded or ignored them. This was on the first day of 'inasi. When it recommenced on the next day, he was not satisfied with his special place in the enclosure and went outside. "I was several times desired to go away, and at last when they found I would not stir, they . . . desired I would bare my shoulders."[47] A special "tabu man" was placed near him to ensure his compliance with Tongan custom, but this restriction too was largely ineffective. Cook knew what "tabu" meant. On the previous voyage he had been sensitive about offending the religious sensibilities of the Tongans.[48] But not now. He boldly walked on consecrated ground and examined sacred emblems without seeking permission.[49]

The Visit to Tahiti and the Destruction of Eimeo

Cook stayed in Tahiti from 13 August to 30 September 1777. Of all the Polynesian people, the Tahitians knew Cook best and had learned how to handle him.[50] For example, during the second voyage, when Cook went in search of a "thief," Tahitian guides took him on long detours till his temper cooled. Here also, on 29 August, when a hatchet was stolen, the chief Tu, fearing Cook's wrath, fled with his family and Cook had to walk three miles to find him.[51] The Tahitians also had a new weapon of the weak. The Spaniards had been there and apparently kept themselves aloof from the native population. No sexual intermingling was permitted and, contrary to English shipboard gossip about their cruelty, they seemed to have behaved with restraint. The Tahitians used the Spanish as an excuse to talk critically about the English. Tahitians told Lieutenant Williamson that "the Spaniards gave them everything they wanted, but if anything was taken from us [the English] by them, everybody was seized upon that we could lay hands of and some practically kill'd, upon the whole we seem to have very little share of their esteem, while the Spaniards have in one voyage the total possession of their affections."[52] It is doubtful whether the Spaniards initiated as idealistic a reign as the Tahitians depicted. But they were a new reference group of Europeans, and Tahitians could use them to carry on a critical commentary on the conduct of the English. Their arguments were so persuasive that Anderson could moralize self-critically: "The consequences of this is that the natives have really acquired a kind of veneration for the people of that nation and seem to respect their moral character still more than admire their power, a proof that tender treatment may sometimes effect more than the force of arms"—an oblique criticism of Cook.[53] This view of the Spanish might have had some effect on cooling the propensity to violence by the English—at least in Tahiti proper.

Cook was concerned about the Spanish presence and was no doubt much relieved when Tu told him that the Spaniards would not be allowed to settle in Matavai "for it [Matavai and Tahitinui] belongs to you."[54] "It belongs to you" is a significant phrase. First, Tu is implying that his traditional foe, the Vehiatua of Tahitiiti, might encourage the Spanish but he (Tu) wouldn't. Second, Tu has learned to boost Cook's ego: "Tahitinui belongs to you" in effect says, "You are the lord of this domain." This flattery also has a political purpose, because Tu was trying to enlist Cook's aid in his projected war against the neighboring Moorea or Eimeo.

This war is the event that I want to focus on. The journal discusses it at length, Cook effectively taking over the narrative from his previous visit in 1774 when Tu and Teto'ofa (Towha) pleaded for his aid.[55] On 30 August, Cook reports that the people of Eimeo were up in arms and Tu's friends "had been obliged to fly to the mountains." He refers to the people of Eimeo as "malcontents." Cook thought of Tu as the "king" of all of Tahiti, a chief like Teto'ofa, his "admiral." It is true that Cook was projecting the British model of kingship to Tahiti; but he superimposes on it another model, that of authority on ship. Mutiny is a horrendous shipboard crime, and Cook looks upon those who defy the authority of the king as mutineers.[56]

Cook records a council meeting in Tu's house where the Tahitians decided to send a strong force to support a group of their friends living in Eimeo. "Those who were for prosecuting the War asked for my assistance and all of them wanted to know what part I would take." Cook declared that he was not acquainted with the dispute and because the people of Eimeo had not offended him, he could take no part in it. This, Cook thought, seemed to satisfy them.[57]

On the morning of 1 September, Teto'ofa (Towha), the prominent chief of the Oropaa division of the country (Cook's "admiral"), sent a message to Tu that he had "killed a Man to be sacrificed to the Eatua [atua], to implore the assistance of the God against Eimeo."[58] Cook thought this a "good opportunity to see something of this extraordinary and Barbarous custom," and with Tu's permission, accompanied him "to the great Morai [temple] at Attahourou [Atehuru]" with Mai, Anderson, and Webber, the artist.[59] Cook's description of human sacrifice (and also Anderson's) is one of the high points of the voyage journals, a superb documentation surpassing anything that Cook had done before. I do not wish to discuss this ritual, because it is not directly relevant to the theme of this book. Cook expressed his repugnance to Tu, and Mai foolishly told Tu that even the greatest man in England would be punished for killing his servant. Thus "we left him with as great a contempt of our customs as we could possibly have of theirs."[60]

What is striking about Cook's behavior is that, contrary to his protestations, he was in fact taking sides. When he felt there was a rumor that some chiefs in Tahiti itself might turn against Tu, Cook wrote that "this called upon me to support my friend [Tu] by threatening to retaliate it upon all who came against him when I returned again to the island."[61] Tu's own father asked Cook whether he and his family could join him on his visit to Eimeo. "This sencible old Man no doubt foresaw that my going down with them must have added great weight to their cause without my takeing any other part whatever in the quarrel. . . ."[62] It is therefore very clear that Cook was fully aware of the political implications of having Tu's father and his family on board on his projected trip to Eimeo. None of this turned out to be necessary, for both sides eventually agreed to a truce, and Cook left Tahiti for Eimeo.

On 2 October, the day after Cook anchored in Eimeo, Mahine, the chief, "approached the ship with great caution and it required some persuasion to get him on board."[63] This is the man who "has made himself in a manner independent of Otaheite [Tahiti]."[64] Mahine was a frail, bald, one-eyed old man but when he visited Cook he covered his baldness with a cloth as if he was "ashamed to show his head." Cook soon realized Mahine's dilemma. People here had seen them "shave the head of one of their people, whom we had caught stealing," and poor Mahine thought that baldness was a disgrace in English society.[65] Perhaps this was reinforced by his people noticing that the ship's gentlemen wore wigs or hats. Not a single shipboard account, as far as I know, refers to this theft and the punishment by head shaving, except this oblique reference by Cook himself. One can make two reasonable inferences from this silence: First, head shaving for theft has been so much routinized that it is taken for granted by the ships' journalists; and second, this punishment was inflicted on the very day he landed in Eimeo, heralding a shift in his attitude toward these Polynesian peoples and their leader, the malcontent Mahine.

The violence commenced with the loss once again of two goats on 6 October. Cook says that it interfered with his stocking other islands with these animals, a lame rationalization, for presumably he could have reduced the number of animals meant for Eimeo itself. Moreover, one animal belonged to the *Resolution*'s lieutenants' mess.[66] Cook thought that the animal was taken to Mahine, the chief. The texts do not reveal how this thought occurred to him, but it is likely that Mai, feeding on Cook's prejudices, was responsible because he was Cook's sole interpreter. Cook sent "a threatening [message] to Mahine if the goat was not delivered up and also the thief."[67] But the people who went to search for the goat never came back, no doubt infuriating Cook further, especially because one was a "she goat and big with kid."[68] Soon the first goat and the culprit were apprehended; the latter did not deny the theft but "said he took it because Captain Cook's men had taken his breadfruit and Coconuts, and refused to pay for them."[69] This man therefore had to be released but Cook's anger did not diminish. Cook sent two petty officers in a boat to look for the other goat, but they returned empty-handed. Mai advised Cook "to shoot every Soul I met with" but, says Cook, "this bloody advice I could not follow."[70] Yet he did go to extraordinary lengths to recover the pregnant goat. "I ordered Lieutenant Williamson with three Armed boats round the western part of the island to meet us. I no sooner landed with my party than the few Natives that had remained fled before us, the first man Omai [Mai] saw he asked me if he should shoot him, so fully was he persuaded that I was going to carry his advice into execution,"—no doubt because Mai sensed Cook's terrible rage.[71] And now the wonderful account of the search for a goat by about thirty-five well-armed Englishmen:

> As we began to ascend the ridge of hills over which we had to pass, we got intellengence that the Goat was gone before us, and as we understood not yet gone over the hills, so that we marched up in great silence in hopes of surprising the party that had her; but whin we got to the uppermost plantation on the side of the ridge the people there told us, she was kept there the first night and the next Morning carri'd to Watea by Hamoah. We then crossed the ridge, without making any further enquiry, till we came in sight of Watea, when some people shew'd us Hamoah's house and told us the Goat was there so that I made myself sure of geting it immediately, and was not a little surprised to find on my geting to the place, the few people we met with deny having ever seen her, even Hamoah himself. On my first coming to the place I observed several Men runing to and from in the woods with Clubs and bundles of darts in their hands, and Omai who followed them had some stones thrown at him, so that it seemed as tho' they had intended to oppose any step I should take by force, but seeing my party too strong droped the design: a nother thing which made me think so, was all their houses being empty. After geting a few of the people of the place together I desired Omai to expostulate with them on the conduct they were persuing, and to tell them, that from the testimony of so many people, I was well assured they had the Goat and therefore insisted upon its being deliv[er]ed up, *if not I would burn their houses and boats.*[72]

Because people did not listen to him or Mai, Cook says he set fire "to six or eight houses which were presently consumed, together with two or three War Canoes that lay [in] some of them."[73] But still no goat. Cook sent a message next morning with one of Mai's men to chief Mahine that "if he did not send the goat I would not leave him a Canoe in the island and that I would continue destroying till it came."[74] True to his word he sent the carpenters to break up three or four canoes that lay ashore at "the head of the harbour." The madness had a method in it: The planks, says Cook, were to be used to build a house for Mai in Huahine![75] But the ravaging, raging, and uprooting went on: "Afterward I went to the next harbour, broke up three or four more and burnt as many."[76] Naturally the goat was returned.

It is remarkable that Cook included this account of massive destruction in his journals, and I can only surmise that by this time he lacked enough judgment to delete such events. There is also a lack of remorse; all he could say is, "Thus this troublesome, and rather unfortunate affair ended, which could not be more regretted on the part of the Natives than it was mine."[77]

Only two journal writers seem to justify Cook's conduct. Samwell thought that the chiefs "brought it upon themselves" and though the reprisals seemed too severe, in fact "they are merciful, as the Natives will be more cautious upon future occasions . . . they had nobody but themselves to blame."[78] Clerke, a bit more critical, nevertheless thought that after all, "every gentle method was taken to recover" the goats.[79] By contrast, our naive midshipman Gilbert astutely noted that Cook was motivated by "his great friendship for Otoo [Tu] to whom these people were professed enemies."[80] What is striking is King's criticisms, because he, like Samwell, idolized Cook. "I doubt whether our Ideas of propriety in punishing so many innocent people for the crimes of a few, will ever by reconcilable to any principles one can form of justice. *At all events plunder should not have been permitted* . . . in future they may fear but never love us."[81] For the first time Cook resorts to plunder, the imagined way of savage warfare, as he kills hogs and dogs and rifles native gardens of coconuts and breadfruit for later shipboard consumption.[82]

On 11 October, Cook left the desolated little island of Eimeo for Huahine, where he was planning to install Mai, and anchored in Fare harbor the next day. But even before landing, King reports that "an Indian we had brought from Eimaio had been caught with something he had stolen, on which the Captain in a Passion ordered the Barber to shave his head and cut off his ears."[83] Luckily for this man, a ships' officer (perhaps Gore or King himself) "convinced that the Captain was only in a Passion," gave fresh orders so that the culprit could get away with the lobe of one ear missing.[84] It seems that the English officers, like the Tahitian chiefs, were devising ways to mitigate the Captain's "passion."

In Huahine Cook assembled the chiefs and, with Mai acting as spokesman, asked them for land to build a house for Mai and his two Maori servants. The response? "A Man rose up and told me that *the whole island of Huaheine and everything in it was mine* and therefore I might give what part of it to Omai."[85] This statement, like that of the Tahitian Tu, might be plain flattery or an idiosyncratic way of attempting to please Cook, but it is likely that Cook took it literally. It is even possible that Cook imagined it all. He was the lord of the islands. "In order to intimidate these [people], I gave out that I should return to the island again after being absent the usual time, and that if I did not find Omai in the same state as I left him all those who had been his enemy would feel the weight of my resentment."[86]

This resentment fell heavily on the man who stole a sextant on 23 October from astronomer Bayly's observatory. Mai tried to intercede with the chiefs but they were watching a play. Cook ordered the play to be stopped. Mai detected the culprit at the show. He was taken on board and clapped in irons. His head and beard were shaved and both his ears were cut off.[87]

The sextant was recovered and the man set free; but soon he had his revenge on Mai by destroying the vines and cabbage plants in Mai's garden. Cook had him seized and clamped again in the same place.[88] Cook and Mai seemed to think alike now: The distinction between the civilizer who had become savage and the savage who had been civilized had broken down in this piece of joint connivance at kidnapping. But either the quartermaster or the sentinel set this man free; consequently both were put in irons and "flogged every day since" and then "disrated for neglect of duty."[89]

Cook's relationship with Mai resembled one model of the long-term relation between an ethnographer and his interpreter (or key informant) who guides the former through the mazeways of the culture. Like the ethnographer and his interpreter, Cook and Mai were in a close, almost symbiotic relationship, such that one seemed to be the alter ego of the other, each feeding the fragments of the dark side of the other's being.

For Mai, coming from a low-status background, and then lionized by the great in England, Cook was the *real* chief. His own position in the islands depended on Cook. Cook had by now taken over the effective lordship of the islands by terrorizing the inhabitants. About Huahine he said that "anarchy seemed to prevail here [more] than any other place, the Earee rahee [*ari'i rahi*] as I have before observed was but a Child and I could not find there was any one man or set of Men who managed the Government for him."[90] The people were troublesome, and it was "only fear" and lack of opportunity that made them behave.

It is no longer necessary to record the litany of punishments inflicted on these islanders. The brutality itself was infectious. On the very day the ships landed in Ra'iatea, after the sojourn in Huahine, Williamson, the moralist, always critical of Cook, "stamped his foot on the side of [a man who had stolen a nail] and broke several of his teeth out and otherwise bruised the Indian very much."[91] In previous visits the people of Ra'iatea showered the crew with feasts and spectacles. But not this time. John Harrison, a marine, deserted and Cook went after him with two boatloads of armed marines and apprehended him in a village house.[92] This was followed by two more serious desertions, that of Alexander Mouat, son of Captain Mouat of the navy, and another of an ordinary seaman, both of the *Discovery*. Apparently all attempts by Cook to find them were futile because they had fled to Borabora. In order to retrieve them, Cook took a most extraordinary step: He invited the chief, Rio, his son, daughter, and son-in-law on board, and asked Clerke to keep them all, except Rio, aboard the *Discovery* as hostages. Rio had once been Cook's friend, and naturally he interceded with him for the release of his family, not believing that Cook had ordered the imprisonment himself. And Cook replied, "If my two men was not brought back I would carry the others away with me."[93] In his previous trip Rio and his family had feasted him, generously supplied the ships' wants, performed shows in his honor; and Cook had a very affectionate farewell from them.[94] But now, says Clerke, "old Oreo [Rio] was half mad, and within an hour afterwards we had a most numerous Congregation of Women under the Stern, cutting their heads with Sharks Teeth and lamenting the Fate of the prisoners, in so melancholy a howl, as render'd the ship while it lasted, which was 2 or 3 hours, a most wretched Habitation. . . ."[95] Rio's men eventually brought the deserters from Borabora and the hostages were released. But now several chiefs planned to kill Cook and Clerke when they went to bathe in a freshwater place, but the plan was revealed by a Huahine woman on board. The two captains did not go to bathe that day.[96]

The Discovery of Hawai'i

The discovery of Hawai'i was neither premeditated nor anticipated by Cook. These islands accidentally and serendipitously appeared before him on his way up north, on 19 January 1778, about five weeks after he left Borabora, his last contact with the Tahitian islands. The visit was very brief, with Cook remaining on land for only three days, but these were momentous days in retrospect. The challenge of the new discovery seemed to have stimulated Cook, fascinated as he was by the enormous spread and dispersal of Polynesian culture.

The first thing that surprised Cook was the orderliness that characterized trade exchanges. There were only a few cases of "theft," and Cook, along with other senior officers, thought that the Hawaiians were probably the most honest of all the South Sea islanders. Because the Hawaiians did not practice theft, there was no immediate provocation for retaliation. Cook was also concerned about the spread of the "venereal" and he issued orders forbidding "all manner of connection with them," knowing of course the futility of these regulations.[97] The episode that I want to focus on occurred on the morning of the 20 January, the day after the sighting of Kaua'i. Cook ordered Third Lieutenant Williamson to look for a place of anchorage. It is then that Williamson killed the first Hawaiian. In his journal he defends his action: He had given strict orders to the ordinary seamen in his boat not to fire owing to "the great wantonness of the inferior people on board a ship, and the idea they posses that it is no harm to kill an indian." But, says Williamson, as they tried to land, over a hundred natives got ahold of the boat and several jumped inside. Williamson bribed them with a few nails and got them out and then tried to seek another landing place, which was impossible because several others were trying to get into the boat. In his desire for iron, one man got ahold of the boat hook;

Williamson offered him a nail, and when he refused, tried to hit him with a rifle butt, to no effect. One Hawaiian "made a stroke at me" while the other man still clung to the boat hook, so that, Williamson says, he was compelled to fire. "The man who was shot was a tall handsome man about 40 years of age and seemed to be a Chief, the ball entering his right pap, he instantly dropt down dead in the water. . . ."[98] It is not clear whether the Hawaiians were trying to steal iron, as Williamson claimed, or simply trying to get the foreigners to land where they were. Because this incident occurred soon after a Hawaiian had stolen a butcher's cleaver from the ship, Williamson simply interpreted their actions as "stealing." Cook, commenting on this event much later felt that Williamson had misunderstood the behavior of the Hawaiians. He thought they had no design "to kill or even hurt any of the people in the boat but were excited by mere curiosity to get what they had from them, and were at the same time, ready to give in return anything they had."[99] Nothing was in fact stolen from the boat. Williamson, who felt he had to justify his action and answer Cook's reprimand, cited a previous authority later on in his journal: "These barbarians must be [initially] quelled by force, as they afterwards readily believe that whatever kindness is then shown them proceeds from love, whereas otherwise they attribute it to weakness, or cowardice, and presents only increase their insolence. . . ."[100] Williamson's rationale is but a minor variation of the views held by the ship's officers, Cook included, to justify creating an initial sense of terror among native populations.

Cook was not aware of the killing when he stepped onshore, that very afternoon, to a place where several hundred natives were assembled. "The very instance I leaped ashore, they all fell flat on their faces, and remained in that humble posture till I made signs for them to rise."[101] It was clear that the native reaction was based on the terror created by Williamson, who was now accompanying Cook. Williamson, boasted that this submissiveness was due to "the good effects of at once shewing our superiority" and therefore a vindication of his own actions.[102] Soon afterward a native guide, like the tabu man in Tonga, escorted Cook wherever he went. Cook clearly recognized that these ceremonies of prostration were of the type "done to their great chiefs."[103] Accompanied by his guide, Cook and some of his officers visited a Hawaiian temple or *heiau* in Waimea and made a brief description of it. From Cook's account it is virtually certain that no major festival was going on at this time in Kaua'i.

I will not describe the long and futile quest for the northwest passage except to highlight Cook's increasing moodiness, isolation from officers and men, lonely rages, and the seeming loss of touch with reality. There were signs of this in Hawai'i. Thomas Roberts, the quartermaster of his ship, died on 27 January; Cook makes no reference to this important event in his journals. Beaglehole's explanation that the business of discovery was taking all his attention is naive, because in times of greater activity during the previous voyages, Cook, a stickler for detail, noted deaths and injuries of his crew.[104] It is as if the death had not touched him. Consider his actions toward Mai, who used to urge Cook to kill various islanders: After installing him in Huahine, Cook left him with a large arsenal of deadly weapons and a liberal store of ammunitions.[105] Another bizarre account in his journal is a detailed description of the Hawaiian sweet potato, as if he had never known it before. "I am told these potatoes are very common in Virginia and other parts of North America and known by the name of spanish potatoes."[106] In fact, he was thoroughly familiar with them, having eaten them regularly in New Zealand; yet he seems to have no recollection of this. Later, up on the Northwest coast, Cook twice took possession of territories on behalf of the Crown in performative acts that were quite meaningless because, unlike the situation on the Polynesian islands, there was no bounded entity, except a desolate bay or river, to take possession of. Anderson, the ship's surgeon, noted the futility of these ceremonials, performed routinely and without a purpose.[107] Another more serious error in judgment, according to Beaglehole, occurred when Cook made four imperfect sightings of the same island and then gave different names to each sighting, such as Clerke's island and Anderson's island. Bligh called this "a gross mistake"; and Beaglehole correctly states that "assuredly the Cook of the second voyage would have disentangled the truth."[108]

Hough, another recent admirer of Cook, adds to this catalogue the hero's ill judgment in navigation itself: "The lapses in the sense of responsibility which—for example—led Gore to persuade him up Cook's Inlet in Alaska, to his casual attitude to his timetable that led to his losing two Arctic summers? ... What explanation can there be for sailing straight towards that reef off Bonavista, and those and other near-fatal errors of seamanship and navigation?"[109] These lapses occurred in the journey up north. Here again Cook acted irrationally toward his men when he asked them to eat walrus flesh, which they hated. When they refused, he cut off all their salt provisions and it was only with difficulty that he was persuaded to "restore salt meat to those who would otherwise have starved."[110] King himself thought that in this instance Cook "was more precipitate than his usual good sense and penetration warrant'd";[111] but Hough more bluntly calls this "force feeding them on stinking walrus flesh."[112]

No wonder their voyage north was a long, cold one without any signs of a breakthrough in the discovery of the passage. The ships gave constant trouble largely due to inferior material and shoddy workmanship. Cook withdrew more and more to himself, almost totally eschewing the company and confidence of his officers. His rages apparently became more frequent: It is during this period that Trevenen referred to his rages as *heivas*:

Heiva the name of the dances of the Southern Islanders, which bore so great a resemblance to the violent motions and stampings on the Deck of Captain Cook in the paroxysms of passion, into which he threw himself upon the slightest occasion that they were universally known by the same name, and it was a common saying amongst both officers and people: "The old boy has been tipping a *heiva* to such and such a one."[113]

In this "damned unhappy part of the world," there was no place to plant gardens and to stock the land with domestic animals. Anderson, the popular ship's surgeon, died of consumption. The approaching winter forced Cook in October to temporarily abandon his project. "The ice had beaten him," says Beaglehole, and Cook himself recognizes this:

> But I must confess I have little hopes of succeeding; Ice though an obstacle not easily surmounted, is perhaps not the only one in the way. The Coast of the two Continents is flat for some distance off; and even in the middle between the two the depth of water is inconsiderable: this, and some other circumstances, all tending to prove that there is more land in the frozen sea than as yet we know of. . . .[114]

There was no way Cook could continue; he decided to go back to Hawai'i (the Sandwich Islands) for the Winter months and try again in the following year for the impossible northwest passage.

The return to warmer climes a month later did not produce a thaw in Cook. His journals do not tell us much about him, but those of others do. The Hawaiian islands were sighted on 26 November 1778. Cook proclaimed the usual orders: Trading should be conducted only by those he authorized, and women would not be permitted on board. The latter was to prevent VD, though Cook himself realized that these people had already got the "Veneral distemper" from the last visit.[115] All of the trading was conducted by natives who came in their canoes and climbed overboard. There was no scarcity of food, though there was a shortage of trade goods on board, for, except for nails and tools, says Cook, "we had nothing else to give them."[116] A third regulation was entirely new and without doubt related to Williamson's conduct and, prior to that, to the Tongan experience. It said that officers carrying firearms have provoked natives to steal, and "it is therefore Ordered that no Officer or other person (not sent on duty) shall carry with him out of the Ships, or into the Country, any fire Arms whatever, and great care is to be taken to keep the Natives ignorant of the method of charging such as we may be under a necessity to make use of."[117] This last regulation was for the most part redundant, because Cook, instead of landing as everyone expected him to do, continued going round the island for a period of about seven weeks! Beaglehole says that "it begins to look as if Cook, for whatever reason, had lost touch with his men."[118]

These men, like Cook himself, had just completed an extremely arduous and physically exhausting voyage. As always, they expected to be compensated by release from the closed and confining conditions on board. Cook's policy had been, up till now, to weigh anchor as soon as it was feasible and release the men. But not now: The men were not only confined on board, but they had no access to women, who were out in canoes, wanting to come in, and when they were turned away, says Riou, "they abused us, (finding that nothing could be done by fair words) most sincerely."[119] There has obviously been a change of policy on Cook's part. "King, waiting at some length until they were safely in harbour . . . thought he could see it; but he could no more than 'presume' his Captain's motives. The policy was to keep the sea as long as possible; and we do not know, either, whether to begin with the Captain was clear about his motives himself."[120] Beaglehole was right: The policy did not seem rational but was consistent with Cook's loss of judgment noted earlier. One might ask whether its basis was in Cook's enveloping *irrationality*, which was paralleled by the lack of curiosity he had exhibited in Tonga, where he had heard about Fiji and Samoa but did not care to visit them even though he had plenty of time. Now here Cook was going round and round the island, forgetting that one of the goals of the voyages was ethnology. He had spent only three days on land during the earlier visit; now he was squandering precious time circling the island when he should have been investigating the lifeways of the Hawaiians. King noted this failure in his journals:

> If it be an object, and if there be one amongst us, whose abilities and leisure would have enabled him to have made enquiries into the Customs of the Natives, and of the produce of the Islands, it certainly by this mode of proceeding was greatly frustrated, our connextions were with the lowest and most ignorant of the people, who were too much occupied in selling their goods and getting on shore again, to attend to our enquiries: and of the land we could speak but very superficially.[121]

Other actions by Cook indicated his continuing forgetfulness and loss of contact with everyday reality. On Monday, 7 December, about two weeks after land had been sighted, the supplies of beer had run out and Cook substituted his own concoction. "Having procured a quantity of Sugar Cane and had upon trial made but a few days before, found that a strong decoction of it made a very palatable beer, which was esteemed by every one on board, I ordered some more to be brewed, but when the cask came to be broached not one of my Mutinous crew would even so much as taste it."[122] "Every one on board" referred, of course, to the officers; the "turbulent crew alleged it was injurious to their health."[123] Cook was using strong language to describe the conduct of the crew, who had sent him a letter remonstrating against it and, according to Midshipman Watts, "at the same time mentioning the scanty Allowance of Provisions serv'd them, which they thought might be increas'd where there was such Plenty and that bought for mere trifles."[124]

What is remarkable about the last statement is that the ship's crew, ever since the voyage up north, had been on a "short allowance." They should have been put on full ration, because they were now in the midst of plenty. Beaglehole's explanation that "Cook seems simply to have forgotten" is patently inadequate.[125] What about Lieutenant King and the other senior officers on the two ships? Surely not everyone could have forgotten. Perhaps none of the ships' officers dared approach Cook to broach this matter; or, if they did, Cook simply ignored them and refused to rescind his order. The discontent over the short allowance could not have arisen suddenly; if it had, some of the officers would have found out and, in spite of their awe, they would surely have approached Cook. In either case Cook was neglectful; had he been aware of the sailors' situation, as I think he was, he was *deliberately* punishing the sailors for a transgression that no one seems to know about. He, the father, was withholding his love. Cook's own reply, according to Watts, was that had he known about it earlier he would have rectified it.[126]

Cook's reaction to the "mutinous" attitude of the crew reinforces my hypothesis that the discourse on food is also a discourse on love.[127] "I gave orders that no grog should be served in either ships," says Watt; "the brandy cask was struck down into the Hold."[128] The shadow of Kurtz has once again fallen on Cook.

Food therefore seems to operate on two levels: the ordinary practical level of everyday reality and the symbolic level of "psychic reality." This is true of the formalized scenarios of the Polynesians and the more informal or provisional scenarios of the British. Cook described the sailors' behavior as turbulent and mutinous; a letter of protest followed by the refusal to eat food could hardly be characterized that way. Their actions expressed the petulance of children toward a father who is both a disciplinarian and a giver (even if rarely) of love. The father is in turn angry at the children's rebellion; he withholds grog, a powerful source of physical and psychic solace which helps one to forget the rigors of shipboard life, to dull its pains. Those who have had their fill become satiated with it; they get "groggy" and go to sleep. Grog is the milk of the father.

The reception the ships received on landing was spontaneous and joyful, both for the islanders and the crew. The ship itself badly needed repairs because "our old ropes and Sails were daily giving way."[129] King estimates that they were greeted by a large concourse on the shore, in canoes or just plain swimming, amounting to over ten thousand people; other estimates are equally impressive.[130] The idea may be true that these people came to see the arrival of their god Lono come in person for the Makahiki festival, but large crowds would surely be inevitable, because the ships had been cruising around the islands for over seven weeks, rousing the curiosity and sense of expectation of the native population.[131] On arrival so many people clambered on board and hung on to the side that the *Resolution* seemed in danger of keeling over. A young chief, Palea, who had attached himself to Cook, "cleared the ship of its incumbrances, and drove away the canoes that surrounded her."[132]

Soon afterward, on the very day of the arrival, an important event took place that many have interpreted as the deification of Cook as the god Lono arriving for the Makahiki festival now under way. I shall deal at length in Part IV with the meaning of these ceremonies for the Hawaiians. Here I am interested in what Cook might have thought about them, and consequently only the briefest description is necessary.

Cook was met on board by an old, kava-emaciated, sore-eyed priest, Koah, who wrapped Cook in a red cloth, and holding a pig in his hand, kept uttering a long oration or "prayer." Then accompanied by Palea, King, and Bayly (the astronomer), Cook was taken to the shrine known as Hikiau (which we now know belonged to the paramount chief or king, Kalaniʻopuʻu). They were soon conducted to a scaffold-like structure by Koah and a younger priest, Keliʻikea. At the foot of the scaffold were twelve images arranged in a semicircular fashion with a smaller image (of the god Kū) in the center. Rather elaborate rites were performed here, the most interesting one being that in which Cook was made to prostrate, with some reluctance, before the central image and kiss it. Some of the ships' officers surmised that it was a welcoming ceremony. Everyone was impressed at the reception accorded him, where "people, except those of the Priesthood, lay ... prostrate or rather on their Hands and Knees with their Heads bowed to the Ground."[133] King thought that these prostrations were a repetition of the ones practiced in Kauaʻi. Because in Kauaʻi Cook thought that he was being treated as one of their own great chiefs, one must assume that he gave the same interpretation to the Hawaiʻi ceremonies.

The tents, including the one for the observatory, were pitched adjacent to the *heiau* (called *morai*, from the Tahitian *marae*, by the ships' journals) in a field of sweet potatoes. The field was tabued by the priests, so that no ordinary people and women could enter. The sail makers were given two houses at the end, and part of one of the houses was used as a hospital or sick bay.

The remarkable feature about the Hawaiian experience is the Hawaiians' extreme generosity with food and provisions. Soon King realized that it was "to a Chief named Kao who would come with Terreeoboo [Kalaniʻopuʻu] to whom we were oblig'd for all provisions."[134] Kao, or Haloa'e, was the chief priest of the king, Kalani'opu'u. Lieutenant King was so touched by the generosity of the priests, including Keli'ikea, that he thought that they had a "separate interest" from that of the king. This was not the case; the priests were probably acting on Kalani'opu'u's orders. It is also clear from Lieutenant King's account that Koah and Keli'ikea, the two priests who performed the rituals for Cook, were also "servants" of the king and indeed went to meet him on 24 January, when he arrived at Hawai'i from his Maui campaign in order to meet Cook.[135]

The impending arrival of Kalani'opu'u meant that the Bay was tabued, and King says "all intercourse with us interdicted!"[136] This meant the end of the supply of provisions. "The next morning [25 January], therefore, they endeavored, both by threats and promises, to induce some of the natives to come alongside; and as some of them were at last venturing to put off, a chief was observed attempting to drive them away. A musquet was immediately fired over his head, to make him desist, which had the desired effect, and refreshments were soon after purchased as usual."[137] "Threats and promises": We are not told anything beyond this. It is also clear that trading tempted ordinary people to violate the tabu. The officers also knew a tabu was in effect, yet they ignored it, firing a musket over the head of a chief who tried to enforce it. We are given a hint that these accounts hide more than they reveal.

That afternoon Kalani'opu'u arrived on board informally, and next day onshore formally "in a grand and magnificent manner," with his chiefs in their "rich feathered cloaks and helmets" followed by Kao and his brethren "with their idols displayed on red cloth."[138] A third canoe was full of hogs and vegetables. Then King Kalani'opu'u went onshore and Cook followed him. "After we had got into the Markee [tent], the King got up and threw in a graceful manner over the Captains shoulders the Cloak he himself wore, and put a feathered Cap upon his head, and a very handsome fly flap in his hand."[139] They exchanged names; and Cook, who sensed the significance of the actions from his previous Polynesian experiences, put "a linen shirt on the King and girt his own hanger [sword] round him."[140] The exchange of names and clothes indicate, from Kalani'opu'u's Polynesian viewpoint, an interaction between equals.[141] Cook, as well as the ships' officers, understood these actions to mean the "strongest pledge of friendship."[142] Soon afterward, the priest Kao wrapped a red cloth around Cook's shoulders and presented him with a pig. King was surprised that Kalani'opu'u was the same "emaciated old man" who had come on board on 30 November 1778 when they were circling the islands. He was now attended by his two sons and his nephew Kamehameha, who, says King, had "the most savage face I ever beheld."[143] "During all this time, not a canoe was seen in the bay, and the natives either kept within their huts, or lay prostrate on the ground. Before the King left the *Resolution*, Captain Cook obtained leave for the natives to come and trade with the ships as usual; but the women, for what reason we could not learn, still continued under the effect of the taboo; that is, were forbidden to stir from home, or to have any communication with us."[144]

III

_____ ❧❧ _____

The Thesis of the Apotheosis

The reception that Cook received when he landed on Kealakekua Bay on Sunday, 17 January 1779, has been interpreted by every biographer and historian of Cook as one accorded to a god. Cook was called "Lono" by Hawaiians, and Lono is the presiding deity of the great Hawaiian thanksgiving festival, the Makahiki. Cook arrived coincidentally during this festival, we are told. Thus, Hawaiians thought he was their god arriving (symbolically to be sure) from Kahiki or Tahiti, the mythic land from beyond the horizon. Consequently, he was ceremonially welcomed at Hikiau, the temple (*heiau*) of the Hawaiian king, Kalani'opu'u. Thereafter, wherever he went, people prostrated before him and made him offerings (some say sacrifices). Even those missionaries who did not like Cook reaffirmed his apotheosis, if only to blame him as an idolator and a latter-day Herod; and native converts concurred. There is little space for disagreement here, even though the major journalists on board Cook's ships who wrote extensively on such matters never once made any of these connections.

The identification of Cook with Lono was attributed to Hawaiians by Western scholars; it seems to have been accepted, at least in part, by native Hawaiian scholars and antiquarians. However, *Fragments of Hawaiian History* recorded by Papa I'i and the rituals described by Kamakau of Ka'awaloa, who might have actually witnessed Lono rituals as a boy, make no reference to either Cook or his deification.[1] Unfortunately, portions of the work of Kamakau of Ka'awaloa are lost; and Papa I'i was born and raised on Oahu, a place Cook did not visit. Consequently, it is possible that Oahu did not produce Cook myths of any significance. This last point is of some importance to the analysis that follows: I assume that the impact of Cook in the Hawaiian islands during 1778–79 was neither uniform nor identical, and therefore the manner in which he was incorporated into Hawaiian "history" must also vary from island to island.

The Hawaiian versions of Cook's apotheosis come from accounts of native scholars and missionaries after the Hawaiians had overturned their tabu system in 1819, and the first American evangelical missions had begun to arrive (the following year). These accounts are used by European writers, historians, and biographers for their own interpretations of the momentous events pertaining to Cook's arrival and sojourn. It is remarkable how most of these versions, including the meticulous and scholarly biography of Cook by Beaglehole, take the apotheosis for granted. For example, no attempt is made to contextualize the myths recorded by the missionaries, even though the earliest (Ellis's) appeared forty-four years after Cook's death and S. M. Kamakau's, the most detailed, over eighty years after.[2] The assumption is that native myths have a timeless character, and what was recorded after 1820 must reflect the events of 1779. I shall question this assumption and show that myths are bound by time and context and reflect controversies or "debates" of the period in which they were recorded. This does not mean that such myths or myth-elements do not deal with the past in any significant way; only that their representation of the past is itself a problem for investigation.

The fact that Western scholarship has accepted the myth of Cook's deification attributed to the Hawaiians indicates that we are dealing with the border zone of history, hagiography, and mythmaking. Insofar as Cook's identification with Lono is taken for granted by Westerners, the myth ceases to be exclusively Hawaiian. It is incorporated into the Western view of Cook and is intrinsic to the perception of him in the European consciousness. In my view the perpetuation of this myth is not primarily Hawaiian, because it is doubtful whether Hawaiians wanted this to happen. The pepetuation is essentially Western. It might well be "history"; it can also be "myth," using myth or legend as I shall always do here, in a nonpejorative sense, as a sacred tale or a story of ancestral heroes.

One of the few histories critical of Cook is by Kennedy.[3] It deals exclusively with the last voyage. Like many writers he does not concern himself with the first visit to Kaua'i in January 1778 but with the second to the west coast of the island of Hawai'i. Kennedy titles the relevant chapter "The Return of Lono." He notes that according to Bligh about a thousand canoes came out and altogether a crowd of about ten thousand people assembled. They brought food and gifts, "a royal, even god-like, welcome."[4] The landing in Kealakekua Bay was significant: The name meant "the pathway to the gods." Cook was thus beginning to fulfill Hawaiian prophecies. "On one level Cook was enacting the Hawaiian legend of the return of Lono, a mythical figure from the lost eons of Hawaiian history who they believed would one day return from the sea. On another level, Cook was replenishing his supplies, repairing his ships and making observations as a European discoverer and scientist."[5] Thus there are two opposed worlds out there: the mythic world of the Hawaiians and the pragmatic, rational one of the Europeans.

The knowledge of the deification of Cook comes from information from missionaries, like Hiram Bingham, whom Kennedy quotes:

In very ancient time Lono dwelt at Kealakekua with his *wahine* [wife] Kaikilanialiiopuna. They dwelt together under the precipice. A man ascended the *pali* and called to the woman. "O Kaikilanialiiopuna, may one dare approach you—your paramour—Ohea the soldier? This to join—that to flee—you and I to sleep." Lono hearing, was angry and smote his *wahine*, and Kaikilanialiiopuna died. He took her up, bore her into the temple and there left her. He lamented over her and travelled around Hawaii, Maui, Molakai, Oahu and Kauai boxing with those he met. The people exclaimed, Behold Lono, greatly crazed! Lono replied, "I am crazed for her—I am frantic on account of her love." He left the islands and went to a foreign land in a triangular canoe, called *Paimalu*. Kaikilanialiiopuna came to life again, and travelled all round the islands searching after her husband. The people demanded of her, "What is your husband's name?" She replied, "Lono." "Was that crazy husband yours?" "Aye mine." Kaikilanialiiopuna then sailed by canoe to a foreign land. On arrival of ships the people exclaimed, "Lo this is Lono! Here comes Lono!"[6]

Lono, the god, was represented in iconography as a "small head on a long pole." Not only did Lono reside in Kealakekua Bay but one of the villages there, Kakooa (now Nāpo'opo'o), was dominated by the priests of Lono and their entourage.[7] Further, during the annual festival of Makahiki, "Lono was represented in his boat by large pieces of draped white cloths, not unlike a ship's sails."[8] Cook's ship coincidentally arrived at this time, and canoes came bearing what looked like white streamers. The Europeans mistook these for symbols of truce, peace, and safe conduct, but they were really symbols of Lono. The massive ships with enormous white sails are recognized by Hawaiians as Lono returning in his mythic ship. Kennedy says that the identification of Cook with Lono must have been a tentative conclusion, but one reinforced by the local priests because the fulfillment of the prophecy enhanced their status. The joyous welcome of the people was an expression of the Hawaiians' excitement at the return of their god during the Makahiki festival.

Kennedy then goes on to describe the "obscure and sometimes revolting ceremony" performed by the priests in an impressive temple or *heiau*, a structure of stone, wood, and straw, about fifteen feet high, sixty feet wide, and one hundred twenty feet long.[9] On it were wooden images; outside it was surrounded by a wooden fence. The ritual was conducted by a priest, Koah, assisted by a younger priest, Kaireekeea [Keli'ikea]. None of the Europeans present (Cook, King, and Bayly) understood its significance, except for the constant chanting of the word "Lono." People prostrated themselves before Cook, and wherever he went he was accompanied by attendants chanting "Lono." On 4 February Cook left Kealakekua Bay, and the send-off was very spectacular. Lono had left. Unfortunately the weather was bad and the *Resolution* sprung its mast. They had to come back, but the Hawaiian reception on the return was not cordial. "Lono had only four days to live."[10]

The more recent writing on Cook makes little change to this story, which is essentially based on work of subsequent investigators who were able to question the natives of Hawai'i. Their accounts simply record the accepted wisdom regarding the deification. No one attempted to erect a theory of society or history on this basis either until the important work of Marshall Sahlins, who used the apotheosis of Cook to advance a certain vision of structural history. Sahlins's theory not only gives theoretical imprimatur to the European versions of Cook's deification but also advances the myth in interesting and unexpected ways. Because my own interpretation of the events following Cook's visit to Hawai'i developed as a response to Sahlins, it is necessary to present both his thesis and theory briefly before I subject it to serious questioning.

Sahlins's empirical thesis can be succinctly stated: Hawaiian ritual annually alternates between the gods Lono and Kū. Lono is "the peaceable and productive god,"[11] whereas Kū is associated with war and human sacrifice. "Coming with the winter rains to renew the fertility of nature and the gardens of the people, Lono's advent is the occasion for an elaborate and prolonged rite of four lunar months called the Makahiki."[12] At the end of this ritual, Lono goes to the invisible land known as Kahiki (or the sky), from whence he came. Then Kū, with his earthly representative, the ruling chief, takes over. "The historic significance of all this is that Captain Cook was by Hawaiian conceptions a form of Lono; whereas the chief with whom he dealt and who would ritually claim his death, Kalaniopuu—he was Ku."[13] This of course is an expansion on preexistent scholarship on Cook's deification. Sahlins claims that virtually every significant event that occurred since Cook's arrival in Hawai'i in January 1779 can find a parallel in the ritual actions of the Makahiki. "The treatment Hawaiians accorded him corresponded to the powerful sequence of ritual events in the Makahiki festival. The correspondence developed into its dramatic *dénouement*: the death of the god."[14] It was an accident that Cook's visit to Hawai'i coincided with the Makahiki festival for the god Lono. The Hawaiians simply fitted his coming to their pregiven structures by escorting him to their principal temple, prostrating before him, and shouting "O Lono." Lono, says Sahlins, was what he was called till his death. "The Lono image of the Makahiki festival is, by most accounts, Lono-makua (Father-Lono) or Lono-i-ka-makahiki (Lono-of-the-Makahiki), names also associated with Cook."[15]

The Makahiki commences with the appearance of the Pleiades on the horizon at sunset. In 1778, this was around 18 November, based on modern computations. What was crucial to the identification of Cook as Lono was the second visit, where he was escorted to the *luakini*, the major temple (*heiau*) of the king, this particular one known as Hikiau. During the first stages of Makahiki, the Kū cult, associated with the ruling chief and with human sacrifice, is held in abeyance to make way for the renewal of nature and fertility by Lono. Lono ceremonially circles the island, thereby symbolically appropriating the land. There can be no war during this period, and the king and chief priest are secluded. The procession of Lono lasts twenty-three days in a clockwise movement with the right hand of the god pointing toward the center of the island. This ritual movement indicates possession or retention of the kingdom by Lono, who goes around in this fashion at each major island. During this circumambulation ceremony, an image of Lono, a crosspiece ensign with white cloth hanging from it and known as the long god, is paraded. Meanwhile another god, known as the short god, makes a tour of the ruling chief's domain in a left or counterclockwise movement, indicating the loss of the kingdom. On the day the Lono image returns to the temple of origin, the king also arrives at the temple by canoe. "Disembarking, he is met by armed attendants of the god, one of whom successfully, though harmlessly, attains the ruler with a spear (rite of *kāli'i*)."[16] This is a sham battle between the king's people and those of the god. This event marks the end of tabus, and the king enters the temple to offer a pig to the god and welcome him to "the land of us-two."[17]

"Within a few days, however, Lono himself suffers a ritual death."[18] This "ritual death" is the dismantling of the Makahiki image "bound up and secluded in the temple, not to be seen until the next year."[19] Then the "canoe of Lono," loaded with offerings, is set adrift to the mythical land of Kahiki, and the temples are progressively opened for the Kū rituals in which Kaho'ali'i, the personal god of the king and a form of Kū, impersonated by a priest, figures prominently. The Kū rituals of Kaho'ali'i are associated with human sacrifice, and at the ceremony one of the eyes of the sacrificed person along with the eye of a bonito fish are swallowed (symbolically) by the Kaho'ali'i priest, putting an end to another set of tabus. There is thus a remarkable concordance between Cook's actions and the Makahiki ritual calendar. For example, prior to the landing Cook went round and round the island in his ship; this parallels Lono's circumambulation of the land. He landed in Kealakekua Bay, "the home of a large body of Lono priests." He was escorted to the temple, "worshipped and adored," according to Sahlins.[20] These rituals exactly paralleled the Makahiki rites for Lono. One example that Sahlins lists: "Cook . . . was made to imitate by his own posture the shape of the Makahiki image while a pig was offered to him, Mr. King and a priest holding his outstretched arms (i.e., the crosspiece of the Lono image)."[21] Elsewhere Sahlins says that "Cook indeed became the image of Lono, a duplicate of the crosspiece icon. . . ."[22]

While all this was happening, the ruling chief Kalaniʻopuʻu was in Maui on 25 January 1779, performing purification rites that would bring the king to Kū status. If the Makahiki festival was on schedule, the closing rituals, including the human sacrifice, would take place between 30 January and 1 February. On 1 February a seaman, William Watman, died on board and was buried in the royal temple known as Hikiau (where Cook was ceremonially received). Cook and King read the divine service with Hawaiian priests in "rapt attendance," and the latter continued to throw pigs and offerings on Watman's grave for three nights. Also on the same day, the British, apparently with the permission of the priests, carried off the wooden fence and images of the temple (save the main image of Kū) for firewood. This is for Sahlins a replication of the ritual dismantling of the shrines. "Everything was indeed proceeding historically right on ritual schedule."[23]

Cook left Hawaiʻi on 4 February, once again not a perfect but a remarkable concordance, like Lono going back to Kahiki in his canoe. The people were aware of it too and were constantly urging the crew to leave. But then an event occurred that upset the "ritual schedule." The *Resolution* sprung its foremast, and Cook was forced to land once again in Kealakekua Bay. People were also no longer friendly and thieving was rife. Given this rupture in the schedule, the events that led to Cook's death (which Sahlins recounts) are expectable. Cook was ritually slain, and upward of a hundred Hawaiians "rushed upon the fallen god to have a part of his death."[24] Within twenty-four hours of his death, two priests took a piece of his body to the ship and asked "with expressions of great sorrow" when Lono would come again, once again acting out a predetermined scenario pertaining to the return of the god. After the death of Cook, Kalaniʻopuʻu, the king, went into seclusion to mourn the death of Lono-Cook. And by the nineteenth century, Cook's bones had become part of the cult of apotheosed chiefs, "being carried around the island of Hawaii by priests of Lono in the annual rites of the Makahiki."[25]

In his first book, Sahlins is reluctant to admit that when Cook visited Kauaʻi and Niʻihau in January 1778, he was also perceived as a god. But in fact his argument requires a stereotypic replication, because the Makahiki would have to have been performed exactly at this time also. Hence, in his later work, he incorporates the first visit also into a Hawaiian mythic structure. Cook and his crew were "extraordinary beings who had broken through the sky beyond the horizon . . . [and were] of a divine nature."[26] Again: "Two years running Cook made his advent during the Makahiki New Year festival of Lono, in the classic Frazerian mode of the dying god."[27] The British themselves admitted they came from Tahiti, which is the way that the people of Kaua'i, in their dialect, pronounced Kahiki, substituting "T" for "K." Thus Sahlins's argument has a perfect symmetry: The arrival, sojourn, death and resurrection of Cook—in his bones that live—are, structurally speaking, the appearance of "the Makahiki in an historical form."[28] Or in the later work: "The irruption of Captain Cook from beyond the horizon was truly an unprecedented event, never seen before. But by thus encompassing the existentially unique in the conceptually familiar, the people embed their present in the past."[29]

The preceding quotation indicates that Cook vindicates Sahlins's structural theory of history. This theory is an attempt to introduce into structuralism something it has always resisted or found difficult to accommodate, namely, history and practical action in the world. The trouble with structuralism is that it cannot easily accommodate history and change, except as a formal, even mathematically elegant, set of transformations. By contrast, Sahlins argues that he can demonstrate by the concrete case of Cook that culture, as a system of signs, encodes practical action and at the same time effects historical transformation and transcendence. The distinction between history and structure, diachrony and synchrony, itself might be redundant. The Saussurean idea of structure can be reconciled with the hermeneutical and Weberian idea of culture. Cultural categories (structures) are pregiven: Events (what one might call the world's messiness) are fitted into these pregiven categories. There are no perceptions that are pan-human, no "immaculate perceptions"; they are ipso facto fused into cultural conceptions. Insofar as these cultural conceptions are finite and pregiven, they are, following Braudel, "structures of the long run." Hawaiian culture is especially amenable to this form of structural analysis, says Sahlins, because it is given to "stereotypic reproduction," a term Sahlins borrows from Maurice Godelier. Stereotypic reproduction is the propensity of a society to replicate its structures continually, such that for example, the theme of a god who returns from beyond the sky can be replicated in a large number of myths that, while sharing substantive differences, embody a single structural theme.[30]

I suspect that Sahlins is aware that this model can be subjected to the same criticisms he levels at his precursors. If cultural categories are pregiven, and events as such do not exist except when categorically framed, where is the room for change, for history? To meet this implicit criticism, Sahlins postulates the idea, also borrowed from Braudel, of the "structure of the conjuncture," where event and structure are synthesized into a new or different structure, or structures. According to this conception, changes must be accommodated into new, evolving, cultural structures or categories. Thus, because Cook arrived during the Makahiki, he was accommodated into a prearranged scenario; coincidentally, his actions, on the empirical level, could be correlated, without too much messiness, into the ritual calendar of Makahiki. Thus Cook was Lono. The individual Cook is irrelevant; Clark Gable could as easily have taken his place. Sahlins does not tell us what would have happened if Cook's actions did *not* fit the cultural scenario; possibly more disjunctive conjunctions of structures would have occurred and produced sudden changes in Hawaiian society.

The "structure of the conjuncture" is Sahlins's attempt to deal with historical change, consonance as well as dissonance. On the one hand, it led Hawaiians to treat Cook as Lono in expectable structural fashion; on the other the British introduced tensions into the vulnerable areas of Hawaiian society, leading to a variety of social and cultural changes such as the abolition of the tabu system and the traditional religion, the shift in the position of women, incorporation of Englishness into Hawaiian chiefly styles, and so forth. But what is peculiar about this notion, as it is applied in the Hawaiian case, is that the initial conjunction of structures starts eroding Hawaiian culture, especially in relation to chiefly authority, women, economic relationships—all in a matter of weeks. Yet no such change affects the Hawaiian view that Cook is Lono returned. Everything flows smoothly according to "ritual schedule," whereas other areas of life have seen immediate, indeed drastic, disjuncture. Even when Cook unexpectedly returns, he must be ritually killed in the Frazerian style of the dying god. Thus, the idea of the conjuncture in Sahlins's thought contains two movements—a strongly conservative one where virtually everything can be pinned down in terms of preexisting beliefs and a ritual calendar, and a parallel radical disruptive movement fostering change. Sahlins does not explain why the very presence of Cook did not entail ruptures in the Lono belief system and ritual calendar, for it is evident from his own analysis that disruptive elements were there from the very beginning—in the behavior of sailors, of women, British reaction to thefts, and so forth. Moreover, and this is where my preliminary critique begins, why did not the Hawaiians react to obvious contradictions in their expectations regarding Lono, and the cognitive disjunctions these must surely have produced?

To begin with, I shall analyze Sahlins's structural theory, not so much as a theory of history or more specifically as an "explanation" of events attendant on Cook's visit to Hawai'i, but as a continuation of the discourse on Cook's apotheosis and death, and in this sense, a new and interesting stage in the Cook mytho-biography. The Western analysis of the events in Hawai'i almost exclusively dealt with his apotheosis; his death is a product of unavoidable events as they developed on the fatal day. This view is shared by Kennedy and Beaglehole and practically everyone writing about these events, using the data of the ships' journals and later missionary accounts. The missionary stories are unequivocal in one regard: The death of Cook proved conclusively to the Hawaiians that Cook was *not* a god, but a mere mortal. True or not, the important thing is that after 1820 a "Hawaiian myth" of Cook's mortality appeared, which nicely complements the accounts of the ships' journals (which I suspect is what they were meant to do). The latent effect of Sahlins's theory, then, is to advance the myth in a new direction: Cook is the god Lono and every significant event during his stay in Hawai'i is explicable in terms of the Hawaiian ritual calendar and belief system. Furthermore, his killing was a "ritual death," according to Hawaiian conceptions. But here's the rub: Hawaiian conceptions, at least as far as we have them, say the very opposite. If so, one must assume that the "ritual death" of Cook is not a Hawaiian belief at all; or it was one acted out by them *on the unconscious level.* Consequently, though unrecognized by Sahlins, the merit of the structural theory is to have elicited this "unconscious infrastructure" that produced Cook's death. But the further merit of the theory is that it enriches the Western discourse on James Cook. Sahlins says that he is the dying god in the Frazerian sense, which, as Frazer recognized, also constitutes the basis of the Christological myth. No wonder the dying god Cook is soon going to suffer dismemberment and a resurrection.

The theory then brings new knowledge into being, which is what a good theory should do; it is also what a bad theory does, if the new knowledge is empirically or evidentially unjustified. I shall deal later with further limitations of the theory, but for now consider two important pieces of new knowledge that the theory unfolds for us: The first pertains to the death of William Watman, an ordinary seaman, who was buried under the paving of the Hawaiian shrine (Hikiau) on the morning of 1 February, at a time when the god Kū was in the ascendance and given a human sacrifice according to Hawaiian beliefs. Watman's death was on ritual schedule: *He* was the sacrifice.[31] But this attempt to see concordance between event and structure, such that the distinction itself becomes redundant, is wildly off the mark! It is hard to believe that the Hawaiians, or anyone for that matter, could ever have made the connection between Watman, who died after a long illness, and a sacrificial victim killed and offered to the gods according to very specific cultural rules. Sahlins might argue that Watman was also a god for Hawaiians, but gods are never killed as a Makahiki sacrifice. Even if these connections were not very clear, or if metaphoric, then it must be presumed that the Hawaiians would have had to offer a real sacrifice, as they have always done during the ascendancy of Kū during Makahiki. But none of the ships' journals make any reference to a human sacrifice, though the remains of former sacrifices were evident. It should be remembered that in Tahiti, before coming to Hawai'i, Cook and his officers witnessed a ritual that required a human sacrifice. They were eager to record such things and attuned to inquiring about them. One must assume that there was no human sacrifice noted in the journals because none took place. Thus a peculiar feature of Sahlins's Makahiki festival: The ceremonies to Kū were carried out without a human sacrifice, but William Watman died very conveniently so that his burial, though substantively different from the normal sacrifice, was structurally similar enough to be a substitute.

A second interesting and novel feature that the theory introduces is that the god Lono suffers a "ritual death," so that he could be viewed as a Hawaiian expression of the dying god theme. But this death of Lono, as far as I can gather, is never enacted in Makahiki, though Kū suffers a symbolic death, according to Valeri.[32] The theory produces another kind of symbolic death of Lono when the image of the god is ceremonially dismantled and removed. This action was also not performed by the Hawaiian priests during this Makahiki year. Instead James Cook, with the permission of the priests, according to Sahlins (and Lieutenant King), ordered the images and the palings of Hikiau to be taken to the ship for firewood! This the British marines did, and even though they could not have performed a *ritual* dismantling, it surely was done on the orders of the god Lono (Cook) himself. I shall analyze the full significance of this important episode later. Suffice it here to say that it is hard to believe that a ritual dismantling at the conclusion of a ceremony, a practice observed in many societies, expresses the death of the deity. Both events also strongly question whether a Makahiki festival was effectively going on at this time. If it was, it was a peculiar Makahiki where the corpse of an Englishman takes the place of a human sacrifice, and the ritual dismantling of the Makahiki at its conclusion is done by marines armed with bayonets. One can as easily say that things were *not* going according to the ritual schedule. Given the present state of scholarly research into the Hawaiian past, it is impossible to show conclusively whether a Makahiki festival was taking place or not during the two visits of Cook in 1778 and 1779. But it is surprising that of the many journal writers who dealt with the events in Hawai'i, not one person mentions the word Makahiki, not even Samwell, who had a flair for names and recorded a lot of names of things, persons, and events. The ships' officers had already witnessed interesting and awe-inspiring rituals in Tonga and Tahiti. They easily figured out the term for the Tongan ritual for the chief's son as 'inasi. The business of inquiry was part of their business, not only as ethnographers but as journalists writing for an avid reading public. It is inherently improbable, therefore, that a major festival was going on in Kaua'i in 1778 and in Hawai'i the following year, and they were unaware of its name or its existence. Missing the festival in Kaua'i was perhaps forgivable because they were there only briefly, but this was surely not the situation in Hawai'i.

For Sahlins Hawaiian culture is specially conducive to "stereotypic reproduction." But it is possible to argue that it is his theory that promotes this form of replication in the empirical record. The examples I have quoted are stereotypic replications entailed by the theory, forcing a peculiar interpretation of events, seeing consonance where there is disjunction or a failure of replication. This is nicely apparent in Sahlins's treatment of the Makahiki festival itself. The extant descriptions of the Makahiki come from the nineteenth century, after the tabu system was abolished in 1819; the ceremony itself was systematized and formalized by the great Kamehameha. Yet, on the basis of these later formalized accounts, Sahlins calculates the exact time period for the Makahiki, in 1778 and 1779, and then further argues that this festival was held on all the major islands at the same time. The Makahiki is stereotypically reproduced at the same time and place everywhere. But this function of the theory ignores the reality that the formalization of this ceremony is a nineteenth-century phenomenon, and that the empirical evidence gathered by Kamakau shows that not only did the timing of the Makahiki vary from one island to another but it might well vary in the same island.[33]

Furthermore, Valeri advances incontrovertible evidence to show that the Makahiki calendar can in fact be altered. When George Vancouver arrived in Hawai'i in February 1794, the Makahiki festival was going on under the auspices of Kamehameha. Vancouver's visit upset the ritual calendar and, says Valeri, "interrupted the progression of the Makahiki rites," forcing Kamehameha to postpone them for one month.[34] Thus it is clear that Makahiki can be altered or adapted to suit political events. To recognize these problems, however, is tantamount to doubting whether the Makahiki was going on in either the first or the second Cook visit or both.

The upshot of my argument is that in the human sciences the scholarly interpretation of the myth can advance the development of the myth. In Sahlins's case new additions to the myth of Cook's apotheosis have been invented. But insofar as Sahlins's Cook is an ancestral hero of sorts for both Europeans and Hawaiians, one can say that the new additions are primarily to the European side of the myth because the Hawaiians flatly deny that Cook was anything but killed in a skirmish; and I shall show later that they also deny that the destruction of the palings of the shrine was a permissible "ritual dismantling." They have no interpretation whatever on whether Watman was a sacrificial victim. Most important is, of course, Cook's own "ritual death" that is said to parallel Lono's (is, in fact, Lono's): A new attribute of divine dignity has been vested on Cook.

The preceding discussion also forces us to reflect on the similarities that underlie the obvious differences between *their* myth and Western history-ethnography. This cannot be done without deconstructing the idea of myth itself. Myth is a term from Western thought: It rarely exists as a category or conceptual term in other cultures. For example, the Sanskrit term *itihāsa* incorporates what in modern thought encompasses history and myth and tradition. We apply the term *myth* vaguely to include genres of story telling that exclude historiography. Yet we know from many societies, including Polynesia, that some stories might be remarkably close to "history," although some are wildly different. Yet they are all "myth" to us. It seems that at best "myth" is a loose and useful term to describe stories of past events about ancestral heroes and gods. But by this token a good part of history is close to myth: Biographies of Cook are developments of older hagiographical traditions, even though expressed and camouflaged in a scholarly idiom. The crucial difference is this: Modern history or ethnography or biography is distinguished from myth and hagiography insofar as its tradition of story telling exclusively deals with what one calls *facts*, using that term to include *meanings*, and indeed all of the empirical data employed by the historian or ethnographer. Though one must question the epistemological status of "facts," the most postmodern of modern thinkers cannot write a history or ethnography if he believes that the data that he has interwoven into a descriptive or interpretive ethnography-history has been invented by him or is implausible or a "fiction." Facts ought to be contestable in any scholarly debate; they surely cannot be incontestably false if they are to be incorporated into a history. Given the importance for scholarship of the validity and contestability of facts, meanings, and data, it seems reasonable to ask whether the ethnography distorts, invents, misreads, or misquotes the factual information.

Facts pertaining to empirical events occupy a peculiar position in Sahlins's work. His major point in relation to facts is that there is nothing called an "immaculate perception," because the empirical world that impinges on one is mediated by cultural values through a consciousness that is also culturally constituted. This is an unexceptionable thesis if it is not carried to an extreme, as Sahlins carries it. "Immaculate perceptions" do not occur, but to postulate "immaculate conceptions" (in the cultural sense) is equally naive, for this is to deny the physical and neurological bases of cognition and perception entirely.[35] I think it quite improbable that the Hawaiians could not make a distinction between the physical shape of Lono's tiny canoe that is floated at the conclusion of Makahiki and Cook's great ships, or that for them the corpse of Watman was a sacrificial victim, or that marines dismantling the palings of the shrine for firewood was a ritual dismantling of the sort practiced by their own priests. One has to balance the facts of physical perception with cultural reality and what I have called "practical rationality."

Further Objections to the Apotheosis: Maculate Perceptions and Cultural Conceptions

I shall now develop my critique of Sahlins further and at the same time criticize the more inclusive Western view that Cook was the god Lono to the Hawaiians. I think it reasonable for Western writers to formulate the hypothesis that Cook was the god Lono returned. But I doubt that Hawaiians could have sustained that hypothesis in historical reality for very long, because there was a *discordance* between the cultural conception of Lono and the physical perceptions of the events as they occurred.

1. The basic argument for the identification of Cook with the god Lono is the myth of the return of Lono quoted earlier and the ritual that enacts this myth, namely, Lono's triangular canoe full of goods being pushed out to sea, and thence to Kahiki. Sahlins employs this myth also, but in a footnote introduced into his first book, he states: "By all evidence, it appears that an explicit myth of the annual return of Lono from Kahiki . . . developed in the latter eighteenth century to early nineteenth century. Hawaiian ethnologists are fairly agreed that such a story is not part of the ancient mythological corpus."[36] This evidence ought to play havoc with his hypothesis, yet Sahlins assumes that there is an *implicit* myth of the god's return even though it was not systematically enacted in Cook's time. Assuming for argument's sake this was so, did the Hawaiians really believe that Cook's two enormous ships with their numerous seamen showed even a remote resemblance to Lono's mast and canoe, represented in the illustrations by Malo and Webber (see Figures 2, 3, and 4). However, it is possible that if Hawaiians had been asked to depict Cook's arrival they could very easily have represented Cook in their own terms, emblematically, in the shape of a canoe and a mast. The myth and the ritual canoe are ineffectual as a vindication of mythic prophecy, for there is little physical resemblance between these and Cook's ships. As a retrodictive enactment of Cook's arrival, the depiction can make sense, because this is an iconically reasonable way for Hawaiians to portray that event. It would be impossible for Hawaiians of Cook's period, given their artistic traditions and technical skills, to construct a model or replica of Cook's ship.

2. It may be possible for Europeans to assume that a British naval captain could be a Hawaiian god, even if he spoke no Hawaiian and did not look Hawaiian. Unlike the European tradition that possesses such myths in its antecedent history, Hawaiians believed that their god Lono was a Hawaiian deity, and presumably looked like them, and spoke their language. Here then is another remarkable discordance that the scholarly debate has ignored totally: an English-speaking, un-Polynesian Lono with a smattering of Tahitian, accompanied by a large crew totally ignorant of the Hawaiian language and lifeways.

3. I find it awfully hard to accept the scholarly view that Hawaiians believed that Cook and company touring their island actually came from Kahiki, the mythic land, when they fully knew that they came from "Brittanee," as the Tahitians and Tongans also knew. Moreover, Charlot convincingly shows that Kahiki could *also* refer to a real land.[37] The British, by

Figure 2. Lono Represented as a Crosspiece Icon

virtue of the official instructions given to them, *had* to inform native peoples where they came from and who their sovereign was. In fact, the priest Koah called himself "Brittanee" from the place of the ships' origin.[38] Thus a peculiar phenomenon that I shall interpret on p. 139: Modern scholars think that the Hawaiians thought that Cook and company came from Kahiki, the mythic land from beyond the horizon; the Hawaiians thought that these people did come from beyond the horizon but from "Brittanee."

4. Here is Sahlins on the Hawaiian perception of European divinity extending to the ships and the objects therein:

Divinity inhered in the relation the Hawaiians conceived to all these strangers with "white skin and bright flashing eyes" come for a far off place. . . . Cook's godliness was a specialization of the generalized re-

Figure 3. The Canoe of Lono Sent Afloat during Makahiki

Figure 4. *HMS Resolution*, pencil drawing by John Webber

lationship the Hawaiians more or less widely entertained to all the
Europeans, not excluding the ships themselves and the objects carried
on them.[39]

I wonder how Sahlins could reconcile these bold assertions with the observations made by King, the man on the spot, who wrote: "No one ever
presumed to land opposite our Observatories, apparently more thro a religious awe and respect for the O'heekeeow [Hikiau, or royal shrine adjacent
the observatory] than for us."[40] Aside from the fact that there is virtually no
evidence in the major journals for Sahlins's assertions, there is also a flat
contradiction between the grandiose mythic image of divine Europeans
and the actual physical evidence of half-starved peoples whom the Hawaiians thought had come from a land where food supplies had run out. James
King states they believed "our visit to them was merely for the purpose of
filling our bellies."[41] How can one reconcile the solar image of the English
with this unflattering view that at least some Hawaiians held and that,
moreover, seems consonant with their physical perceptions of these for-

eigners? Further, given the Hawaiian opinions about physical cleanliness, what would they have thought of those people in the lower depths of the ship? Hawaiians need not be told of the relationship between godliness and cleanliness.

5. For Sahlins there is a crucial isomorphism between what Cook did and the rituals for Lono, and this is Cook going round the island of Hawai'i before casting anchor in Kealakekua Bay. This parallels the circuit of Lono, in the form of the long god. But does this parallelism have any validity according to Hawaiian cultural conceptions? The circuit of Lono is on land in a clockwise direction where the right side of the god faces the area being encircled, an act very much like the Hindu ritual of *pradakṣiṇā*. Sahlins rightly says that this act incorporates these lands as Lono's. One might add, following Valeri's information, that Lono or the "long god" incorporates the irrigated lands.[42] Sahlins omits the reverse circumambulation of the "short god" that places the *sea*, another source of Hawaiian economic well-being, on the right side, and also according to some accounts the uncultivated wilds, another important source of economic sustenance for the islanders.[43] How does the ship "circumambulating" the islands by sea during a period of seven weeks parallel the ritual functions of the two forms of Lono? Where is the key right movement with its positioning of the right shoulder? And what about the short god and the structural opposition crucial in the Hawaiian ritual, between him and the long god? Finally, Sahlins postulates an isomorphism between sea (Cook's actions) and land (Lono's actions) when these are distinctive oppositional categories everywhere, and in Hawai'i symbolized by the differential circuits of the long god and the short god.[44]

6. Another extremely significant fact that virtually proves that the Hawaiians did not perceive Cook as a god pertains to the famous ritual that Cook had to undergo in the Hawaiian *luakini* shrine (Hikiau). Here Cook had to prostrate himself before the image of Kū and kiss it. Kū is the powerful god of the ruling chief and however one interprets this ritual sequence, it is clear that even an important person like Cook (who is at least analogous to a Hawaiian chief, if not a god) must prostrate before Kū. Further, if Cook, the living god Lono, was present in person (or even as an incarnation of Lono) at the Makahiki festival, it is strange that local chiefs did not prostrate before him. It was the commoners who performed these prostrations as they did to their own chiefs.

7. Sahlins seems to assume that the arrival of Lono-Cook at Makahiki time was right on ritual schedule. But in fact this is a totally *unprecedented* event, for no Hawaiian god is supposed to arrive as a physical person during

these ritual festivals. As in other societies, the gods are invoked in chants and prayers to be "present" in the ceremony; they may also appear in various forms, as for example, a wind. Thus, the arrival of the god Lono in person would have upset their ritual schedule, compelling them to make readjustments and alterations to deal with this unprecedented and unexpected event.

8. The most pathetic disjuncture is between the vision that Hawaiians had of Lono as the benign god of fertility and of Cook. During the second visit, the venereal infection from the first visit to Kaua'i had spread among the Hawaiians, and the ships' doctors, when they were off the coast of Maui in late 1778, were besieged by those with inflamed genitalia. King notes: "Three of the natives have apply'd to us, for help in their great distress: they had the Clap, their Penis was much swell'd, and inflamed."[45] This was an understatement, for a few months later Clerke notes that "many of these good Folks both Men and Women about the ship were miserably afflicted with the Venereal disease, which they accuse us of introducing among them during our last visit";[46] and this is confirmed by King who said that many men and women were killed by it.[47] According to Valeri, Lono was not only the god of fertility par excellence but he was emblematically represented as a phallic icon.[48] It is indeed possible for gods to strike people with illness and disaster, but not Lono, who comes at Makahiki to bring peace and prosperity to the land. Surely Hawaiians must have been forced to reflect why the British divinities attendant on Lono alias Cook were afflicting Hawaiian natives with diseases of the very organs that represented fertility. This, in combination with the violence unleashed by the ship's crew, ought to have made the mythopoeic Hawaiians postulate a different symbolic equation: that Cook was the violent, warlike god Kū, especially because there was a phonological similarity here! I am not being entirely facetious because the Cook = Kū identification is warranted by one part of the logic of Sahlins's analysis. According to his calculation of the Makahiki for 1779, through modern computer methods, the terrifying reign of Kū begins around 1 February. Thus, part of Cook's visit coincided with the hegemony of Kū; that this should have at least led to Hawaiian puzzlement is not considered by Sahlins. When Cook arrived, Koah the priest threw on Cook's shoulders a piece of red cloth and later Cook was swathed round with red cloth. We know that Koah was a priest of the Kū cult and red is Kū's color.[49] The ritual death of Cook is intelligible if we postulate the Kū = Cook equation, because Kū, unlike Lono, *is* in fact ritually killed at Makahiki in the ritual known as Kāli'i, at least according to Sahlins.

The evidence thus far adduced suggests very strongly that the postulated concordance between Cook and Lono, between the actual events and their cultural encapsulation, must be questioned. The only truly significant evidence that still resists criticism is that Cook was indeed called Lono by the Hawaiians and that they practiced prostrations before him in a manner that might well befit a divinity. I shall soon provide in Part IV an alternative and more complex interpretation of these recalcitrant facts.

Anthropology and Pseudo-History

Pseudo-history is the term made famous in the history of anthropology by Radcliffe-Brown, who used it primarily as a critique of the speculative histories of the late nineteenth- and early twentieth-century culture historians and diffusionists who attempted to reconstruct the histories of "peoples without history."[50] Anthropologists no longer share Radcliffe-Brown's vision of tribal peoples, and they now, rightly, use a variety of sources, internal and external, to deal with the history of those they study. Nevertheless, anthropological training and experience in fieldwork barely qualifies us to examine historical texts and archival material in a critical manner, our basic problem being that we tend to conflate these with interview data. But the trouble with interview data is not only that they are fluid or boundariless, if not boundless, but they also constitute for the most part a "private archive" of the ethnographer. The private archive becomes public only after the ethnography is written; consequently there are only a few ways to question the validity of the data on which the interpretation rests. What provokes disagreement and debate is the theory or the interpretation—the public part of the ethnography. This methodological dilemma is an embarrassment to ethnography. Ethnography is supposed to be an empirical discipline based on fieldwork that, for the most part, remains in private archives. By contrast, historians contesting the validity of a particular interpretation end up inevitably arguing about evidence and the validity of the sources used.

The sources used in Cook studies are "archival" in the public sense, mostly journals and logs, published and unpublished. An ethnographic historiography ought to be suspicious of this material written on the basis of observational data collected by naive fieldworkers at a time when critical scholarship in ethnography was virtually nonexistent. One must probe into the hidden agendas underlying the writing of these texts. Take the voluminous journals written by the ships' officers about Cook's last voyage to Hawai'i. On every single previous trip, they had the benefit of Tahitian interpreters who could help translate cognate Polynesian languages into basic Tahitian, which some officers could comprehend. But there was no native interpreter on this phase of the voyage. Only Anderson, the ship's surgeon, knew enough Tahitian to perhaps vaguely comprehend Hawaiian. Cook was the most experienced journalist; yet his journals end in 17 January 1779, so that we do not have the benefit of his views for the second landing in Hawai'i and the momentous events that followed. Moreover, in this last voyage Cook relied exclusively on Mai, the Tahitian interpreter who knew some English, and consequently his own Tahitian might well have fallen into disuse. Anderson died on route to Hawai'i on 3 August 1778. King and Samwell had a basic knowledge of basic Tahitian; their accounts are perhaps the most reliable when it comes to Hawaiian ethnography. Rickman, Ledyard, Gilbert, and others are useful only as far as they describe the actions of the English or gossip on board and, with some reservations, what they actually saw or participated in. All these writers knew that their material must eventually be handed to the Admiralty. Those who kept journals, with an eye to eventual publication, must have had a vision of their audience. Consequently, their writing must contend with what the reading public wished to hear.

Let me now make explicit my methodological critique of Sahlins. The assumptions underlying the anthropological approach to informant statements are transferred in toto to the new data, such that there are virtually no instances in Sahlins's corpus where a source is critically examined, beyond two references to Ledyard labeled as unreliable without any reason given for this judgment. Information from any text is used as long as it fits the structuralist thesis, the assumption being that because it fits the theory it must be factually correct. A variety of early native histories and missionary texts are given the same prominence as are the ship's journals. Brief visits by seamen in the nineteenth century are mined for useful information. There is no real probing into the agenda underlying the writing of different kinds of texts.

Example 1: Uncritical Reading of Texts

Let me illustrate this with one example from over a dozen cases of erroneous uses of source material that I have discovered. Here is Sahlins describing what happened on board when, after Cook's death, the British set fire to the village, including the royal temple and the residences of priests:

> The women on board the British ships thought it all a fine show: "It is very extraordinary that amidst all these disturbances, the women of the island, who were on board, never offered to leave us, nor discovered the smallest apprehension either for themselves or for their friends ashore. So unconcerned did they appear, that some of them, who were on deck when the town was in flames, seemed to admire the [s]ight, and frequently cried that this was *maitai*, or very fine." . . .

The translation here is correct, and Samwell, who heard the same on the *Discovery*, adds "at the same time we could see the Indians flying from their homes all round the Bay, and carrying their canoes and household goods on their backs up the country."[51]

The first quotation Sahlins employs is central to his thesis on Polynesian women, tabu and sexuality, but does it provide reliable information? The quotation is from King's "official" journal of the last voyage. Cook's and King's journals were edited by Rev. John Douglas, canon of Windsor, with the active cooperation of King to produce the three official volumes of 1784. One must remember that these journals were aimed at a reading public avid to hear the details of Cook's death. King, with Douglas's editorial help, consequently used all sorts of other sources in writing. Fortunately, thanks to Beaglehole, we now have King's "unofficial" shipboard journal and log.[52] This version has no reference whatever to the incident quoted above. As far as I know, no other source refers to it, except Samwell. Consequently, it is likely that King used Samwell's material, here as elsewhere in the official journal. Thus, Sahlins is wrong when he says "Samwell heard the same"; there is only one source and that is Samwell. Consequently, in these texts, when two writers refer to the same event, it does not imply that the one is a confirmation of the other. Not only were opinions and gossip circulating on board collectively formed, but the journal writers also did not hesitate to borrow each other's ideas without acknowledgment.

Now let me quote Samwell's observations that appear immediately before the second quotation (Samwell's) that Sahlins uses: "We had two or three girls on board all this Day, *one of them* looking at the Town burning said it was *maitai* or very fine at the same time. . . . "[53] This one girl in Samwell's account becomes "the women on board" in King, who forgets to inform the reader that the sum of women on this occasion is three. Between King and Sahlins appears the shadow of Beaglehole who, in his introduction to the (unofficial) journals of the third voyage, writes: "Women had never entirely abandoned the ships; they had even admired the flames of a burning village."[54] Sahlins uncritically accepts the line of prejudice coming from King through Beaglehole and inadvertently omits the crucial sentence that precedes the Samwell quotation he uses. In any case it is naive to unambiguously state that expressions like "very fine," be it in Polynesian or English, can be divorced from the context of utterance and given a literal interpretation. One must heed what Bakhtin calls their "expressive intonation."[55] From reading Sahlins, one gets the impression that the decks of the ships were crowded with women gleefully shouting, "very fine" as the houses of their priests and fellow countrymen were being consumed by flames.[56]

EXAMPLE 2: COOK AND THE
HAWAIIAN LANGUAGE

The next example is much more complex and concerns the notorious Hawaiian (and Polynesian) propensity to "theft," nowadays understood by anthropologists as gratuitous taking from the English, either because they were not part of official exchange networks or, in Sahlins's terms, because Hawaiians felt they had a right to the ship's produce. Why so? Let me once again quote Sahlins:

> Still, for Hawaiians, centuries of sacrifice had been rewarded: the very first man from Kauai to board HMS *Resolution* proceeded—without hesitation or the least trouble to conceal it—to pick up the ship's sounding line and carry it away. Halted by British incantations of private property, he was asked where he thought he was going. "I am only going to put it in my boat, " he said. . . . The cargo cult Melanesians later dreamed about these Polynesians for one fleeting instant realized: "They thought they had a right to anything they could lay hands on," wrote Cook. . . .[57]

Here Sahlins uses two sources, first Cook's own shipboard journal that makes reference to the theft of the sounding line and second the 1784 official journal (volume 2), which does not. Because Cook was dead, Douglas, the editor of the official journal, took all sorts of liberties with Cook's own journal.[58] Hence the Douglas rendering of Cook simply cannot be used (except very advisedly) as a source. By contrast Douglas consulted King extensively while preparing volume 3 of the official journal that deals with the last part of the voyage, and King must be held accountable for any discrepancies between the official journal and his own unofficial shipboard version. But one cannot blame Cook for Douglas's emendations; hence one must rely almost exclusively on Cook's own *unofficial* journal now available in Beaglehole's scholarly edition. In the Douglas edition, the references to the sounding line are omitted and instead you hear the following: "There was another circumstance, in which they also perfectly resembled those other [Polynesian] islanders. At first, on their entering the ships, they endeavoured to steal everything they came near; or rather to take it openly, as what we either should not resent, or not hinder."[59] This is Douglas; Cook by contrast never made this statement in his unofficial journal.

Now let me get back to Sahlins's first quotation from Cook's unofficial journal. An important sentence is missing in Sahlins's use of it, for Cook completes the sentence thus: "nor would he quit til some of his countrymen spoke to him."[60] The second quotation from the Douglas edition is virtually the same as in the unofficial journal, but the two preceding sentences are missing. Let me supply them from Cook's own (unofficial) journal: "No people could trade with more honisty than these people, *never once attempting to cheat us*, either ashore or alongside the ships. Some indeed at first betrayed a thievish disposition, or rather they thought they had a right to anything they could lay their hands on but this conduct they soon laid aside."[61]

Cook himself only reports two cases of "theft"; there must surely have been more. "Theft" was the English term that embraced a variety of behaviours and no more satisfactory than Sahlins's substitution of Hawaiians gratuitously partaking of Lono's largesse. Take the case of the first Hawaiian who came aboard and simply took the sounding line without even "by your leave." Sahlins never asks the obvious question, How could Cook have possibly translated the Hawaiian's utterance? This is Cook's first day at Kaua'i; he didn't know a word of Hawaiian; his smattering of Tahitian would have been of no use in the bustle, confusion, and noise of shipboard activity. In translating the Hawaiian so confidently into English, he was following an implicit convention in these journals: *Cook translated the man's actions into words*. He inferred what the thief said from what he did. The only thing we are sure of is that, when his fellow countrymen talked to him, the "thief" returned the sounding line. Why he stole it in the first place is something we will never know for certain, but alternative interpretations are possible. Let me hazard a guess: The previous day, before the ship anchored, people traded with the ship's crew from their canoes. It is likely that a crew member bought something from this man without a return payment, because seamen had by now exhausted their supplies of trade goods. When no return is made, we know from other Polynesian cases, an especially bold person might simply take something from the ship as compensation.[62] Such actions are then defined by the English as "theft." If, for example, Hawaiians felt they had a right to the goods on board, it is strange that the thief's fellow citizens would have persuaded him to return the object. Key statements in the journals cannot be taken at face value but must be seen in the varying contexts in which they occurred.

Now take Cook's assertion that the Hawaiians, in general, were *not* given to "thieving," however one defines it. The very first visit to Kaua'i was in 19 January 1778. People came in canoes but were reluctant to come on board. "They exchanged a few fish they had in the canoes for anything we offered them, but valued nails or iron above any other thing. . . ."[63] Cook mentions the orderly nature of trade, people taking whatever was given to them. "Several small pigs were got for a sixpenny nail or two apiece."[64] If the anthropological view posits the ship as the harbinger of "cargo," the British also make a parallel claim for Hawai'i, such that the delighted Cook, after a long spell on the high seas without fresh provisions and water, thought they had "found themselves in the land of plenty."[65]

Every single source emphasizes the "honesty" of the Hawaiians. Bayly, the astronomer, says, "They exceeded anyone we ever met in point [of] their honesty both in their trading and otherwise never deviating from their agreement, nor was scarcely a theft committed by them."[66] Captain Clerke in the sister ship, *Discovery*, although noting an attempt to steal his hammocks, added this proviso: "They did commit some thefts, tho' but few, but in general were very honest fair traders."[67] Samwell, in the same ship, recording the only other case of theft, where a man tried to steal a clamp, rightly noted that "Iron was their principal object";[68] and indeed the overwhelming cases of theft pertained to that precious metal, needed to make daggers to be used in their endemic wars. The officers had no reason to change their opinion when, a year later, they were cruising off the Hawaiian islands. Cook writes, "These people trade with the least suspicion of any Indians I have ever met" and adds, "It is also remarkable that they have never once attempted to cheat us in exchange or once to commit a theft."[69] Even the cat that fell overboard was returned by them.[70] Thus, the ships' officers were impressed by the fact that the Hawaiians, unlike some Polynesian groups, were *not* given to gratuitous taking. Quite the contrary, the ships' journal constantly record that Hawaiians, especially the priests, often gave *without* expectation of return. Thefts did increase somewhat during the last few days of Cook's sojourn; but one must solve that problem in relation to the conditions prevailing at that time in the interaction between Hawaiians and Englishmen. Thus, contrary to Sahlins, the evidence of the journals suggest that gratuitous taking was not the Hawaiian style; the very opposite, gratuitous giving, was.

EXAMPLE 3: LOG AND JOURNAL COMPARED

Often there is no mitigating reason for inclusion of a text in a scholarly study, owing to its blatant unreliability. It is used only because it nicely fits the scholar's theoretical position. Here is Sahlins in an extremely important discussion of the Hawaiian perception of the white man as a wonderful, shining being, coming from the sun: "The Kauai chief who discussed these matters with Lt. Rickman of the Cook expedition was convinced that, as beings from Kahiki, the British had journeyed to the sun between their first and second visits to Hawaii."[71] An important statement no doubt, but reading Sahlins one thinks that Rickman was engaged in a "discussion" with Hawaiian chiefs on local cosmology. The fact is that Rickman published his work anonymously in 1781;[72] and for a long time scholars thought this was written by that nasty Connecticut Yankee, Ledyard. Rickman's log is now available, but it was not available to Rickman when he wrote his journal, because by law all logs had to be handed over to the admiralty. Unfortunately, there are serious discrepancies between the journal and the log.[73]

At best Rickman might have had parts of his log recopied before he left the ship. If there did exist some concordance between the log and the journal, then one might place some credence on the latter. It appears that the "discussion" that Sahlins refers to occurred, according to Rickman's journal, on 1 March 1779. The *log* entry for that date laconically says that they "were moored in the old Road at Towy [Kaua'i]"; and then goes on to say that, far from being treated as sun-like beings, the crew were subjected to "every mark of uncivility and buffoonery"![74] Nor could I find the sun reference anywhere in the log entries for the whole of March and April. Furthermore King, in his unofficial journal, confirms that "the Natives were conscious of having us in their Power, and that there was no other way of proceeding if we meant to get ourselves and things safe [than] to finally suffer their Insolence."[75] King's official journal reiterates that the natives behaved "in a most teasing and provoking manner."[76]

That Rickman did not have access to his log for this part of the voyage is clear from his journal. He says there that on 1 March "we arrived at the Island of Ne-hu [Ni'ihau]," whereas the log rightly says it was Kaua'i.[77] But Sahlins ignores this error in the journal and says that Rickman talked to a chief of *Kaua'i*, named Noo-oh-a. Now let me quote the journal for Rickman's cosmological conversations with Noo-oh-a of Ne-hu: "Pointing to the sun, [he] seemed to suppose that we should visit that luminary in our course, and that the thunder and lightning of our guns, and that which came from the heavens were both derived from the same source."[78]

My own guess is that some such event did occur, either in Hawai'i or even in Tonga or the Tahitian islands, where full-scale terror was launched against the native population. The context of the discussion is also stated in the journal: Guns were fired above the heads of natives; "two were seen to drop, and by the shrieks and cries of the women, more were supposed to have been killed or wounded."[79] In light of this context of utterance, let me reexamine Rickman's statement. It seems perfectly reasonable for a frightened chief to *point* to the sun and then to the guns in a metonymic or metaphoric sense; but from this *conversation of gestures* there is no way that any detailed information could be elicited, such as Rickman's imputation that Hawaiians thought they [the British] were going to visit that "luminary." And nowhere in Rickman's journal is there the view imputed to him by Sahlins that "the British had journeyed to the sun between their first and second visits to Hawaii,"[80] or that they came from Kahiki.

The very day of Rickman's purported entry, Samwell, a more reliable if somewhat immodest journalist, noted the difficulty of eliciting even simple information from the Hawaiians. "It must be remembered, that there is not much dependence to be placed upon these Constructions that we put upon Signs and Words which we understand but very little of, and at best can only give a probable Guess at their Meaning."[81] Time and again Cook himself noted the impossibility of getting any complex information on religion and cosmology except what could be empirically observed; and this applied to places like the Tahitian and Tongan islands he was most familiar with. Rickman, at best, had a mere smattering of Tahitian, but this is of no use in carrying on cosmological conversations with Hawaiians. We know from Dutton's important essay that during first contact (or later in the case of those who did not know the native language) signs were the almost exclusive mode of communication between natives and whites.[82] With greater familiarity, as Samwell says, there develops a combination of "signs and words" that, in the case of a skilled interviewer, could be put to good use. Rickman unfortunately did not fall into this category.[83]

EXAMPLE 4: TRUNCATED TEXTS

Real clarity could have been achieved if Sahlins had completed the quotations he employed or placed them in context, as for example when he missed the first part of the Samwell quotation pertaining to the number of women on board ship. Take the following experience of George Little in 1809:[84] Along with two comrades who "spoke the language of the islands," he made a pilgrimage to the place where Cook was killed. In a recent essay Sahlins uses Little to illustrate what he calls "the divine career of the deceased Cook." He says that Little's Hawaiian companions approached Cook's burial place with "profound reverence" and uses the following quotation from Little as illustration: "Once a year all the natives assemble here to perform a religious rite in memory of his lamentable death."[85] Had Sahlins included the first part of his own Little quotation, he would surely have had doubts about Cook's divinity because, says Little, "they expressed unfeigned sorrow at the unfortunate circumstance which caused the death of *this great chief*, as they termed him. . . ."[86] "Mirror on mirror mirrored is all the show," said William Butler Yeats.

IV

Politics and the Apotheosis:
A Hawaiian Perspective

I start my alternative interpretation of the facts pertaining to the apotheosis with Sahlins's own recognition that the traditional European and late Hawaiian interpretation of the myth of Lono's arrival in a canoe might well be wrong. It is doubtful whether there is a protracted four-month Makahiki cycle, until Kamehameha's time. A scholar like Barrère goes so far as to say that the famous rite of Lono is an "iconic representation of Cook's voyage."[1] Yet this new interpretation (which I do not find wholly plausible) makes sense only if one considers the powerful impact of Kamehameha's rule.[2] For the first time in Hawaiian history, Kamehameha brought all of the Hawaiian islands under a single rule, at enormous human cost.[3] A strong personality with a profound vision of the future, Kamehameha was influenced by the British example and probably during Cook's own visit formed his own conception of the British monarchy. The unitary nature of his state was paralleled by uniform policies and above all by the adoption and systematization of the Makahiki festival as the main national ritual of integration. David Malo, whose book has the best descriptions of Makahiki, was born during Kamehameha's time and may even have witnessed some of these rites. But his older informants gave him the version that was already formalized as the state cultus. The systematized nature of the Makahiki is apparent in Malo's account. For example official collectors gathered Makahiki taxes "for the districts known as *okana, poko, kalana* . . . into which an island was divided," and officials known as *konohiki* levied taxes for the king on the eighteenth day of Makahiki; on the twentieth this was completed and the collected properties displayed before the gods.[4] This was done all over the island at the same time, at least in principle.[5] It seems that the Makahiki was systematized, universalized, and articulated to state polity by Kamehameha. This also meant, Sahlins says, the eventual legitimization of the peaceful Lono as the dominant deity which, in turn, diminished but did not eradicate, the cult of Kū, who was associated with interisland warfare and human sacrifice.[6] Unfortunately Sahlins, instead of recognizing the implications of this finding for his hypotheses, continues to believe in the correspondence between events of the Cook visit and the Makahiki festival. I shall present a different interpretation of these events that downplays the significance of the Makahiki and show that the designation of Cook as Lono and the so-called worship extended to him had nothing to do with his apotheosis.

Let me begin with an important statement by the anthropologist Te Rangi Hiroa (Peter Buck), who is himself half-Polynesian:

Another popular fallacy associated with Captain Cook is the theory of his alleged deification by the people of the island of Hawaii. The theory that Cook was regarded as a god seems to have been based primarily on the fact that the Hawaiians gave him the name of Lono. However David Malo [*Hawaiian Antiquities*, 2nd ed., Honolulu, 1951, p. 145] stated that the name of Lono was given to Captain Cook because of the resemblance the sails of his ship bore to the tapa of the god. In the course of time, however, Lono the man and Lono the god have come to be identified as the same individual. The popular version is that Cook was thought by the Hawaiians to be the god Lono, returned. A ceremony conducted on a heiau and the acts of prostration before Cook have been accepted as further evidence that he had been deified. These incidents, however, may be interpreted in another way.

Proper names which had been applied to the gods were given to chiefs, and the ceremony conducted with religious ritual, including offerings of pigs, was also observed in the installation of high chiefs. The prostration attitude, termed *kapu moe*, was given to mortal chiefs of the highest rank, and it is certain that Captain Cook was elevated to the highest rank of chieftainship. On the other hand, the contention that a living man was made a god does not accord with native custom and usage. If he was thought to be a god, why should the heiau ceremony be conducted to make him one? The fact that the Hawaiians eventually killed Cook does not detract from the fact that he was made a high chief, for high chiefs were killed when circumstances demanded. When the Hawaiians took away Cook's body and stripped the flesh from the bones, he was nearer deification than he had been in life, for the Hawaiian custom of deification of selected high chiefs was a post mortem event, not an ante mortem one.[7]

I will spell out the implications of Te Rangi Hiroa's statement in detail because I think his is a basically correct interpretation of the historical events that is consonant with the Hawaiian ethnographic data. At this point let me state that except for Zimmerman and Rickman, not one of the ships' journal writers stated that Cook was perceived as anything but a man.[8] According to James King, Hawaiians thought of him as a being of a "superior nature" and on occasion at least their attitude "seemed to approach Adoration,"[9] but then King shows that this "remarkable homage" was also extended to Captain Clerke of the *Discovery*.[10] Samwell's account agrees with King's.[11] Even though the attitude of "inferior chiefs" to Cook was more than "ordinary devotion," he was also perceived as "a Mortal much their superior," according to King.[12] Yet King added that ordinary people approached their own superior chiefs in much "the same manner they did when C. Cook first came on shore."[13] Samwell makes similar observations: "The Ceremonies seem to have been intended as a welcome reception to Captain Cook into this Country."[14] In fact Samwell thought that the second ceremony to Cook was a kind of installation rite: "Today a Ceremony was performed by the Priests in which he was invested by them with the Title and Dignity of Orono [Lono], which is the highest Rank among these Indians and is a Character that is looked upon by them as partaking something of divinity."[15] Samwell made a clear distinction between the god Lono (Orono) and Cook-Lono but seemed to see a connection between Cook and *another Lono* with qualities of divinity whom I shall later identify. Priests clearly identified for Samwell the Lono shrine in front of which, "on a pole stuck in the ground hung a small dead pig, and round the pole a heap of Cocoa nuts and Plantains as an offering to the God Orono [Lono], who they told us lived in the Skies."[16] They showed him an image of this deity. I shall show later that according to shipboard gossip among ordinary seamen the Hawaiians did deify Cook. Yet in spite of this popular propensity and a clear knowledge regarding the god Lono and his priests and shrines, the ships' officers and major journal writers did *not* make the connection that Cook who was called Lono was also an incarnation of the *god* Lono.

Even more striking is the fact that King thought that Lono was a title given to others also.[17] Samwell was more restrictive: "The Title of Orono which is esteemed sacred among them belongs only to Kario poo [Kalaniʻopuʻu] and his Family, upon whom likewise they bestow the title of Hemairee . . . the A-ree [*aliʻi*] is next to these in rank. . . ."[18] Ledyard also refers to Kalaniʻopuʻu as "their Orono, La Hai or greatest Chief"[19] and writes that Lono "implied royalty."[20] He also made an elaborate threefold classification of the Hawaiian aristocracy with Lono as the foremost category.[21]

The ships' officers were right that the name Lono was given to other highly placed people. In Hawaiian myth and history there were many characters with that name generally prefixed to a longer one; and some with that name were also present during the period of Cook's visit. The name Lono was interpreted as a title (which is strictly speaking inaccurate, because Lono is a given name). Beckwith points out, as did Te Rangi Hiroa and Malo much earlier, that the chiefs were named after the gods. She then specifies: "Each man worshipped the *akua* [god] that presided over the occupation or profession he followed, because it was generally believed that the *akua* could prosper any man in his calling."[22] For now let me state that insofar as Lono is the god of plenty and some myths associate him with the sea, it is reasonable for Cook to have been invested with this name or title. The ceremonies of prostration before Cook (Europeanized as "adoration" by the journal writers) represented, as Te Rangi Hiroa notes, the way they treated the most important chiefs; high European officials visiting other colonized nations were treated in a similar manner.

These prostrations were therefore not confined to Hawai'i. During the second voyage, Cook was accorded a great deal of honor by ordinary Tongans, though not the sort reserved for their sacred chief; during the last voyage the Tongans were more deferential. On one occasion during a fireworks display, Ledyard (and others) observed the reaction of people: Some ran off and "some of those who remained fell prone upon the earth with their faces downward" and, adds Ledyard, might have "worshiped Cook as a being of much superior order to themselves" while chiefs "entreated him not to hurt them or their people."[23] We have already noted that the first act of prostration before Cook occurred in a similar context in Kaua'i in 1778 when Lieutenant Williamson who had been sent ahead fired at a group of people and killed a man. This was the Hawaiians' first contact with the British and their dreaded firearms. Remember that Cook was not aware of this killing when he landed later: "The very instant I leaped ashore, they all fell flat on their faces, and remained in that humble posture till I made signs for them to rise."[24] To sum up the evidence thus far: It seems virtually certain that Cook being called Lono can be accounted for without attributing to Hawaiians the belief that he was the god Lono arrived in person during the Makahiki. The latter belief, as Te Rangi Hiroa points out, is against Hawaiian cultural logic, though fully consonant with European beliefs, as I shall soon show.

The objection to Te Rangi Hiroa's thesis was formulated very clearly by Beaglehole: "If the *heiau* ceremony was merely for the installation of high chiefs, in what capacity was Cook being 'installed'? Certainly not as a high chief of Hawai'i. Malo, like other Hawaiian writers, is silent on any such ceremony of installing, or even honouring, a high chief thus.... As by hypothesis he was a god already he could not be 'made' into a god, but he could be formally recognized and honored as a god...."[25] It is this objection that I shall now address by examining in detail the political conditions of Hawai'i prior to, during, and after Cook's visit. I will discuss the motivations for the Hawaiian chiefs for formally installing Cook as one of their own chiefs.

First let me formulate the set of assumptions with which I operate: There is no way to directly verify the motives of the Hawaiian chiefs, but one can do this *indirectly* with verifiable evidence from Cook's contacts with *other* Polynesian cultures, specifically Maori, Tahitian, and Tongan. It is reasonable to assume with most scholars that Hawaiian culture was in a broad sense Polynesian, and judicious comparison might shed light on the Hawaiian events. For present purposes the significant fact is that in all of the aforementioned places the native chiefs tried to enlist Cook in their tribal wars. In his last visit to the Maori, Cook wryly observed that if he had listened to tribal importuning he would have had to exterminate the whole race.[26]

During the second trip, Tu and Teto'ofa [Towha] of Tahiti tried to enlist Cook's support against the people of Eimeo or Moorea; and ordinary Huahine folk wanted him to destroy the chief of Borabora.[27] This propensity was even more evident in the last trip, as we have already seen, illustrating once again the interplay of practical rationality and "the pragmatics of common sense" as Polynesian people tried to assess how newcomers and their weaponry could serve for their own political ends. Many Polynesians wanted to go to "Brittanee," not only to see King George but also to collect firearms to destroy their enemies.[28] Practically all exchanges with Western traders coming soon after Cook were, everywhere in Polynesia, geared to this single-minded purpose.

Hence my hypothesis: Kalani'opu'u, the "king" of Hawai'i at the time of Cook's arrival, as if following general Polynesian practice, tried to enlist Cook's aid in his wars with Maui. The only direct evidence for this would have been Cook's own logs and notes, but these have inexplicably been lost;[29] Lieutenant King officially takes over the journal from Sunday, 17 January 1779, the day of the landing. There was plenty of time for Hawaiians to reflect on Cook. Cook first sighted the islands on 19 January 1778; then after the fruitless quest for the Northwest passage, he came back almost a year later on 26 November 1778 but went round the islands for about seven weeks before coming ashore at Kealakekua Bay on 17 January 1779. When Cook arrived, Kalani'opu'u the king was engaged in a war in Maui, according to at least one journal account that is confirmed by Hawaiian sources, particularly Kamakau's, collated by Fornander.[30] Let me now describe the Maui wars waged by Kalani'opu'u, which will in my view render intelligible the events pertaining to the purported apotheosis of Cook. I summarize Fornander's superb and graphic account of these wars.[31]

Let me begin with the account of these wars after Kalani'opu'u had defeated chiefly rivals to become the paramount chief (or "king") of the island of Hawai'i and then, for several years, his hoarding of arms and war canoes for eventual war with Maui. He invaded eastern Maui, according to Fornander, in 1759 and attacked the Hāna district. Kamehamehanui the ruler could make little resistance, and Kalani'opu'u was able to take the valuable districts of Hāna and Kipakula and the important fort of Ka'uwiki overlooking Hāna harbour. He placed his man Puna in charge of these areas and returned to Hawai'i. Meanwhile Kamehamehanui carefully mustered his forces and with the help of the neighboring islands of Moloka'i and Lana'i confronted Puna's forces and defeated them, except for Hāna and Ka'uwiki, which successfully resisted a siege. The Hawaiians continued to hold Hāna.

Not much of great significance happened till the death of Kamehamehanui circa 1765. This led to a period of internal conflict in Maui, when the deceased king's brother, Kahekili, took effective control, and a fresh war erupted between Hawai'i and Maui circa 1775. Led by Kalani'opu'u, Hawaiian forces from Hāna attacked the Kaupō district, which suffered great destruction of property and loss of life. When Kahekili learned of this he dispatched forces to support the Kaupō people. "Kalaniopuu's army was utterly routed and pursued to their fleet . . . [they] barely escaped on board and returned to Hana."[32] Kalani'opu'u went back to Hawai'i; it was in this war that the great Kamehameha first made his name as a warrior.

Kalani'opu'u spent the next year (1776) in preparation for war. He reorganized his army and also sought the help of his god Kū-kā'ili-moku, the special protector of the king. He repaired several temples, "and the high priest Holoae was commanded to maintain religious services and exact all his knowledge and power to accomplish the death and defeat of the Maui sovereign."[33] This priest was known as Kao to Cook's crew.[34] In retaliation, the Maui king took parallel action of the same symbolic order: Because there was no one in Maui with priest Holoa'e's ability and power, he sent a mission to Oahu and persuaded their powerful high priest Kaleopu'upu'u "to come to Maui and take charge of the religious rites and magical processes whereby to counteract the incantations and powers of the Hawaii high-priest."[35]

This event is central to my interpretation and I must develop it further. "This Kaleopuupuu," says Fornander, "stood high in the Hawaiian priesthood, being a descendant of Kaekae, Malui, and Malea, the foreign priests whom Paumakua of Oahu is said to have brought with him on his return from foreign voyages about seven hundred years previously."[36] These foreign priests are described as "foreigners of large stature, bright sparkling eyes, white cheeks, roguish, staring eyes, large white hogs [a poetic expression] with reddish faces."[37] The priestly families of Oahu traced their descent to this group of foreigners. With one or two exceptions on Kaua'i, they flourished exclusively in Oahu. The importation of the chief priest Kaleopu'upu'u belonging to this line was obviously an act of momentous significance for both contending parties. Under this priest's instructions, Kahekili repaired and consecrated the *heiau* called Kaluli on the north side of Wailuku. Kaleopuʻupuʻu assured the chief that the Hawaiʻi forces "would be caught like fish in a net."[38] Apparently Kaleopuʻupuʻu was both priest and counselor, helping Kahekili to plan his strategy.

The priestly magic and planning worked. In 1776 Kalaniʻopuʻu landed in the Honuaula district and plundered and despoiled the local population, who fled into the mountains and ravines. Another detachment of eight hundred men known as the *ālapa* went by water to Kiheipukoa, and then on to Wailuku where Kahekili was residing.[39] This force, according to legend, contained the bravest and best of Kalaniʻopuʻu's army "with their feather cloaks reflecting the sunshine and the plumes of their helmets tossing in the wind."[40] But the wily Kahekili made several strategic moves and finally fell upon this regiment as it entered the sandhills southeast of Kalua near Wailuku. The whole *ālapa* regiment was annihilated and only two among the eight hundred lived to tell the tale.[41]

Kalaniʻopuʻu, shattered by this defeat, summoned a council in which several chiefs participated. They decided to march the entire army to Wailuku in a bold move to retrieve the previous day's fortunes. But Kahekili was prepared; and once again Kalaniʻopuʻu's forces were routed, though Kahekili also suffered severe losses.[42] Kalaniʻopuʻu decided to sue for peace and ultimately sent his own son Kiwalaʻo (whose mother was Kahekili's sister) to obtain favorable terms. The local histories do not mention the conditions of the peace, but the two rulers met and peace was concluded.[43]

But the peace did not last. In late 1777 Kalaniʻopuʻu carried his campaign of "war and desolation into Kahekili's dominions."[44] He had some initial successes but was eventually repulsed with considerable losses. He landed on the adjacent island of Lanaʻi, the only place where he had success, taking the main fort and killing some of the chiefs. From Lanaʻi he landed once again on Maui at Hāmākualoa, "where he plundered the country, and committed fearful barbarities on the people."[45] But Kahekili arrived there and "after several encounters, drove Kalaniʻopuʻu on board of his fleet."[46] From this time onward, the protracted war continued, with victory vacillating back and forth, for several months.

Now for the other set of crucial events: It was in the early part of this last campaign that Cook arrived in Kauaʻi in 1778. Then again, after his northern sojourn, he approached the Hawaiian islands and after going round, he anchored in Kealakekua Bay. Fornander also makes it clear that according to native accounts Kalaniʻopuʻu and his priest Pailiki, son of Holoaʻe alias Kao, was in Maui as officiating priest of that expedition; the accounts do not mention the whereabouts of Kao. Even Sahlins in a later paper says that Kalaniʻopuʻu was warring in Maui in late November.[47] According to one version of the Makahiki calendar, this would be a violation of the Lono tabu. However, according to the December Makahiki, Lono's circuit is between 14 December and 4 January, and presumably Kalani'opu'u was not warring at this time. Fornander's sources contradict this, however, for after Cook had anchored on 17 January two chiefs (Palea and Kanina) came aboard and said that Kalani'opu'u was in Maui and would be back in a few days. Samwell also noted that the king was in Maui and "will be here in three or four days" and, according to Rickman, "settling the terms of peace."[48] Because it is not likely that the Hawaiians read European reports one must assume the authenticity of indigenous history in Fornander's account. If on or around 17 January Kalani'opu'u was negotiating the peace, then it is very likely that he was in fact fighting during the period 14 December–4 January when the peace of Lono was supposed to prevail. It is even more likely, however, that Kalani'opu'u was negotiating the peace at this late stage precisely because of Cook's arrival off the shores of Hawai'i on 26 November. It should be noted that on 1 December Kalani'opu'u himself visited the ship, accompanied by his nephew Kamehameha, and probably with Pailiki, the priest of the Maui expedition. None of the officers knew his importance except that he was "a great Chief."[49] There was no ritual calendar obstructing Kalani'opu'u from assessing the situation for himself.

Let me now look at Cook's arrival in light of the preceding background. Kalani'opu'u has suffered severe defeats in spite of his fine army; the native histories emphasize this. It would seem then that part of his misfortune is due to the superior priestly powers of Kaleopu'upu'u, Kahekili's priest. This priest is from the lineage of white foreigners; now another group of white foreigners arrive. They resemble very nicely the mythic image of the founders of the Oahu priestly lineage. There is enough resemblance between the myth and the event for Kalani'opu'u to make a pragmatic decision that these white foreigners must be enlisted to help him against Kahekili of Maui. The action is dialectical: Kahekili's priests failed and he enlisted the aid of Kaleopu'upu'u of the foreign (white) lineage; Kalani'opu'u now has a chance to counteract this by enlisting the aid of a parallel group of foreigners who resemble the mythic image. But this does not conform to any prophecy or the workings of a ritual schedule; it is based on the "pragmatics of common sense," in order to enlist the foreigner to turn the tide in a conflict mired in a hopeless impasse. Given Kalani'opu'u's situation, it is hard to believe that he would have done otherwise; Cook's assistance was sought by other Polynesian peoples for less pressing reasons.

I have tried to provide the missing link in Te Rangi Hiroa's argument, namely, the motivation to install Cook as a chief in the Hawaiian aristocracy, through the symbolic mode of ritual. Once again the motivation and the ritual of installation are an interplay of practical power politics and

Hawaiian symbolic values. If my hypothesis is correct, then I should be able to interpret the famous ritual of Cook's "deification" as an "installation ritual." Sahlins, it should be noted, has an elaborate point-by-point description of the concordance between this ritual and the predications of the Makahiki calendar. My alternative interpretation brings it into serious question. The very possibility of a plausible alternative interpretation is at the very least a demonstration of the folly of attempting any rigid interpretation of symbolic forms.

The best account of the installation of Cook is by King, an eyewitness of the proceedings, who described it in some detail but admitted to not understanding it. Let me briefly fill in the background information: Hawaiians possessed an extremely complex pantheon that, like parallel cases elsewhere, was being pushed toward formalization and systematization by a powerful priesthood. It is possible that there were considerable interisland differences, but the general scholarly consensus is that there were four major gods, Kū, Kanaloa, Kāne, and Lono and a very powerful goddess, Pele, associated with the volcano. As was true of other polytheistic pantheons, there were a multiplicity of lesser dieties, spirits, and ghosts that were propiated in a variety of ways by different religious specialists. According to Beckwith, following Malo, "Lono seems to have come last and his role to have been principally confined to the celebration of games" while, at least during the period of Cook's arrival in Hawai'i, the "priests of the strictest religious order followed the Ku ritual."[50] Each god, however, had a multiplicity of forms or manifestations, such that even the generally peaceful Lono or the warlike Kū might have other opposed characteristics. Beckwith, possibly in relation to the island of Hawai'i, asserts that "according to the Ku worship any public calamity which threatened the whole people, like prolonged drought, was to be averted by the erection of a special form of heiau (luakini) in which was observed a prolonged ritual involving the whole people as participants and demanding exorbitant offerings to the gods in the shape of pigs, coconuts, red fish, white cloth and human victims."[51] The ruling chief alone could erect such a site; this site at the *heiau* at Kealakekua Bay was called Hikiau and correctly identified as such by Samwell and King.[52] Hikiau was the site of the installation ceremony.

When the *Resolution* landed, the two chiefs, Kamina and Palea, who had been helpful mediators, introduced the ship's officers to the priest Koah (I shall retain this erroneous spelling in order not to confuse him with Kao, the principal priest). After clothing Cook with the red cloth, Koah held a pig in his hand and repeated a ritual formula in which the word *Lono* appeared, "the name by which the Captain has for some time been distinguish'd by the Natives."[53] Koah led him ashore and "as he went along a Herald walked before him repeating some Words and the Indians cleared the way and prostrated themselves on their Faces before Captain Cook."[54] Greeting chiefs with incantations is perfectly intelligible according to both Hawaiian and Tongan custom. Here, as in Tonga, the tabu man or herald accompanied Cook everywhere, for the same reason: Hawaiians knew that Cook was unaware of their customs, and the tabu man had to ensure that Cook conformed to them, especially in sacred spaces.

> We were conducted to the top of the pile of stones [Hikiau]; It was on one side raised about 8 feet from the ground, but on the opposite from the Nature of the ground was twice that height. I judge it to be about 20 yards broad, and more than twice that in length, the top was flat and paved with Stones; *there was a stout Railing all round on which were stuck* 20 Skulls, the most of which they gave us to understand were those of Mowee [Maui] men, whom they had killd on the death of some Chief.[55]

It is likely that the chief referred to here had died in the Maui wars and his funeral rites were celebrated with the sacrifice of Maui victims. King describes the physical aspects of the shrine in some detail, which I shall skip. Cook and his officers were then escorted to the top of Hikiau by Koah.

> At the entrance we saw two large wooden images, with features violently distorted, and a long piece of carved wood of a conical form inverted, rising from the top of their heads; the rest was without form, and wrapped round with red cloth. We were here met by a tall young man [Keli'ikea] with a long beard, *who presented Captain Cook to the images* and after chanting a kind of hymn, in which he was joined by Koah, they led us to the end of the Morai.[56]

It is clear that Cook is being introduced to the Hawaiian deities, but not as the god Lono. This particular temple [Hikiau] was the shrine of the king and sacred to the war god Kū, and as Sahlins says, "It was a temple of human sacrifice, specially forbidden in the peaceful rites of Lono."[57] It is strange that if Cook was considered to be the god Lono himself he would have been invited to this place antithetic to his persona. From here they were led to the end of the area where a raised platform was located.

> At the foot of this were 12 Images ranged in a semicircular form, and fronting these opposite the Center figure was a corrupt'd hog, placed on a stand, supported by post[s] 6 feet high, exactly resembling the Whatta of Otaheite [Tahiti], and at the foot were many pieces of Sugar Cane, Coco nuts, breadfruit etc. Koah led the Captain under this Stand, and after handling the hog and repeating a prayer, he let it drop, and conducted him to the Scaffolding which they asscended, not without great risk of tumbling, Koah kept hold of the Captains hand;

We now saw coming round the rail, a procession of 10 men, who brought with them a hog and a large piece of red Cloth: they approachd to where a piece of a wall, and the Scaffolding of a house, which together seperates this part of the Area from the rest, and there prostrated themselves, Kaireekeea taking the red Cloth and carrying it to Koah, who wrapt it round the Captain, afterwards the hog was handed up to him.[58]

These offerings have been misinterpreted as given to Cook (as god Lono); it is reasonably clear that they are offerings to the deities of the shrine. Cook is being introduced to these deities and Koah is addressing a chant on his behalf. The hog is also offered to the deities on Cook's behalf by Koah. When they come down from the shrine, they are ceremonially greeted by ten men carrying the red cloth. It is true that red is associated with Kū,[59] but more often it is the color of chiefly apparel. The two priests perform the crucial ceremony of wrapping Cook with it; he was "swathed round with red cloth,"[60] that is, dressed as a Hawaiian chief in a red cloak (*malo*). Note that Cook was wearing his officer's uniform. The red cloth covers this foreign mundane dress and renders it appropriate for the crucial ritual that will follow soon after when Cook is presented to Kū, at the center of a cluster of images. My interpretation, then, is that Cook is being installed as a Hawaiian chief.[61] The Hawaiian custom of virtually obliterating the foreign dress of the visitor was also adopted in Tahiti. King says that in Tahiti, during the ceremonial exchange of names, it was the custom "to rowl round you a large piece of Cloth,"[62] thereby coverting the foreigners into acceptable personae for ritual purposes.

For some time Kaireekeea and Koah kept repeating sentences in concert and alternately, and many times appeard to be interrogating; at last Koah let the hog fall, and he and the Captain descended, and Koah led him to different images, said something to each but in a very ludicrous and Slighting tone, except to the Center image [of Kū]; which was the only one coverd with Cloth, and was only three feet high, whilst the rest were Six; to this he prostrated himself, and afterwards kiss'd, and desird the Captain to do the same, who was quite passive, and sufferd Koah to do with him as he chose; this little Image Pareea nam'd Koonooe-akeea, [Ku-nui-akea, "the great Kū"] the rest they nam'd indiscriminately Kahai.[63]

It is also clear that, passive or not, Cook, covered in red cloth, prostrated himself before the similarly attired Kū and kissed him. In the crucial rite Cook is made to acknowledge the superiority of the great Hawaiian god. He is now formally installed as a chief who is, like others, subservient to Kū. Following this is a different part of the ritual in which commensality is emphasized:

We now were led near the Center of the Area, where was a space of 10 or 12 feet square, dug lower by 3 feet than the level of the Area; On one side were two wooden Images; between these the Captain was seated; Koah support'd one of his Arms, while I was made to do the same to the other. At this time a second procession of Indians carrying a baked hog, Breadfruit, sweet Potatoes, plantains, a Pudding and Coco Nuts with Kirikeeah at their head approachd towards us, he having the pig in his hand, and with his face towards the Captain he kept repeating in a very quick tone some speeches or prayers, to which the rest responded, his part became shorter and shorter, till at last he repeat'd only two or three words at a time and was answerd by the Croud repeating the Word Erono. When this Offering was concluded, which I suppose lastd near a Quarter of an hour, the Indians sat down fronting us, and began to cut up the hog, to peal the Vegetables, and break the Coco nuts; whilst others were busy in brewing the Yava by chew[ing] it in the same manner they do at the other Islands. The Kernel of the Coco nut was chewd by Kaireekeea and wrappd in a piece of cloth with which he rubbd the Captains face, head, hands, Arms, and Shoulders, and did the same to Mr Bailey and myself, Pareea also was just touchd and Koah. These two now insist'd upon Cramming us with hog, but not till after taseting the Kava; I had no objection to have the hog handled by Pareea, but the Captain recollecting what offices Koah had officiated when he handled the Putrid hog could not get a Morsel down, not even when the old fellow very Politely chew'd it for him. We rose as soon as we could with decency, and the Captain gave some pieces of Iron, and other trifles which he said was for the Eatooa at which they were well pleas'd, but took care to divide the Spoil between them.[64]

What now is happening is the *formal* bestowal of the chiefly name Lono to Cook. As we have already noted, chiefs are named after gods, and moreover each man worshiped the god related to his calling, and "chiefs & Kings, addressed their worship to the gods who were active in the affairs that concerned them."[65] People now acclaim his new designation, "O Lono!" Sahlins says that the ritual action where Cook's arms are supported by Koah and King is an attempt to imitate the crossbar by which Lono is represented. This is quite implausible: If Cook was the god Lono himself, it is strange that he should be asked to imitate his own form as the god of sports. The raising of arms is a standard attitude of praying in Hawai'i. Cook naturally was ignorant of this and he is therefore *made* to pray to the Hawaiian gods, the priests uttering "speeches or prayers" on his behalf. Cook is given the name Lono after the god Lono who is, to borrow a term not strictly applicable to Hawai'i, a kind of "guardian deity" to him. The coconut dedicated to the gods (perhaps even Lono) is now chewed by the priest and applied on *Cook as well as on King and Bayly*. If this ceremony repeats the anointing of the Lono image with coconut oil as in Makahiki (as Sahlins thinks), it is strange that King and Bayly were also thought of as incarnations of Lono! The ritual just described uses the pre-masticated kernel of the coconut—the milky sap of fertility, I would guess. Sahlins's view that Cook was anointed with *oil* is of course a continuation of the Western canonization of the great explorer.[66] The culmination of the ceremony, where the priest Koah feeds the three Englishmen with food and kava blessed by Lono, indicates that the English are in a sense reborn as the children of the Hawaiian gods. It is likely that the installation ceremony had the effect of imbuing Cook with the mana of the war god Kū himself. Because Hawaiian chiefs do possess such "divine qualities," it seems natural for them to impart these to the English chief, particularly in the context of the political motivations sketched earlier. James King, in his official journal, recollected people telling him that the little image at Hikiau was that of Kū, and "it was Terreoboo's [Kalaniʻopuʻu's] God; and that he [Kū] also resided in us."[67] It is therefore entirely possible that the installation rituals helped effect this "residence," both in Cook and in the other gentlemen present, thereby converting them into Hawaiian chiefs, though of varying degrees of ritual status and mana.

Thus far the rituals of installation are appropriately at the great shrine for Kū, the war god and also the deity of Kalaniʻopuʻu, the ruling chief. That this ritual should be conducted in the ruler's shrine is significant in that its deity, Kū, assists the king in his wars against Maui. That the king and his chief priest are not present is also significant: This ceremony of installation could be allocated to priests of lower rank. Moreover, it is puzzling that the ruler and chief priest would not be present if the god Lono had indeed arrived in person, Makahiki or no.

Two days after this ceremony, Cook participated in another whose sense was better understood by Samwell:

> To day a Ceremony was performed by the Priests in which he was invested by them with the Title and Dignity of Orono, which is the highest Rank among these Indians and is a Character that is looked upon by them as partaking something of divinity; The Scene was among some cocoa nut Trees close by Ohekeeaw, before a sacred building which they call 'Ehare no Orono' or the Temple of Orono [*he hale no Lono*, a house of Lono]. Captain Cook attended by three other Gentlemen was seated on a little pile of Stones at the foot of an ill formed Idol stuck round with rags and decayed Fruit, the other Gentlemen sat on one side of him and before him sat several Priests and behind them a number of Servants with a barbequed Hog. As an introduction he who appeared to be the Chief Priest took a small Pig by the hinder Legs and struck it's head against the Ground, after which

he held it over a blaze without the Circle till it expired. He then laid it at Captain Cook's feet and put his own foot upon it, singing a Song in which he was accompanyed by all except the Servants who were carving the barbequed Hog. The Officiator had wrapt up some cocoa nut meat chewed in a clean Rag which he applyed to Captain Cook's Head, Hands and feet, and wou'd have anointed his Cloaths with it but that he begged to be excused, *he likewise applyed it to the Heads of the other Gentlemen.* The Song was all this while kept up, interrupted now and then by short Speeches made by the Priest, which were sometimes repeated after him, at other times assented to by short responses from the Under Priests and Servants. One of the Priests rose and made an Harangue while the Chief Priest held Captain Cook by the Finger. After this the Priests dined on the barbequed Hog; when they had done the Company dispersed except two of the Priests that took Captain Cook to another part of the Island about 5 Miles off, where much such another Ceremony was gone through. In their Way thither a Herald went before them singing, and thousands of people prostrated themselves as they passed along and put their Hands before their Faces as if it was deem'd Vilation or Sacrilege to look at them.[68]

I no longer need to analyze these ceremonies; basically Cook and his officers are now brought symbolically under the aegis of Lono, the god of the Makahiki. This last ritual also illustrates an aspect of Cook's character: From King's account it seems that Cook passively and reluctantly performed the ceremony of prostration before Kū; but when he is later invited to a parallel ceremony he does not refuse. By contrast Captain Clerke avoided these "honours" as a "very disagreeable kind of amusement" and then asked the chiefs to withdraw them since he "disliked exceedingly putting so many people to such a confounded inconvenience."[69] The thesis that Cook was an ethnographer of the modern sort, as Beaglehole seems to suggest, is quite improbable. Cook was fascinated by native custom, as in Tonga, but his was not the fascination of a scholar. Withey rightly points out that Cook seemed to enjoy these ceremonies and on one occasion at least "went so far as to have some of his crew carry him on their shoulders when he visited the village."[70]

I have attributed to Kalani'opu'u, an important political motivation that is not arbitrary but based on the political situation in Hawai'i at that time and on the motivations all major Polynesian islanders shared regarding Cook. By contrast the apotheosis of Cook, if it did indeed occur, is uniquely Hawaiian because no other Polynesian society seemed to have thought that he was a divinity. Let me pursue the logic of my analysis further, even though the only confirmation would be the lost notes of Cook (see note 29, p. 216). In the events following the "installation," as I shall now designate that ceremony, Cook was being socialized into Hawaiian culture.

The tabu man went ahead of him, both to honor him and to guide him in the intricacies of Hawaiian culture, particularly its areas of tabu. He was called Lono, but this was not an exclusive designation; he was also Tuute, the Polynesian rendering of "Cook." Thus, when Kalaniʻopuʻu visited Cook on board ship on 26 January, he exchanged names with Cook, "Captain Cook taking upon him the Name of Kariopoo [Kalaniʻopuʻu] and the king calling himself Co-kee [Tuute]."[71] Much later, the Hawaiian chief Palea fearful that he would be accused of theft, asked the officers "if Co-kee [Tuute] would kill him," clearly using Cook's personal name.[72] It seems as if the name Lono was used by the multitude, whereas chiefs generally called him Tuute (Cook). At a critical point when Cook tried to take their ruler hostage, some people (probably chiefs) asked whether "Tu-tee was about to carry off their king to kill him";[73] and this was also the name they used when they agreed to return Cook's remains.[74] In other words Cook was both Lono and Tuute for Hawaiians, fitting in very nicely with the Hawaiian tradition of having alternative (even multiple) names.

I noted earlier the need to assume that Kalaniʻopuʻu sought Cook's help in his Maui wars. Though there is no way of verifying this, a parallel request was made soon after Cook's death. On 6 March 1779 on their way up north, Captain Clerke, while cruising around Kauaʻi, recorded that one chief sought their aid in a conflict among chiefs of that island: "They have been making many large offers and fair promises to some of my People to induce them to run away and assist them in their Battles, but the idea of turning Indian which was once so prevalent among them as to give us a great deal of trouble is now quite subsided."[75]

It therefore seems reasonable to assume that Kalaniʻopuʻu did ask for Cook's aid and that Cook refused, as he almost always did, even if equivocally. For this and other reasons, including the depletion of food supplies—a critical problem for these islands—people were anxious to see the English leave. When Cook returned because of the sprung mast, he found a tabu imposed on the bay, and people were not trading. Perhaps Kalaniʻopuʻu was acting according to the ritual schedule of Makahiki; it also nicely fitted Polynesian strategies since imposing a tabu on the Bay was also an effective way of controlling the food supply and simultaneously controlling Cook. The lack of warmth among the ordinary people was expectable: To feed the British for an extended period of time meant starving themselves. People who, under the threat of constant warfare, were aware of the reality of food shortage must surely have been concerned over the demands made by chiefs to provide as many provisions as possible for the foreigners. The return of Cook's ship was a real threat to them as it was to Polynesian islanders everywhere.[76]

In spite of this, there was virtually no overt hostility among the general population and Samwell, who made a journey into the interior, was impressed by the courtesy and hospitality of the people.[77] But the even tenor of these last days was rudely broken by the violence that erupted, even though the actions of the Hawaiians do not seem to be premeditated at all (I shall discuss this in detail later). All the journals correctly noted this. Cook was in a rage over the loss of the ship's cutter and he did exactly what he had done on previous occasions—confront the ruler to hold him responsible. As in Tahiti, the people tried to distract Cook in several ways, but ultimately he did confront the ruler. Cook apparently thought he was "quite innocent of what happened."[78] Briefly, what happened was that Cook's rage and the fears of the Hawaiians for their chief escalated into violence resulting in Cook being stabbed to death. For present purposes what is relevant are the events pertaining to the disposal of Cook's remains.

On 15 February, the day after Cook's death, the tabu man came on board and told Lieutenant King and the other officers that the body was "cut up to pieces and burnt; but that the head and all the bones, except what belonged to the trunk, were in the possession of Terreeboo [Kalani'opu'u] and the other Erees [ali'i, chiefs]."[79] The tabu man brought with him a nine-pound portion that belonged to the chief priest, Kao, "to be made use of in some religious ceremony."[80] To prove his innocence, he had sent this piece of flesh. Two days later a friendly chief provided further information: The limbs of the marines were divided among the lesser chiefs while Cook's head went to a great chief, Kahoo-opeon [Hu'opio?]; the hair went to Kamehameha and the legs, thighs, and arms to the ruler, Kalani'opu'u.[81] Then two days later (20 February), under the threat and practice of massive retaliation, many other parts of Cook's body were restored, viz., both hands identified by a scar in one of them; the whole length of the metacarpal bone; the skull minus the scalp and the facial bones; the scalp with the hair cut short and the ears adhering to it; the bones of both arms with the skin of the forearms hanging on them; the thigh and leg bones joined together but minus the feet. "The lower jaw and feet which were wanting. . . . [They] had been seized by different chiefs and that Terreeboo [Kalani'opu'u] was using every means to recover them."[82] These were supplied on the twenty-first morning along with "the barrels of his gun, his shoes, and some other trifles."[83]

These accounts make one thing absolutely clear: Cook's body was ritually dismembered, burned, and distributed among chiefs as if he were an important chief. It is true that after these rituals were practiced the bones could not all be returned. The important thing is that some were and whether they were actually Cook's bones or not is immaterial, for almost all later accounts are unanimous concerning the cult of Cook's bones. Once again I must give an interpretation of how this cult developed, taking into account the interplay of rational pragmatics with powerful symbolic formations in Hawaiian society and consciousness. Central to my argument is that there was no way that Cook would come to the aid of Kalaniʻopuʻu in his Maui wars. Cook's death was also totally unanticipated. But with his death it was possible to use his *power* to benefit the Hawaiian polity, for according to Hawaiian thought a chief (or even a commoner) on his death could be converted into a deity by prescribed rituals. Given Cook's extraordinary status, one can assume that any rituals for converting him into a deity would be analogous, if not identical, to those that applied to the ruling chief. Malo has an excellent account of how this is done,[84] and Luomala has a summary of the proceedings:

> The corpse of a king or paramount chief received special attention, particularly if he had been much loved and was to be deified. His leaf-wrapped corpse was laid in a shallow grave over which a fire burned for ten days while Lolupe-worshiping kahunas chanted continuously. When the remains were removed, the flesh and soft parts were deposited in the ocean on a tabooed night. For the skull and bones of a king, Hawaiians invented a casket plaited of sennit, shaped to have a head with shell eyes, a short neck, and a somewhat cylindrical torso without arms or legs. Two caskets found at Hale-o-Līloa, now kept in the Bernice P. Bishop Museum to prevent further deterioration, may be those for King Līloa and King Lono-i-ka-makahiki. The completed casket was probably taken to the chapel in the *mua* or to a heiau, where a priest's prayers transformed the spirit into a real god. The taboo imposed when the king died was then lifted, and the king's successor returned from the exile imposed on him to prevent his pollution. A shrine was built for the casket, and the new god was worshiped with prayers and offerings. A commoner could be deified, but the ceremony was longer and more arduous.[85]

It is hard to believe that Cook's remains were not treated in similar fashion. Moreover, according to Luomala, this actually happened to a previous chief who was also a Lono, that is, the famous Lono-i-ka-makahiki. It should also be remembered that "the life of Lono the god seems to have been mixed up with the quarrel of the chief Lono-i-ka-makahiki with his wife Kaikilani."[86] This mix-up is apparent, as I show later, in European and missionary retelling of the Lono myths, parallel with the mix-up of latter-day Europeans and anthropologists regarding the confusion of Lono-Tuute, the chief, with Lono, the god. Going back to Luomala's account it should be noted that the soft parts of the body are to be deposited in the sea. The astute priest Kao probably sent the tabu man with nine pounds (if not of soft parts) of the superfluous parts of Cook's flesh, "without any bone at all" in a small bundle;[87] and the ships' officers ceremonially performed what the Hawaiians required by depositing it in the sea! What was not expected is the unleashing of British terror. Thus, some or all parts of the body were returned but it is most likely that the unidentifiable parts came from the corpses of the ordinary marines. How could it have been otherwise? The logic of our analysis brings us back to Te Rangi Hiroa's idea that, according to Hawaiian beliefs, deification is a postmortem and not a premortem feature.

Luomala's account is derived from Malo, who uses a key phrase: *"The apotheosis of the dead king being accomplished, he was worshipped as a real god."*[88] Malo's account emphasizes that the Hawaiians, like Hindus and Buddhists, recognized shades of differences in "divine attributes" (or qualities of mana). We noted earlier that no Hindu would mistake the king who is, let us say, an embodiment of Śiva for the same Śiva whom they worship in the temple. To do so is to transfer a monotheistic bias to pantheistic and polytheistic religions. So with Hawaiians; as Malo says, the dead king has to be deified and then only can he be worshipped "as a real god." If indeed the king was already a god, it would be senseless to deify him after death. Because deification at the death of a chief was nothing unusual, one can perhaps assume that Cook was also deified in the Hawaiian manner, so that his mana could be enlisted for the welfare and strength of Kalaniʻopuʻu's kingdom. As a result of the preceding analysis, I shall hereafter use the term *deification* for the Hawaiian custom of converting dead chiefs into gods and *apotheosis* for the European myth of the redoubtable white man as a god to natives. Later on in this work, I shall examine the cult of the apotheosized or deified Cook from the viewpoint of both Europeans and Hawaiians.

On the analytical level, the strategy employed here refutes the idea that Hawaiians (and other preliterate people) are given to a form of "mythopraxis," as if they were acting out a cultural schema without reflection. By contrast I have shown how the pragmatics of common sense, practical rationality, and improvisational creativity result in the choice of a cultural scenario from a variety of possible ones. Yet it can be argued that, although I introduce some flexibility into the analysis, I have nevertheless attributed to the Hawaiians a single scenario, one that reflects the political motivations of Kalaniʻopuʻu and perhaps the ruling class of Hawaiʻi. Following my stated assumption that there are multiple structures being manipulated in terms of rational pragmatics, I shall show that these structures and motivations are by no means confined to the political life. Cook's arrival was a powerfully unsettling experience and people must have reacted to it in a variety of ways. It is, for example, difficult to believe that the women and lower classes shared the chiefly interpretations; but even if they did, owing to the power of the establishment and its priests, they must have had other ideas about Cook and his crew.

The Other Lono: Omiah, the Dalai Lama of the Hawaiians

The ship's journalists observed that Lono was also a "title" or "rank" given to others, or they erroneously believed that Lono was a category term reserved for high chiefs or for Kalani'opu'u and his family. I think these views are persistent and cannot be dismissed as a figment of the journalists' imagination. The fact is that the journals refer to a very important person known as Omiah and also called Lono. King in his official journal reports:

> . . . yet we had never met with a regular society of priests, till we discovered the cloisters of Kakooa in Karakakooa Bay. The head of this order was called *Orono*; a title which we imagined to imply something highly sacred, and which, in the person of Omeeah, *was honoured almost to adoration*. It is probable, that the privilege of entering into this order (at least as to the principal offices in it), is limited to certain families. Omeeah, the *Orono*, was the son of Kaoo, and the uncle of Kaireekeea; which last presided, during the absence of his grandfather, in all religious ceremonies at the *Morai*. It was also remarked, that the child of Omeeah, an only son, about five years old, was never suffered to appear without a number of attendants, and such other marks of care and solicitude, as we saw no other like instance of. This seemed to indicate, that his life was an object of the greatest moment, and that he was destined to succeed to the high rank of his father.[89]

This information has led scholars to assume that there was an order of priests of the Lono cult in this area. But the evidence suggests otherwise. Kao or Holoa'e, as we noted in the preceding section, was the chief priest of the king and was very likely the head of the cult of Kū. His son Pailiki was the priest in charge of Kalani'opu'u's expedition to Maui (perhaps because the father was too old for the task). Now we learn that Omiah, a powerful priest also named Lono, is also Kao's son. In this case Omiah is none other than Pailiki (or a brother of his.) Keli'ikea was a grandson of Kao and an uncle of Pailiki-Omiah, while Vancouver informs us much later that Koah, who along with Keli'ikea performed the installation ceremonies for Cook, was Kao's son-in-law.[90] Thus this powerful line of priests can be depicted as in Figure 5.

This genealogy is the most likely one, because Omiah's power and influence suggests that he is none other than Pailiki, the priest of Kalani'opu'u in the current Maui war. He seems a powerful priest who could cope with the prestigious high priest imported from Oahu by Kahekili. The use of multiple names is very common in Hawai'i, and Freycinet notes "that the Sandwich Island chiefs are accustomed to frequent changes of name, some-

Figure 5. Genealogy of Kalaniʻopuʻuʻs Priests

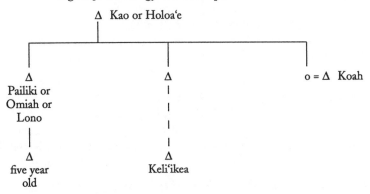

Broken lines indicate the possibility of
a classificatory relationship.

times for the most trivial reasons."[91] And King in fact says that this Lono "has another name."[92] Moreover, if Pailiki and Omiah were different persons, it is strange that the former, in spite of being an important priest, is never mentioned in the ship's journals.[93]

This powerful line of priests, both Samwell and King erroneously thought, were opposed to the king. Samwell and King were also unaware of the close relation between Koah (whom King thought was a treacherous fellow) and Kao-Holoaʻe, the head of this priestly lineage. The fact that Omiah was called Lono, plus the fact that other chiefs also have the name of Lono, led the journalists to assume that Lono was a category term. This is evident in Samwell's important statement that I shall quote once again: "Today a ceremony was performed by the Priests in which he [Cook] was invested by them with the Title and Dignity of Orono [Lono], which is the highest Rank among these Indians and is a Character that is looked upon by them as partaking something of Divinity."[94] This sentence has led to a great deal of scholarly misunderstanding, because Samwell's statement is taken to mean that either Cook was a character partaking of divinity or that Samwell was thinking of Cook in relation to the *god* Lono who partook of divinity. In fact Samwell is referring to the other Lono, Omiah; and he agrees with King that Omiah *partook* of divinity. The verb *is* clearly indicates that Samwell was using "character" in the sense defined in the Oxford English Dictionary as "a possessor of special qualities: a personage, a personality." Samwell was also correct in surmising that this was a ceremony of investiture. Furthermore, because Omiah was obviously not a god and yet called Lono, Samwell inferred that Cook was somehow or other being brought in line with Omiah, and his rank was parallel to the Omiah's. Even

King seems to concur. Hence, King, after his discussion of the extreme respect extended to Omiah and his son, adds that "the title of Orono, with all its honours, was given to Captain Cook."[95]

The power and sacredness of Omiah-Pailiki is well stated by King in a footnote in his official journal:

> Captain Cook generally went by this name amongst the natives of Owhyhee; but we could never learn its precise meaning. Sometimes they applied it to an invisible being, who, they said, lived in the Heavens. We also found that it was a title belonging to a personage of great rank and power in the island, who resembles pretty much the Delai Lama of the Tartars, and the ecclesiastical emperor of Japan.[96]

Thus it is very clear that the priest Omiah alias Lono was a powerful and sacred person and treated with extraordinary deference. It is not surprising, then, that one of the ships' surgeons, Law, confused the deference given to Omiah with that given to Cook. Here is Law describing an event on 1 February during a display of sports and boxing for the ships' crew:

> I had an opportunity of seeing this afternoon the respect shown to CJC [Captain James Cook] by the natives who was coming to view this sight. Mented [guided?] by the High Priest and a Young Boy Nephew or Grandson to the King. Directly the Signal was given of his Approach which was done by one Continual Murmuring of the Word *Orono* (signifying Chief). Every Body layed flat before him as he passed. He Entered Into the Ring and sat down when their (sic) was a kind of Song sung 3 or 4 times in a Chorus which I believe was in honour of him.[97]

It is as likely that people prostrated and were murmuring, "Lono," not primarily for Cook, but to Omiah who was accompanied by his son (not the king's son as Law thought). This incident probably led King to conclude that Omiah was a figure like the Dalai Lama. That Omiah-Lono should be here is not surprising because these sports were conducted under the aegis of Lono as the god of sports, *akua pa'ani*. A comment by King much later clearly says that Omiah was in fact present "at one of the entertainments of boxing."[98] Incidentally, it should be noted that Law translates the title "Lono" given to Cook as "signifying chief." He too joins the major journal writers in thinking that Cook was treated by Hawaiians as a chief and not as a god.

Considerable implications flow from our identification of Omiah as none other than Pailiki, the powerful priest of the Maui campaign. Insofar as Omiah was the priest in the Maui wars, one could see a justification for Cook also to be called Lono, someone who also might help the king in his present campaign. Moreover, the ceremonies of installation reported earlier now begin to make greater sense. Cook is made to acknowledge the superiority of Kū and is converted into a Hawaiian chief; then at the second ritual at the Lono temple he is brought under the aegis of the god Lono. If Cook was the god Lono arrived in person, it is strange that the ships' journalists, in spite of constant probing, could not find this out; or that Hawaiians, in response to constant probing, would not simply state this as a fact.

Cook, Lono, and the Makahiki Festival

Once one restores the dimension of reflectiveness and rationality to Hawaiian thought, the question of why Cook was called Lono, after the god of the Makahiki festival, can be answered. In Western mytho-logic, Cook was identified with the god Lono because he arrived at the time of the Makahiki festival. Hence these anthropological debates have focused almost entirely on whether a Makahiki festival was going on or not during the two periods of Cook's arrival in 1778 and 1779, in Kaua'i and Hawai'i, respectively. Thus, a group of Danish scholars have argued that the Makahiki was a minor festival that was refashioned later into a state cult by Kamehameha I and that there is no evidence that a Makahiki festival was going on when Cook was in Hawai'i.[99]

Unfortunately, this argument does not resolve the issue of why Cook was called Lono. Sahlins replies vigorously that, although Kamehameha formalized the cult, Makahiki was an ancient and continuing ritual of fertility.[100] But Sahlins cannot show how the formalized Makahiki calendars of Kamehameha's time can be retrospectively used to reconstruct the timing of the Makahiki festival in the period of Cook's arrival in Kaua'i and Hawai'i in the pre-Kamehamehan era, when the islands were under independent chiefdoms.

I think it is virtually certain that there was no Makahiki festival during Cook's visit to Kaua'i in 1778. But it is not clear whether or not Cook's second visit coincided with Makahiki time. My own guess is that the existence of boxing and other festivities associated with the god Lono probably indicated that some form of the Makahiki was operative, but this does not warrant the inference that this coincidence prompted Hawaiians to think that Cook was their god Lono. Those who argue for and against the Makahiki hypothesis are in fact continuing the Western debate over Cook's "divinity," because both arguments assume that *if Cook arrived during the time of Makahiki, then the Hawaiians had to think that Cook was their god Lono* for, it is assumed, Hawaiians, unlike Europeans, do not understand that coincidences do occur, even occasionally. No European will make this mistake; but Hawaiians did, initially at Cook's arrival during Makahiki, and they continued to do so until Cook's death (according to missionary and native Christian versions) and, according to Sahlins's account, long after his death. The logic of the argument is as follows: Cook was named Lono by the Hawaiians; he was subject to prostrations and worship; he arrived at Makahiki; *therefore* he was called Lono because Hawaiians thought he was the god Lono of the Makahiki. This logic apparently does not apply to Hawaiian chiefs, several of whom were also called Lono. Thus Omiah was called Lono; he was subject to prostrations and "worship"; but it is quite impossible for Hawaiians to confuse him with Lono, their god. Hence, according to Beaglehole: "The name 'Erono' or Lono given to this chief [Omiah] does not imply that he was a god, even if it implied honour 'almost to adoration'. His status was not parallel with the status conferred upon Cook."[101] Beaglehole and European scholars refuse to see the connection that Samwell and King made, namely to envisage that Cook's status was in fact parallel to Omiah's and that Cook being called Lono did *not* imply that he was a god.

To resolve this problem, let me consider alternative reasons why Cook was called Lono.

1. There is good reason, according to the logic of Hawaiian naming procedures, for Cook to be called Lono simply because he came at the time of the Makahiki festival or close to it. In Hawaiian thought, as in many other cultures, a person is given a name that is associated with an event involving him. Such commemorative names are mentioned in that compendium of Hawaiian custom, *Nānā I Ke Kamu* [Look to the Source]:

> When Dr. Gerrit Judd performed his historic operation on the breast of Kapiolani, a child born to a relative about then was given the name *Ke-'oki-waiū-o Kapi'ōlani*, meaning, "the cutting of the breast of Kapiolani." Queen Emma's name was not even used when her trip to Europe was noted by naming a child *Ke-li'i-holo-i-ka-hiki*, "the ali'i who went to foreign lands." . . . Christian events also inspired commemorative names. When the first Communion service was held in Kona, a baby was named Ka'aha-'āina'a-ka-Haku, or "the Lord's supper."[102]

Cook coming in at Makahiki time was sufficient reason for him to be called Lono, a name that other Hawaiian chiefs of the time also possessed. In other words, this was a reasonably conventional naming procedure.

2. There might have been another reason why it was apt for Cook to be called Lono: In Hawaiian mythology another important chief has the appellation Lono and his life resonates with Cook's own arrival, more so than the myth of Lono-i-ka-makahiki. This is Lono Kaeho, an ancient chief of

the southern islands (Kahiki). Fornander quotes a chant in which a chief, Makuakaumana, invites Lono Kaeho to come to Hawai'i:

> E Lono, E Lono! E Lono Kaeho!
> Lono Kulani, chief of Kauluonama!
> Here are the canoes, get on board
> Come along, and dwell in Hawaii-with-the-green-back,
> A land that was found in the ocean
> That was thrown up from the sea . . .
> The canoes touch the shore, come on board
> Go and possess Hawaii, the island [motu];
> An island is Hawaii
> An island is Hawaii, for Lonokaeho to dwell on.[103]

Here too a Lono is depicted as coming from Kahiki and is urged to stay on in Hawai'i. In Hawaiian myth, Lono Kaeho declines the invitation but instead sends Pili, from whom are descended the Hawaiian chiefs of the Ulu line. I think it possible that this myth and similar ones are responsible for Cook's ships being labeled "floating islands," a fine trope, because the ships looked like the southern islands themselves being "thrown up from the sea."

3. Most importantly, if my analysis of Hawaiian politics is correct, the high priest Pailiki, or Omiah, is also called Lono and accorded extraordinary respect. It is therefore apt that the new arrival, who might help Hawai'i in her Maui wars, was also called Lono.

Thus the designation Lono accorded to Cook is related to neither an error in Hawaiian perception nor to a Hawaiian misconstruing of coincidence. It is a product of what one might call *situational overdetermination*, whereby a particular conjunction of events renders appropriate a specific definition of the situation. In this case the conjunction of events are the arrival of Cook in or near Makahiki time, the activation of prior myths of foreigners coming to Hawai'i from Kahiki and elsewhere, and the Maui wars and the chief priest Lono in charge of their spiritual progress. The events all converge on an extraordinary episode, namely, the arrival of Cook, who is then appropriately designated Lono. By contrast, the idea that Cook was the god Lono because he arrived at Makahiki time is a continuation of a Western mythological tradition that was also accepted by recently converted Hawaiians during a moral and spiritual interregnum where the old religion and morality had been voluntarily renounced in 1820 and new ones barely put in their place. To put it differently: The moral and spiritual malaise that followed the destruction of the tabu system and the burning of idols and temples set the stage for the Hawaiian acceptance of a variety of European and missionary reinterpretations or misinterpretations of Cook's arrival. Early histories like Bingham's and Jarves's, and the more recent ones by professional historians, simply converted myth into fact. In a world dominated by the myths of empiricism, fact, of course, is synonymous with truth.

What, then, is the relevance of the Makahiki festival to the arrival and sojourn of Cook during his second visit to Hawai'i? Because I have already argued that the existence of a Makahiki festival did not necessitate the apotheosis of Cook, I now return to the subsidiary question as to the type of Makahiki festival that, if at all, was in progress around the time of Cook's arrival. Take Vancouver's visits in 1793 and 1794, both of which occurred during the Makahiki festivals of Kamehameha's regime. Vancouver was aware that his arrival was during Makahiki, but this did not produce any recollection on his part that the last time he was with Cook on Kaua'i and Hawai'i he was also in the midst of a Makahiki festival. The problems I now address are whether there was a Makahiki festival going on during Cook's two visits and furthermore, if there was a Makahiki during the second visit, what kind of festival was it? I shall answer these questions once again as a response to the Sahlins position.

I noted earlier that Sahlins argues that the Makahiki festival was formalized and given uniform calendrical validation for all the islands during the reign of Kamehameha I. All the major descriptions of Makahiki by scholars such as Malo, Kamakau, and I'i come from this period. Because several accounts state that the commencement of the Makahiki was marked by the sighting of the Pleiades, Sahlins can, with the help of modern computers, calculate the exact time the Makahiki would have been held in the years 1778 and 1779. His conclusion is that both of Cook's visits coincided with the Makahiki festival.

The trouble with this hypothesis is its sheer improbability. Consider again my previous critique of Sahlins. He assumes that the formalized and universalized Makahiki calendar of Kamehameha's rule could be retroactively used to calculate the exact Makahiki calendar of a period when each island (or a set of islands) was ruled by independent chiefs who had their own priests and temples and resisted domination by others. Sahlins's theory is also contradicted by Kamakau, who says: "The way in which the Makahiki was observed in the time of Kamehameha I was in some ways different in the ancient days. For one thing, the months of the people of ancient times were not the same as when he ruled; they were changed to be according to the counting of the Hawaiian island people perhaps."[104] Furthermore, the Sahlins hypothesis also assumes the unalterability of the Makahiki calendar in spite of endemic wars, famines, or other vicissitudes of fortune. Such a propensity is expectable among people given to "stereotypic reproduction and mythopraxis."

What is plausible in my view is that Kamehameha formalized and universalized for all of the islands the type of calendar or calendars that were operative in his own native Hawai'i. Thus a retrospective calculation of the Makahiki may well be accurate in the case of Cook's visit to Hawai'i (December 1778–February 1779) but not applicable to his visit to Kaua'i (January 1778). Sahlins never gave up the idea that Cook visited Kaua'i also in the time of Makahiki, but he is forced to recognize in his later work that the empirical evidence does not warrant a single Makahiki calendar. Thus he has recently come up with two standardized Makahiki calendars for the period of Cook's visits, which I reproduce in Figure 6:[105]

Figure 6. Optional Calendars of Major Makahiki
Events, 1778–79*

	Ikuwa	24 Welehu	16 Makali'i	15 Ka'elo
	Makahiki begins	Lono appears	End of Lono's circuit	End of Makahiki
"November Makahiki"	Sept. 22, 1778	Nov. 14, 1778	Dec. 6, 1778	Jan. 3, 1779
"December Makahiki"	Oct. 21, 1778	Dec. 14, 1778	Jan. 4, 1779	Feb. 2, 1778

* All Gregorian dates are c. ± 1 lunar.

The new flexibility is more apparent than real. The two optional calendars are also based on information available from Kamehameha's time, such that instead of a single formalized calendar we now have two! Although this might suggest that a Makahiki festival was going on in *Hawai'i* during the period 1778–79, it renders even more remote the idea that other islands, independent of or hostile to Hawai'i, were going to practice these same calendars. The existence of *two* calendars for the Kamehameha period may well indicate the existence of multiple calendars in other islands during the pre-Kamehameha period.

The position I take is that ritual calendars are much more flexible than anthropologists make them out to be. Moreover, the existence of ideal calendars does not mean that they are *unalterable* in the face of difficult events. I find it hard to believe that Kamehameha, who was fighting with neighboring islands, could have rigidly followed either calendar unalterably during his wars of consolidation, especially because these calendars took almost three to four months to complete. There is evidence for the practice of emended or shorter Makahiki festivals, generally lasting one month, in some years of Kamehameha's reign.

1. Corney says that the Makahiki commenced in November with the ritual of Kāli'i where the King wards off the spears aimed at him; and in 1817 it ended on 24 December "while I was here."[106] "This is the season for dancing, boxing, feasting, and all kinds of amusement. When the god arrives from the place when he first started, the Taboo is taken off. They are

about thirty days going round, calling at all the villages and plantations, to remind the people that it is time to bring in their taxes, which they do twice a year."[107] Eight years previously, in 1809, Campbell, a long-term resident, reported: "During the period called Macaheite, *which lasts a whole month*, and takes place in November, the priests are employed in collecting the taxes. . . . The people celebrate this festival by dancing, wrestling, and other amusements."[108]

2. There is unequivocal evidence that the Makahiki festival could be *suspended* in the face of untoward circumstances. Vancouver's third visit was in January 1794 during the height of the Makahiki season, when Kamehameha himself was under a tabu that prevented him from dining with Vancouver or traveling abroad. Vancouver not only made Kamehameha dine with him but says Bell "at last told him that if he would not accompany him round, he would instantly quit the Island, and proceed to Mowee, where all the presents intended for him should be given to Titeree [Kahekili]: this stagger'd him, and he consented to go, provided he could get the permission of his Tahouna or High Priest who was then on shore."[109] I noted earlier that Kamehameha resolved the problem soon after by temporarily suspending the Makahiki. Thus, the hula dance was part of the Makahiki, but the king and queen were forced to withdraw, for, said Vancouver, "they are prohibited by law from attending such amusements, except on the festival of the new year" and that day's performance "was contrary to the established rules of the island."[110] Vancouver thought that the king and queen were prohibited from witnessing the hula *except* on religious festivals. This seems most unlikely. They withdrew because this particular dance *ought* to have been held in association with the Makahiki whereas now it was not. Hence Kamehameha had to withdraw from participating in it. There was nothing unusual in such interruptions either. Valeri, following Malo, writes that "it was a traditional custom to repeat a rite that had been interrupted"; in this particular case the suspended rituals were resumed in the following month.[111]

Once one is emancipated from the view that the Makahiki is a calendrical festival that is rigidly and inexorably enforced, one can, I think, have a better grasp of this same festival during December 1778–February 1779, the period of Cook's second visit. It *is* indeed likely that this was Makahiki time. There is evidence, marshalled by Sahlins, to show that the traditional tabu on fishing, especially for the *bonito*, was operative.[112] On the other hand, the tabu on trading, ideally expected during part of this period, was inoperative. The Hawaiians traded practically without interruption. Sahlins adopts the simplistic explanation of the Hawaiian text, the *Mooolelo*, compiled by the missionary Dibble, "that because this was Lono [the god] the people decided the tabu could be violated."[113] People never decide such things; their chiefs would have decided that it was acceptable to enforce the fishing *tabu* and yet relax the tabu on trading. Trading was clearly to their advantage—another illustration of at least a partial relaxation of tabus because of practical considerations and the weighing of issues.

Given the flexible nature of the Makahiki, it is entirely possible that, when Cook actually landed in Hawai'i, there was a real crisis that upset the ritual schedule as Vancouver's arrival did for the 1794 festival. I suggest that when Cook arrived the ceremonies were suspended and that the politics of the suspension were similar in both instances. Kamehameha desperately wanted and sought Vancouver's help to fight his enemies; Kalani'opu'u had even more pressing political motivations. The postponement or suspension of the ritual calendar meant that neither the required human sacrifice nor the ritual dismantling of the shrine could be carried out. Furthermore the sports, dances, and other activities had a "profane" character, some of them performed at the request of the ship's officers. Kamehameha faced a similar, if less stressful, dilemma with George Vancouver. In relaxing his tabu on dining and postponing the ritual schedule he was, I think, following the example of his predecessor, Kalani'opu'u. It must be remembered that the arrival of large numbers of foreigners in Cook's (and Vancouver's) ships meant that there was no way that the integrity of Hawaiian religious norms, especially those pertaining to tabu, could be maintained. Sahlins's thesis that Cook was killed because he violated a tabu by returning at the inappropriate time has little merit. Cook and his crew were violating tabus from the very start. Hence, it seems to me that Kalani'opu'u (like Kamehameha after him) had little choice but to temporarily suspend the Makahiki ritual schedule. The merit of my alternative interpretation is that it can explain the following: the Hawaiian attempt to bring some order to the relationships between ordinary Polynesians and the ship's officers by incorporating the latter into a Hawaiian hierarchical scheme; the absence of ritual dismantling of the Lono shrine by Hawaiian priests when the ritual calendar, in principle, required it to be held around 1 February when Cook was still around; and the absence of that crucial feature of Hawaiian religious life, the human sacrifice, which should also have occurred at the same time.[114]

V

———— 〰️ ————

The Narrative Resumed:
The Last Days

On the morning of 4 February 1779, the ships unmoored and sailed out of Kealakekua Bay only to be confronted with huge gales that damaged the *Resolution*'s foremast. Cook had little choice but to head back to Kealakekua Bay on 8 February, and on 10 February they were a few miles from their old harbor. King omits considerably important events on this day and the next few days, and we have to rely on Samwell. On 10 February, Koah, the priest who performed the welcoming ceremonies on the first round, "brought a small Pig and Cocoa nuts in his Hand and repeating a few words presented them to Captain Clerke as a peace offering and welcome again to this part of the Island, after which he left us and went on board the other ship to perform the same Ceremony."[1] Many canoes kept circulating around, one of them navigated by the king's nephew, the "savage looking" Kamehameha, dressed in an elegant feathered cloak. Samwell noted that chiefs of late refused to part with anything of value except for iron daggers—not even hatchets that they once valued. "All the large Hogs they bring us now they want Daggers for and tell us they must be made as long [as] their arms, and the armourers are employed in making them instead of small adzes. Kamehameha got nine of them for his Cloak."[2] It is clear that iron, which the Hawaiians greatly desired, was now more or less exclusively being used for deadly weapons—daggers—no doubt for the war with the people of Maui.

The ships anchored the next day, but the day after (12 February) a tabu was imposed on the bay because Kalaniʻopuʻu, says Samwell, "was paying his first visit to day" and arrived "with several Presents for Captain Cook."[3] The next morning, however, the tabu was taken off the ship. King says that "in a short time the bay was crowded with Indians. The ships surrounded with Canoes, full of Hogs and roots of all kinds, such was the Situation of affairs on the 13th at Noon."[4] King's official account, however, adds an interesting observation: "Upon coming to anchor, we were surprized to find our reception from what it had been on our first arrival; no shouts, no bustle, no confusion; but a solitary bay with only here and there a canoe stealing close along the shore."[5]

In this account King clearly recognizes that perhaps this was simply due to the tabu imposed on the bay by Kalani'opu'u; yet some on board "were of the opinion, or rather, perhaps, have been, by subsequent events, to imagine, that there was something, at this time, very suspicious in the behavior of the natives."[6] He adds that the conduct of Kalani'opu'u next morning was "unsuspicious" and that the "consequent return of the natives to their former friendly intercourse with us, are strong proofs, that they neither meant, or apprehended any change of conduct."[7]

Yet clearly, after Cook's death, there were retrospective assessments of native conduct and some were of the opinion that their behavior had altered. The tabu imposed by Kalani'opu'u and the absence of welcoming canoes added fuel to this speculation. In fact, it is likely that the return visit was not too welcome for a variety or reasons, including Cook's own behavior vis-à-vis the palings and, as I noted earlier, the more pragmatic reason of diminished food supplies. Moreover, as King himself recognized in a journal entry of 4 February, familiarity itself might breed all sorts of things including contempt. "They regard us as a Set of beings infinitely their superiors; should this respect wear away from familiarity, or by length of intercourse their behavior may change."[8] It is likely, therefore, that there was a cooling of Hawaiian attitudes, but it is hard to believe that the Hawaiians, experienced navigators that they were, could not understand the plight of the English forced to return to repair their ship. Any hesitation they may have had was counterbalanced by the enormous desire of a people with a Stone Age technology to have access to iron.

"However true or false our conjectures may be, things went on their usual quiet course, till the afternoon of the 13th," says King.[9] Actually, trouble started on the *Discovery* on the morning of the very day Kalani'opu'u visited the *Resolution* and rescinded the tabu on the ships. "An Indian stole the Armourers Toungs from the Forge but having been detected he was ordered to be seized up to the Shrouds where he received a very severe flogging."[10] The motivation was clear: Iron was being specially valued for daggers, and Hawaiians were taking risks to get it. As for the flogging, note that it was the playful Clerke who ordered it, which we know was forty lashes, as usual over three times the authorized limit. In spite of this, owing to the strong demand for iron, a second theft occurred. King Kalani'opu'u had visited Clerke and given him a present of a cloak and a hog. Later the chief Palea, who had often befriended the crew, arrived on board and while he was there "another Indian . . . had the boldness to snatch the same tongues and a Chizel off the Forge before the Armourer's face and jumped overboard with them."[11] Clerke ordered "the People to fire at them and at the same time Mr Edgar the Master put off in a small cutter in chase of the Canoe."[12] Cook had apparently seen the incident from the shore and ran to intercept the canoe.

Cook's anger was thoroughly expectable. Before these events occurred, an officer who was filling a water cask for the *Discovery* told King that a chief had hindered the natives from assisting him and wanted King to send help. King sent a marine with side arms only; but "Mr Hollamby soon returnd and said the Indians had now arm'd themselves with Stones and *were still more insolent.*" King went there with an armed marine and managed to restore order. Cook had come on shore and learning of the incident, says King, "gave orders to me that on the first appearance of *throwing stones or behaving insolently,* to fire ball at the offenders: this made me give orders to the Corporal, to have the Centries pieces to be loaded with ball instead of shot."[13] A serious change in orders had taken place: Loading of muskets with ball instead of shot has an obviously literal and a not so obvious hidden meaning of "shoot to kill." During the second voyage, for instance, some crew members fired at Melanesian faces with small shot, which would deface but not kill people.[14] The change to ball meant that Cook had begun to view the situation as serious, warranting the killing of people.

It was then that the armourer's tongs and chisels were stolen from the *Discovery.* Cook and King were at the observatory when they saw a canoe paddling toward the shore and the firing of muskets from the *Discovery.* Assuming that this was a case of theft, Cook, accompanied by King and two armed marines, tried to intercept the canoe. King outran the rest, but he also failed to intercept the boat because it had landed much earlier. Now consider this significant statement by King:

> The Captain instead of coming towards me or nearer the Discoverys boat, kept walking at a great rate along shore . . . I must then have lost the Captain, for it was with great difficulty I could at all join him; on coming up to him I askd him if he had any tidings of the thief or thing stolen, he said no, but that they point'd a little farther. We kept running on till dark and I believe more than 3 miles from the tent, sometimes stopping and enquiring after the thief, the Captain threatning to make the Centry fire, if they did not bring the man. Whenever the Marine made any motion of presenting [arms], the Croud would recoil back, but it was observable enough that they began to laugh at our threat. . . .[15]

A familiar manic Cook emerges from this account: walking and then running to catch an elusive thief, threatening destruction in a language that the Hawaiians did not understand, though they without doubt understood his tone and mood. Beaglehole commenting on this passage says, "It is not at all clear where the canoe and the small boat landed, but quite clear that

Cook in his fury completely ignored them."[16] In other words, Cook's "passion" was of such an overpowering nature that he lost all sense of direction, and according to Beaglehole, blindly finished "up or near the village called Keei, on Palemano Point."[17] The bizarre nature of the quest comes out inadvertently in King's account of frantic Englishmen running in the wrong direction for the lost chisel and tongs.

Clearly the Hawaiians were giving false instructions, and because they could not comprehend the meaning of Cook's threats, they laughed at them, says King.[18] It was dark, and Cook realized the futility of further pursuit and decided to return. "They conducted us back a very different rout, which was further from the Sea, and which as we afterwards jugd was designedly done."[19] According to Samwell, the Indians had deliberately led Cook astray from the very beginning. Hawaiians seem to have learnt by sheer experience to handle Cook in the Tahitian style in order to deflect Cook's anger and prevent his wrathful lash descending on the thief. But they were also laughing at his discomfiture. By all shipboard norms, this is "insolence" and something that cannot be tolerated. One must also assume that Cook, given his self-perception as effective lord of the islands, "worshipped" by natives, could not possibly tolerate such insolence. Hence the fateful statement reported by King: "In going on board, the Captain expressd his sorrow, that the behaviour of the Indians would at last oblige him to use force; for that they must not he said imagine they have gained an advantage over us."[20] It is likely that the substance of King's *words* paraphrase Cook's own; the *tone* is the lieutenant's deliberate reformulation for English audiences of his captain's angry mood.

What happened to the tongs and the chisel? Palea, the friendly chief, "promising to bring the things back," set off after the thief and soon, probably because of his persuasion, the precious objects were returned "together with the Lid of the Water Cask which our people knew nothing of its being stole."[21] Unfortunately, Edgar, the Master of the *Discovery*, who had gone earlier in pursuit of the thief, having seen Cook, King, and the two marines also similarly engaged, decided he should confiscate the canoe that brought the goods back. He was of course anticipating Cook's own possible line of action in this type of situation. Samwell has a graphic description of this episode:

> [Edgar] accordingly landed and was pushing her off himself when Parea made his Appearance and desired him to desist as the Canoe belonged to him, but no heed being given to his remonstrance, he laid hold of the Officer and pinnioning his Arms behind him held him fast by the hair of his Head. Upon this one of the Resolution's people struck him on the head with an oar which made him loose his prisoner, he then seized on the Oar, wrenched it out of the Man's Hand and broke it in two before his face; there was a great Croud gathered

about them on the Rocks, who now began to pelt them with Stones. The Boats crew took the stretchers and an Oar or two in their Hands, landed and made a shew of Resistance, but the Indians poured upon them so fast that they were soon driven back to the Boat, where the Stones came so thick among them that they were all obliged to jump out of the Pinnace and swim to the small Cutter, which lay a little way off the shore with two men in her who took them in. The Master and the Midshipman, not being able to swim, retreated upon a small Rock in the Water where they were attacked by the Indians with stones, the broaken Oars & Sticks; one man advanced close to them with a broaken Oar in his hand and made a push at the Master, but his foot slipping he missed him and slightly hit the midshipman, the Indians all the while pelting them with stones from which they both received some hurts, and would perhaps have been killed had not Parea just at this time made his Appearance and ordered them to desist. The Indians then fell to plundering the Pinnace, took out all her Oars and Gangboard and endeavoured with large Stones to knock out the bolts and other iron about her. The Midshipman got into the Pinnace and was beat by them and had his cap stolen. They complained to Parea of the Usage they received from his Contrymen; he interposed his Authority and gained a Cessation of Hostilities, he then desired the Gentlemen to go on board, but being told that all the Oars had been taken away he went and brought back two whole ones and one broken with which they rowed off to the Tents, where Captain Cook arrived soon after and was informed of what had happened. He was much displeased at our People for attempting to land among the Indians and seize a Canoe without having any Arms, and more especially with the Pinnace's Crew having intermeddled in this affair and left their Station without orders. As the Boats were going towards the Tents, Parea came up with them in his Canoe and delivered the Cap which had been stole from the Midshipman; *he asked them if Co-kee would kill him for what had happened* and the Gentlemen told him that he would not, with which he seemed satisfied and left them and crossed the Bay to the Town of Kavaroa.[22]

It should be remembered that all of these incidents took place on the *Discovery*. Clerke himself comments on its implications: "This was an unfortunate stroke as matters now stood, as it increas'd the confidence of these People which, before was *too much bordering upon insolence*."[23] Clerke and Samwell thought, unfairly, that Palea himself engineered the whole theft. What is extremely interesting, however, is Palea's fear that Cook would kill him for what he had done. Such statements give us a clue that chiefs like Palea were hardly afraid of the officers, superior beings though they might be; their dread and esteem was for James Cook.

The next morning, 14 February, Lieutenant Burney informed Clerke that the *Discovery*'s cutter was stolen (for its nails and iron, we know from later information supplied to King). Clerke reported the matter to Cook. When King met Cook on board, he found "the marines arming and Captain Cook loading his double barrelled gun":

> It had been his usual practice, whenever any thing of consequence was lost, at any of the islands in this ocean, to get the king, or some of the principal Erees [chiefs], on board, and to keep them as hostages, till it was restored. This method, which had always been attended with success, he meant to pursue on the present occasion; and, at the same time, had given orders to stop all the canoes that should attempt to leave the bay, with an intention of seizing and destroying them, if he could not recover the cutter by peaceable means. Accordingly, the boats of both ships, well manned and armed, were stationed across the bay; and, before I left the ship, some great guns had been fired at two large canoes, that were attempting to make escape.[24]

There is not the slightest doubt that, once we look beneath the surface of this official account, Cook, in his wrath, was attempting to replay the drama at Eimeo. He had decided already to take the king or principal chiefs captive; the natives' canoes were not to leave the bay, and there was no question whatever that if the lost object was not found the canoes were to be destroyed.

The time was about seven or eight in the morning when, according to King, Cook left the *Resolution* in search of Kalani'opu'u, whom he planned to take as hostage. Cook went in the pinnace with Lieutenant Phillips and nine of his marines toward the residence of the king in Ka'awaloa. Lieutenant King, before he went on shore in a small boat, gave orders to the marines "to load their pieces with ball, and not to quit their arms:"[25]

> I found, that they had already heard of the cutter's being stolen, and I assured them, that though Captain Cook was resolved to recover it, and to punish the authors of the theft, yet that they, and the people of the village on our side, need not be under the smallest apprehension of suffering any evil from us. I desired the priests to explain this to the people, and to tell them not to be alarmed, but to continue peaceable and quiet. Kaoo asked me, with great earnestness, if Terreeoboo [Kalani'opu'u] was to be hurt? I assured him, he was not; and both he and the rest of his brethren seemed much satisfied with this assurance.[26]

King's promises were empty and false. He knew that Cook was going to take Kalani'opu'u hostage and if the cutter wasn't returned canoes would be destroyed. Either way the Hawaiians were bound to suffer harm from the British. The significance of Cook going toward Ka'awaloa with armed marines meant, to Kao and his priests, that their sacred king might well be hurt. It is doubtful whether they were satisfied with King's "assurance." By contrast, Samwell reports Cook's intentions in a much clearer fashion: Cook had confidence in the power of firearms, saying that the Hawaiians "would not stand the fire of a single musket"; therefore, Cook "resolved to go ashore himself at the Town of Kavaroa and if Kariopoo [Kalani'opu'u] should be there to get him on board the Ship and detain him till the Boat was returned . . . *but if he found that he and his people had fled as there was reason to suppose, his intention was to retaliate upon them by burning their Houses and seizing upon the large Canoes which we hauled up upon the Beach.*"[27] There was method in Cook's wrath; he knew from his previous experience that chiefs fled or hid rather than confront him in this state. If so, there was no question whatever that Hawai'i would suffer Eimeo's fate. In fact, even before Cook was killed, his future desires were being anticipated by Captain Clerke when he asked Lieutenant Rickman "if he had made any seizures of Canoes to send them to the Ship by the Jolly Boat."[28]

It is also possible that the priests sensed the deadly mood that Cook was in. The ships' surgeons certainly sensed its obsessional quality. Harvey calls it "an infatuation that is altogether unaccountable."[29] Says Ellis, "There seems to be a degree of infatuation attending him, which rendered him deaf to everything!"[30] Cook in his wrathful mood had lost all sense of perspective. This puzzles his modern biographer. Beaglehole asks, "Why should Cook now lose his sense of proportion as one is compelled to think he did: why should he act with less than real foresight? There can hardly be doubt that, if he wanted to take Kalei'opu'u hostage, he could at a more normal hour and in a more normal manner, easily get him into the ship." Beaglehole's Cook apparently was regretful of what happened in Eimeo and "wished he had not started this miserable business." More puzzlement: "Unless the Hawaiians were already convinced that the muskets were loaded with ball, what use would Phillip's ill-trained men be?" Perhaps, says Beaglehole, a slight show of force was all he intended. "But that does not tally with loading ball. If he was serious about the ball then he had parted with his general theory that it was better to frighten than to slaughter the unsophisticated."[31] In fact, we know that Cook had loaded his gun with ball the previous day, and all of Cook's actions seem consistent with his behavior during this voyage.

One of the fascinating problems that the events of 13 and 14 February reveal is the presence of the elusive Omiah alias Pailiki, the other Lono. Unfortunately, there is no way to assess the significance of his presence. He first appears in King's account of the thirteenth evening soon after he (King) had reported people laughing at the sentry attempting to present arms: "They began to laugh at our threat; we also remarked that he they called Erono [Lono], received some intelligence which two or three times made the whole body fly to some distance, and we remarked large bodies collecting in all parts. . . ."[32] For whatever reason people were getting organized into groups, and Omiah-Pailiki was associated with these movements. The next day, after the cutter was stolen, he appears again on the scene. Cook had ordered all canoes to be intercepted and to fire if any attempted to escape the blockade. At this time, reports Samwell, the following incident occurred:

> The master was dispatched in the large cutter, in pursuit of a double canoe, already under sail, making the best of her way out of the harbour. He soon came up with her, and by firing a few muskets, drove her on shore, and the Indians left her: this happened to be the canoe of Omea, a man who bore the title of Orono. He was on board himself, and it would have been fortunate, if our people had secured him, for his person was as sacred as that of the king.[33]

It is a pity that there is no information on Omiah's reaction to being fired upon, but he could not possibly have been favorably disposed to the British. The case of Omiah suggests a very important feature about the journals, namely, that they possess an illusion of fullness and narrative continuity, but it is clear that much is missing in them.

The Death of Cook: British and Hawaiian Versions

In anthropology death is never a simple biological event nor even a more complex one where the set of relations clustering around the dead man has to be rearranged and the death itself given public meaning and significance. Often enough the personal and the public are fused in the beliefs and the ceremonials of death as, for example, when my love for the dead person can be expressed in the wish that he is not really dead but lives in some "heaven-haven of the reward." When Cook was killed, both the Hawaiians and the English performed formal obsequies. The English, once they collected whatever body parts were left of him, gave him a decent sea burial. The Hawaiians distributed his bones among chiefs and deified him in accordance with their customs.

The performance of customary obsequies lends recognition to the fact of death in the case of ordinary persons dying under ordinary circumstances. But when extraordinary persons die in unusual and unexpected circumstances, that death cannot easily be defined; its meaning is left open. One keeps asking questions about its meaning, and this quest for meaning, though contained within the broad parameters of the cultural tradition, cannot be wholly encapsulated by the standardized rituals and beliefs pertaining to death and mourning. The rules of ordinary death are not sufficient for comprehending the extraordinary one, which is open to continual symbolic elaboration and debate. There is also no true or empirically correct account of Cook's death. Even those who wrote about it soon after it happened could not possibly have ignored the larger, even cosmic, significance of his death to the European consciousness.

The account of Cook's death I employ is that of Phillips, Lieutenant of the Marines, who was with Cook when he was killed. His version of the death was taken down by Captain Clerke, who was now the commander. Molesworth Phillips provides a dry, factual, "official" documentation; yet it helps us to pick up the thread of the narrative from where we left off:

> Captain Cook landed at the Town situate within the NW point with his Pinnace and Launch, leaving the small Cutter off the Point to prevent the escape of any Canoes that might be dispos'd to get off, at his Landing he order'd 9 Marines which we had in the Boats and myself onshore to attend him and immediately march'd into the Town where he enquir'd for Terre'oboo [Kalani'opu'u] and the 2 Boys (his sons who had liv'd principally with Captain Cook onboard the Resolution since Terre'oboo's first arrival among us). Messengers were immediately dispatch'd and the 2 Boys soon came and conducted us to their Fathers house. After waiting some time on the outside Captain Cook doubted the old Gentlemans being there and sent me in that I might inform Him. I found our old acquaintance just awoke from Sleep when upon my acquainting him that Captain Cook was at the door, he very readily went with me to Him. Captain Cook after some little conversation observ'd that Terre'oboo was quite innocent of what had happen'd and proposed to the old Gentleman to go onboard with him, which he readily agree'd to, and we accordingly proceeded towards the Boats, but having advanc'd near to the Water side an elderly Woman whose name was Kar'na'cub'ra one of his Wives came to him and with many tears and intreaties beg'd he would not go onboard, at the same time 2 Chiefs laid hold of him and insisting that he should not, made him sit down, the old Man now appear'd dejected and frighten'd.[34]

Kalani'opu'u's fear and dejection was an ironic commentary on the cultural definition of the Hawaiian king as a sacred being, untouchable as it were. Here he was an emaciated kava-worn old man, susceptible to his wife's pleas and held down by two chiefs. We know, however, that Kalani'opu'u was once an impressive person, but now effective power seemed to be in the hands of his nephew, Kamehameha. Meanwhile Cook's own conduct was, to say the least, morally dubious. He knew that Kalani'opu'u was "innocent," yet he decided to take him hostage.

The threat to the king brought a lot of Hawaiians to the scene. The situation was compounded by the firing of the ship's great guns, soon followed by the news that "the boats [under Lieut. Rickman], which had been stationed across the bay, having fired at some canoes, that were attempting to get out [of the blockade], unfortunately killed a Chief of the first rank," and this news had now reached the village.[35] Phillips continues:

It was at this period we first began to suspect that they were not very well dispos'd towards us, and the Marines being huddled together in the midst of an immense Mob compos'd of at least 2 or 3 thousand People, I propos'd to Captain Cook that they might be arrang'd in order along the Rocks by the Water side which he approving of, the Croud readily made way for them and they were drawn up accordingly: we now clearly saw they were collecting their Spears, etc., but an Artful Rascal of a Priest was singing and making a ceremonious offering of a Coco Nut to the Captain and Terre'oboo [Kalani'opu'u] to divert their attention from the Manoeuvers of the surrounding multitude. Captain Cook now gave up all thoughts of taking Terre'oboo onboard with the following observation to me, "We can never think of compelling him to go onboard without killing a number of these People," and I believe was just going to give orders to embark, when he was interrupted by a fellow arm'd with a long Iron Spike (which they call a Pah'hoo'ah) and a Stone; this Man made a flourish with his Pah'hoo'ah, and threaten'd to throw his stone upon which Captain Cook discharg'd a load of small shot at him but he having his Mat on the small shot did not penetrate it, and had no other effect than farther to provoke and encourage them, I could not observe the least fright it occasion'd; immediately upon this an Aree arm'd with a Pah'hoo'ah attempted to stab me but I foil'd his attempt by giving him a severe blow with the Butt End of my Musket, just at this time they began to throw stones, and one of the marines was knock'd down, the Captain then fir'd a ball and kill'd a Man. They now made a general attack and the Captain gave orders to the Marines to fire and afterwards called out "Take to the Boats." I fir'd just after the Captain and loaded again whilst the Marines fir'd; almost instantaneously upon my repeating the Orders to take to the Boats I was knock'd down by a stone and in rising receiv'd a Stab with a Pah'hoo'ah in the shoulder, my Antagonist was just upon the point of seconding his blow when I shot him dead, the business was now a most miserable scene of confusion—the Shouts and Yells of the Indians far exceeded all the noise I ever came in the way of, these fellows instead of retiring upon being fir'd at, as Captain Cook and I believe most People concluded they would, acted so very contrary a part, that they never gave the Soldiers time to reload their Pieces but immediately broke in upon and would have kill'd every man of them had not the Boats by a smart fire kept them a little off and pick'd up those who were not too much wounded to reach them. After being knock'd down I saw no more of Captain Cook, all my People I observ'd were totally vanquish'd and endeavouring to save their lives by getting to the Boats. —I therefore scrambled as well as I could into the Water and made for the Pinnace which I fortunately got hold of, but not before I receiv'd another blow from a stone just above the Temple which had not the Pinnace been very near would have sent me to the Bottom.[36]

There is little reason to doubt the main outline of Phillips's account insofar as it pertained to the actual devolution of events. This objective and largely "value free" account is based on the conventions of shipboard writing that are in this case carried to an extreme for purposes of impartial documentation. In reality this seeming verisimilitude is itself a technique of ignoring or sidestepping Cook's own responsibility for his death, and the dubious actions, or inaction, of the crew. Several commentators have, I think fairly, accused Clerke, the new commander, of a cover-up. For example, Bligh was openly contemptuous of the marines, whom he thought were an ill-disciplined bunch who fled precipitately into their boats and failed to come to Cook's aid.[37] Williamson was the more serious case. He did not like Cook and at the critical juncture either refused to come to Cook's help or was paralyzed into inaction. He was unpopular with many crew members and there was talk of court-martialing him. Rickman, who shot an important chief and thereby angered the Hawaiians, emerges as a responsible, even dedicated, officer.[38] There is also no criticism of Cook either by Clerke or Phillips. However, we know that Phillips himself, in a manuscript now lost, put much of the blame on his captain. J. E. Taylor, who saw this manuscript, wrote, "You will find Phillips account of the death of Captain Cooke interesting I think . . . it shows that *he* (not the Islanders) was the assailant."[39] Even Clerke, commenting on Phillips's account, recognized that "matters would not have been carried to the extremities they were had not Captain Cook attempted to chastize a man in the midst of this multitude," believing from experience elsewhere "that the fire of his Marines would undoubtedly disperse them."[40] The official journal of King merely summarizes Phillips and redeems the actions of the crew by emphasizing Phillips's own bravery: "On this occasion, a remarkable instance of gallant behavior, and of affection for his men, was shewn by that officer. For he had scarcely got into the boat, when, seeing one of the marines, who was a bad swimmer, struggling in the water, and in danger of being taken by the enemy, he immediately jumped into the sea to his assistance, though much wounded himself: and after reaching a blow on the head from a stone, which nearly sent him to the bottom, he caught the man by the hair, and brought him safe off."[41]

Regarding Cook's death, King's official account slants Phillips's in order to impose a meaningful history on the death of the hero. Here Cook asks a native who was threatening to throw a stone (a breadfruit by other accounts) to desist. But because the man "persisted in his *insolence*," Cook fired small shot. Later he fired his second barrel loaded with ball "and killed one of the foremost of the natives."[42] And here is Cook's final noble gesture, that officially expresses his "tenderness and humanity":

> Our unfortunate commander, the last time he was seen distinctly, was standing at the water's edge, calling out to the boats to cease firing, and to pull in. If it be true, as some of those who were present have imagined, that the marines and boatmen had fired without his orders, and that he was desirous of preventing further bloodshed, it is not improbable that his humanity, on this occasion, proved fatal to him.[43]

This last gesture has been beautifully captured in a famous painting, *The Death of Captain Cook*, by Webber, the ship's artist. It depicts a tall, youthful, and slender Cook, his right hand raised, gesturing to the marines to hold their fire while a Hawaiian chief, his dagger raised, is waiting to strike him from behind (see fig. 14). King continues: "On seeing him fall, the islanders set up a great shout, and surrounded by the enemy, who snatching the dagger of out each others hands, showed a savage eagerness to have a share in his destruction."[44] Those writing about Cook as the humane personification of the Enlightenment utilized and elaborated this account in various ways. In paintings, poetry, and theatrical presentations, Cook comes close to the European conception of the tragic hero. He even possessed a tragic flaw. "His temper," says King, "might perhaps have been justly blamed, as subject to hastiness and passion, had not these been disarmed by a disposition the most benevolent and humane."[45]

Unfortunately, there is no near-contemporary Hawaiian account of the death of Cook that might supplement Phillips's. Most accounts we have are from the post-1820 period, after the Hawaiians voluntarily gave up much of their traditional religion and then came under evangelical influence. However, in 1793, fourteen years after Cook's death, Lieutenant Puget of Vancouver's squadron interviewed the chief priest of the very shrine where Cook was ceremonially received. This priest said that Cook was killed because of his sacrilegious conduct in ordering the fence around the shrine to be used for firewood for the ships. Puget's interpreter, Issac Davis, a resident of Hawai'i for the past five years, had some knowledge of the language:

> In the Afternoon I went on Shore with Davis and my Friend Terrymiti [Keli'imaika'i, Kamehameha's brother], where we were joined by Mr. Whidbey and the high Priest, who immediately conducted us to the Morai from which Captain King had taken the Wood, this he

explained through Davis to have been the original Cause of this Dispute with Captain Cook, for at that time though sanctioned by the Chiefs, yet it gave great offence to the Populace, who bigotted superstitiously to this Morais, never forgot the Depradations being committed on its fence; but the Malancholy Consequences which followed deprived this Morai of its Sanctions [Sanctity] as a Place of worship, whether that proceeded from the circumstances of the Wood or the Ceremony through which Captain Cook went, within its Walls on his first Arrival, Davis could not inform me. It has ever Since been Taboo'd the priest informed us, *they* had predicted the Death of Captain Cook from the moment the Wood had been carried away; this appears to be their Province, for they are generally right nine times out of Ten; however this is easily accounted for; they work the Minds of the People up to any Spirit of Revenge and then foretell the sudden dissolution of a Chief for having committed some Offense against their Religion or Morais and it is pretty certain, that person will shortly be found dead. This no doubt was the case of Captain Cook, for I am convinced it was not the Events of the Morning on which he was killed, that intirely was the Cause of his Death, but the Chiefs and People were prepared to lay hold of the first Opportunity of fulfilling the predictions of the Priests incensed against him for the Circumstance of the Wood. . . .[46]

It should be noted that Puget fully accepts the priest's version, albeit as an example of a self-fulfilling prophecy. For us the priest's statement is very important as an early attempt to give meaning to Cook's death by the Hawaiians themselves. As an "explanation" of Cook's death, it is unsatisfactory because it postulates that Cook was killed for a ritual reason alone, that is, his desecration of the temple. For example, we know that if Cook had not gone on a wrathful search for Kalani'opu'u as a hostage, he would not have been killed. Yet it is indeed possible that Hawaiians, angered by the desecration of the shrine, were motivated to kill him, and Cook's attempt to take their king hostage provided them the opportunity or the excuse. It should be remembered that there had been unsuccessful attempts to kill Cook in Tonga and in Huahine for lesser reasons. Because social action is largely overdetermined, it is possible that the Hawaiian anger at Cook's sacrilege was a part of a complex pattern of motivation that, in greater or lesser measure, influenced the death of Cook. Sacrilege, however, was no more the cause of Cook's death than was his anger, or no less.

It is clear that by 1793 Hawaiian priests provided a cultural reason for killing Cook, a reason that goes totally against the mythology of Cook as the humane embodiment of the Enlightenment. Surely this act could not be the work of "a disposition most benevolent and humane"? Thus, an impressive defense of Cook's action has been undertaken by scholars. The most powerful argument is by Thrum, followed by Stokes, Beaglehole, Sahlins, and others, which states that the fence was not sacred and that Hawaiians themselves took the palings for firewood.[47] Moreover, the fence itself was in a state of decay. It is true that the crew who were ordered to remove the fence also took away the images in the central shrine, but after all, they argue, the main image of Kū was returned. Sahlins carries this argument to an extreme: The British sailors were doing what the Hawaiian priests would eventually do, and that is to ritually dismantle the shrine at the conclusion of the Makahiki. Moreover, the journals are clear that Cook not only sought the permission of the chiefs but also paid them a good price. None of this scholarship, however, addresses a critical issue, namely, how is it that Cook, the child of the Enlightenment, decided in the first place that it is perfectly all right to use for ships' firewood the fence of a Hawaiian temple that contained the impaled heads of twenty sacrificed Maui chiefs? Firewood was hardly a scarce item and presumably the ships had a regular supply. Consequently, one must assume that the need for firewood was a rationalization for actually *wanting* to destroy the fence of the temple. But the puzzle does not end there: Apparently the British took *all* the images in the central shrine and only returned the image of Kū when, on the priests' intercession, King ordered them to do so. That ordinary sailors would have been permitted to enter the temple is not likely. It is also highly unlikely that they would do so on their own volition, defying Cook's own orders by ransacking the temple of its images. During this voyage, on several occasions, Cook imposed stern punishments on ordinary sailors for minor infractions of his orders, such that Trevenen could speak of his "hasty and somewhat tyrannical disposition to his inferior officers and crew." The puzzle remains; to unravel it, let me get back to the ships' journals.

Here is King's official version, which substantially agrees with the entry in the unofficial journal for 1 January 1779:

The ships being in great want of fuel, the Captain desired me, on the 2d of February, to treat with the priests, for the purchase of the rail, that surrounded the top of the *Morai*. I must confess, I had at first, some doubt about the decency of this proposal, and was apprehensive, that even the bare mention of it might be considered, by them, as a piece of shocking impiety. In this, however, I found myself mistaken. Not the smallest surprize was expressed at the application, and the wood was readily given, even without stipulating for any thing in return. Whilst the sailors were taking it away, I observed one of them carrying off a carved image; and on further inquiry, I found, that they had conveyed to the boats the whole semi-circle. Though this was done in the presence of the natives, who had not shewn any mark of resentment at it, but had even assisted them in the removal, I thought it proper to speak to Kaoo, on the subject; who appeared very indifferent about the matter, and only desired, that we would restore the centre image, I have mentioned before, which he carried into one of the priest's houses.[48]

There is something suspicious about King's account. That the natives assisted the British to remove images of their gods is very doubtful. King says in his unofficial account that the palings were decaying and part broken, which is also strange because only some days before, at Cook's installation ritual, he describes the "*stout* Railing all round, on which were stuck 20 Skulls."[49] These skulls were those of recent Maui captives sacrificed to Kū; it is quite unlikely that they were stuck on a decrepit fence. What is interesting about King's account is that all the images of the gods were in the very place where the central rituals for Cook had been performed. Now they were taken for firewood. Only the center image of Kū, the god whom Cook kissed and before whom he prostrated, was returned on Kao's request.

Let me now quote an alternative and radically different version of this episode by Ledyard, the American corporal of the marines who had been accused by Beaglehole of fabricating this episode.[50] Ledyard is so much persona non grata that his book is not even mentioned in Beaglehole's biography of Cook. Beaglehole thinks that because Ledyard was an American he was writing an anti-British tract. Yet there is not the slightest reference to such feelings in his journal. In fact, soon after publishing this work, Ledyard joined a British expedition organized by Banks in 1788 to explore the course of the Niger.[51] Ledyard seemed to have got on well with Cook, because Cook, on Gore's recommendation, gave Ledyard the important task of exploring Unalaska island and establishing contact with Russians who were supposed to be there.[52] There is no criticism of Cook in Ledyard's journal prior to their arrival in Hawai'i. Indeed Ledyard, unlike King, has no condemnation of Cook for his violence in the Tahitian islands. His first criticism comes when Cook kept circling the Hawaiian islands without landing, effectively refusing his crew the food, exercise, and relaxation they needed. "This conduct of the commander in chief was highly reprobated and at last remonstrated against by the people on board both ships . . . Cook's conduct was wholly influenced by motives of self-interest, to which he was evidently sacrificing not only the ships, but the healths and happiness of the brave men, who were weaving the laurel that was hereafter to adorn his brows."[53] This is hardly reason to fabricate stories about Cook. Ledyard's account is, I think, extremely plausible, especially now that we are aware of Cook's precipitate and irrational behavior.

[Cook] came to Kireekakooa with his boats to purchase and carry off the fence around the Morai, which he wanted to wood the ships with.

When he landed he sent for the Priest Kikinny [Keli'ikea] and some other chiefs, and offered them two iron hatchets for the fence. The chiefs were astonished not only at the inadequate price, but at the proposal and refused him.

Cook was as much chagrined as they were surprised, and not meeting with the easy acquiescence he expected to his requisitions gave immediate orders to his people to ascend the Morai, break down the fence and load the boats with it, leading the way himself to enforce his orders. The poor dismayed chiefs dreading his displeasure, which they saw approaching followed him upon the Morai to behold the fence that enclosed the mansions of their noble ancestors, and the images of their gods torn to pieces by a handful of rude strangers without the power, or at least without the resolution of opposing their sacrilegious depredations. When Cook had ascended the Morai he once more offered the hatchets to the chiefs. It was a very unequal price if the honest chiefs would have accepted of the bribe, and Cook offered it only to evade the imputation of taking their property without payment. The chiefs again refused it. Cook then added another hatchet and kindling into resentment told them to take it or nothing—Kikinny, to whom the offer was made turned pale, and trembled as he stood, but still refused. Cook thrust them into his garment that was folded round him, and left him immediately to hasten the execution of his orders. As for Kikinny he turned to some of his menials and made them take the hatchets out of his garment, not touching them himself.[54]

Ledyard's account shows Cook in his destructive persona, as in Eimeo, Huahine, and Ra'iatea. We see a familiar wrathful Cook in action: It is he who negotiates the deal, and he leads the way, exactly as he did in other places and also soon afterward in Hawai'i on his way to death on the beach at Ka'awaloa. We must remember that in Tonga also Cook violated tabus, though in a cavalier, not wrathful, manner. The flavor of Cook's presence is unmistakable here—if we ignore Ledyard's own moralizing. This is the kind of thing that the ships' officers could *not* possibly put into writing. Midshipman Trevenen, for example, recognized that "it might not be right to expose the rougher part of his character."[55] It would be impossible for them to say that their captain, who had recently been killed, actually *did* destroy part of a native shrine. King had good reason to cover up this event; Ledyard had none. The easy dismissal of Ledyard's account illustrates the power of scholarship in fostering the conventional mythology of Cook. Ledyard adds, "By this time a considerable concourse of the natives had assembled under the walls of the Morai, where we were heaving the wood down, and were very outrageous, and even hove the wood and images back as we threw them down, and I cannot think what prevented from proceeding to greater lengths, however it so happened that we got the whole into the boats, and safely on board."[56]

I find this account, in its basic outlines, extremely plausible. It can also be reconciled with a reference to this event in the log of the *Resolution*'s surgeon, John Law: "*Both* Captains went on Shore and purchased from the Priests part of an old Morai [shrine] for firewood—a Sign that for the Sake of a little Iron they would sell both Church and Burying Ground (sacred as they call it)."[57] This is partially confirmed by Edgar of the *Discovery* who says that his captain, Clerke, went ashore to purchase part of a "burying place for firewood."[58] The only way to reconcile Ledyard and Law with King is to assume that Cook ordered King (and other officers perhaps) to negotiate for the palings, but when this failed he and Clerke took over. Clerke was of course very ill and was perhaps a mere witness to Cook's "negotiations."

From all accounts it seems that Cook's stated rationale was that the ships needed firewood and because the fence was old, it should be purchased for that purpose. Most of the crew, naturally, accepted their captain's version at face value. However, Zimmerman says that "the removal of the poles had caused a good deal of indignation amongst the people, although it was not given expression, on account of their King having given his sanction to the action; nevertheless, it was easy to read their feelings in their faces."[59] Zimmermann, who did not witness the actual event, belonged to the sister ship, the *Discovery*. Yet his observation of Hawaiian resentment is probably correct. That there was public resentment, whether or not Ledyard's account is true, seems virtually certain from Puget's 1793 interview with the priest of this shrine. I think it also certain that the memory of this event prompted Kamehameha to request Vancouver in February 1793 to "give the most positive orders that none of our people, on any account whatsoever, should be suffered to enter their morais [temples] or consecrated places, or be permitted to infringe on their rights or sacred privileges."[60]

Now let me interpret, in terms of deep motivation, the inner relationship between the ritual in Hikiau in which Cook participated and the later removal, for ships' fuel, of the palings with their line of skulls and the "idols" from that very shrine. Only connect: *It seems as if the last act annuls the significance of the first*, such that it is simultaneously a physical and psychical "undoing." However one interprets the Cook rituals at Hikiau—as an apotheosis, as a welcoming, or as a ceremony of installation—it is very clear that Cook was at least treated as a chief by Hawaiians on a par with their own. What did Cook think of this? We know that he appreciated similar rituals among the Tongans; they supplemented the poorly ritualized hierarchies on board. The Hawaiian rituals would have indicated to Cook that, even more than in Tahiti, *he* was the captain of the ship and the lord of these isles. *He* was the chief of chiefs. He certainly could not have anticipated the rituals performed at Hikiau. Here *he* is made to prostrate before the Hawaiian gods and kiss the image of their deity, Kū. It is unlikely that at that time Cook was aware of the implications of his subservience to the Hawaiian gods: nor could he have foreseen it. Cook must have later reflected, favorably or unfavorably, on these occurrences. He was not a believing Christian, but he was no disbeliever either. He must have been socialized in a home and in a village society where Christian values were important. I am therefore suggesting that the later destruction of the palings and images of the *heiau* was motivated by Cook's guilt in addition to his violated self-esteem. The objects chosen for destruction are significant. The palings are not just a fence round the *heiau*; they contained the skulls of twenty sacrificial victims. In Tahiti Cook witnessed a human sacrifice and expressed his horror and resentment against it to Tu, the Tahitian chief. Yet in Hawai'i Cook was made to kiss the image of the very gods for whom these sacrifices were made and prostrate before them. It is hard to believe that his conscience and his sense of guilt and revulsion would *not* have surfaced sooner or later. Consequently, the palings with their sacrificial heads and their semicircle of images had to be destroyed. Obviously, Cook could not actually set the temple on fire without adequate provocation: This was done later by the ships' crew in an act of retaliation for Cook's death. Instead, these idolatrous objects were to be used for the pragmatic purpose of ships' fuel. Everything, we are told, was nicely done with proper consultation with the priests and proper payment, with properly behaved natives assisting the sailors in their task. (See Appendix 1, "The Destruction of Hikiau and the Death of William Watman," for further details.)

VI

———— ❧❧ ————

Language Games and the European Apotheosis of James Cook

I have made a case for the deification of James Cook in a specifically Hawaiian manner in accordance with their cultural structures and rational pragmatics. It is now necessary to inquire how the myth of the apotheosis arose, namely the European belief that Hawaiians thought that Cook was their god Lono, arrived in person. Some say he was from Kahiki, the land beyond the horizon; others embellish the myth further with many more divine beings in the two ships. I remind the reader that the term *apotheosis* refers to the European myth and *deification* to the Hawaiian one. What, then, is the genesis and evolution of the European myth of the apotheosis of James Cook?

What impressed Europeans was the abject ceremonials and prostrations performed by the Hawaiians toward Cook. These practices, when seen from a European perspective, look like "worship," or "adoration," or "devotion," so that even modern scholars like Kennedy, Beaglehole, and Sahlins are misled. But let me quote Captain James Clerke of the *Discovery*: "The respect they pay the King and two or three chiefs here is, whenever they see one of them coming they fall flat upon their faces scarcely daring to look up, and in this position they continue till he is twenty or thirty yards past them; if in their canoes, they leave off paddling and prostrate themselves along the boat."[1] It is clear, then, that Cook was simply accorded the ceremonial obeisance known as *kapu moe* by which their own important chiefs were honored. As I noted earlier, this same obeisance was extended to Captain Clerke, but never to ordinary seamen. A highly hierarchical society, Hawaiians were sensitive to hierarchies not their own.

The ceremonial prostrations expressed the great political and social gulf between chiefs, especially the king himself, and commoners. The term for "sacred" is *kapu*, or tabu in other Polynesian cultures. The king was sacred and could not be touched by ordinary people. The very interaction with outsiders, such as the British officers, would be a violation. When Clerke, in the very first visit at Kaua'i, put his friendly arm around an important chief, the chief's attendants were appalled.[2] Thus, there is no question that if the Hawaiian chiefs were to interact with officers and maintain their authority with their own people or if chiefly women were to sleep with white officers, then it was in fact necessary to "sacralize" the officers. Cook's installation was a major ceremony, highly overdetermined by a variety of other meanings and motivations. The lesser ceremonies performed everywhere for lower British officers represent a more general political motivation, namely, to render them "untouchable," to convert them into a class similar to that of native chiefs. Rules of interaction are provided for both commoners and chiefs in their relationships with British officers, strictly Hawaiian rules designed to counter the emergence of a set of double standards that might erode commoners' attitudes toward their own chiefs or at least produce a severe clash of values—one set practiced by the British, the other by the Hawaiian chiefs. The rules applied only to the areas where the chiefs had jurisdiction, that is, the island itself and the adjacent seas. Beaglehole writes, "There is no mention of such abasement among people who thronged the ships," at least in Hawai'i, a phenomenon thoroughly expectable in terms of my preceding analysis.[3] Incidentally, this would not have been the case if Cook was indeed the god Lono, for one would expect even greater prostrations in the very domain where Lono had indisputable sway.

None of these traditional ceremonies of obeisance amounted to "adoration," "worship," or "devotion" in the Christian sense. Quite the contrary, they were highly formalized and expressed abjection and sometimes fear. The "fear" noted by journal writers caught the spirit of the prostrations. But, for the most part, the major journal writers used a "language game" borrowed from Christianity. This language game, I shall show, also corresponded with "a form of life" that existed onboard ship vis-à-vis the living persona of James Cook.

Let me briefly recapitulate this familiar language game: In the conclusion of the discourse on cannibalism, James King mentions the frequent query of the Hawaiians regarding the return of the (dead) Cook and adds, "They considered him a being of a superior nature."[4] During the ceremony of installation, King conjectures, "As far as related to the person of Captain Cook, they seemed approaching to adoration."[5] Again, "the adoration that was paid to Captain Cook" and the frequent ceremonies performed before him are "a sort of religious adoration."[6] All this was in the 1784 edition that contemporary British readers used. Now juxtapose the following account by Samwell of the reaction of the crew when they beheld Cook's remains: "Such was the Condition in which those, who looked upon Captain Cook as their father and whose great Qualities *they venerated almost to adoration*. . . ."[7] Samwell says elsewhere also that he held Cook in "great Veneration."[8] And this is Trevenen: "The fact that I (as well as many others) had been so used to look up to him [Cook] as our good genius, our safe conductor, *and as a kind of superior being*, that I could not suffer myself, I did not dare, to think he would fall by the hands of Indians, over whose minds and bodies, also, he had been accustomed to rule with uncontrolled sway."[9] Trevenen, in the context of harsh shipboard discipline, also considered Cook a "despot"; similar sentiments were expressed by others. Thus, Cook was both kind and stern: the embodiment of the Father. "He is," says Roberts, another crew member, "such an able Navigator, equalled by few and excelled by none, justly stiled the father of his people."[10] At his death seamen cried, says Samwell, "with Tears in their Eyes that they had lost their Father."[11] One of these seamen is Zimmermann, who felt that "we had lost a father."[12]

The preceding analysis shows that the language game in which the Hawaiians were supposed to adore or worship Cook is in fact a projection of the attitude of the ships' officers and crew toward Cook. Underlying it is a form of life on ship: Cook is the loving yet stern father, aloof and idealized by the ship's crew as their guide and genius. Yet, in spite of this attitude, I noted that none of the officers (except Rickman) made the connection that Lono-Cook was the same as Lono the god, even when they were fully aware that there was a Hawaiian god by that name. They were baffled; they recognized that he was placated in the same manner as was a chief, but they never claimed that the Hawaiians thought he was Lono or any other deity.

Only two journal writers made the connection. One was Lieutenant Rickman, the first to appear in print anonymously in 1781. His work was hastily written and he did not even get the chronological sequence of events correct. Yet he cannot be dismissed entirely, as Beaglehole dismisses him. Even the romantic stories that he included in his texts were probably not deliberate inventions or fabrications but a record of shipboard gossip.[13] It is also as gossip that his references to Cook are significant. He never witnessed the installation ceremony, yet he says that Cook "was seated in a kind of throne, and addressed in a long oration by a priest clothed in a vestment of party-coloured cloth . . . *this part of the ceremony over they fell at his feet, the king acquainting him that this was now his building*, and that he was henceforth their Ea-thu-an-nueh."[14] Rickman added that a special chief waited on him always to "conduct him to his house, which the sailors now called Cook's Altar."[15] This account is sheer nonsense, since the king was not present and it is Cook who fell at Kū's feet. But shipboard gossip reverses the reality in order to convert Cook into a Hawaiian deity. So it was with Zimmermann, an ordinary seaman who wrote his short volume in German also in 1781. "The inhabitants . . . raised Captain Cook to the dignity of a god and set up an idol in his honor which they called after him 'O-runa no te tuti,' 'O-runa' meaning god, and 'tuti' Cook."[16] When old

William Watman died, Zimmermann once again echoed popular gossip: "The death of our quartermaster destroyed their previous belief in our immortality, and, this belief being lost, their reverence for us was gone."[17]

It is virtually certain that Zimmermann's idea that the Hawaiians thought of the European as immortal, or that Cook was a god, comes from their own popular shipboard traditions. Similar views were held by Wallis's men, the first European group to discover Tahiti in June 1767. After having terrified the Tahitians in their canoes by firing at them and killing several, Robertson, the master of the *Dolphin* wrote:

> How terrible must they be shockd, to see their nearest and dearest of friends Dead, and toar to peces in such a manner as I am certain they neaver beheald before—to Attempt to say what this poor Ignorant creatures thought of us, would be taking more upon me than I am able to perform.
>
> Some of my messmates thought *they would now look upon us as Demi Gods,* come to punish them for some of their by past transgrations, but I think they were not yet fully confirmed in that oppinion, altho afterwards we hade some reason to believe they were partly in that oppinion, from some circumstances that happened soon after.[18]

This was written even before landing; hence the idea of white gods is almost certainly part of shipboard traditions. That the savage or native looks upon the European as a deity is the stuff from which the apotheosis of James Cook was constructed by ordinary seamen. The officers were surely aware of this tradition and were therefore cautious in accepting the popular shipboard equation that Cook was a god for Hawaiians, even though they themselves looked upon their captain with feelings of "adoration" and "veneration" as befits "a superior being" (see Figure 7).

This idea that the European is a god to savages is not just shipboard tradition (though it must be very strong there) but also a structure of the long run in European culture and consciousness. I can only highlight the tradition here very briefly. As is well known, Cortés and possibly Columbus were apotheosized; Cortés had a profound impact on the European imagination as the indigenous god Quetzalcoatl, also a god who returns following his disappearance. Here is Todorov's summary:

> According to Indian accounts from before the conquest, Quetzalcoatl is a figure at once historical (a leader) and legendary (a divinity). At a given moment, he is forced to leave his kingdom and flee to the east (toward the Atlantic); he vanishes but, according to certain versions of the myth, he promises (or threatens) to return some day to reclaim his own. We may note here that the notion of a Messiah's return does not play an essential role in Mexican mythology; that

Figure 7. Natives Worshiping Captain Cook, illustration from
A. Kippis, *A Narrative of the Voyages Round the World,
Performed by Captain James Cook*

Quetzalcoatl is merely one divinity among others and does not occupy
a privileged place (especially among the Aztecs, who perceive him as
the god of the Cholultecs); and that only certain narratives promise his
return, whereas others are content to describe his disappearance.[19]

The question whether this apotheosis is also a European invention I shall
leave to others to pursue. But the event itself was treated as a true occurrence by Europeans. Thus, the very beginnings of the voyages of discovery
carried with them the tradition of the apotheosis of redoubtable European
navigators who were also the harbingers of civilization. This cultural structure occurs against a larger background of ancient Indo-European values
pertaining to euhemerism, to gods in human shape appearing among mor-
tals, to men becoming gods and gods becoming men and so forth. The
Christian cult of the saints is a continuation of older euhemeristic traditions or that of the apotheosis of those who die violent deaths. The popular
shipboard narratives of Europeans who were divine figures to natives is
thus an old tradition, and one that has continued to this very day in popular
cartoons (see Figure 8) and in pseudo-historical writing like Van Daniken's
and in some forms of science fiction. It is also the backdrop against which
the shipboard narratives of the divinization of Cook and his crew make
sense.

In spite of this cultural background (or perhaps because of it), the journal
writers did not connect Cook with divinity because their empirical observations did not warrant it. Yet there are clear indications that the reading of
texts by Zimmermann and Rickman and debates in England regarding
Cook's death have affected the writing of the third volume of the journals
by King, which is not surprising because writers are affected by the defini-

THE FAR SIDE   By GARY LARSON

With a little luck, they may revere us as gods.

Figure 8. "The Far Side" cartoon by Gary Larson

tion of a situation in a particular time and place. Thus, King in the official edition describes the deference paid to Cook as follows: "This ceremony [of prostration and offering of a pig] was frequently repeated during our stay in Owhyhee, and appeared to us, from many circumstances, to be a sort of religious adoration."[20] This reference to "religious adoration" is not in King's *unofficial* journal. Again the official journal says: "Their presents were made with a regularity, more like a discharge of a religious duty than the effect of mere liberality. . . . "[21] The unofficial makes no reference to "religious duty"; instead: "All this seemed to be done as a duty . . . either as a peace offering or to a Mortal much their superior."[22] And Trevenen, scribbling comments on the edition of 1784, refers to Cook as the "idolized man," because by the time he wrote, the debate that Cook was idolized had appeared in London in Evangelical circles and even on the English stage.[23] King's idea that the offerings to Cook were "religious" led Ellis and later historians of Hawai'i to believe that sacrifices were offered to Cook-Lono in order to propitiate him.

125

The official journal was published under the editorship of Douglas in 1784, five years after Cook's death. That very year William Cowper, the poet, wrote to a friend, the Reverend John Newton:

The reading of these volumes afforded me much amusement, and I hope some instruction. No observation however force itself upon me with more violence than one, that I could not help making on the death of Captain Cook. God is a jealous God, and at Owhyhee [Hawai'i] the poor man was content to be worshipped. From that moment, the remarkable interposition of Providence in his favor was converted into an opposition that thwarted all his purposes. He left the scene of his deification, but was driven back to it by a most violent storm, in which he suffered more than in any that had preceded it. When he departed, he left his worshippers still infatuated with an idea of his godship, consequently well disposed to serve him. At his return, he found them sullen, distrustful, and mysterious. A trifling theft was committed, which, by a blunder of his own in pursuing the thief after the property had been restored, was magnified to an affair of the last importance. One of their favorite chiefs was killed too by a blunder. Nothing in short but blunder and mistake attended him, till he fell breathless into the water, and then all was smooth again. The world indeed will not take notice or see that the dispensation bore evident marks of divine displeasure; but a mind, I think, in any degree spiritual cannot overlook them. We know from truth itself that the death of Herod was for a similar offence. . . . Besides, though a stock or stone may be worshipped blameless, a baptized man may not. He knows what he does, and, by suffering such honors to be paid him, incurs the guilt of sacrilege.[24]

This is Cowper reading the text as a European and a Christian mythmaker. He picks up two themes that are central to later Cook hagiography, namely, his apotheosis and its sacrilegious nature. Cowper had no access to the Hawaiian myths of Lono, for these trickled to England very much later. The tradition of mythologization that Cowper represents is a European one constructed on the basis of the European past and a special reading of the journals. I doubt that this is Cowper's own unique reading either; it must be based on a variety of "debates" going on in England and Europe following the dramatic death of the famous explorer. Given European traditions and the ambiguously seductive nature of the texts describing the "religious adoration" paid to Cook by Hawaiians, it would be surprising if explicit debates over Cook's apotheosis did not take place.

Thus, there seems to have developed soon after Cook's death several European versions of a Cook myth. These versions deal with Cook as a god to savages or, in the Evangelical version, as an idolater. A third and very important strand is the intellectual mythologization of Cook as the humane embodiment of the Enlightenment. This form of idealization commenced in Cook's own lifetime and was fully mythicized after his death. It appears in popular poetry, in eulogies, and in the theatre. The last takes over the idea that Cook might well have been literally a god to savages and at the same time affirms that he was, metaphorically, an immortal in the European galaxy of great men. Let me now briefly deal with this humanist mythicization of James Cook.

Kippis's biography (1788) quotes several verses composed soon after Cook's death. One French poet refers to his ship as "the sacred vessel," and the "ingenious and amiable Miss Hannah More" wrote:

> Had those advent'rous spirits, who explore
> Through ocean's trackless wastes, the far sought shore,
> Whether of wealth insatiate, or of power,
> Conquerors who waste, or ruffians who devour:
> Had these possess'd, O Cook! thy gentle mind,
> Thy love of arts, thy love of humankind;
> Had these pursu'd thy mild and lib'ral plan,
> DISCOVERERS had not been a curse to man!
> Then, bless'd Philanthropy! thy social hands,
> Had link'd disserver'd worlds in brothers' bands;
> Careless, if colour, or if clime divide;
> Then lov'd, and loving, man had liv'd, and died.[25]

This is plain hagiography that has little to do with Cook, but it does represent in extremis the idea of Cook as the humane civilizer, a child of the Enlightenment to the European consciousness. Kippis says that other poems, especially an elegy by Miss Seward "admirably represented the principle of humanity by which the captain was activated in his undertakings."[26] As we have seen earlier, this vision of humanity is expressed in symbols of growth and the fertilization of alien lands with English plants and domestic animals, including John Bull himself (see Figures 9 and 10):

> To these the hero leads his living store,
> And pours new wonders on th' uncultur'd shore;
> The silky fleece, fair fruit, and golden grain;
> And future herds and harvests bless the plain.
>
> O'er the green soil his kids exulting play,
> And sounds his clarion loud the bird of day;
> The downy goose her ruffled bosom laves;
> Trims her white wind, and wantons in the waves;
> Stern moves the bull along th' affrighted shores,
> And countless nations tremble as he roars.[27]

Figures 9 and 10. Captain Cook and His Domestic Animals,
two illustrations from A. Kippis, *A Narrative of the
Voyages Round the World* . . .

These idealizations are matched by the vision of the almost sacred nature
of his death:

> Ye, who ere while for Cook's illustrious brow
> Pluck'd the green laurel, and the oaken bough,
> Hung the gay garlands on the trophied oars,
> And pour'd his fame along a thousand shores,
> Strike the slow death-bell!—weave the sacred verse,
> And strew the cypress o'er his honour'd hearse;
> In sad procession wander round the shrine,
> And weep him mortal, whom ye sung divine![28]

More research is required to better analyze the popular literature and
debates characteristic of the period after Cook's death. Of perhaps more
interest are the theater and paintings that deal directly or indirectly with

this theme. I refer to *Omai, or a trip round the world . . .* performed as a pantomime in Covent Garden on 20 December 1785. The producer was Jacques de Loutherbourg, a major technical innovator in theatre who employed John Webber, the ship's artist on the last voyage, as a consultant. The plot of *Omai* is a total travesty of the journals. Let me present its fascinating conclusion from the original text in the Huntington Library.[29]

There appears on stage a huge procession of chiefs and ordinary men and women from fifteen countries visited by Cook, wearing their exact native clothes, according to the playbill.[30] The rest of the cast are an English sea captain, Omai [Mai], Oberea [Purea]—the famed Tahitian "queen" of Wallis's and Cook's first voyage but now converted into a "sorceress"—and a chorus of Indians. The English sea captain gives a sword to Omai.

CAPTAIN: Accept from mighty George, our Sovereign Lord
                A sign of British love, this British sword.

OBEREA: Oh, joy! away my useless spells and magic charms
                A British sword is proof against the world in arms.

CAPTAIN: [To the Indians] Ally of joy! Owhyee's (27) fatal shore
                Brave Cook, your great Orono (28) is no more.

CHORUS OF   Mourn, Owhyee's fatal shore

INDIANS: For Cook, our great Orono, is no more

At this point, "*a grand painting descends, and the* English Captain *sings*."[31] The lowering of this painting—*The Apotheosis of Captain Cook Being Crowned by Brittania and Fame* (Figure 11 of this volume was inspired by it)—is an important technical accomplishment in the English theater. The English captain now sings:

> Ye chiefs of the ocean your laurels throw by,
> Or cypress entwine with a wreath;
> To prove your humanity heave a soft sigh,
> And a tear now let fall for his death!
> Yet the Genius of Britain forbids us to grieve
> Since Cook, ever honor'd, immortal shall live.[32]

The next stanza compares Cook to "the hero of Macedon," but unlike Alexander, who brought about death, Cook "taught mankind how to live." And the final stanza:

> He *came*, and he *saw*, not to conquer but save;
> The *Caeser* of Britain was he;
> Who scorn'd the ambition of making a slave
> While Britons themselves were so free.
> Now the Genius of Britain forbids us to grieve
> Since Cook, ever honor'd, immortal shall live.[33]

The numerals 27 and 28 appearing in parentheses in the sea captain's speech quoted earlier indicate references to two key footnotes found in the printed version of the text (not, however in the handwritten manuscript also in the Huntington Library). The first appearing after "Owhyee" says that it refers to "the Island [Hawai'i] where Captain Cook was killed"; the second says that "Orono" [Lono] is "A Demi-God, or hero, and the distinguished title with which the natives honoured Captain Cook."[34] The printed text appeared in 1785, a year after the publication of the official journals. The footnotes tell us that a) Cook was a demigod, the view enshrined in popular shipboard gossip, or b) that he was a hero; and he was given a "distinguished title [Lono]," which is the view of the enlightened journalists. After Cook's death the first voyage to Hawai'i by Europeans was in 1786, and there is no way that information on a cult of James Cook could have reached London the year before. The playwright was using *European* views of Cook as demigod or as a hero honored by Hawaiians. The debate is still open: There is yet no decision by the theatre producers whether he was one or the other to the Hawaiians. The production also makes clear that the "Indians" also join the English in mourning the loss of the great Orono. The ambiguous texts of the voyage have been given unambiguous meaning as Hawaiians begin to mourn for Cook on the English stage.

Inspired by *The Apotheosis of Captain Cook* (that is, the theater painting used with the play *Omai*), several paintings with that title appeared between 1785–93, the most interesting being a depiction of the allegorical trio of Cook, Britannia, and Fame hovering in the clouds above a view of Kealakekua Bay where Cook was killed (see Figure 11). Needless to say, there is nothing remotely Hawaiian about them, because the painters simply capitalized on previous European traditions and the current debates over the apotheosis and death of James Cook.

I do not think that the paintings of the apotheosis can be taken literally. Rather like the idealizations of the poets, they are an allegorical expression of the European view of Cook as the arch civilizer and child of the Enlightenment. It is unlikely that educated eighteenth-century Europeans thought that Cook was "deified" like a European saint or that at death he ascended to heaven. Contrast with this, however, the European perception of savage people: *They* were capable of direct and unabashed deification of the intrepid explorer in their midst. Furthermore, at least among ordinary English sailors, this process of projecting onto the savage their own fantasies must be seen in the context of their hatred of the Spaniards. The Spaniards had their Cortés who was deified by the Aztecs; now the English had their Cook, their own hero who also explored and opened up a new world. Cook is the avatar of Cortés.

Figure 11. *The Apotheosis of Captain Cook*, engraving by Philip Wouvermann

The Humanist Myth in New Zealand History

The Enlightenment view of Cook that appeared in various forms at that time and later is what I call the humanist myth. This version is extremely important in Australia and New Zealand, where he was perceived as a kind of founding ancestor of the white colonizers. Let me deal with the humanist myth of Cook insofar as it appears in New Zealand, using as my primary text a recent work, *Captain Cook and His Times*, that claims to make a

131

modern critical revaluation of this remarkable man.[35] The distinguished scholar of the art of Cook's voyages, Bernard Smith, does recognize, as I do, that Cook was a mythic figure of the Enlightenment and that his tragic death "propelled his memory far beyond the level of mere fame to those exalted realms of the human imagination where only saints, heroes and martyrs dwell."[36] Shortly after his death, Smith continues, "his reputation was submitted quite consciously and deliberately to a heroizing process, not by his fellow voyagers but by academicians, poets, and artists, whose imagination had been gripped by the power of his achievement."[37] Smith proceeds with a fine scholarly account of this construction of a humanist mythology of Cook by intellectuals. I think that this humanist mythology has been perpetuated into the present by the various histories of these voyages and the biographies of Cook.

Another side to the Cook mythology, also part of the humanist myth that Smith explores, pertains to his significance to the new Europe. "After his death, Cook's life and achievements provided the material from which a new kind of hero, one admirably adapted to the needs of the new industrial society of Europe and its global expansion was fashioned . . . or to put it rather bluntly, the prototypical hero of European [post-eighteenth-century] imperialism."[38] But why Cook? Why not Nelson or Wolfe? Smith says that the new imperialism claimed to be a humane one and Cook's own life fitted the conception of "a world wide empire dedicated to the arts of peace (a *pax Britannica*), not one based on war."[39] And beyond that, for intellectuals of the Enlightenment and after, a vision of *Pax Universitas* was erected on the principles of free trade, which Cook in his own way introduced into the South Seas through his contact with Polynesians.[40] "Cook was in a sense Adam Smith's global agent, for he developed markets and spread the notion of enlightened self-interest, bringing to prehistoric cultures the disguised checks and balances of a market economy."[41] He is also the Promethean hero who brings metallurgy and its related forms of culture to primitive man.

THIS is as far as Smith's "revaluation" goes. He acutely diagnoses the multiple facets of Cook's mythic persona for Western man, but he does not critically examine whether these mythic images have any relation to the character of Cook as they are revealed in his and others' extensive shipboard journals. Instead, he seems to suggest that it was possible for Europeans to mythologize Cook in this manner because Cook, in his actual life, fitted this conception. For Smith there is a consonance between Cook the man and Cook of the humanist myth: "There is little reason to doubt that Cook on any reading was a man of great virtue; my point is rather that we should recognize the sociality, the timelessness of his array of virtues, his inborn capacity to exercise an ethics of situation. . . . When he was most himself, he was most in harmony with the new, secular, industrial order that was emerging as the new world order in his lifetime."[42]

It seems, then, that the most recent scholarship on Cook in fact reinforces the older view of Cook as the humane embodiment of the Enlightenment, a new type of hero that emerged into world history, permitting us to critically reflect on the earlier violent Spanish expansionism.

Smith's article then purportedly attempts to redefine Cook, the man and the voyages, and ends by reifying them in the manner of earlier scholarship. It tries to critically move away from the monumental biography of J. C. Beaglehole, *The Life of Captain James Cook.* Beaglehole, assessing Cook's character, has this to say: "The humanity that is kindness, understanding, tolerance, wisdom in the treatment of men, a quality that is practised naturally as well as planned for is what gave Cook's voyages their success, as much as the soundness of his seamanship and the brilliance of his navigation."[43] But Alan Frost, in the first essay in the very volume that claims to be a revaluation, continues in even more adulatory terms: "When we think of the majesty and mystery of this extraordinary man's achievement . . . we may also know that, in giving the reality he did to the world beyond Europe, he marked the imagination of his age in a manner of a Newton or a Darwin."[44] In my view both the adulation and the assessment are wildly exaggerated and yet endemic to Cook scholarship.

In the summer of 1990, I was in London researching the archival materials on Cook when I had an opportunity to participate in a celebration of Cook in a one-day seminar at the Royal Society, organized by the New Zealand Universities' Graduate Association, to commemorate the 150th anniversary of the signing of the Treaty of Waitangi, by which the Maoris effectively gave up all sovereign claims to New Zealand. During the lunch break, all of us left the crowded hall and walked to the Pall Mall to lay a wreath at Captain Cook's statue. The event celebrated the humanist myth of Cook. In the seminar, the chairman of the committee, Admiral of the Fleet, Lord Lewin of Greenwich, raised the troublesome issue of Cook's behavior during the third voyage and reiterated the view of Sir James Watt, a noted physician, that Cook's erratic behavior was caused by roundworm infestation![45] A more pathetic attempt to exonerate Cook from responsibility for his actions could scarcely be invented.

Though Tasman was the first Westerner to discover New Zealand, Cook is spiritually the founder of that modern nation. David Mackay, a New Zealand historian, in his presentation at the celebration, said that the Maoris "generally portray him [Cook] as a figure of considerable stature; a distinguished, firm, yet compassionate individual. Contemporary Maori leaders [of Cook's time] seemed to regard him as a person of some nobility; the obvious one to negotiate with, or to complain about depredations."[46] It is baffling how Mackay could have made inferences about Maori views of

Cook from the ship's journals. His is an attempt to show that Maoris loved Cook, who was the founder of the nation for both Maoris and Whites.

> That strong sculptured face ... is better known than that of any past politicians, governors general, military leaders, or even rugby players. Cook's name graces more streets, suburbs, parks, motels, hotels, schools and other public institutions than that of the present or any previous sovereigns. His ship, the *Endeavour*, is on the reverse side of our 50 cent piece, and even more significantly, when we hold our paper money up to the light we see in the water mark that stern face again, as the guarantor of the integrity of our currency.[47]

Mackay also implies that Cook could be what he is made out to be because in reality that is what he was. He admits, however, that during the third voyage "the flaws were evident; lapses in judgement, irritability, an erosion of his sense of balance and proportion," yet he has "survived the ravages of both time and historians."[48] Why so? Among other reasons, "he embodied the pioneer virtues, qualities and skills in developing a new settled land. Adaptability, resourcefulness, endurance and doggedness. ... Physically he was a big, rawboned individual, the epitome of the pioneer or frontier type ... a self made man, who had eschewed the easy road to success and pushed himself to the top largely by his own efforts."[49] Especially remarkable is that Cook could survive intact in the egalitarian traditions of Australia and New Zealand. "James Cook however has remained sacrosanct. In historical terms it is a remarkable achievement."[50]

THE scholar, then, is both historian and mythmaker, a mythmaker qua historian. Mackay says that in New Zealand, a country without "liberation heroes," Cook is "sacrosanct." But what about the Maoris? Mackay recognizes that Maoris are intimately part of this new nation, quite unlike the Australian aborigines who have been excluded from the white nation from the very start. This again is made possible because Cook, in his journals, created an image of the fearless, independent Maoris who had their own ideas of sovereignty and nationhood. Consequently, the British decided to colonize Botany Bay as their penal colony, and the colonization of New Zealand "was delayed for more than fifty years and occurred in a more humane age."[51] He adds that in 1851 a hydrographer, John Lort Stout, impressed by Cook's navigational skills, suggested that "New Zealand's most distinctive landmark should be named after him. The Maori name for Mt. Cook is Aorangi—cloud piercer—a peak which stands above the rest in the monumental southern alps. It is a fitting New Zealand memorial to a navigator without peer,"[52] a man towering over both Maoris and whites, a true founder. History in this account is fully myth.

The sources used by historians to depict Maori perceptions of Cook's nobility are derived not so much from the ship's journals as from Maori narratives. Here is probably the most famous one recounted by Sinclair in his *History of New Zealand*:

> To picture how these undreamed-of strangers must have appeared to the Maori we must imagine what our reaction would be if we suffered a Martian invasion. According to one Maori chief, Te Horeta Tani-wha, who as a small boy was present when Cook came to Mercury Bay, the Maoris at first thought the white men were goblins and their ship a god. Eighty years later the old man recalled the astonishment when one of the goblins pointed a walking stick at a shag and amidst the thunder and lightening the bird fell down dead. "There was one supreme man in that ship. We knew that he was the lord of the whole by his perfect gentlemanly and noble demeanour." This chief goblin gave the little boy a nail which he long kept with great care as a tool and a god.[53]

This is "history," and practically every source I have read recounts it. This account of a Maori's reminiscences was first taken down at Lieuten-ant-Governor Wynyard's direction (by an unknown person) in 1852, pre-sented in Chapman's New Zealand Magazine in 1862, and then again by White in his *Ancient History of the Maori*.[54] The story has a wide diffusion from popular culture to orthodox history. Sinclair's brief summary excludes some fascinating details: The Maoris mistake ships' biscuits for pumice stones; they disliked whale blubber (which the journals report they en-joyed.) The ship was a *tupera*, a god; and the wonderful creatures on board had eyes at the back of their heads.

> When these goblins came on shore we (the children and women) took notice of them, but we ran away from them into the forest, and the warriors alone stayed in the presence of those goblins; but as the gob-lins stayed some time, and did not do any evil to our braves, we came back one by one, and gazed at them, and we stroked their garments with our hands, and we were pleased with the whiteness of their skins and blue eyes of some of them.[55]

These goblins are kind. A Maori was shot by one of them, but this man "was a noted thief."[56] Cook himself is wonderfully kind and paternalistic to them: "He was a very good man and came to us—the children—and patted our cheeks and gently touched our heads . . . he came up on deck again and came to where I and my boy companions were, and patted our heads with his hands . . . and again patted our heads with his hands and went away."[57]

WE do not know whether Te Horeta, known to whites as Old Hooknose, was the Uncle Tom he is made out to be. But what is striking is that this myth was recorded by god knows who in 1852. Cook's first visit was in 1769, and therefore Te Horeta in 1852 would have been an 83-plus old man reminiscing about an event that supposedly occurred when he was probably under five years old! Sources such as this are distorted many times over, but they eventually become history as well as public knowledge. They soon become a tradition that influences the scholarly writing about Maori perceptions of whites. Thus when Marsden, the first missionary, arrived in New Zealand, how did the Maoris perceive him? "When Marsden mounted his horse and rode up and down the beach he was, by common consent, given the status of more than a mortal."[58] And a sophisticated scholar, Withey, writes about a Maori presenting a green branch to Cook in Queen Charlotte Sound during his second voyage, as "perhaps an attempt to conciliate the English god."[59] There is no Maori voice here: It is a European one imputing to the Maoris a special kind of voice. And consider another historian, Harrison Wright, mixing Te Horeta's tropes with others developed in early New Zealand history. According to him, when New Zealanders first saw the *Endeavour* on the horizon they thought it was an enormous bird and they talked with wonder about its huge beautiful wings. As it came closer, they saw a smaller bird without wings descend to the water, and "a number of party-coloured beings, but apparently in the human shape" descended into it. The large bird contained "a houseful of divinities." The amazed New Zealanders thought that these were gods in human shape capable of unleashing thunderbolts at will.[60] It must be remembered that the Maori perceptions of the white man related only to Cook and his English crew. The Frenchmen Marion de Fresne and de Surville were also here. None of them were deified; indeed poor de Fresne, a thoroughly decent man, ended up being eaten by the Maoris.

The myth related by Te Horeta soon became part of a tradition and began to possess an axiomatic and taken-for-granted quality, such that it emerges in a variety of ways in popular and scholarly culture. In some cases there is a collaboration between native and white in the construction of myths, but in an unequal power structure the white version triumphs and is eventually accepted by the subaltern culture. I doubt whether Maoris, unlike Hawaians, possessed the many versions of myths that Hawaiians did, that managed to surface in print in the early years of colonization or missionization. The Te Horeta myth itself is nothing new: It is based on the myth model discussed earlier, that of the redoubtable white harbinger of civilization, but given a peculiar application in New Zealand. These myths provoke debates that result in new renditions and variations of the old, as for example the various versions of the Te Horeta myth and William Cowper's Evangelical version of the myth of Cook as demigod.

The Evangelical myth of Cook the idolator, popularized by Hawaian missionaries after 1821, is not a comfortable one for those who believe in Cook as the founder of a modern nation. Thus Mackay tells us that the Australian aborigines have a devastating myth of Cook as "a malevolent figure who killed their ancestors and took their land."[61] His diagnosis, I think, is correct, that this myth emerged as a consequence of the terrible treatment of the aborigines by the white settlers, whereas the more benign version of the Maori myth reflected better interracial relationships. We know that Cook's contact with aborigines was brief and nonviolent. But the contrast permits Mackay to argue that the aboriginal myth is a *myth* of the sort that primitives possess, because such myths have no basis in *reality*. By contrast, the story of Te Horeta (and similar myths of white gods) is true. It is *fact* and therefore could be incorporated into modern histories. It is also consonant with the facts about Cook the man. Here, then, is an intrinsic feature of modern mythmaking: A story such as Te Horeta's is justified and reasoned on the basis of fact, of evidence. It therefore can be disguised as history and for the most part *is* history. What I have done is to reveal the myth model buried in a specific history or in the popular traditions of a modern nation that claims to construct such traditions out of history.[62]

The Resurrection and Return of James Cook

Let us leave the English stage and the humanist myths of the great explorer in order to examine the fate of his bones in Hawai'i and in the imagination of later sea captains. The journals refer to an intriguing question that priests asked of James King and others soon after the death of their Captain: When will Lono (Cook) return? The conception of the return, like that of the apotheosis itself, was in all likelihood influenced by biblical messianic notions. Hawai'i, like many other cultures, believed that a spirit of a dead person may return in a variety of ways, but this variety has been narrowed down and synthesized in European accounts as the return of James Cook as the god Lono. Let me try to disentangle some of the contexts in which Hawaiians could, within their own scheme of things, speak of the return of Lono-Cook:

The crucial event pertaining to the return of Cook which Sahlins highlights occurred when two priests came on board the *Resolution* bearing a piece of Cook's body. "Handing it over to the British with expressions of great sorrow, they asked when 'Lono would come again.'"[63] Sahlins adds, "It was a question British navigators would hear from other Hawaiians, not only at this time but again in later years."[64] This initial query is recorded in detail in the official edition of 1784, which substantially agrees with King's unofficial journal and with Samwell's account.

Let me examine the full account of the event by Lieutenant King. Naturally the ship's officers were appalled at the sight of the grisly object, but they soon overcame this; the were, after all, the first ethnographers, imbued with a scientific curiosity. They could easily change into their white coats for let it not be forgotten they were representatives of the Royal Society. King reports:

> This [meeting] afforded an opportunity of informing ourselves, whether they were cannibals; and we did not neglect it. We first tried, by many indirect questions, put to each of them apart, to learn in what manner the rest of the bodies has been disposed of; and finding them very constant in one story, that, after the flesh had been cut off, it was all burnt; we at last put the direct question, Whether they had not eat some of it? They immediately shewed as much horror at the idea, as any European would have done; and asked, very naturally, if that was custom amongst us? They afterward asked us, with great earnestness and apparent apprehension, "When the *Orono* would come again? and what he would do to them on his return?" The same inquiry was frequently made afterward by others; and this idea agrees with the general tenour of their conduct toward him, which shewed, that they considered him as a being of superior nature.[65]

Let me examine the context of this utterance in some detail. The priests who brought the disposable remains of Cook knew quite clearly that his chiefly bones were separated for customary disposal. If our hypothesis is correct, Cook would now have been subject to rites of deification. But in the present context, the ships' crew activated another set of anxious questions imputing to the Hawaiians the custom of cannibalism. This inquiry was reasonable from the British point of view, for, if the Hawaiians had burned Cook's body, they might well have "eat some of it." But because the Hawaiians were not anthropophagous, they simply assumed, says King, that cannibalism was the custom of the British! This was probably a current rumor anyway, because Cook had asked this same question the previous year in Kaua'i and Ni'ihau, provoking Hawaiians to worry that the strangers asking these questions were cannibals.[66] In any case it is clear that this context provoked the Hawaiians to ask with "great earnestness and apparent apprehension" when Lono would come back and, then, "what he will do to them on his return?" It is very clear that their feelings were not of "great sorrow," as Sahlins says, but fear of Cook's "ghost" or his return as an avenging diety. It seems that the anxiety about cannibalism has focused the Hawaiian discourse on the fearsome aspect of Cook's character that they were familiar with, a fear reinforced by the terror unleashed on the Hawaiians by the British as reprisal for Cook's death, which, in turn, would have activated childhood fears of cannibal monsters that exist in the Hawaiian imagination. Some of these monsters in fact come from foreign lands.[67] Moreover, we have noted already that according to King Hawaiians believed that the British came from a country where food supplies had run out, which explained their huge and avid consumption of the island's produce. Such beliefs could, temporarily at least, aggravate the Hawaiian fear of cannibal strangers coming from the land of "Brittannee." In any case, I think this cannibalistic discourse in the larger context of terror, activated the Hawaiian priests' concern that the person whom they had just deified might turn out to be a vengeful spirit. One must recognize that different Hawaiians might have had differing views about the "return" of James Cook, depending on context, social position, and involvement in ongoing events.

Samwell, in his journal entry for 20 February, notes: "In the Night an Indian came to the guard boat of the Resolution and gave the Midshipman in her some burnt bones which he said belonged to the Orono. The Indians have a Notion that Captain Cook as being Orono will come amongst them in a short time."[68] This statement in context means that because Cook was deified his spirit will return shortly. However, again one must remember the further context of terror here: Many Hawaiians had been killed on 17 February, the priests' quarters and most of the tower were gutted, and wrathful sailors brandished before the terrified people two decapitated Hawaiian heads that they stuck on the deck of the Resolution. It is hard to believe that this context would have produced an image of the benevolent Cook coming once again as their peaceful god Lono to bring blessings on their land. To deify Cook was the expectable and conventional thing for them to do; yet the later context would have produced fears of the return of the spirit of a feared and fearful person. As Beckwith notes, "Hawaiians believe in the power of spirits to return to the scene they know on earth in the form in which they appeared when they were alive."[69] Corney in 1817 recorded a related belief: "The natives . . . believe that the spirits of the departed are permitted to revisit this world," and he gives graphic examples of fearful revisitations.[70] Thus the anxious question asked by the Hawaiian priests, and perhaps by Samwell's informants, pertained to their dread of the return of Cook's spirit. Beckwith continues: "Especially is this true of the procession of gods and spirits who come on certain sacred nights to visit sacred places, or to welcome a dying relative and conduct him to the 'aumakua world. . . . They are seen on the sacred nights of Ku, Lono, Kane, or Kanaloa, or they may be seen by day if it is a procession to welcome the soul of a dying relative. To meet such a procession is very dangerous."[71] Many Hawaiians were killed or lay dying: The context is right for people to ask anxious questions about the return of Cook-Lono. One must not assume, as Sahlins does, that this question implies the return of Cook as Lono, the god of the Makahiki. Sahlins's position is derived from missionaries like Ellis who, without being aware of it, framed this issue in Christological terms as the return of the dead god.

Even the very term for a god, *akua*, is, says Beckwith, of "indeterminate usage."[72] To appreciate the diverse kinds of *akua*, one has only to glance at the *Hawaiian Dictionary* edited by Pukui and Elbert or consider Kamakau's discussions in *Ka Po'e Kahiko*, such as the following: "An ancestral god was called an *'aumakua* or a *kumupua*, not an *akua 'unihipili* (a deified spirit) or an *akua kaku'ai* (a corpse transfigured into the form of his source *'aumakua*), or an *akua ho'ola'a* (a spirit made into a god through consecration), or an *akua makemake* (a god created through desire or need), or an *akua makemake ho'oula* (a god acquired by being inspired by one), or an *akua malihini* (a newcomer god), or an *akua haole* (an introduced god)."[73] Then there are *kupua* (incarnated spirits), and even ghosts (*lapu*) can on occasion be called *akua lapu*, according to Beckwith. "Nonhuman spirits who dwell in the myriad forms of nature are the little gods (akua li'i) regularly invoked in prayers for protection."[74] It is therefore not surprising that later Western missionaries and travelers, when they heard of Cook referred to as an *akua*, translated that word as "god" and assumed that he was the god Lono to Hawaiians.

There are other hints that the return of Cook was misinterpreted by the first sea captains visiting Hawai'i after 1786. Writing in 1788, only nine years after Cook's death, Meares says that the Hawaiians call the English "the people of the Brittanee" and adds: "As they believed that the commander of every European ship, who had touched at their islands, since the death of Captain Cook, were the sons of that illustrious navigator, they, in the most affecting manner, deplored the event...."[75] It seems that Meares took the phrase "sons of the navigator" literally when the Hawaiians probably either used "sons" in an extended or classificatory sense or, more likely, idiomatically to mean "descendants of the illustrious navigator" as, for example, when Buddhist texts refer to monks as "sons of the Buddha." At least one British officer in Cook's ship, Bligh, thought that the "return of Cook" simply referred to the possible return of naval officers in British ships.[76]

Other conceptions of the "return" could also coexist in Hawaiian culture and consciousness. Consider the following statement by Colnett in 1791:

Indeed they have constantly been at war since Captain Cook was kill'd, and also have had a great deal of Sickness which never before his time afflicted them which they allege to having kill'd him. They made strict inquiry of me, if ever he would come back again, and when I saw him last, I told them: having been constantly in their part of the world, I could not tell, but this I knew, the Spaniards were coming to take their Country from them and make them Slaves. They inquired if Captain Cook had sent them, and how long he would be angry with them, and what they should do to get Captain Cook to get his area [*ali'i*, i.e., the King of England] to send and assist them against the Spaniards.[77]

It is not likely that Colnett, who was obsessed by the Spanish presence, was attuned to Hawaiian modes of thought. But if at least some of his statements are correct, they do not lend much support to the thesis that Cook was the god Lono. By this time, it is obvious that Hawaiians know that Cook came from "Brittanee" and that he was under another chief (the King of England) who would help the Hawaiians get rid of the Spaniards. Yet if Cook went through a postmortem deification, he was "alive" in some sense as a deity and might even be a guardian of British sailors.

Other interpretations of Colnett are also possible as, for example, one of spirit possession, whose complexity has been noted by Kamakau:

Nothing is impossible to god spirits, *akua*. Persons are possessed, first, when the gods desire to reveal hidden things and to foretell important events that will come to pass (persons so possessed are called *kaula*, or prophets); second, when persons are chosen by the *'aumakua* and directed to take care of their physical forms (*kino*) and the things pertaining to these forms; third, when *'uhinipili* (*'unihipili*) spirits directed by the *'aumakua* possess; fourth, when spirits that have been consecrated (*'uhane ho'al'a*) possess at the desire of these spirits; fifth, when *'unihipili* spirits, combined with spirits of the *po pau 'ole* [that is, evil spirits], possess.[78]

Insofar as Kamehameha himself encouraged and gave a filip to possession and healing cults, one cannot rule out the possibility that in many contexts, including Colnett's interpretation, the "return of Lono" simply meant the return of his spirit, either in disembodied form (spirit transfer) or by possession of someone else (spirit possession). A case of spirit transfer was reported by Campbell who lived in Oahu and wrote in 1809 about a Welshman, William Davis whom the Hawaiians thought "had been one of their own countrymen who had gone to Caheite [Kahiki] or England after his death, and had now come back to his native land."[79] If Charlot is correct, the most fascinating case of spirit transfer is that of Liholiho (Kamehameha II), who visited England and died there. In the Fornander collection there is a chant, *He Kanikau no Liholiho I Kono Holo Aua i Biretania* ("A dirge for Liholio On his trip to Britain"), where the spirit of Liholiho is asked to return from England to his native land to see his chiefs.[80] This would mean that some Hawaiian discourses on the "return of Lono" simply referred to spirit transfer. In any case I am suggesting that the Hawaiian concern with the "return of Cook-Lono" might well have meant different things to different people in differing situations. To freeze Hawaiian thought into a single scenario is once again mistaken.

The Versions of the Apotheosis in the Traditions of Sea Voyagers

To free our conception of Hawaiian thought from the simplistic interpretations of early voyagers and come to understand its more complex ramifications is only a preliminary strategy; we must perform a parallel action in relation to the European readings of Cook's apotheosis. Sahlins is correct in saying that some shipboard writings mention the apotheosizing of James Cook by native Hawaiians but it is wrong to assume that these statements "confirm" the hypothesis of the apotheosis. The sea captains who reported these myths were influenced by a variety of debates, both Hawaiian and European, that were circulating after Cook's death, and it is not always clear whether the sources they used were Hawaiian or European or peculiar combinations thereof. Let me illustrate this difficulty by examining some of the finest narratives about Hawai'i by the Russian explorer Otto Von Kotzebue during his two voyages round the world in 1815–18 and 1823–26.[81]

In his first voyage Kotzebue visited the Hawaiian islands in November 1816 and September 1817. He wrote that the "Hawaiians adored him [Cook] as a god, and still piously revere his memory."[82] Kotzebue was thoroughly familiar with the Russian translations of all of Cook's voyages and refers to them at length in his work. He was fully aware of the fact that "neither Cook nor his companions seemed to have any notion that they were saluted with divine honours ... [Cook] contented himself with the conjecture, that the appelation was a title of honour, signifying chief or priest."[83] But not for Kotzebue; for him Cook's being called Lono was proof that Cook was a god. Now it is possible that Kotzebue got his information from Hawaiian sources, as Sahlins thinks. I think he could as easily have been influenced by European sources, for we have already shown that these ideas were developed in Europe even before the first European ships, since Cook's death, reached Hawai'i. Thus, Kotzebue's statement can be read as an efflorescence of the European dialogue that developed after the death of the great navigator and the publication of the official journals. In other words, a *tradition* of Cook's apotheosis already existed in Europe, and later accounts, even in the well-intentioned investigations of sea captains, were easily contaminated by this tradition. What is therefore impressive is the persistence of views that qualified this tradition or differed from it. Thus, Adelbert von Chamisso, the naturalist on Kotzebue's ship the *Rurik*, often critical of Kotzebue, made an important qualification about his captain's account: "They honored him *like a god*, and they still honor his memory piously."[84] Chamisso's observation is not based on interviews with Hawaiians either; he confines himself entirely to King's 1784 official account.

Later on, Chamisso makes a more insightful and original comment: "Formerly every white person was immediately regarded as a member of the *nobility*, but now his condition depends on his personality."[85] By contrast consider the following statement of another famous Russian, V. M. Golovnin, a contemporary of Kotzebue, aboard the *Kamchatka*. Golovnin says that unlike Cook, Vancouver was not considered a supernatural being and then adds his own view of primitive peoples that comes straight from prior shipboard traditions: "Among the primitive people there are undoubtedly some gifted with penetrating minds and unusual strength of spirit. Such people, *though at first considering the Europeans as supernatural beings*, soon discovered in them the same defects they saw in themselves and realized that they were equal in all respects."[86] Here Golovnin is tapping a tradition that antedates Cook and takes us back to shipboard myths such as Robertson's on Wallis's voyage and beyond that to myths concerning Cortés and Columbus. It should be noted in fairness to Golovnin that, unlike contemporary scholars, he did at least recognize the capacity of preliterate intellectuals to soon figure out the error of this attribution.

When Kotzebue revisited the islands in December 1824 during his second voyage, he documented the momentous changes that had already occurred in Hawaiian society, including the death of Kamehameha I, the abolition of the traditional religion and the spiritual malaise that followed, and the increasing power of the missions. Consequently, the accounts about Hawai'i in the *New Voyage round the World* are influenced by the debates of this later period and especially by the myths "recorded" by the missionaries Ellis and Bingham. "When Cook appeared they took her [the ship] for a swimming island, and believed that Etua-Rono [Akua-Lono], for whom they always retained the most profound veneration, had at length fulfilled his promise and returned to them."[87] Here Kotzebue adds a new mythic element to his previous account: Lono is the god who returns "to restore the Golden Age upon the island."[88] Kotzebue says that his informants were Kalaimoku (Billy Pitt), the powerful chief in charge of the country's affairs after the death of Liholiho (Kamehameha II), and the Spaniard Marini, a long-term settler and innovative farmer. Kalaimoku had become the foremost interpreter for practically all Europeans of note till 1827 (the year of his death). However, he was also Hawai'i's first Christian having been baptized as a Roman Catholic by a priest during Freycinet's expedition of 1819. This was probably a formal conversion, but it is also a powerful piece of symbolic action indicating a special attitude toward Western values. Soon Kalaimoku effectively became a Protestant under the influence of the American missionary Bingham. He liked his English name, Billy Pitt; he wore European clothes, adopted European mannerisms and food, and in general admired Western ways. It would not be surprising if he gave his Western informants versions of the Cook myth that they were already familiar with or at the very least helped accommodate the Hawaiian deification of Cook to the European apotheosis.

Kotzebue was one of the most intelligent and interesting of the sea captains who visited Hawai'i after Cook did and also one sympathetic to native Hawaiians. Yet his accounts, like those of others, cannot be uncritically accepted. Though well-read, he was no scholar and did not critically differentiate among the several sources that he used. For example, he has an extensive quotation from King's official account of Cook's death, but then immediately after this he says that Kalaimoku related these events to him![89] It is likely that Kalaimoku did tell him a story of Cook's death, but because it was similar to King's (or so he thought), Kotzebue found it more convenient to quote or summarize King himself. He also talked to Bingham, as he did with missionaries in other places he visited, and it is possible that Bingham's own views appear masked in his rendering of Kalaimoku's and Marini's accounts, reinforced by his own prior European presuppositions regarding Cook's apotheosis. It should also be remembered that by now there was a large European expatriate community in Hawai'i who were not averse to fostering a myth that implicitly legitimated European superiority and hegemony.

It seems reasonable to assume that there existed a variety of views pertaining to Cook's apotheosis and deification expressed by visiting ships' journalists. Consequently, it is wrong to think that these are empirically correct renderings of what occurred in history. Rather, they pertain to what occurred in the *construction* of history. Hence, such accounts have to be *deconstructed* before they can be effectively *reconstructed* as reasonable history. Viewed in this light, many of the sources used by Sahlins to prove Cook's apotheosis could be read in a variety of ways.

I have already noted that, contrary to Sahlins, George Little's informants thought that Cook was a "great chief." Then there is Mariner's account, based on conversations with Harbottle, Kamehameha's harbor master, and Hawaiian residents in Tonga in 1807. The latter apparently believed that Cook could not be killed "as they considered him a supernatural being." He was killed by a "carpenter" who struck Cook "not knowing him to be the extraordinary being of whom he had heard so much, for he lived a considerable distance up the country."[90] Unfortunately, Mariner's is a piling up of hearsay accounts, complicated by the fact that Mariner "communicated" his experiences in Tonga to his "editor" John Martin in London, in 1811, at a time when the Cook myth was popular there. Mathison, another authority Sahlins uses, visiting Hawai'i in 1821 after the tabu system and native ritual were abolished, says that Hawaiians repented for having killed Cook and "to perpetuate his memory, they resolved to deify him."[91] This could indicate a tradition of a postmortem deification rather than a premortem

apotheosis. Vancouver's voyages (1791–94) are especially interesting because, in spite of extended accounts about Hawai'i, he never once refers to
Cook's apotheosis. If Cook was indeed the god Lono and a cult of this god
existed in Hawai'i, it is strange that Vancouver would make no reference to
it. Lieutenant Puget interviewing the priest of Hikiau, says that Cook's
bones were placed alongside Kalani'opu'u's but once again makes no reference to an apotheosized Cook. On the contrary, Puget says that the god
Lono "bore the same name given to Captain Cook," implying a clear sepa-
ration of these two beings. Puget adds that Cook was "treated with the
greatest Veneration by all Ranks of People, and his Name is still mentioned
with a Sort of Enthusiastic Respect."[92]

Let me now consider two major sources that antedate the missions used
by Sahlins and that seem, on the surface, to confirm that Cook was the god
Lono. The first is Joshua Lee Dimsdell, who lived in Hawai'i during the
period 1792–1801. One would like to know more about him, because he
unequivocally says that "the term Oroner [Lono]" intimates that Cook is a
"third god."[93] One must, however, be cautious about accepting the words
of Dimsdell, because we know that Lono does *not* mean "third god."
Dimsdell is also, unconsciously, recasting the mythology of Cook in Eurocentric trinitarian terms. More reliable are these words of the French explorer Freycinet, who was in Hawai'i in 1819:

> Rono [Lono] was an ancient king of Owhyhi who, when on the point
> of leaving this island in a canoe promised to return. Not seeing him
> reappear, the inhabitants began to worship him like a god. Later,
> when Captain Cook arrived on these shores, believing it was their god
> Rono who had returned, the natives prostrated themselves at his feet.[94]

Now this would seem to be a pre-missionary account but is actually a footnote reference, most probably added in or around 1839, when Freycinet
published his Hawaiian material. It is simply taken over from the missionary Ellis, whom he uses extensively as a source.[95]

Some sources cited by Sahlins give us no clue whatever to the apotheosis,
deification, or "return" of James Cook.[96] Other sources could as easily prove
the existence of a postmortem cult of Cook as that of a deified chief. Consider Byron's visit in 1825, to return the remains of Liholiho [Kameha-
meha II], who had died in London. Even at this late date, the statements
of Byron's officers, collated by Graham, are highly ambiguous and do not
warrant an easy inference of a premortem apotheosis:

> He [Kalaimoku, Billy Pitt] is one of the oldest of the chiefs . . . and
> confirms the conjecture hazarded by Captain King, that the whole
> affray was accidental, and as much lamented by the natives as by us. Of
> the respect, according to their natives, paid to his remains, and of their

belief, *that though once dead, he might, as their deity Orono [Lono] come again* among them, Karaimoku's testimony is hardly necessary.[97]

I have already stated reasons for being cautious about Kalaimoku's "testimony." However, his testimony here could be interpreted either as a premortem apotheosis or a postmortem deification, which suggests once again that this ambiguity is his way of reconciling the two myths of Cook for the benefit of European audiences. A journal entry a few days later on 12 July could more clearly be read as an account of deification: "His death was purely accidental and truly lamented by the natives who conferred every honour on his body which was in their power, and regarded him as a deity whose spirit might one day return to them."[98] And Andrew Bloxam, the naturalist on the *H.M.S. Blonde*, after visiting the place where Kamehameha I died, noted that his bones were carefully preserved and divided among the chiefs, and then added, "These were the customary honours paid to deceased chiefs, the same also were paid to Captain Cook's remains."[99]

The political condition in the islands following the death of Kalani'opu'u and the rise of the power of Kamehameha further suggest the impossibility of Hawaiians *maintaining* that Cook was their god Lono who has returned and will return again in a "second coming." After 1786 European and American vessels came into Hawaiian harbors regularly, and Hawaiians rapidly began to understand Western technology and lifeways. The crucial technological obsession was Western military hardware and expertise. Kamehameha, at the very start, tried to get European guns and early European traders were invaluable to him (and to other Hawaiian chiefs) for this purpose. Kuykendall says that in December 1794 King Kalanikupule of Oahu sought and obtained the help of an English ship to assist him in repelling an invasion from Maui.[100] In 1789 Captain Douglas supplied Kamehameha with arms and ammunition and a swivel gun mounted on a platform on a large double canoe; and that same year Kamehameha detained John Young of the *Eleanora*, who together with Issac Davis, the sole survivor of the schooner *Fair American*, became his close advisor and effectively his construction engineer.[101] Soon afterward Hawai'i became a favorite stop for American traders. As early as 1804, the Russian captain Lisianskii was told by his informants that the Oahu ruler had many guns and that Kamehameha had a force of seven thousand Hawaiians and fifty Europeans; in addition he possessed six hundred muskets; eight guns capable of carrying a ball of four pounds; one company carrying a ball of six and five with a ball of three; not to mention forty swivels; six small mortars; and adequate powder, shot, and ball—[102]an awesome force that was augmented in the following years by the further development of naval and artillery power.[103]

Parallel with the development of the technology of warfare, and influenced by it, were other advances. Hawaiians themselves became excellent sailors in the Western style, and they were especially favored by American traders. Berkh, during the Russian expedition of Lisianskii-Kruzenshtern in 1804, met an American who had hired a dozen Hawaiians to supplement his crew. "Within eight weeks, he told me these young natives had turned into such proficient sailors that he could not have wanted better."[104] Hawaiians picked up Western ways very fast. Meares refers to a Hawaiian woman who stayed on board his ship bound for China for two years, at the end of which it was hard to tell she was not an Englishwoman![105] Langsdorf of the Lisianskii expedition says that Hawaiians have "more affinity with Europeans than the Nikugivans [Marquesans] do, no doubt because of more frequent intercourse with European visitors."[106] The Russians also found that they could use English in their relations with the Hawaiians more effectively than the Marquesan of their interpreter. Langsdorf adds that Kamehameha "brought English into general use among his people . . . that few natives of Owaichi [Hawai'i] of any rank and distinction do not speak the language now."[107] This is small wonder, for Campbell reports that in Oahu alone there were sixty Englishmen and Americans, many of them servants of Kamehameha. He had white carpenters, joiners, masons, bricklayers, and blacksmiths, some of whom in turn trained native Hawaiians in their arts.[108] Both Campbell and George Little could not report a single case of human sacrifice during their stay. Instead, newer spectacles seem to have come into vogue. Thus, James Beattie, the King's blockmaker who was "one time on the stage in England," produced plays and Campbell saw a mimetic production of *Oscar and Malvina*.[109]

What are the implications of the preceding summary of political-economic events for a later cult of the bones of James Cook? It is quite improbable that a plurality of Hawaiians by now would not have known, on the basis of their European contacts and experiences on board foreign ships, that James Cook was an English sea captain. Hence, there is no way that they would have *persisted* in the belief that Cook was their god Lono and that he would once again return. Even Sahlins has to admit that by Vancouver's time (1792–94) no Hawaiian believed that Europeans were gods—for him the only exception was James Cook, who "alone was able to preserve his divinity."[110]

What is striking about Sahlins's insistence is that the very "native" sources he approves unanimously state that at least when Cook died, they knew he was a human and mortal. Thus, contrary to Sahlins, it is virtually certain that any elevation of Cook's ritual status must have occurred as a postmortem deification.

What is the basis of this persistent error? I think that Western writers, including Sahlins, have for the most part imagined the subsequent cult associated with Cook's bones as a kind of ritual worship of the type found in ancient and medieval Christianity. The cult of saints' relics and cults associated with Christ's passion are only remotely similar to the Polynesian cult of the bones of chiefs and ancestors that were treated either as objects of vilification and contempt or as objects of the ʻaumakua (ancestor) cult that bestow dignity and power (mana) upon the possessor. One might call them sacred objects if one does not confuse the more generalized Polynesian concept of sacred (tabu) with the Christian one. Thus Sahlins, following the misapprehension of Europeans, thinks that Cook's bones were subject to "actual worship."[111] That there was a cult of Cook's bones is indisputable but it is the logical result of his treatment as a chief. Thus, the bones of Kalaniʻopuʻu and Kamehameha were treated in a similar manner not because they were gods, but because they were chiefs who were deified at death and converted into "real gods." In other words, the cult of Cook's bones does not prove that Cook was the god Lono who arrived in person during the Makahiki festival.

One must, however, not commit the reverse fallacy and assume that the bones of all chiefs were equally important. The various foreign observers such as Little, Mariner, and others attest that Cook's bones were treated with special respect. Here one can agree with Sahlins, who has argued that Cook's bones had considerable significance for Kamehameha. For us to fully appreciate the significance of the Cook cult and its relation to the Lono cult, let me get back to Lieutenant Puget's important observations that a) Cook's bones were in the *heiau* with those of Kalaniʻopuʻu and b) Kamehameha felt especially close to the god Lono and, most importantly, in Puget's words, "this Divinity always accompanied the King on his excursions."[112] Kamehameha did take the images of various gods on his excursions, but Puget's "always" suggests a special interest in Lono. To fully grasp the significance of these two cults, one must view Kamehameha's attitude toward traditional religion.

In his political life and activities, Kamehameha was a superb strategist skillfully manipulating realistic means to achieve his goal of a unified Hawaiian state. Nevertheless, he remained essentially traditionalist in his religious beliefs, firmly convinced that they were true and efficacious. The one institution he excluded from the newly emergent nation was human sacrifice. There is no doubt his contact with the West influenced his decision to allow this important cult of the traditional state to simply die. But, as Kamakau records, he encouraged other religious rituals—especially possession, prophecy, and healing—and was firmly committed to the tabu system as applied both to his own person and regulations concerning men and women dining together.[113] He was a radical reformer and yet a traditionalist: His religious reforms that paralleled his systematization of state polity were based on traditional Hawaiian religion. Observers noted his typical Polynesian fears of sorcery, because of which attendants carried his spittoon wherever he went. He ate by himself and all exuviae were secreted away to avoid ensorcelling. He told Kotzebue in 1816: "These are our gods, whom I worship; whether I do right or wrong, I do not know; but I follow my faith, which cannot be wicked, as it commands me never to do wrong."[114] Thus, though a traditionalist, he did let go human sacrifice; and when gods failed him, he could act in a very pragmatic manner. V. N. Berkh reported in 1804, "The King had taken numerous idols along in his expedition against Tomari, and had burned them all publicly on his return, because they had given him no aid."[115] This kind of pragmatism is not uncharacteristic of other religions, though perhaps not to such an extreme. Given Kamehameha's presumed commitment to traditional religion, and his pragmatism, it is not surprising that Cook's bones, unlike those of other chiefs, would be assigned considerable significance in the state cultus. They lent power and prestige to the ruler and above all a kind of legitimacy to the new state in which Western ideas diffused from sea captains played a prominent part. But it is a mistake to exaggerate the importance of the Cook cult and to confuse it with that of Lono. The latter was central to the personal convictions of the king and to the state cultus.

Essential to the state cults, according to Kamakau, were two priestly orders. The first was the order of Holoaʻe, which we have already discussed in relation to Kalaniʻopuʻu's reign (Part IV). The priestly deity of this order was Kū, the god of war and the sacrifice, in his various forms. The other priestly order was that of Kualiʻi, and its rituals were dedicated to Lonoikaʻoualiʻi, who was a visible manifestation of the god Lononuiakea. This latter cult was thus associated with the god Lono and his various manifestations. Among the many chiefs who belonged to the Kualiʻi order of Lono was Lonomauki *ma*, according to Kamakau.[116] Kū was associated with the sacrifice; it is not surprising that Kamehameha's abandonment of the sacrifice led to a decline in the Kū cult and the rise of Lono, the latter as the personal god of the King and as a crucial element of the state cultus. Sahlins says that "during the first decade of the nineteenth century, the Makahiki festival of Lono in fact completely superseded the sacrificial rites of Ku, which had been the traditional prelude to war."[117] This is an exaggeration, because Kamehameha did not abandon Kū, but he probably had a personal commitment to Lono, whose cult seemed more suitable to the new regime. Hence, he systematized and regularized the Makahiki festival in honor of Lono. Lono, insofar as he appears at Makahiki, was also called Lono-i-ka-makahiki, but this deity must not, says Kamakau, be confused with the legendary chief of that very name. "The real man Lono-i-ka-makahiki was different from the god, but he too was covered (*uhi*) with bird feathers on the head and had a *kaʻupu* (bird) for an ensign (*lepa*), as a flag of privilege *(hae no ka lanakila)*."[118] I do not know whether Kamakau is right, or whether Lono-i-ka-makahiki the chief became identified with Lono the god. It seems, however, that in Kamehameha's time the peaceful Makahiki became the state cultus and undermined the centrality of the older Kū rituals, especially those associated with the sacrifice. However, there is little evidence to suggest that the god Lono worshipped at the newly reorganized Makahiki was the Englishman James Cook. It was quite impossible at this time for Kamehameha to make this mistake.

Lono, I noted, was not only the god of the state cult of the Makahiki but he was also the personal guardian of Kamehameha. As early as 1793, Kamehameha was moving away from the older deity, the war god Kū, who was the guardian of his uncle and predecessor, Kalani'opu'u. Hence, Puget's observation that Lono went everywhere with the King. Mathison in 1822 uncovered an "ancient relic" of a custom when his informant(s) referred to Lono as the "wandering god." However, Mathison made the obvious European error that Lono was none other than Cook! By Mathison's time the tabu system had been abolished, the missions had already arrived and begun to redefine the cult of Lono as the worship of the idolatrous James Cook. Mathison says that this god

> for many years was actually carried in procession round the island of Owhyhee, under the appellation of *The Wandering God*. This image, during the procession, was immediately preceded by a person bearing in his hand a spear, to which was prefixed an instrument containing twenty lashes, each a yard in length, woven with the same sort of feathers that are used in the manufacture of cloaks and idols. He brandished it before the image, as it were to clear the way; and any person who had the misfortune to be touched by it, was summarily put to death as guilty of violating the tabu regulation.[119]

The source of this error can now be clearly located. For the Hawaiians the wandering god is Lono, the god of the Makahiki who has now assumed special prominence. Lono was termed "the wandering god" because Kamehameha took him wherever he went. For Mathison, as for the missions, there was an added part to this equation, namely, that Cook is also the god Lono for the Hawaiians. Thus, it is almost inevitable that the Europeans would close the equation by assuming that the wandering god Lono is none other than their immortal explorer, James Cook, also called Lono.

It therefore seems that the cultural and political conditions in Hawai'i during and after the reign of Kamehameha I gave an impetus to the special reading of King's official journal and reinforced European traditions about Cook's apotheosis. The processes, though not the chronological sequence of events, that fostered these developments can be illustrated by several examples. Consider the reactions of one of Puget's fellow officers in Vancouver's squadron. On 25 February 1793, the day before Puget interviewed the priest of Hikiau, Thomas Manby, Master's mate of the *Chatham*, visited the area of Kamehameha's palace and shrine. He was not permitted inside but was allowed to visit the residence of the chief priest. At the entrance to the residence, he says, "stands the great Oroona [Lono] or God of Owhyee. The Oroona is a huge figure cut out of wood to resemble a Man's face, with an enormous large mouth, stuck full of teeth; with two large Mother of Pearl Eyes."[120] He describes at length the huge "dinner" served to this god and other deities, and the greedy priests who actually ate it, thus having "the gratification of a good supper every night and laugh at the credulity of country-men."[121] The snide comments aside, Manby appears to confirm Puget's belief that the god Lono had come into full prominence as Kamehameha's personal deity as well as the major god of the island. A week later Puget, Manby, and Edward Bell (a clerk on board the *Chatham*), and other gentlemen, accompanied by Keli'imaika'i (Terrymiti), brother of the King, visited the "rock" where Cook was slain. Bell observed that the death was so powerful an event that "every child able to prattle can give you an account of it" and then adds: "at that time they look'd up to him as to a supernatural being, indeed call'd him the 'Orono' or great God, nor has he lost any of his character or consequence with the Natives they still in speaking of him style him the Orono. . . ."[122] Bell is also not conducting an interview with natives. He is adapting the account of Cook's death in the 1784 official edition to accord with his present experiences. Bell, following the official edition, says that Hawaiians look upon Cook *as to* a supernatural being, clearly showing the connections with the similes employed by King and Samwell. Yet Bell compares Cook to a supernatural being, the great god Lono—a mistake that the earlier journalists never made. The reason is that by now the Lono cult has come into full prominence, and Bell compounds the issue by connecting Lono Cook with Lono "the great god." The identity of names easily leads to a comparison of personae.

Thirty-two years later, at least one journalist on Byron's ship, the artist Robert Dampier, clearly closed the equation that Cook was a god to Hawaiians. He claimed that his information came from a chief, Naihe, who was a boy when Cook died. "According to his [Naihe's] account, as long as Cook kept his face towards the natives they, respecting him as a God, would not venture to attack him as a person. The man who wounded him first when in the act of desiring his men to cease firing was a common Kanaka, coming from a distant part of the island, and ignorant of Cook's attributed Divinity."[123] Obviously this account is a mélange of different sources: Cook desiring his men to cease firing is inspired by King's portrayal of Cook as compassionate, and the commoner assailant is a version of Mariner's carpenter from the upcountry who also killed Cook out of ignorance.

Not all of Dampier's fellow travelers, we noted, shared his view of Cook's death. Yet such views were expectable at that time (1825), because the missions had been there for five years and, prior to that, a diverse variety of Europeans who held a variety of views on the subject. Byron's officers, we know, were also influenced by missionary views, especially those of Bingham and Ellis. Bingham by now had "thrust himself into all the political affairs of the island, and acts as secretary of state, as governor of the young princes, director of consciences, controller of amusements. . . ."[124] We should not, therefore, be too surprised if after 1825 it is almost impossible to come across any account of Cook's death, Hawaiian or European, that did not include his apotheosis.

A rather startling, and incongruous, example of the apotheosis comes from a later folklorist, Westervelt, writing in 1929. If Manby says that "the huge figure cut out of wood" is the Hawaiian god Lono, Westervelt connects the Lono idol with James Cook himself! The frontispiece to his book, *Hawaiian Historical Legends*, has a photograph of these sculptures with the caption "Idols by which Captain Cook was worshipped."[125] (See Figure 12.) These idols in turn, Westervelt tells us, were the very ones used

Figure 12. Idols by Which Captain Cook Was
Worshiped, illustration from W. D. Westervelt,
Hawaiian Historical Legends

in the temple where Cook was worshipped. And here is Westervelt, writing on Hawaiian historical legends, retelling that event:

Lono went to the western bay Ke-ala-ke-kua and the priest took him into the temple, thinking he was their god. There they gave him a place upon the platform with the images of the gods—the place where sacrifices were laid. The priest stepped back after putting on Captain Cook the *oloa* (the small white tapa thrown over the god while prayer was being recited) and the red cloak *haena*, as was the custom with the gods. Then he offered prayer thus:

"O Lono! your different bodies in the heavens, long cloud, short cloud, bending cloud, spread-out cloud in the sky, from Ulunui, from Melemele, from Kahiki, from Ulunui, from Haehae, from Anaokuul-ulu, from Hakalanai, from the land opened up by Lono in the lower sky, in the upper sky, in the shaking bottom of the ocean, the lower land, the land without hills.

"O Ku! O Lono! O Kane! O Kanaloa! the gods from above and from beneath, gods from most distant places! Here are the sacrifices, the offerings, the living things from the chief, from the family, hanging on the shining cloud and the floating land! *Amama* (amen); *ma noa"* (the tabu is lifted).[126]

Thus, by 1929, the accounts of Cook's apotheosis have assumed a definitive character. The antecedents are clear: They lie in the missionary renderings and in travelers' accounts like Dampier's and Mathison's that converted the identity of names into an identity of persons. By 1929 this segment of European mythmaking had been fully accepted as historical fact, such that Cook was the god himself. He was given "offerings" and "sacrifices" (see Figures 7 and 12); and the chants that Cook's officers confessed were incomprehensible are now recovered through the assiduous work of subsequent investigators and incorporated into texts such as Westervelt's. Needless to say, these chants are considered to be prayers offered to that immortal English navigator, James Cook, the god Lono of the Hawaiians.

VII

————————— ❦❧ —————————

Cook, Fornication, and Evil:
The Myth of the Missionaries

Earlier in this book (Part III), I drew attention to the missionary view that Cook's arrival was the reenactment of the myth of Lono returning to Hawai'i in a triangular canoe. This myth itself is suspect: First, it confounds the myth of Lono with that of a famous chief of Hawaiian legend, Lono-i-ka-makahiki and his wife Kaikilani; second, the myth is quoted by a missionary, Bingham, who in turn obtained it from a compilation from the students of the Lahainaluna seminary in Maui and published it in 1838 as *Mooolelo Hawaii*.[1] Famous Hawaiian scholars like David Malo attended this school, and Kamakau was in the second batch of Lahainaluna scholars. Kamakau's version of the Cook mythology is partly derived from *Mooolelo Hawaii*. Although Malo contributed to this project, his own work *Hawaiian Antiquities* seems to be quite removed from it and is probably the only truly scholarly account, but applicable almost entirely to the period of the Kamehameha reformation. Further, Malo was much more alienated than the others; strongly Christian, he, like other native historians, was also patriotically Hawaiian and sympathetic to Hawai'i's past, and he resented the increasing takeover of Hawai'i by foreigners.[2] Malo does not explicitly deal with the apotheosis. In a very brief statement he simply states, "Captain Cook was *named* after this god, because of the resemblance the sails of his ship have to the *tapa* of the god," an interpretation that can now be entirely discounted.[3]

One of the disconcerting features of the contemporary scholarship on Cook, and this applies to Beaglehole's work, is the cavalier manner in which bits and pieces from the missionary and *Mooolelo Hawaii* narratives are taken to prove the hypothesis of the apotheosis. I think these procedures are endemic to the scholarship pertaining to nonliterate peoples who cannot strike back. Such sources would either be shunned or at least critically examined were they to be used in the reconstruction of European history. *Mooolelo Hawaii* can be used only if it is placed in the historical context in which it was written. Far from describing pre-contact culture, for the most part it advances the debate about James Cook in the direction anticipated earlier by William Cowper.[4]

I think that it is impossible *not* to translate the Hawaiian language game of Cook's "deification" into a Western "apotheosis" in the context of early cultural contact. The summary features of the Hawaiian postmortem deification of Cook can now be stated in a few propositions:

1. Cook for whatever reasons was called Lono when he arrived in Hawai'i for the second time.

2. There was a complex ceremonial for Cook performed by priests at the *heiau*.

3. There was also a well-known god called Lono.

4. Prostrations (adorations) were performed before Lono-Cook.

5. After Cook died, he was deified in the Hawaiian manner.

6. There was a state cultus associated with Cook's bones in the early part of the nineteenth century.

It would have been impossible for a native Hawaiian to "explain" or give a narrative account of Cook embodying these propositions to a white person who invariably possessed only a smattering of the language, and least of all to the missionaries who, I shall soon show, have their own agenda for Cook. The Hawaiian "language game" simply cannot make sense to them. When appropriated into the Western "form of life," it must mean that Cook *was* the god Lono; he *was* worshipped by Hawaiians; his bones *were* relics that lived. The Hawaiian postmortem "deification" must, by the logic of the translation of language games, be converted into a European "apotheosis." From here it is only a short step to develop a variety of other myths that are developed from earlier ones. These later myths, products of historical debates that were going on in Hawai'i, are those I will now tentatively explore.

The first missionaries, mostly American Calvinists (a notable exception being Ellis) arrived in Hawai'i in 1820, a year after the native tabu system and "idolatry" were abolished by Liholiho, son of Kamehameha I.[5] The first foreigners after Cook were British and American traders who had already widened the fissures that existed in Hawaiian society. I noted earlier the important attempt by chiefs to separate what went on in the ships from events in their own domain. But this could not last, for the mere fact that rules were being violated on the ships must necessarily have its repercussions on the larger society. Everywhere in the Polynesian islands, this applied most dramatically to common women, who now could have relations not only with lower-class seamen but also with "gentlemen." Women were soon induced to violate a basic interdiction of their society—that of commensal relations between men and women. Thus, in an ironic way, it was the very coming of the Europeans that helped "liberate" Polynesian women—ironic, because these women had no standards of comparison at all except the ships and their "manners and customs." But for the areas of interdining and food restrictions, they were in many respects much more liberated than their European counterparts, and in the long run their new freedom was followed by restrictive (or at least confusing and anomic) Calvinistic norms.

A further difficulty arose in relation to Hawaiian notions of the sacred or tabu. How does one adopt the earlier procedures of formally converting white officers and sea captains into chiefs when they were coming in increasingly large numbers? With increasing numbers and the increasing conflicts between and among Hawaiians and Europeans, there was no way that the ceremonials of deference could be maintained. Lisianskii, the Russian explorer, who arrived there in 1804, thought that in a twelve-month period the islands were visited by no less than eighteen vessels.[6] As Kuykendall says, these visitors did not respect the complex ideas pertaining to tabu, which they consistently violated without any serious misfortune befalling them. The Tahitian ruler Pomare II had abolished the Tahitian tabu system, and the time was ripe for Hawai'i also. It was no accident that the movement toward liberation from the traditional religion was led by the ruler's mother and other powerful females and was focused symbolically on interdining, the Western norm of correct intersex behavior.[7] This was expressed in a powerful, mythicized scenario, a feast where King Liholiho invited chiefs, select foreigners, and women, with two tables arranged in the European fashion, but one for women and one for men.

After the guests were seated, and had begun to eat, the king took two or three turns round each table, as if to see what passed at each; and then suddenly, and without any previous warning to any but those in the secret, seated himself in a vacant chair at the women's table, and began to eat voraciously, but was evidently much perturbed. The guests, astonished at this act, clapped their hands, and cried out, "*Ai noa,*—the eating tabu is broken."[8]

At the end of the meal, Liholiho issued orders to destroy the *heiau*s and burn the idols all over the nation. Whether the orders were fully implemented was doubtful, but it was nevertheless a revolutionary event that took place in the first week of November 1819.

The social psychological effect of the abolition of tabu and the destruction of idols and temples must surely have been profound. Significant elements of the old religion were displaced and the new religion was not yet established. The loss of faith in the old religion by the most powerful elite of the society did not occur suddenly but was heralded by psychological demoralization reflected in excessive alcohol consumption and a general appearance of decay and physical neglect. The dirty conditions of living

were noted by Freycinet, who was in Hawai'i in 1819 just prior to the abolition of tabus. He also noted the addiction of the royal family to alcohol: "It
is not too much to say that these royal guests drank and carried away,
during a period of two hours, enough to take care of a mess of ten persons
over a period of three months."[9] These observations were confirmed by
Mathison, who also noted the demoralization caused by the loss of the
old religion.[10] In my view this was fertile ground for some Hawaiians to
accept the European view that James Cook was their god Lono. The
first missionaries arrived on 30 March 1820. Soon after, practically every
source—Hawaiian and European—began to affirm that Cook was the god
Lono and furthermore, that in acquiescing in this role he was an idolater.

The Lahainaluna seminary or high school was established in 1831, but
missionary teaching, preaching, and conversion went on very rapidly from
1820 onward. Hence the earliest mission account of Cook, that of Ellis,
does not come from *Mooolelo Hawaii*. Ellis was an English missionary who
arrived in Tahiti in 1816 and then went to Hawai'i in 1822. In the following
year he undertook a two-month tour of Hawai'i with some American evan-
gelists, which resulted in his book *A Narrative of a Tour Through Hawaii*
and his later *Polynesian Researches*.[11] Ellis is also more sympathetic to Polynesian culture than most missionaries. Yet his native informants, as in all
works of this sort, are mostly nameless and featureless. His information, he
says, comes "from a number of persons . . . who . . . were present themselves at the unhappy dispute . . . or are well acquainted with the particulars
of that melancholy event." He adds that "they all agree in the main facts
with the account published by Captain King, his [Cook's] successor."[12]
King, however, did not say that Cook's was a case of "apotheosis," but
Ellis does, though briefly. He seems to have accepted an interpretation of
Cook's death that is reflected in Cowper's work. It seems very likely, therefore, that any informant statements regarding the complicated events that
led to Cook's installation and deification would simply be fitted into the
preconceived English view of his apotheosis.

In Ellis's account the legend of Lono-i-ka-makahiki, the famous Hawaiian chief, has been assimilated into that of the god Lono. This may not
have been Ellis's own contribution to the myth; it is more like a product of
the Kamehameha reform. However Ellis, more than anyone else, fully incorporated the former into the latter and systematically rationalized it.[13]
This is accepted strategy in practically all such accounts prior to the development of modern ethnography. Native informant versions are systematized into an ideal type, eliminating contradictions or differing viewpoints
and complex native exegeses. Here is Ellis's account:

> We may also mention here, the reason for which the remains of
> Captain Cook received, as was the case, the worship of a god. Among
> the kings who governed Hawaii, or an extensive district in the island,

during what may in its chronology be called the fabulous age, was *Rono* or *Orono*; who, on some account, became offended with his wife, and murdered her; but afterwards lamented the act so much, as to induce a state of mental derangement. In this state he travelled through all the islands, boxing and wrestling with every one he met.

He subsequently set sail in a singularly shaped canoe for Tahiti, or a foreign country. After his departure he was deified by his country-men, and annual games of boxing and wrestling were instituted to his honor. As soon as Captain Cook arrived, it was supposed, and re-ported, that the god Rono was returned; the priests clothed him with the sacred cloth worn only by the god, conducted him to their temples, sacrificed animals to propitiate his favor, and hence the people pros-trated themselves before him as he walked through the villages. But when, in the attack made upon him, they saw his blood running, and heard his groans, they said, "No, this is not Rono."[14]

We no longer can take this account seriously. Consider the various ele-ments that constitute this history: Not only is the identification of the legendary chief Lono-i-ka-makahiki with the god Lono problematic for the period of Cook's sojourn, but there is also little justification for the other statements. The idea that Lono-i-ka-makahiki sailed in a peculiarly shaped canoe is based on the enactment at the conclusion of the Makahiki ritual where a miniature canoe is released into the ocean. But this ritual enactment, according to Barrère, is an invention of Kamehameha's reign. There is not a trace of evidence to suggest that "priests clothed him with the sacred cloth worn only by the god," except on the assumption that because Cook was Lono, and because he was draped in a red cloth by a priest, that cloth must be the god's own vestment.[15] That animals were offered to Cook by ordinary Hawaiians in order to propitiate him is at best a wild interpretation of Hawaiian behavior toward Cook. Finally, the last sentence probably introduces a piece of Western mythologization, for it should be remembered that when old Watman died members of Cook's crew thought that this occurrence "destroyed the belief in our immortality." Likewise, Cook's death was also seen to have disproved Hawaiian beliefs about his immortality. This view was probably attributed to Hawaiians by Europeans who had their own notions of body and spirit. One must also assume that Hawaiians were reworking their conceptions of Cook throughout the period of Kamehameha I and very likely incorporating European conceptions into their own.

Regarding the apotheosis itself, Ellis has only a very brief statement: "After he was dead, we all wailed. His bones were separated—the flesh was scraped off and burnt, as was the practice in regard to our own chiefs when they died. We thought he was the god Rono, worshipped him as such, and after his death reverenced his bones."[16] It should be noted that all of Ellis's preceding narrative was incorporated almost in toto into one of the earliest histories of Hawai'i, that of Jarves, and converted into fact.[17]

After Ellis, *Mooolelo Hawaii* is the crucial work, written by students at the Lahainaluna seminary in Maui. It is likely that there is a preliminary filtering through a Maui lens of the Hawai'i events. The preface states that the students gave the accounts they had written to a teacher who edited them and "who himself inserted some remarks."[18] This teacher was the Reverend Sheldon Dibble, who states that the whole idea of writing *Mooolelo Hawaii* came from him. Ten of the best scholars, individually and separately, went out and collected information from old inhabitants, and these data were read aloud at school meetings. Dibble adds that "discrepancies were reconciled and corrections made by me, out of which I endeavored to make one connected and true account."[19]

It is hard to believe that Dibble was not influenced by his own terrible prejudices. In his *History* he speaks of the obstacles faced by missionaries in trying to communicate the true religion. Hawaiians, he said, present "an almost entire destitution of the power of reflection—of originating thought, or of carrying on a continuous chain of reasoning. Among the uneducated heathen . . . instances are very rare of those who have strength and discipline of mind enough to connect three links of a chain together, to come to a satisfactory conclusion."[20] "The ignorant mass, except when operated by God's spirit, exhibit a vacant and unmeaning stare, which indicates the emptiness within." Like other missionaries (Hiram Bingham was no better), he wrote of the "utter ignorance, the entire destitution, and deep degradation of the Islanders."[21] The data for *Mooolelo Hawaii* were gathered by his students and then emended and edited by him. In several places the editor interpolates his own dissent into the text. "It is certain that these accounts are lies"; or "what a lie," and so forth.[22] Stokes says of the *Mooolelo*: "It seemed more of an instrument designed to excise from the minds of his immature and impressionable scholars, all thought and respect for their own history."[23] Yet it is this work that is used by Sahlins for information on the apotheosis of James Cook.

I shall only present a very brief analysis of *Mooolelo Hawaii* to show that it is in part a deliberately constructed "myth charter" for modern evangelical Christianity, and Cook's mythic role is as a symbol of false worship or idolatry that the missions wanted to expunge from its very roots from Hawaiian soil. If *Mooolelo* was a product of the traditional priests of Kamehameha's time, as Sahlins implies, they must have been a peculiar lot. Consider this section entitled "What Hawaii was like a long time ago":[24]

When foreign vessels arrived at these islands Hawai'i's people were living in great darkness. They were idolaters, and, in amusements and in all evil activities they had been taught and were well prepared. They were led by Satan to do his will. Because of long experience in sinful living the light had been extinguished, the heart had been darkened, and indifference had increased and they had sunk very low—were very degraded—animals were higher, they were lower.[25]

This state of abysmal darkness could not have existed at the very beginning, because Hawaiians like everyone else "are descendants of Adam and Eve; and people after the flood are descendants of Noah."[26] Thus their early ancestors knew the true God, but later this knowledge was lost "because men prefer sin, and . . . care not for God and his commandments." Hawaiians thus "sank so low" that they became "idolators, pleasure seekers, easily provoked and quick-tempered."[27] Apparently, the traditional priests of Kamehameha's time who composed all this could also quote a large chunk from the Bible (Rom. 1:21–25, 28) to justify their views of their own past degradation.[28]

The real moral change, according to this Evangelical myth, came with the missions. *Mooolelo* also provides a neat justification for why the missions did not arrive earlier (and for why they abandoned the country, presumably, to the depredations of traders and whalers who came there after Cook). The *Mooolelo* says that if the missions had come earlier God's word could not have been successfully proclaimed because there was no unity anywhere with chiefs fighting each other. "Therefore, God exercised considerable foresight and caused the successful combination of all the islands into one kingdom."[29] But how did God accomplish this end? Through Kamehameha, of course. Kamehameha foolishly thought that he was fighting wars to obtain a kingdom for himself, but in reality he obtained one for God. "He did not realize God was achieving his purpose through him (Kamehameha). But Kamehameha's success in combining the islands into one kingdom came from God, and that is how the missionaries found peace when they came and the word spread successfully from Hawai'i to Kaua'i."[30] In fact, the abolition of the prohibitions was also preordained, and "God's will was fulfilled—all entanglements were removed before the arrival of the missionaries."[31] No wonder then that this section of the myth is entitled "Concerning God's clearance of the way for the arrival of the missionaries."

Cook is central to this evangelical charter, because his mythic persona can incorporate a variety of moral lessons. Fundamentally he resolves the important question, How is it that white sailors, who also believed in God, were so different from the missionaries? Cook exemplified the "bad whites" in extremis: He made himself into a god, he had sex with a Hawaiian chiefess that in turn led to wholesale fornication, and he also introduced the deadly venereal disease into these islands. Hence, the importance of the section entitled "About the arrival of Lono (Captain Cook)" followed by "About the landing of Cook at Kealakekua and his death." The myth of Lono's arrival is quoted almost verbatim by Dibble in his *History*, and I shall deal with it later. It is the one on his apotheosis and death that I shall briefly consider here. Part of the myth seems to have been taken from King's account such as the date of Cook's arrival, while other parts deal with standard "historical" views of Cook such as his arrival at the Makahiki, his death and the subsequent disposition of his bones. The section relevant for my analysis follows:

> Because the people believed Lono—Cook—was a god they worshipped him and exalted him. They gave him hogs and vegetables, clothing and all sorts of things in the same manner they gave to their gods—they did not sell. The priests bowed low when they approached him, placed a feather cape on his shoulders, drew back a little, gave hogs and this and that thing, spoke slowly, spoke rapidly. That was prayer and worship.
>
> If Cook went ashore many of the people ran away in fright and the rest bowed down in a worshipful manner. He was led to the house of the gods and into the temple also and he was worshipped there. He allowed the worshipping like Herod did. He did not put a stop to it. Perhaps one can assume that because of this error on the part of Lono—Cook—and because he caused venereal disease to spread here, God struck him dead.[32]

The *Mooolelo* explicitly carries on the discourse initiated by Cowper by comparing Cook with Herod. The introduction of venereal disease as a mark of fornication, evil, and sin is the specific Calvinistic addition to the myth. The latter part of the myth also introduces the Western idea of the deity as an immaterial being. Hence, "the people believed Cook was a god and would not die. But because Cook cried out when he fell, Kālaimāno-kaho'owaha [a chief who was slashed by Cook during the melee] decided he was mortal. He no longer considered Cook a god. Then he put Cook to death."[33]

The themes of the *Mooolelo Hawaii* are taken up again by Dibble in his *History*, and the influential missionary Hiram Bingham develops them further:

> The great and acknowledged superiority of Captain Cook and his associates over the natives would, had they taken the wisest course, have given them an enviable moral power for good, in making the earliest impressions from the Christian world highly salutary. Had this distinguished and successful navigator, conscientiously resisted, through jealousy for the honor of the Most High, every token of religious homage wrongfully offered to his own person by the infatuated natives, and with his party insisted on the propriety and duty of their leaving their horrid idols and vain oblations, and tabus, and acknowledging the living Jehovah alone as God, they might have prepared the

way for the overthrow of the foolish and bloody idolatry of the land. But that was not the object of the expedition; and if the influence of it had been nugatory it might be passed by with little notice.

But we can hardly avoid the conclusion, that for the direct encouragement of idolatry, and especially for his audacity in allowing himself like the proud and magisterial Herod to be idolized, he was left to infatuation and died by the visitation of God.

How vain, rebellious, and at the same time contemptible, for a worm to presume to receive religious homage and sacrifices from the stupid and polluted worshippers of demons and of the vilest visible objects of creation, and to teach them by precept and example to violate the plainest commands or rules of duty from Heaven—to encourage self-indulgence, revenge, injustice, and disgusting lewdness as the business of the highest order of beings known to them, without one note of remonstrance on account of the dishonor cast on the Almighty Creator![34]

"Dishonor cast on the Almighty Creator": This was a major topic of missionary discourse in the post-1820 period. In fairness to Cook and his officers, they rarely thought of native religion in as disparaging a manner. Native ritual specialists were given familiar, even complimentary, designations: Thus, "curate," "pastor," and "bishop" were used to describe Polynesian priests by Samwell and others; Cook refers to Tongan priests as Reverend Fathers and compares one of them to the Archbishop of Canterbury![35] A Tahitian ritual object used in the sacrifice is "the ark of the Eatua."[36] Not that any of Cook's officers were avowedly atheistic, but they had assimilated enough of the spirit of the Enlightenment and of eighteenth-century science that they could compare alien beliefs to their own with a degree of detachment, even if this perspective was an ethnocentric evolutionary schema that placed Europeans on the top. In their discourses on such topics as cannibalism and human sacrifice, Cook's officers were willing to recognize that even European society might well have practiced such customs in prehistory. Cook and his officers, relative to the missions, tolerant of *cultural* beliefs; their intolerance was to a large extent based on their conscious and unconscious ideas of Empire and their sense of innate cultural and racial superiority in the evolutionary scheme of things in this pre–Darwinian era.

Viewed in this light, *Mooolelo Hawaii* operated as a mythic charter for the new vision of Hawai'i of the evangelical missionaries. This does not exhaust the content of the text, because it also contains important historical information on Hawai'i's past. Yet Dibble and the Lahainaluna scholars recast the mythology of Cook in their sermons to illustrate the evils of idolatry and the terrible consequences of fornication. Their discourse on the venereal continued into the nineteenth century in a new direction; that is, Cook and his crew were godless creatures who introduced this terrible affliction on the already benighted savages. Thus, Cook was not at all popular with Hawaiians for most of that century. "The result [of the venereal] was death and indescribable misery to the poor Hawaiians," says Fornander "and no wonder that the memory of Captain Cook is not cherished among them."[37] *Mooolelo Hawaii* is at best only a partial historical source book for the past of Hawaiian history and myth; it is primarily a compendium of myths and new discourses on sin, evil, and idolatry.

On Native Histories: Myth, Debate, and Contentious Discourse

Historians like Kamakau wrote down native histories from a variety of sources that were not critically disaggregated. All these histories must be taken seriously but also considered relative to the goals of the present enterprise to determine whether certain occurrences did in fact take place. Thus, for scholars like Sahlins, and for me also, one has to resolve the crucial empirical problem whether Cook was treated on arrival and thereafter as the god Lono. A further empirical issue that is central to Sahlins's theory (but not for me) is that Cook's arrival during the Makahiki explains why Hawaiians mistook him for Lono. Thus, the purpose of our initial look at native histories is not to deny their legitimacy as diverse, even contradictory, Hawaiian visions of their past, but rather to determine whether these histories help illuminate the empirical question of Cook's apotheosis by Hawaiians. Some native histories collected and collated by Kamakau, Malo, and Fornander show family resemblances to modern historical writing; others do not. Everywhere these histories pose serious problems precisely when they deal with Cook because they get locked into the missionary agenda. Take the case of Kamakau: Barrère says that "Kamakau was an ardent, vehement, and highly vocal Christian convert . . . [and this led him] to show a comparable background of belief between the Hawaiian and Christian concepts of God and man."[38] If Malo reacted against the missionary demeaning of Hawaiian culture with an almost "purified" ideal typical account of Kamehameha's time, Kamakau sometimes reacted by articulating Hawaiian culture very deliberately within a frame of Christian beliefs. Kamakau's Hawaiians, when they beheld Cook coming from beyond the horizon (Kahiki), joyously exclaim, "Now shall our bones live," which is influenced by Ezekiel 37, especially 37:3: "And he said unto me, Son of man, can these bones live?"[39] Incidentally, Ezekiel 37:23 contains one of the most powerful charters for missionization: "Neither shall they defile themselves any more with their idols, nor with their detestable things, nor with any of their transgressions: but I shall save them out of all their dwellingplaces, wherein they have sinned, and will cleanse them: so shall they be my people, and I will be their God." This and other apocalyptic texts were very important to both the early Evangelical movements and to the later American Calvinistic missionaries, including those of the Lahainaluna seminary where Kamakau, Malo, and others studied. To assume as Sahlins does that these reflect pre-contact beliefs is, I think, quite untenable.

Kamakau has excellent accounts of native cosmology and historical genealogies, but his Evangelical prejudice forces him to translate Hawaiian cosmology into a kind of pantheism with a supreme being at the top.[40] Furthermore, Kamakau has serious problems of identity. His strong Evangelical conviction has the passion that one associates with recent converts. In fairness to him, he makes no bones about it (if I may continue a popular metaphor). In his chapter on Cook, Kamakau says: "Now it is doubtful whether Captain Cook consented to have worship paid him by the priests. He may have thought they were worshipping as in his own land. But he was a Christian and he did wrong to consent to enter an idolatrous place of worship. He did wrong to accept gifts offered before idols and to eat food dedicated to them. Therefore God smote him."[41] This *is* a native history, but one self-consciously influenced by the Evangelical charter that Kamakau himself, along with other Lahainaluna scholars, helped Dibble to construct. Because Cook's apotheosis is central to this charter, any indigenous Christian vision of Hawaiian history has to cope with it. Some, like Malo, can effectively *ignore* it, while others, like Kamakau, make it the key event. Kamakau can give splendid renditions of native storytellers' versions of the pasts of Hawai'i. He can also idealize this past because it is distant in time and remote from his emotional involvement in the new religion. But regarding Cook he reiterates Ellis, Dibble, Bingham, and others. Thus, native priests offered "sacrifices" to Cook and "worshipped" him, and Cook, the idolater, permitted it.

Further problems arise with Kamakau's handling of these events, for unlike the pre-European past, he has to contend with the European statement of that history, including the journals of James Cook. This is apparent from Chapter 7 and onward of his *Ruling Chiefs of Hawaii*. Thus, for example, "Captain Cook left Kauai and sailed northwest of America through Bering strait to seek lands to the north" is clearly Western history incorporated into this native history. Even more startling is a speech by a Hawaiian named Kila about the ship and its crew:

> Great and strong Pakaku' is the chief of this canoe, and his astronomers are Roving-eyes (Na-maka-oka'a) and Great-eyes (Maka-loa). As they sailed along in the ocean great Pakaku' called out to Roving-

eyes and Great-eyes, "O Roving-eyes and your comrade, peer and listen! Climb the mast of our ship, gaze about, seek and look for any mischievous one who could trouble our ship. Haʻehaʻe-ke!" "O great and strong Pakaku'! we have gazed and gazed. Lo! here is the mischievous one. Oho! oho! here is Ku-long-dog (Ku-ʻilio-loa) with wide-open mouth before us. Here is the upper jaw of the dog extending above us; his lower jaw is beneath us. One more huge wave and we shall be devoured!" Then Pakakuʻ called out to the people of the ship, to Lono-of-the-volcanic-fires (Lono-pele), to Lightning (Ka-huila) and his company, to Flash ('Anapu) and his company, to Kane-of-the-thunder (Kane-hekili), to Father Lono (Lono-makua) and his company, to Steam (Mahuia) and his company . . . and to Little-flame (Lapalapa-iki) who was in charge of the fires, "O Little-flame, Little-flame! Gaze about you, gaze about! Ready! Pause! Charge! Hoi-he-ke! Hoi-he-ke!" Then the great and mighty Pakakuʻ called to Shooting-water and to Exploding-water, "When I shoot, leap! when I shoot, leap! . . . O smooth pebbles of Great Britain! hard-grained pebbles of Great Britain! Oh, exploding waters of America! when I shoot, leap forward! when I shoot, leap!" A bullet sped forth striking Ku-long-dog on the forehead, splitting his skull apart. The hide here was his. The coconuts lying here are the remains of Traveling coconut. The ropes on this ship are the intestines of Great-black-turtle (Ka-honu-nui-mae-loku). The points of the anchor are the foreheads of Lono-ka-ʻeho, Ku-anuenue, and Lele-ia-naha. Thus all the gods of the ocean have been destroyed.[42]

Kamakau adds his own comment:

At the conclusion of Kila's story the people said, "It is true, this is Lono, our god! this is Lono, our god!" (Perhaps this man Kila had heard Cook's name from the chiefess with whom Cook slept and had corrupted 'Captain Cook' into Paka-kuka or Pa-kuka.) Then the people brought hogs, taro, potatoes, bananas, fowls, everything he wanted, thinking him to be their god Lono.[43]

Kina's speech is, from the perspective of the text itself, something that occurred while Cook was on board. But it is clear that at least part of it was composed *after* the event, when Hawaiians got to know more about America and perhaps after they had voluntarily destroyed their own gods. Kamakau's own comment refers to a well-known myth that when Cook arrived in Kauaʻi for the first time a famous chiefess, Ka-maka-helei, gave her own daughter to Cook alias Lono. This, I suggested earlier (p. 160), is a charter-myth to give legitimacy and dignity to the fact that Hawaiian girls slept with English sailors. The prototypical mythic act is that of Cook himself sleeping with a chiefess. So it is with the divine persona of Cook himself. It remains the Evangelist charter whose lines I traced earlier. Here is Kamakau concluding his chapter on Cook:

> Captain Cook was a [man of] Britain famous for his explorations in the Indian, Atlantic, and the Pacific oceans. He discovered lands in the ocean which were [previously] unknown. He had been but a short time in Hawaii when God punished him for his sin. It was not the fault of the Hawaiian people that they held him sacred and paid him honor as a god worshiped by the Hawaiian people. But because he killed the people he was killed by them without mercy, and his entrails were used to rope off the arena, and the palms of his hands used for fly swatters at a cock fight. Such is the end of a transgressor. The seeds that he planted here have sprouted, grown, and become the parents of others that have caused the decrease of the native population of these islands. Such are gonorrhea, and other social disease; prostitution, the illusion of his being a god [which led to] worship of him; fleas and mosquitoes; epidemics. All of these things have led to changes in the air which we breathe; the coming of things which weaken the body; changes in plant life; changes in religion; changes in the art of healing; and changes in the laws by which the land is governed.[44]

I have some sympathy for this thesis of a "fatal impact" formulated by a native historian, but it does not illuminate any of the empirical theses favored by Sahlins at all. For example, the disparaging uses of Cook's bones and entrails fit nicely with general Polynesian ways by which defeated chiefs are contemptuously treated. But it introduces a new debate on the fate of Cook's bones, quite different from the one favored by Sahlins, for whom Cook's bones were worshipped as relics in a temple along with Kalani'opu'u's. Yet Sahlins urges us to take Kamakau's history as literally true, at least insofar as the apotheosis of James Cook is concerned. Can we?

Though not literally true, Kamakau's texts can be used to illustrate a feature of Hawaiian discourse, namely, its contentious or argumentative nature. Let me therefore get back to some of the Hawaiian discourses on Cook, collected by Kamakau, which, though collated and written down at a later date, clearly show that Hawaiians, in these mythic discourses of the past, had no single view regarding the divine persona of James Cook that European scholars so readily attribute to them. However, for argument's sake one might treat these texts *as if* they were contemporaneous with Cook's arrival. Even so, it is easy to demonstrate that these discourses, precisely owing to their argumentative nature, attest to a variety of "debates" regarding the person, presence, and arrival of James Cook. The discourses are also not exclusively about James Cook, because there were Hawaiian legends about other foreign visitors, including white men, long before Cook. I refer to my previous discussion about Fornander's account of the lineage of white priests and that of Lono Kaeho's representative, Pili (Part IV). There are also detailed myths about Paao, a priest-chief from Samoa, while Ellis recorded other myths, including that of white men arriving in the time of Opiri, the son of Paao, and these the "natives knew not whether to consider . . . as gods or as men."[45] In other words, there existed previous myths about foreign visitors, including "white" ones, and consequently traditional discourses about their nature, as for example whether they were gods or men. Thus, the discourses on Cook gathered by Kamakau are, I think, conditioned by a preexistent tradition. It is difficult to say when they were composed; they were not invented *de novo* on Cook's arrival.

Let me get back to Beckwith who, on the authority of Kamakau, says that when asked whether Cook's party were gods or men the *kahunas* [priests] expressed the opinion that they were "men from the land of Kaekae (Kakae) and Kukanaloa."[46] Strangers from these places were supposed to have landed in the Hawaiian islands previously. After relating a myth about those people Beckwith, summarizing Kamakau, states that "their speech was unintelligible as that of the late birds that live in the hills."[47] I think this tradition is a later crystallization by a professional priesthood of a variety of *debates* that were provoked by the arrival of a strange people. By contrast, the ships' journals refer to a less figurative and more straightforward form of discourse, though equally argumentative and inquisitive. Consider this example of a chief of Kaua'i who met King when he anchored there in early 1779 on their return trip. King says:

> That man [Ka'eokulani] whose figure I have mentioned as having so Commanding and pleasing a Countenance, was very inquisitive about our Manners and Customs; the Questions that he ask'd would alone be a proof that these people have a great Variety of Ideas, he ask'd after our King, our Numbers, how our shipping was built, and our houses, the Produce of the Country, if we ever fought, Who was our God, and such like.

In fact, this man and his wife "wanted much to go and see Brittanee"![48] It is these very people of Kaua'i who sought Clerke's help in their internal wars. Earlier that very year, in Hawai'i itself, King generously reflected on a Hawaiian chief who was killed in the melee following Cook's death:

> Our unfortunate friend, Kaneena, possessed a degree of judicious curiosity and a quickness of conception, which was rarely met with amongst these people. He was very inquisitive about our customs and manners; the method of building and ships; our houses; the produce of our country; whether we had wars; with whom; on what occasions;

and in what manner they were carried on; who was our god; and many other questions of the same nature, which indicated an understanding of great comprehension.[49]

It is on the basis of such close rational ethnographic inquiry stimulated by prior British questioning of Hawaiians on similar lines, that decisions regarding Cook and his crew were made, especially how they could be used in practical alliances against enemies. This kind of rational pragmatics cannot be easily reconciled with the post-1820 myths that say Cook was Lono coming in his triangular ship from Kahiki.

Mooolelo Hawaii and missionary accounts provoke a debate about the myth of James Cook that has come down to our own time. The Evangelical accounts are valueless as a "history" or as a repertoire of traditional myths. At best these accounts can give us a glimpse of what *later* Hawaiians thought about earlier Hawaiian views of Cook. Yet they can be read in other ways, for there is in them much that is hidden, waiting to be brought to the surface. I shall now show that an examination of Kamakau's text with a gaze of suspicion sheds considerable light on the nature of an indigenous Hawaiian discourse that is the very opposite of the evangelical. Though Hawaiians have been portrayed as thinking mythically, their mythic thought is considerably more flexible than the inflexible discourse of the missions, which can tolerate almost no internal debate. By reexamining Kamakau's work, I shall also show that the Hawaiians were far from given to "stereotypic reproduction." Rather, they were asking questions and carrying on debates about the advent and presence of Cook in their island. For convenience I have italicized the elements of the myths that express these debates.

> 1. Some chiefs cried, "Let us kill these people for killing Ka-pupu'u!" but the kahuna Ku-'ohu said, "That is not a good thought, for they were not to blame. The fault was ours for plundering, for Ka-pupu'u went to plunder. I have told you that we live under a law; if any man rob or steal, his bones shall be stripped of flesh. The proper way to do is to treat these people kindly. *For listen, you chiefs and people! I do not know whether these are gods or men. Here is the test of a god*: if we tempt them and they do not open their gourd container which holds their ancestral gods (*'aumakua*) then they are themselves gods, but if they open the sacred gourds (*ipu kapu*) [that is, if they yield to the temptation of women] then they are not gods—they are foreigners (*haole*), men from the land of Ka'eka'e and Ku-kanaloa and their companions." *Many of the old people felt doubtful, for they had heard of foreigners, but the majority of the people and the young men shouted*, "A god! a god! Lono is a god! Lono is a god!" Thus the name Lono spread from Kauai to Hawaii.[50]

It is immaterial whether this account is true or not; what matters is that this text helps us focus on the argumentative nature of Hawaiian discourse on the mythological.

2. Ka-'eo, chief of Kauai, sent Kane-a-ka-ho'owaha and Kau-ka-pua'a to Ka-hahana on Oahu to relate all that had happened at the coming of Captain Cook to Kauai and to describe the appearance of the white men. They said that their speech was like the twittering and trilling of the *'ō'ō* bird, with a prolonged cooing sound like the *lali* bird, and a high chirping note. They said that they [the foreigners] were clothed from head to foot, wore triangular shapes on their heads, and shoes on their feet. *Said Kane-a-ka-ho'owaha, "They were not gods for they opened the sacred netted gourd; Ka-'eo caused Lele-mahoa-lani, the chiefess, to sleep on the heiau." The leading kahuna of Ka-hahana, Ka'opulupulu, said, "They are foreigners from Hi'ikua, Uliuli, Melemele, Ke'oke'o—they are men who will possess the land." Some said, "Perhaps they are the people whom Kekiopilo, the prophet (kaula) of Kupihea, prophesied would come, white men, having dogs with long ears which men would ride upon." Others said, "These are the men spoken of by Kekio Pilakalo in the time of Kuali'i:*

> A messenger is Ku from the heavens
> A stranger is Ku from Kahiki.

There was a great deal of talk about Captain Cook.[51]

Here the tradition of debate ("a great deal of talk") that the myth crystallizes is even more contentious, a set of discordant voices. The last couplet is especially fascinating, for it implies that some thought, even at a late stage, that Cook was not Lono but his opposite, Kū, arriving from Kahiki! "Dogs with long ears" are of course horses, but I doubt there were any on board at the time of Cook's arrival. The chief Ka-'eo [Kaeo, Ka'eokulani] who initiated the discourse here is the same chief who inquired from Captain King about English "manners and customs." Here he is engaged in making similar inquiries, but his discourse is re-represented in tropic form by Kamakau's priestly informants much later.

3. To the Hawaiians he [Cook] gave gifts of cloth, iron, a sword, knives, necklaces, and mirrors. The cloth they called "foreign fiber" (*a'a kahiki*) because it resembled coconut fiber. Glass they called *kilo* [from the practice of the *kilo*, or soothsayer, looking into a shallow bowl of water where he was supposed to see reflected the persons or acts about whom inquiry was made], and iron they called "dagger" (*pahoa*). *They ceased to believe the foreigners to be gods. At first they had taken their cocked hats to be a part of their heads and their clothing to be wrinkled skin.*[52]

Now we see the operation of "the pragmatics of common sense" and the significance of ordinary perception, as if the Hawaiians said ironically: "If they appear in a mirror they are human; we thought their hats were part of their heads and we were mistaken. They are like us."

4. On February 4, Lono sailed away in his ship and had got beyond Kawaihae when he discovered that one of the masts was decayed and he had to put back to Kealakekua to repair it. The natives saw him return, and the women took up once more their association with the sailors, but not in such numbers as before. *The natives had begun to be suspicious, and some said, "These are not gods; these are men, white men from the land of Ku-kanaloa." Others declared them to be gods. Still others said, "The legends of Kane, Kanaloa, Ku, and Lono say that they came from Kahiki; they do not lie with women. Lono-i-ka-makahiki was a defied man, not a god." One man said, "The woman [Lele-mahoa-lani] who was on the ship says that they groan when they are hurt. When the woman sticks her nails into them they say, 'You scratch like an owl; your nails are too long; you claw like a duck!' and more that she did not understand." The natives tried to provoke Lono to wrath to see whether he would be angry.* They reasoned, "Perhaps the god will not be angry because he has received offerings of hogs, clothing, red fish, bananas, and coconuts, and the god Lono has been propitiated."[53]

More argumentative voices, even practical experiments of the sort traditionally used to test ghosts, in order to find out whether the foreigners react like themselves to pain and anger. The substantive contents of these accounts are later creations, but what they illustrate is a Hawaiian mode of contentious discourse and multiple interpretation illustrating their capacity to weigh the actuality of myth and event against the pragmatics of common sense. It is hard to reconcile these discourses with the missionary view that the Hawaiians are incapable of rational and connected thought and the structuralist view that they acted according to prearranged scenarios and, more specifically, that they saw history as a simplistic enactment of the myth of Lono even when these concordances violated other beliefs that they possessed and their physical perception of the events that unfolded before them during those two fateful years. Culture may botch the physical perception, but the physical perception in turn botches any immaculate (cultural) conceptions.

Debate, I have shown in an earlier work, is a contentious discourse that erupts in history and affects the direction in which a myth develops.[54] Thus the missionary discourses produced debates about sin and evil that changed the content and significance of Cook's mythic persona. My contextualizing myth in a particular time, place, and tradition does not mean that myth elements do not send tentacles into the past. This is not self-evident, however, and only a critical reading of myths permits us to make tentative historical inferences.

Let me now reflect back on the two types of discourse that I have presented above. It seems that the inquiries by the two chiefs about the customs and manners of the Europeans and especially their fire power have an inquisitive, almost ethnographic, thrust. The chiefs attempt to find out about the lifeways of the new arrivals. They are especially curious about the new weapons, perhaps trying to assess their value for interisland conflicts. The questions are direct and forthright. Contrast these voices with Kamakau's priestly informants: Their statements are indirect, tropic, and cast in a story or anecdotal form. It seems to me that the voices of the first set are those of "counselors" and the voices of the second set belong to priests and other religious specialists.

Both priests and counselors in their own ways must be able to coordinate and strategically manipulate culturally defined means to achieve desired goals, but perhaps the counselor has greater leeway in manipulative choice and action. The counselor is the exemplar of practical rationality and his discourses reflect this orientation.

The critical difference between the two types lies in the realm of discourse. The statements of both priests and counselors are, or can be, the precipitates of arguments or debates, except that the argumentative nature of priestly discourse occurs within the frame of indirect, metaphoric, tropic, or mythic thought. The discourse of the counselor is more literal, less indirect, and more readily comprehensible to us, whereas priestly discourse cannot be interpreted without special knowledge of the symbolic forms in which it is expressed. In the particular case of the priestly discourse presented above, a further complication arises, because Kamakau's informants probably made tropical statements about Cook long *after* his arrival and sojourn. By contrast, the statements of the counselors reported by King occurred at the time of Cook's visit. I am not suggesting that priests and counselors are different breeds of *persons*, but that in embodying different traditions they engage in different kinds of discourses. It is indeed possible for the same person to be a counselor in one context and a priest in another.

Monterey Melons; or, A Native's Reflection on the Topic of Tropical Tropes

Sheldon Dibble, directly following the tradition of *Mooolelo Hawaii*, has this account of the new mythicization of James Cook, as he (Cook) approached Hawai'i for the second time:

The people inquired of the messenger respecting the strangers. He replied, (as tradition says, with grains of exaggeration no doubt), "The men are white—their skin is loose and folding, (mistaking their garments for their skin, as they themselves in their ignorance of civilized manners had no conception of a well-fitted garment), "their heads are strangely shaped,"(mistaking at a distance their hats for their heads, as they in their rude condition had no idea of such a covering)—"they are gods, volcanoes, for fire and smoke issue from their mouths," (a mistake gathered at a distant view from the smoking of cigars)—"they have doors in the sides of their bodies," (mistaking their pockets for openings into their bodies), "into these openings they thrust their hands, and take thence many valuable things—their bodies are full of treasure." Then standing up he thrust a piece of gourd shell into his malo at his side and drawing it thence in imitation of the foreigners, endeavored to give some idea of the unintelligible nature of their language. He then gave a terrific account of the discharge of cannon and the display of fire-works which had been exhibited at Kauai.[55]

And then, those melons from Monterey:

Captain Cook proceeded from Maui to the large island of Hawaii, and appeared (December 2nd) off the district of Kohala near Kukuipahu. As he approached the island, some of the natives ventured off in canoes, and gazed at the ship at a distance. They saw the strangers eating something red, and pronounced it the flesh of men; they saw fire about their mouths, and supposed it, as they had heard, to issue from their bodies. They returned to the shore, and reported that the men on board were gods—gods of the volcano. That which they supposed to be the raw flesh of men was the red core of the watermelon, brought from Monterey, to which they were then entire strangers; and the fire, of course, was from cigars.[56]

Unhappily, Cook was never in California; but Vancouver was in Monterey several times between 1792 and 1794, and he might well have brought watermelons from there to Hawai'i. Dibble's informants did know of Vancouver's ships. They were "coral rocks . . . floating hither." Vancouver and his crew were also gods for them. But when a Hawaiian threw a stone and hit the chin of a sailor, they knew otherwise. Says Dibble, "The white man cried out with the pain inflicted, on which the natives said—'They cry indeed—they are men perhaps—we thought them gods, their eyes were so bright.'" One remonstrated, "Be not in haste to kill the Lord Lonoikaoualini—for great Lono being slain in Hawaii, this one remained, the great and powerful Pekeku—he is a god."[57] Dibble must have had peculiar informants, for even Sahlins says that it is virtually certain that by Vancouver's time practically no one in Hawai'i believed in any kind of apotheosis or deification of the white man; nor did any Hawaiian practice ceremonial prostrations before Europeans.

Let me deal with the first part of these so-called Hawaiian myths of the white man. For Dibble these are "mistakes"; for Sahlins they express a mythic reality that permitted Hawaiians to gratuitously take goodies from the ship.[58] I want to suggest such discourses are *tropes*, and it is the failure to understand their nature that has led to scholarly (and popular) literalization of the tropic and an attribution to the native, at least in popular Western discourse exemplified in Dibble's work, of a stark credulity.

Let me begin with my critique of the misunderstanding of native tropics with a reminiscence about my own childhood: In the 1930s many of us Sri Lankans, children and adults, used to sing a refrain when the train rushed past our houses in Colombo:

> *Aṅguru kakā vatura bibī—kolaṁba duvana yakaḍa yakā.*
> Eating coals and drinking water, the iron demon that
> runs to Colombo.

And the up-country train that slowly chugs its way to Kandy sings:

> *Uḍa raṭa mānikeṭe—paṭa kuḍa dekadeka.*
> To the lady upcountry, two, two, silk umbrellas.

In the first refrain the words are important: The train is physically visualized eating coal and drinking water. It is a demon, the text says, though no one ever seriously thought of it quite that way. "Iron demon" was for most of us somewhat funny because the train is *not* a demon. It is the incongruity that is startling. In the second refrain, the words are not significant: What is important is the rhythmic nature of the utterance that matches the rhythm of the train as it chugs uphill. Another nonsensical refrain, with the same rhythm, could and did take its place. Every time I went to Kandy, even as an adult, I could still hear the train sing, *"uḍa raṭa mānikeṭe—paṭa kuḍa dekadeka!"* (curse those diesel trains that came later). I treat these examples as illustrative of a larger process of misunderstanding of language use by those (including natives) unfamiliar with native tropes.

Like our Hawaiian informants, the *Rājāvaliya* ("dynasty of kings"), a Sri Lankan chronicle, says of the Portuguese that they are a group fair of skin and the sound of their cannons was like the thunder that bursts over the cosmic mountain Yugandara. And then the text adds that these foreigners eat stone and drink blood.[59] Western and modern Sri Lankan historians took this example literally as an error in perception or the simple credulity of people who mistook bread and wine for stones and blood. Many years ago when I was doing fieldwork in a remote village in Sri Lanka, an informant told me how the villagers met their first Englishman, a government

173

official on circuit seated on a rock. "And you know, he was eating stones and drinking blood, ha! ha! ha!"; and others who were there started laughing. The decontextualized reference in the *Rājāvaliya* now began to make sense: The utterance is a joke that emerges from incongruous juxtapositions. Here is an implied reference to demons; demons drink blood, but what kind of demons eat stones! The basis of the trope is physical resemblance, but its significance is that it makes a parody of those resemblances that are not resemblances.

These two tropes also appear in other Polynesian cultures. Remember that the Maori Te Horeta said that the English ate "pumice stones";[60] and in the second voyage the Tahitian chief Tu, on board the *Resolution* with the redoubtable Teto'ofa (Towha, the "admiral"), joked with the latter that the wine he drank was blood, no doubt to Teto'ofa's discomfiture.[61] However, a trope can be much more elusive in its significance because irony is elusive. For example, when I was in the field in 1958 some children had tantrums when I approached them, sprawling on the floor and crying uncontrollably. I soon realized that I was being used as a bogey man by mothers to scare their children into obedience. I was a *sanyasin* (improbable as it may seem to those who know me), who will gather a child in a bag and kill it as a sacrifice to obtain a hidden treasure. Now transfer this idea to the white foreigner: It is possible to scare children by saying that the white man is a demon eating stones or drinking blood—but there is no "ha! ha! ha!" So with Tu, Teto'ofa and the funny equation (at least for Tahitians) that blood equals wine. But this equation need not remain funny. When people talk about it often enough, it can attach itself to situations that cause anxiety. For example, in several places, people, even chiefs, were hesitant to go on board, specially into the lower depths of the ship, for fear that they might be killed. These fears were reinforced by the fantasy of some Polynesians that the British were cannibals. Now a joke like "The English drink blood" can get attached to these anxious contexts and beliefs and cease to be a joke, at least for some people. Thus it is with pumice stones and watermelons: Adult villagers might laugh, but solemn historians can treat them solemnly, as they did with Hawaiian tropes about white men issuing fire from their mouths, their hats part of their bodies, their pockets full of treasures (if not rye), and so on. I do not know enough Hawaiian to deal with them. These tropical statements must await the research of native scholars familiar with the nuances of their own language, though sometimes this is not necessary because the parodic nature of the utterance is obvious.

Consider this statement by Reynolds, a missionary, writing in 1824, at a time when Hawaiians were thoroughly familiar with things European:

Natives put a story in circulation that the Mission houses were burnt at Mawee [Maui] the mission sent off. Pitt [Kalaimoku, the "Prime

Minister"] gone to Owhyhee [Hawai'i] to send them forever from that Island, because the mission gave the young prince [Kauikeaouli, later Kamehameha III] and princess [Nahi'ena'ena] shit to eat. It appeared that they were at the mission house and were offered bread and butter—the natives who were standing about the Prince not being acquainted with butter raised the report as above.[62]

The missionaries in their dead earnestness have totally misread the parodic nature of the Hawaiian utterance. But perhaps there is more to it than butter or shit: For Sahlins it indicates "the Hawaiian categorical opposition between food and excrement."[63] I suppose there must exist societies where food and excrement are not categorically opposed.

This problem of literalizing tropes is endemic to ethnography, because very few outsiders can pick the nuances of utterances insightfully discussed by Bakhtin and more recently by Searle as "utterance meaning."[64] The statements, "The white foreigner drinks blood" or "eats pumice stones," or "eats shit" gain their significance, I might add, in a "context of utterance." This context of utterance, though confined to the bounds of a speech community, can be very stable, but it can also as often be fluid, shifting ground according to time, place, and history. For example, as Europeans become familiar to a community the trope can become dead. In such a changed historical context, it is easy to falsely attribute credulity to a previous speech community. The credulity is ours and lies in our failure to recognize the context of utterance and the processes that lead to the literalization of tropes.

The upshot of my remarks is not to deny "mythopoeic thought," but to affirm that the world of myth is not closed. The structures through which experience is filtered are multiple; these structures are not mechanically followed but are manipulated in accordance with rational reflection. Sometimes the actions of Polynesian peoples may seem "prelogical," custom bound, and so forth, but closer examination dispels these illusions. For instance, during the third voyage Samwell noted how the Hawaiians incorporated English astronomical routines into their mythic structures: "The Indians always called the clocks and watches which they saw in the astronomers' observatories by the name of Etua [atua, a god] and supposed they were our God and that we worshipped them."[65] It was the same in Tahiti where Polynesians made offerings to the English flag after Wallis had unceremoniously taken the land ceremonially on behalf of the English king.[66] But the Polynesians were pragmatic and sensible in the way they incorporated the English practices into their own mythic structures. After all, the ceremonies of taking over were, to any observer, ritualistic, and because the Polynesians did not have an exclusivist view of religion, they very pragmatically continued to propitiate the flag by incorporating it into their own forms of life. The observatory provides a better example. The

British in fact had a tabued space in a potato field given to them next to the *heiau* and, says King, "we made Parea understand that that field (edged out and separated as it was by a stone wall [of the *heiau*]) was to be tabooed." This was done "by the priests sticking upon the Walls their Wands."[67] Thus, it would seem a reasonable and rational inference that astronomical instruments were sacred objects to the British. Moreover, the British did perform "peculiar" actions, for example, staring at the heavens in routine fashion with instruments. The Hawaiians were probably closer to the truth than the British realized, because astronomical routines were mechanically performed for the most part and had little serious or practical significance. There was no professional astronomer on the *Resolution*, and Lieutenant King had to take over these tasks. Hawaiians were trying to make rational sense of British ceremonials (and no doubt they erred) as the British were trying to rationally figure out Hawaiian ceremonials (and they also erred most likely). When the functions and mechanism of the clock were explained, a Tahitian chief understood without any difficulty.[68]

There is also evidence of creative improvisation that even the British journalists could admire. The outstanding case is the brilliant Tupaia, who had an extensive geographical knowledge of this vast region and not only gave Cook a detailed list of the islands but also drew them on a chart for Cook's benefit, even though he had no familiarity with pen and ink.[69] Tuaha, another Tahitian encountered during the second trip, was as sharp. "Cook shewed him a map of Tahiti [without telling him what it was], and although Tuaha had never seen a map before, he immediately picked out and named every district on the island. He pointed to the spot where the European [Spanish] ship had anchored, just north of Vaitepehu Bay."[70] And here is that wonderful Boraboran, Hitihiti, Cook's interpreter on the second voyage, freezing in the Antarctic, yet keeping his own ship's journal in his inimitable style with a bundle of twigs of different lengths. "At every island they visited he selected a twig to represent the discovery, and although the twigs all looked alike to the Englishmen, he could recount every bit of land sighted, in the proper order, by referring to his bundle."[71] One could go on and on.

VIII

—— ✦ ——

Myth Models in Anthropological Narrative

I have suggested that the myth of Cook as the god Lono is fundamentally based on the Western idea of the redoubtable European who is a god to savage peoples. This was further transformed in European thought in the Evangelical idea of idolatry. The later Hawaiian acceptance of this idea is not proof that it was the Hawaiians' idea in the first place. To put it differently, the divinization of Cook is a structure of the long run in European thought, inasmuch as his chiefly deification is a Hawaiian example of the same phenomenon. I am now suggesting that Sahlins's anthropological narrative of the life and death of Cook is not only a theoretical vindication of structural continuity and conjuncture, as he claims, but it is also a continuation, albeit unwitting, of the European myth of the apotheosis of James Cook. Theoretical thought is often enshrined in nontheoretical traditions.

My analysis of the myth of the dying god, James Cook, elaborated by Sahlins, requires a close examination of language use, because the empirical accounts of the ship's journalists have been subtly, and sometimes not so subtly, rephrased or altered in Sahlins's rendering. Let me begin with the account of James Cook's trying to reach Kalani'opu'u, the king, on the fateful day of Cook's death. "In the beginning, as he went, 'to find the King,' pigs were pressed upon him; and as he waited for Kalaniopu'u to awaken, more offerings of red tapa cloth—proving that the English sea captain was still the image of the Hawaiian god."[1]

The only eyewitness account we have of this is Phillips's, and nowhere in Phillips's account is Cook given pigs or "offerings" of red tapa cloth. King in his unofficial journal makes no reference to these offerings either, but he does mention that on the previous evening, when the cutter was stolen and the troubles got started, people were becoming more and more "insolent." Cook threatened to make the sentry fire but "whenever the Marine made any motion of presenting, the croud would recoil back, but it was observable enough that they began to laugh at our threat."[2] Cook was also taken on a wild goose chase and had to come back on board, frustrated and angry, hardly the kind of treatment accorded someone cast in the image of a god.

The question then is, From which source did Cook receive his "offerings?" This comes from Samwell: "As Captain Cook passed along the Indians prostrated themselves on their faces before him and showed him the same Respect as usual. . . . They asked him if he wanted any Hogs or Roots, he told them that he did not, but that he wanted to see the King . . . they came out several times and presented some pieces of red cloth to him. . . ."[3] It should be noted that Samwell was nowhere near this scene. However, there is nothing inherently improbable in this account. King, in his official version used Samwell's data extensively, but he converted the event of the Hawaiians asking Cook whether he *wanted* hogs or roots into something quite different. "He immediately marched into the village, where he was received with the usual marks of respect; the people prostrating themselves before him, and bringing their accustomed offerings of small hogs."[4] These two references are compressed into a single event by Sahlins: Cook, as a divinity, is given pigs and offerings of red tapa cloth.

To continue Sahlins's narrative:

> The King came away willingly and was walking by Cook's hand to the waiting ship's boat when he was stopped by his favored wife Kaneikapolei and two chiefs, pleading and demanding that he not go on. By all accounts, British as well as Hawaiian, they told him such *stories of the death of kings* as to force him to *sit upon the ground*, where he now appeared—according to Lt. Phillips' report—"dejected and frightened."[5]

Because there were no contemporary Hawaiian accounts of these events, one must rely on the British ones. Not one British account even remotely indicates that Kalani'opu'u's wife and the two chiefs told the king "stories of the death of kings." Quite the contrary, this was a tense and moving scene and no time for story telling. Phillips says that Kaneikapolei "came to him with many tears and intreaties beg'd he would not go onboard, at the same time 2 chiefs laid hold of him and insisting that he should not, made him sit down, the old Man now appeared dejected and frightened." Phillips's account reflects a poignant human situation; Sahlins's myth is about kings and gods opposed to each other and engaged in symbolic battles of the sort noted by that great mythmaker, Frazer. Consequently, Sahlins has Kaneikapolei and the chiefs tell Kalani'opu'u "stories of the death of kings," not unlike Shakespeare's King Richard II, who laments,

> For god's sake, let us sit upon the ground
> And tell sad stories of the death of kings
> > (*Richard II*, act III, sc. 2)

The British accounts emphasize the firing of the ship's canons, the confiscation of canoes, the killing of a chief of "first rank" and that the news reached the village, so that two or three thousand people armed with spears had assembled. In Sahlins's account the unsuspecting king suddenly becomes symbolically opposed to God Cook:

> The transition comes suddenly, at the moment the King is made to perceive Cook as his mortal enemy. This is the structural crisis, when all social relations begin to change their signs. Accordingly, the material exchanges now convey a certain ambiguity, like those Maori sacrifices that pollute the gods in the act of placating them. An old man offers a coconut, chanting so persistently that the exasperated Cook cannot make him lay off. A supplication begging the release of the King? Lt. Phillips considered that "the artful rascal of a priest" was carrying on to divert attention from the fact that his countrymen, gathering to the number of two or three thousand, were now arriving to defend their King. About this time, a report comes that an important chief has been killed by the British blockading the Southern end of the Bay. The King is still on the ground "with the strongest marks of terror on his countenance," . . . but he soon disappears from the scene.[6]

Let me first note an error that arises from Sahlins's uncritical reading of texts, namely, the reference to the king still on the ground "with the strongest marks of terror on his countenance." The phrase is from King's official journal and is found nowhere else, not even in his unofficial journal. Sahlins also inadvertently omits the words "and dejection" that appear after "terror." Thus, King's phrase "terror and dejection on his countenance" is borrowed from Phillips's description of the King ("dejected and frightened"), but while Phillips's king is in this state when the chiefs force him to sit down, King's king has this experience much later. Sahlins borrows King's version and adds that the king "soon disappears from the scene." Not one account confirms this. Rather, the king's exit is required by the dramaturgical view of these events that is at the heart of Sahlins's thesis. Consequently, like a character in a play, Kalani'opu'u "disappears from the scene."

But not before he is made to realize by his chief that Cook-Lono is his "mortal enemy." A further puzzle for the uninitiated: Because Sahlins's own theory postulates that the king and the god are symbolically opposed, the king ought to have understood this opposition himself by virtue of his role. He does not require the chiefs to make him realize what he is by virtue of being a divine king. The fact is that Sahlins has to accommodate the messy events noted by the journalists. Here the king seems a helpless old man, quite happily agreeing to go with Cook on board (as hostage), till he is forced to do otherwise by his queen and his chiefs. Converted into Sahlins's ritual drama, this means a sudden transition and that "the king is made to perceive Cook as his mortal enemy." Now this suddenly realized opposition between King Kalani'opu'u and God Cook produces a "structural crisis" because all social relations change their signs. But not yet; before this crisis, there is a period of uncertainty or ambiguity expressed as "material exchanges." Actually, Sahlins refers to one such material exchange only where the priest offers a coconut and a chant to Cook. I am at a loss to figure out the ambiguity here. However, Sahlins's interpretation that this might be "a supplication begging the release of the king" fits nicely with the Western mythologization of Cook. Phillips, the only eyewitness, says that the priest sang and made "a ceremonious offering of a Coco Nut to the Captain *and* Terre'oboo [Kalani'opu'u]."[7] It doesn't make sense for the priest to offer a coconut to Kalani'opu'u to obtain his [Kalani'opu'u's] release, unless of course this is a case of ambiguity that precedes a structural crisis. My own guess is that we will never know why this offering was made jointly to Cook and Kalani'opu'u, and any number of hypotheses are possible and plausible. It is in the nature of interpretation that some things are impossible to interpret.

The confrontation between the two opposed parties now takes a dangerous turn, with "each side responding to the perceived threats of the other" till the fatal end. But these events are by themselves meaningless, we are told, unless they take "systematic or positional value in a cultural scheme."[8] The decisive moment has come and Cook and Kalani'opu'u, the god and the king, "will confront each other as cosmic adversaries." This is like the ritual of Kāli'i where, during the new year celebration and other important occasions, the king wards off the spears aimed at him by a party representing the god. However, it is now "played in reverse," with the god taking the part of defender. Thus, says Sahlins, for the Hawaiians the confrontation between the god, James Cook, and the king, Kalani'opu'u, was a ritual enactment—not a post-hoc interpretation either, but perceived as such as the events were being played out.[9] (See also Appendix 2, "Kāli'i and the Divinity of Kings.")

The god Lono (Cook) was wading ashore with his warriors to confront the King. Rather than the reinstitution of human sacrifice by the King under the aegis of Kū, news came that Lono's people had killed a chief. . . . Now the King would be taken off to sea—instead of the canoe of Lono sent adrift. And did not the other actors play out their legendary roles? Recall that Kalaniopu'u was prevented from accompanying Cook by the intercession of the favored wife, Kaneikapolei. For one brief and decisive instant, the confrontation returned to the *original triad* [of Hawaiian myth] of the god, the man, and the woman, with the issue again determined by the woman's choice.[10]

I think the analysis here is fundamentally flawed and Sahlins comes perilously close to implying that Hawaiians did not perceive events *except* ritualistically. When Cook's crew kill a Hawaiian chief, it is Lono's people killing a victim for the sacrifice that the king should ideally have performed. This is also presumably "played in reverse," a neat way of accommodating recalcitrant facts. The idea of a sacrifice involving ritual procedures that the British could not possibly employ should go counter to Sahlins's hypothesis, except that Hawaiians seem to relax their own rules whenever Lono-Cook does anything! Furthermore, Sahlins has to alter the British accounts to make them fit his myth. Thus, "the god Lono was wading ashore with his warriors to confront the King." This is not found in any account, because Cook landed on shore with Phillips and nine marines and *then went to the village of Ka'awaloa where they met the king*. Sahlins has to distort the evidence because this is the Kāli'i played in reverse and the Kāli'i is enacted on shore.[11] It is indeed the case that Cook was killed later on near the seashore, but then he was *not* wading ashore but going in the *opposite* direction with his "warriors" who, according to Bligh at least, were running helter-skelter to their boats to save their lives.[12] A peculiar Kāli'i indeed, certainly played in reverse in more senses than Sahlins imagined!

Another reversal takes place in Sahlins's account: The king will be taken off to sea instead of the canoe of Lono being sent adrift. The reference is of course to the conclusion of Makahiki, when a miniature canoe, fitted with provisions, is pushed into the sea. But the isomorphism is vague. Kalani'opu'u voluntarily agreed to go on board; this is something he has done before and there is no implication that he was going out to sea. Moreover, if, as Dorothy Barrère asserts, the ritual of the canoe was nonexistent in Cook's time, having been invented by Kamehameha much later, then there is little merit to Sahlins's argument.[13]

The idea that the drama played out in the village of the king enacted a Hawaiian myth of an original triad is also wrong. The idea of an *original triad* is, I think, influenced by Christian ideas and a misreading of the eighth chant of the great Hawaiian creation myth, the *Kumulipo*.[14] But this aside, Sahlins again misunderstands the evidence. For him, Kalani'opu'u was prevented from going with Cook by his wife and she is therefore the decisive player. But Phillips, the man on the spot, tells us that the wife pleaded with the king with "tears and intreaties" while the decisive role was taken by two chiefs who "laid hold of him, insisting that he should not [go], made him sit down, [and] the old Man now appeared dejected and frightened."[15] The king even now might have been willing to go with Cook, but, says King in his official account, "whenever the king appeared inclined to follow him, the Chiefs, who stood around him interposed, at first with prayers and entreaties, but afterward, having recourse to force and violence, insisted on his staying where he was."[16] Sahlins reproduces a primordial Hawaiian mythical triad in the king's village by eliminating these two chiefs. His data are derived from Samwell, who was nowhere around. "An old Woman came crying to the King and *throwing her arms round his neck*, with the assistance of two of the Chiefs attending him made him sit by the side of the double canoes hauled on the Rocks."[17]

Let me now resume Sahlins's narration of the myth of the dying god, James Cook. As we said earlier, this is a cosmic drama in the form of Kāliʻi in reverse. Thus, in Kāliʻi the king himself either wards off the spears aimed at him (as Kamehameha did) or in most cases has a "champion" to take his place. This is Lt. Molesworth Phillips. "Cook was accompanied everywhere on shore by his second, Lt. of the Marines Molesworth Phillips."[18] And then there is the death of the god beautifully described by Sahlins in his first book. Cook's death was a "ritual murder, in the end collectively administered: *upwards of a hundred Hawaiians* rushed upon the fallen god to have a part in his death."[19]

Cook, in this account, is more a hero from Western myth than a performer of the Kāliʻi—he is even a Christ-like figure on occasion. Molesworth Phillips is also Europeanized into a "second," associated with European duels that end in death. By contrast all sources insist that the Kāliʻi is a "mock battle" or "sham battle" where no one gets killed.[20] In the present case, Cook dies along with five of his "warriors," not to mention the many Hawaiians killed, wounded, or maimed. Is this a ritual drama on the model of the Kāliʻi? Sahlins says that over a hundred Hawaiians participated in Cook's death. Aside from the fact that this numerical indicator is entirely Sahlins's invention, is there any resemblance here to Kāliʻi? "Ritual murder" is *ritual* and never murder.

One of the serious problems that Sahlins faces in his mythic interpretation of Cook's death is that there is nothing in Hawaiian culture that recognizes a "Kāliʻi in reverse." At best one might say that in the Kāliʻi the king is symbolically killed, never the god. But for Sahlins, Cook is the dying god of Frazer's West Asian and Christian religions. Where is the Hawaiian parallel? Sahlins seeks this in the rite we discussed earlier (Part V), where at the end of Makahiki the gods are brought into the king's temple and dismantled for storage.[21] Unfortunately Valeri labels this somewhat inappositely as a "symbolic death" of the deity. Sahlins picks up this idea: The dismantling and storage of the Makahiki images (the long god and the short god) is the death of Lono enacted yearly. But he refuses to face the fact that this ritual dismantling or "symbolic death" hasn't the foggiest resemblance, substantively or structurally, to the Kāliʻi or to the cosmic confrontation of the royal Kalaniʻopuʻu and the divine Cook, which resulted in a "structural crisis" that led to the latter's "ritual murder."

Who killed Captain Cook? Sahlins recognizes that there were many claimants to this distinction. It is quite impossible for a commoner to kill

Cook, says Sahlins, because "the sociological category is wrong."[22] As Molesworth Phillips was identified as Cook's second, we must "likewise search for the slayer of Cook among the companions of the King's retinue: the one who parries the spear of the god?"[23] But here Sahlins seems to have forgotten his own thesis that Cook's death is Kāliʻi in reverse, and consequently the king's place is taken by Cook and his champion who is Phillips. There is no room now for another champion on the king's side, unless this is a peculiar Kāliʻi with a champion on both sides, on the Western model of a duel or knightly combat. Thus, in Sahlins's myth there are two sets of participants: the king and his champion and warriors versus the god with his champion and warriors. The battle has been inadvertently Europeanized. Sahlins has identified Phillips as Cook's champion; but who is Kalaniʻopuʻu's? "I hope to show, the key to the mystery is elementary categories (my dear Watson)."[24] "We have been doing the cultural analysis of an historic event (or vice-versa). By all rights, it should lead to a solution of a 'murder mystery.'"[25] This solution is especially important when we remember that none of the later Hawaiian accounts say that Cook's death was either the Kāliʻi or even premeditated.

The anthropologist by contrast can tell us exactly what went on: "The identity of Cook's assailant is deducible, in Holmesian fashion, from the elementary categories"—my dear Watson.[26] The same strategy that led Sahlins to postulate the isomorphism between Cook (Lono) and Makahiki, between the Kāliʻi and Cook's death, now permits him to identify the killer. This is Nuʻa [Nuha], and it is Samwell, among the major journalists, who correctly identified him as a near relation of the king.

Samwell has been singularly impressed with Nuha's physical appearance from first he saw him in the King's retinue: "he was tall and stout, with a fierce look and demeanor, and one who united in his figure the two qualities of strength and agility, in a greater degree, than I ever remembered to have seen before in any other man." . . . Thus Nuha would be one of the *kaukau aliʻi* or lesser chiefs of the royal entourage, a man whose privileges were contingent on his service. He was a warrior, and on that day he was everything he should be.

In status and appearance, this is exactly the figure of Cook's assassin depicted by John Webber, artist of the expedition, in his well-known "Death of Captain Cook" [Figure 14]. We should not ignore the graphic evidence. Indeed, the painting's chief artistic merit is generally acknowledged to be its effort at accuracy. Consider, then, Webber's characterization of Cook's attacker. He is a young man, of exceptional size and athletic build. Perfect for the *kāliʻi* part. Besides, he wears—in warrior fashion, over one shoulder—a distinctive cloak, made primarily of blackcock or frigate-bird feathers, by contrast to the fine, multi-

Figure 13. *Cook Meeting Inhabitants of Van Dieman's Land,*
painting by John Webber

colored feather garments and helmet seen on the right side of the
painting. The latter are made of rare mountain birds. . . .[27]

It is indeed possible that, among the many claimants, Nu'a was the person who gave the fatal blow. But the confirmation of this hypothesis on the
basis of Webber's "accurate" portrait, engraved by Bartolozzi, can be discounted. According to Bernard Smith:

> Although Webber drew exotic landscapes with great accuracy his fig-
> ure drawing retained the facility and attenuated proportions of much
> late eighteenth century draughtsmanship, particularly in Switzerland.
> When engravers like Bartolozzi and Sherwin came to engrave the
> plates for Cook's third voyage such stylistic features became even more
> pronounced and natives were seen for the most, as noble savages, de-
> spite contemporary criticism of the engravings in Hawkesworth.[28]

A contemporary critic noted that Webber, in contrast to Hodges of the
second voyage, "seems to have sacrificed the realities before his eyes to a
faint reminiscence, and stale repetition of Cipriani-Beauties."[29] As an example of the attenuation of features, Smith uses the painting *Cook Meeting
Inhabitants of Van Dieman's Land* (reproduced in Figure 13). You will no-

Figure 14. *The Death of Captain Cook*, engraving by F. Bartolozzi,
after a drawing by John Webber

tice that Webber's Australians (Tasmanians) haven't the remotest resemblance to them: The tall, elongated figures are not too different from the Polynesians depicted in his *The Death of Captain Cook*. Sahlins thinks that Webber's is an exact representation of Nu'a; but if one looks at this painting (also reproduced in Figure 14 above), *all the Hawaiians depicted there seem to have the same proportions as Sahlins's Nu'a*. They also resemble the Australians in their proportions, except that they are much more muscular ("stout"), which is not at all surprising because, according to Joppien and Smith, lean and elongated figures are Webber's manner of depicting nobility.[30] Even the noble Cook seems to have the same physical proportions that the noble N'ua has! It should also be remembered that the melee in which Cook was killed took only a few minutes and by all accounts was a scene of confusion. It is hard to believe that Phillips could have made the nice sociological distinction between a minor chief, Nu'a the killer, and a major aristocratic chief next to him, on the basis of the two kinds of bird feathers they wore. And how did Webber the painter, who wasn't there, make an "accurate" representation of this event? Joppien and Smith again provide us with the answer for, it seems, *The Death of Captain Cook* was not painted in Hawai'i but "invented after the voyage" very likely in the context of the European mythologization of Cook.[31] And the bird feathers? "Several feather objects had been traded with the Hawaiians and it is interesting that the cape worn by the assailant on the right was copied from the specimen in Webber's own collection."[32]

Who then *really* killed Captain Cook? I think most people identified by the ships' crew, or by themselves, could have killed him. All accounts, British and later Hawaiian ones, agree with Trevenen's judgment that it was a "sudden and confused transaction" rather than an orchestrated ritual. One can reject the flagrantly absurd suspects, like Mariner's killer who was a carpenter from the upcountry who hadn't seen Cook before, but not Trevenen's killer, "an old chief, whom Captain Cook himself had kicked out of the ship the day before with many expressions of anger, for having committed a theft. . . ."[33] He may not have been in the right sociological category, but given Polynesian notions of status honor and sensitivity to public humiliation, he had the right *psychological* motive. And the elusive Omiah, the other Lono, who was organizing people into groups for who knows what? He had good sociological reason because, as high priest of the king, he would not have been very pleased with the dismantling of the images of the royal shrine. And he fitted the right cultural category; what better example of "ritual murder" could there be than one Lono [Omiah] killing another Lono [Cook]? He also seemed to have the right psychological motivation: "At the first boxing match," says King, "the wife of a chief they called Erono [Lono] sat herself down by an officer, and on the Company's breaking up, she walked down holding his Arm. The enrag'd husband, with all the fury of Jealousy, seized her by the hair of the head and before he could be stopped beat her unmercifully."[34]

Lieutenant Puget of Vancouver's squadron thought it was "the chief *Paheah* who terminated the existence of that much celebrated Navigator Captain Cook." The man himself admitted it, some Hawaiians agreed, and the ships' crew were so impressed that several wanted to possess a lock of his hair.[35] Sahlins will be pleased to know that he too fitted Samwell's description of Nu'a, "being about thirty four years of age, tall stout and well made . . . ," according to Puget.[36] Puget omits Samwell's description of Nu'a as a person "with a fierce look and demeanor." This is obligingly supplied by Bell, Puget's clerk on the *Chatham*, about another possible killer of Cook: "In one of the Canoes that here came off to us, a man was pointed out to us, as being the principal hand in the murder of Captain Cook, and as such, it is natural to be supposed, he was not a little stared at, which he observed, and stole away, and we saw nothing more of him. He was a tall stout man, of a *fierce countenance*. . . . "[37] But then "tall, stout and well made" is so commonly used to describe Polynesians in the ships' journals, that it is as stereotypic of them as are Webber's representations. The one is a translation of the other.

The Mourning and the Aftermath

After death there is mourning. There is no conventional Polynesian model for the mourning of a dead god because, prior to Cook, no other god had been killed by the Polynesians. Unlike Frazer's West Asian Attis, Adonis, and Osiris, there is no ritualized mourning for a god ritually killed in a enactment. Nor is there a bleeding Christ and the *mater dolorosa*. However, Polynesians do have a model for the mourning practices associated with the death of kings or chiefs. Archibald Campbell, who was present when Kamehameha's brother died, wrote:

> The natives cut off their hair, and went about completely naked. Many of them, particularly the women, disfigured themselves by knocking out their front teeth, and branding their faces with red hot stones, and the small end of calabashes, which they held burning in their faces till a circular mark was produced; whilst, at the same time, a general, I believe I may say an universal public prostitution of the women took place; the queen and the widow of the deceased alone exempted.[38]

Corney, much later, describes the reactions to the death of another chief in much the same way, except that there is no reference to sexual license though "both men and women [were] going about quite naked, to demonstrate their grief."[39] At Kamehameha's death, even though times had changed, similar reactions took place.[40]

If Sahlins's hypothesis is correct, one would expect the Hawaiians to react to Cook's death in similar fashion. But the evidence of the journals suggest that they treated him as an opponent killed in a battle. Hawaiians expressed defiance and "insolence," and there were only a few priests like Keli'ikea to act as mediators and pacifiers of tempers on both sides. According to King, one man had "the Insolence to turn up his backside"; he took up his musket to fire but Burney prevented it.[41] There were other Hawaiian reactions: a constant blowing of conches ("a sign of Defiance").[42] In his 1784 official version, King states that some natives were "parading about in the clothes of our unfortunate comrades; and among them a chief brandishing Captain Cook's hanger, and a woman holding a scabbard."[43] Trevenen, in a marginal note inscribed in a copy of this book, adds that he saw a man with a bloody hanger and that "he told us he had been cutting up the body of our Chief, and if we came ashore he would serve us in the same manner."[44] Captain Clerke, now in command, could not stand any of this. It was "too gross an insult to bear," and because "this multitude being a fine large mark I fired several of the 4 Pounders at them when they dispersed in a great hurry." This "frightened them confoundedly" and "in the evening two Arees [chiefs] came off, and beg'd we would fire at them no more, and expressed their wishes for a peace."[45]

Their wish for peace was never realized, as we know from the British reactions to the death of Cook which were in fact not entirely dissimilar to the Hawaiian reactions. After the first stunned silence, when they realized that Cook, the father of the crew, was dead, the ship's officers tried under threats to get back the body parts of their captain for decent burial at sea. We noted earlier that the body parts were collected in two stages and the remains were committed to the deep in accordance with naval tradition. But this formal ceremonial of death and mourning is only cursorily mentioned in the texts. What is significant is the explosive anger that Cook's death provoked, which made all normal mourning almost redundant. It seems that with the occurrence of a powerfully unsettling and unexpected event the normal routines break down and multiple reactions take place, but these are still standardized or culturally expectable.

What added fuel to the rage was the unbearable "insolence" of the Hawaiians—a word now appearing with increasing frequency in the ships' lexicon. Especially unbearable was the sight of Hawaiians wearing Cook's clothes and hat. Samwell describes this temper well:

> This intolerable Insult added fresh fuel to our passion already in a flame; the Circumstance of the Hat being shewn to our people, like the Mantle of Caeser to the Romans, inflamed them even to madness and nothing was heard among them but a cry for revenge. They went in a body to Captain Clerke, told him they could bear these Insults no longer and desired that he would suffer them to revenge the Death of Captain Cook. This he promised that they should do the next day, and a plan was laid for all the Boats to land and burn the Town of Kavaroa [Ka'awaloa] to morrow and to warp the Discovery in shore to cover them, which spread an universal Joy over both Ships; however Objections were made to it by the new Commander of the Discovery [John Gore] and so the business is postponed to a future day. . . .[46]

None of this, needless to say, appears in the journals of Clerke or King.

The postponed action in fact took place the very next day, 17 February. The town of Ka'awaloa was not the target, though, but the village where the royal temple (Hikiau) was located in Kealakekua Bay. Clerke wanted water for the ships and ordered the infamous Lieutenant Rickman and Lieutenant Harvey to protect the watering party with orders "not to let any of the Natives come near them, by no means to molest them if they first did not give provocation by acting offensively."[47] A dangerously ambiguous order, considering the decision of the previous day. Provocation in the present charged atmosphere was inevitable, as inevitable as the reaction of the crew, already readied for revenge. People threw stones at them and this, says Watts, "induced Mr Rickman to order fire to putt to the Houses, which was done with so much spirit that in half an hours time about 150 houses were consumed and the place evacuated. . . ."[48] This is Law:

"During this fire ½ a dozen men were shot by our people in a Most Brutal Manner. . . . Others of the Natives who stayed in their Houses were run thro' by Bayonets and some poor People Making their Escape were Shot. . . ."[49] But worse: Two people were decapitated, their heads "stuck on poles, and waved to the crowd of Indians assembled on the hills about a ½ of a Mile off."[50] And then Trevenen's Conradian touch: "A cry of horror, and an involuntary motion or starting back was instantly observ'd amongst them. . . ."[51] Frightened people on the hill, says Watts, "soon after from every quarter hung out ensigns of peace and sent their girls and boys to us with presents."[52] One such was an old man who brought a bundle of coconuts and plantains to propitiate the dreaded aggressors. He was bound and bundled in the boat along with the heads of his countrymen. They "shaked the two heads of his Countreymen . . . reeking with blood in his face" (Samwell), and told him "he would be like it."[53] When the old man was brought on board, says King, "I never saw horror as truly pictur'd as in his face, nor a sudden transition, when he was unty'd and told he should not be hurt; he went on shore, brought off what he was bringing when he met with such severe treatment, and afterwards continued a most constant friend."[54]

Some of the officers were upset by the fact that "the House of Kaireekea [Keli'ikea] the priest was burnt down with the rest and all the sacred Buildings and Images about it."[55] When Keli'ikea came aboard, the officers apologized to him, for it was Keli'ikea and the priests who constantly befriended the crew, providing them food and provisions, often gratuitously. "He expostulated a little with us on our want of friendship, and on our ingratitude. . . . On coming on board, he had seen the heads of his countrymen lying on the deck, at which he was exceedingly shocked, and desired with great earnestness, that they might be thrown over-board."[56] According to Trevenen, the old man who was made to face these bleeding heads, was also on board at the time, when Clerke, in deference to Keli'ikea, ordered the ghastly objects to be thrown overboard.[57]

The rage was expectable, but it was certainly not normal mourning! But there is something else going on in the deadly British game of revenge that I want to briefly explore here. In this situation of fear, rage, and sorrow, *they were behaving in a manner that seemed to render fuzzy the distinction between the savage and the civilized.* This is of course a distinction made by the civilizer himself. Kurtz was present in these savage lands long before Conrad. Psychoanalysts practicing group therapy use the term "resonance of fantasy" to depict the process whereby one member in the group reacts to the fantasy of another by reproducing it himself, a process also noted by Bettleheim in extremely disturbed children.[58] A parallel process was occurring here. In this crisis situation the civilizer unconsciously takes over the attributes of the Savage Other. It is the savage who cuts off human heads. The palings of the temple had the impaled heads of twenty Maui chiefs, a living proof, one might say rather ineptly, of savage-ness. Now the British sailors cut off the heads of two Hawaiians and wave them at the terrified savages on the other side and then stick them on the ship's deck. This echoing of the imputed cultural attributes of the Other can be usefully labeled as "symbolic psychomimesis."

Meanwhile the ships' officers perform a less obvious mimesis of savageness in a strange event reported by neither King nor Clerke. Edgar says that on the afternoon of 15 February "was Sold the Effects of Captain James Cooke."[59] This is confirmed by Samwell, who says that "Cook's Clothes were sold in the Cabbin to the gentlemen of both Ships."[60] This event is omitted in almost every biography owing to its bizarre and inexplicable nature. A modern authority, Gould, says: "I have never come across another instance of the same practice being employed in the case of a commissioned officer," let alone a beloved captain recently killed by savages.[61] "Sell" also is a euphemism for simply dividing the clothes among themselves; the owner was Cook, who was dead; no money ever went to Cook's widow from this transaction. According to Samwell, this "sale" took place even before part of Cook's body was recovered, or by Edgar's account, after the flesh from the thigh, but not the rest of the bones, was brought onboard. How does one interpret this piece of symbolic action? I suggest that here also is a case where the psychic qualities attributed to the savage were taken over by the civilized, the immediate cue for civilized action being a parallel action performed by the Other. What attribute of the savage though? *The savage who kills the redoubtable white civilizer wears the latter's clothes.* Thus, when the Frenchman Marion was killed by the Maoris, they wore his clothes and brandished his sword and pistols in triumph.[62] Cook learned about Marion's misfortune on the way home after the second voyage. I believe this story and others like it form parts of shipboard narratives and gossip. In Cook's second voyage, Rowe and company were massacred; only a few of their clothes and belongings were recovered by Burney, and it is easy for the crew to presume they too were worn by the Maoris. The immediate trigger was clear: Triumphant Hawaiians were wearing Cook's hat and brandishing Cook's sword. This produced an immediate reciprocal symbolic imitative action on board: The officers sold Cook's belongings in order to wear the clothes of the dead redoubtable navigator, thereby introjecting the power or mana of the dead man—symbolic psychomimesis produced on the unconscious level by a parallel action on the other side.

The preceding account makes clear that conventional mourning barely occurred on either side. It is not surprising, therefore, that Sahlins does not discuss the public reaction to the death of Cook in his work. He does ask a related question, namely, How is it that Hawaiians could treat Cook as the embodiment of their own divinity who left at the appropriate time, only to come back at a ritually unscheduled moment to suffer a ritual death for this wrong move? Echoing Bernard Smith, he says that this happened because "Cook must have been the first European to practice successfully on a global scale the use of tolerance for the purpose of domination. So if the Hawaiians were willing to receive him as their own god, he was willing to accept the honors."[63] Alive or dead, of course. Thus, in the new stage of the Western myth that Sahlins adumbrates, there has to be a ritual mourning for this dead god, who, he says, "makes the earth bear fruit for mankind: a seminal god, patron of the peaceful and agricultural arts."[64] The ordinary Hawaiians do not fit this requirement, but their king does. Having killed "the divine Cook," the king, Kalani'opu'u, began to mourn for him, in isolation, away from it all. It is Kalani'opu'u, in Sahlins's version, who seems to say, with the players in Covent Garden:

> Mourn, Owhyee's fatal shore
> For Cook, our great Orono, is no more.

And how did Kalani'opu'u mourn? He withdrew, says King, "into a cave in the steep part of the mountain, that hangs over the bay, which was accessible only by the help of ropes, and where he remained for many days, having his victuals let down to him by cords."[65] He might have been mourning for Cook; but what about the five chiefs killed, probably kinsmen of his, and many more *ordinary* people killed then and later on in the day?[66] And the pollution—not just the pollution of death, but the earlier pollution at the shrine where British seamen handled and mishandled the sacred images, including the central image of Kū, the deity who represented the king himself in his sacred role. And then the burning and the further destruction of the village and the royal temple, the later toll of many more ordinary people killed in brutal fashion—Kalani'opu'u had cause to mourn. In a not untypical liminal enactment, Kalani'opu'u removed himself temporarily from the social world; he withdrew into a cave in the hidden steep recesses of the hillside, symbolically becoming an infant in the womb.[67] His food was conveyed in ropes lowered from above, fed through a kind of umbilicus, as it were. Eventually, after the invaders were gone, he would reemerge into a new birth, cleansed of the pollution of death and sacrilege to rule a new kingdom from the embers of the old. History, however, would not remain the same.

AFTERWORD
ON DE-SAHLINIZATION

───────────────── ❧❧ ─────────────────

The Argument Revisited

In the years since the first edition of this study was published, a number of reviewers have raised issues about the arguments I have presented.[1] Preeminent among these is the book-length study by Marshall Sahlins, *How "Natives" Think*. It is Marshall Sahlins himself who says that "one might better characterize Obeyesekere's objections as 'de-sahlinization'" (N. 228). I agree that this is not a bad characterization of my reanalysis of his work on Captain Cook in Hawai'i. But the task of "de-sahlinization" might perhaps be an impossible one: To quote a New Testament saying, "if the salt has lost its savor wherein shall it be seasoned" (Luke 14:34).

My disagreement is primarily with Sahlins's recent "culturological" approach that has superseded his earlier Marxist-influenced thinking. This culturology, with its "mythopraxis," a theory of how natives think, is based on the Saussurean semiology that sees the world as we know it as constituted by an interconnected system of signs and as the main task of ethnography as the decoding of these sign systems. If for Saussure sign systems pertain to *langue*, Sahlins's challenge is to extend it to culture. His strategy is close to that of Tzvetan Todorov, who believes that formal sign systems are characteristic of most non-Western ("cold") societies, whereas the modern West has by and large emancipated itself from signs. In his earlier work on Captain Cook as well as in his most recent book, Sahlins's focus is primarily on myth, a special form of organized signs. Myth structures human action in the world, and much of it can be explained in terms of the practice of myths or mythopraxis. For Sahlins, this is a structural theory; for me, it is a special one, more in tune with Todorov than Claude Lévi-Strauss. At least in Sahlins's work on Cook there is little place for unconscious infrastructures; structures are surface ones and these easily explicable surface structures exist in the long run in native thought.

I shall restate Sahlins's criticisms and respond to them insofar as they affect the central argument of the present work. Sahlins treats this as if it is about Hawai'i, whereas it is about Europe and specifically about the contradictions in the Enlightenment's self-imaginations represented in the person of Cook and the voyages of discovery sponsored by the Royal Society. Cook's voyages intersected with Polynesia, itself a construction of that period, culminating in the final and tragic death of Cook in Hawai'i. Insofar as this last intersection is critically important for my thesis, it is perfectly reasonable for Sahlins and others to criticize my knowledge of Hawai'ian ethnography. Nevertheless, even that ethnography was formulated by navigators who had no previous knowledge of Hawai'i and were there only for a very short period filled with turmoil. I do not want to lose sight of my central thesis that the apotheosis of Captain Cook is a European myth of imperialism, civilization, and conquest. In this sense, the crucial part of my argument is whether the Hawai'ians did or did not perceive Cook as their returning god Lono. If Sahlins can demonstrate with new evidence that Cook was the god Lono for Hawai'ians and he suffered a "ritual murder," then my hypothesis has suffered a severe blow.[2] Parallel with the defense of my central thesis, I want to respond to methodological, ethical, and political issues that emerge from our respective positions.

Sahlins's basic strategy in How "Natives" Think is to produce more and more "empirical" evidence to substantiate his view that Cook was indeed the god Lono to the Hawai'ians, that he came during Makahiki, that the members of his crew were also viewed as divinities, and that similar processes of "deification" occurred in other cultures, most notably in Melanesia. The reiteration of old information and the advancing of new data help to substantiate the underlying theory of mythopraxis, namely, the idea that native peoples tend to act out their myths and, more sensibly, that the discordance between myth and event might produce new structures of thought. As I understand him, the underlying assumption is that if we know the "myths" of native peoples, we can understand their behavior, that is, the practice of their myths (mythopraxis). Throughout this afterword, I shall also deal with the nature of Sahlins's "language game" of how natives (including native anthropologists) think and then critically examine the "form of life" that underlies that language game. My basic criticism can be summarily put thus: None of the new evidence substantiates Sahlins's thesis that the apotheosis of Cook is a Hawai'ian rather than a European phenomenon; nor has he dealt adequately with the methodological criticisms that I made of his previous work, particularly those pertaining to source material. Finally, it seems to me, that piling up more examples of Hawai'ian mythopraxis only reinforces my criticism that he continues to believe more strongly than ever that Hawai'ians, like other natives, were incapable of commonsensical inferences and a reflective form of practical reasoning, capacities that are for Sahlins not only a prerogative of the West but also, more restrictedly, of its bourgeoisie.

While Sahlins never acknowledges that he has been influenced by my work, except on very minor matters of detail, there is some evidence that he has. For example, in his previous work, he takes the journalists' statements that Cook was treated as a "superior being" or that "they regard[ed] us a set of beings infinitely their superiors" as indicative of the "divinity" accorded to Cook. I show that these are standard phrases used by other writers such as Henry James. In *Portrait of a Lady*, the heroine is described in several places as a "superior being" and idealized as "descended from the gods"; in *The Bostonians*, Basil Ransom says of Olive Chancellor that "she was doubtless a superior being."³ As for adoration, surely Sahlins ought to know that it could be used in religious as well as secular ways in European literature. For the most part, the ships' journalists were simply using standard phrases related to class distinctions, not to religion.

It is therefore not surprising that the major journalists of the voyages— Cook, Samwell, and King—made no reference to an apotheosis in their unofficial texts, though they noted that Cook was not only called "Lono" but that he was accorded the honors (*kapu moe*) given to their high chiefs. Cook himself noted this in his journal entry for 21 January 1778, during first contact at Kaua'i where he was accorded ceremonies of prostration. "This, as I afterwards understood, is done to their great chiefs," the word "afterwards" clearly implying that this is something he learned later.⁴ I then showed that in the official version edited by John Douglas and James King, words such as "religious adoration" are inserted into the text, and this I related to the ongoing mythologization of Cook in England and the introduction of the popular mytheme—that the European navigator is a god to savages—now foisted on the public about Cook (A, 121–22).

Let me now discuss the manner in which Sahlins examines a text pertaining to Cook's "divinity" in the official edition, which he and I dispute. I will begin with a passage from Samwell's journal: "Today a Ceremony was performed by the Priests in which he [Cook] was invested by them with the Title and Dignity of Orono, which is the highest rank among these Indians and is a Character that is looked upon by them as partaking of something of divinity."⁵ I have shown that the "Character" referred to here is not Cook but the important priest Omiah who had not surfaced in any of Sahlins's texts. Sahlins now reacts with the argument that, because Omiah was "something of a divinity" and Cook was compared to him, he too was something of a divinity. Any doubt apparently is resolved by King, who in a footnote to the official edition of the voyages said: "Captain Cook generally went by this name amongst the natives of Owhyhee; but we could never learn its precise meaning. Sometimes they applied it to an invisible being, who, they said, lived in the Heavens. We also found that it was a title belonging to a personage of great rank and power in the island, who resembles pretty much the Delai Lama [*sic*] of the Tartars, and the ecclesiastical emperor of Japan" (N, 134; A, 94).⁶ Sahlins goes on to say that King "must have been aware" of texts such as Thomas Astley's *New Collec-*

tion of Voyages, published in 1741, which described the Dalai Lama as "God incarnate" living in Tibet. In fact, King was probably unfamiliar with that text because he refers to the Dalai Lama as a Tartar. (Incidentally, statements such as "must have been aware" are anathema when used by Obeyesekere but permissable for Sahlins)(N, 118). Hence Sahlins's skewed logic: Omiah the priest was called Lono; he was a god incarnate like the Dalai Lama; Cook was called Lono; therefore Cook was also a god incarnate (sort of). Unhappily, this logic is not that of Captain King, who asserts categorically that as far as the term "Lono" was concerned he could "never learn its precise meaning," that the name referred to a deity in the heavens and that Omiah was called Lono. King, however, did not make the final erroneous conclusion that Sahlins makes but instead simply says, "Captain Cook generally went by this name." Nor does King say that Omiah himself was a divinity. Like Samwell, he says Omiah had the "title" Lono and he "resembled" the Dalai Lama—unless Sahlins wants to change the meaning of "resemble" and "partaking of something of divinity" to one of identity.

Unlike in his previous work, Sahlins now no longer depends on the major journalists for his hypothesis of the apotheosis. At best, he can say that these journalists grasped the fact that Cook was given "religious adoration" and that he was a Dalai Lama of sorts, but they did not know he was a god, much less the god Lono, arriving at Makahiki time (N, 21). Sahlins gives the English considerable linguistic and ethnographic skills; why, then, were they incapable of figuring out that Cook was the god Lono when he was called by that name, when they did know there was a god called Lono and also a priest called Lono, Sahlins's "god incarnate"?

Having said that the English failed to make these connections, Sahlins has somehow to fill the lacuna in the texts. First, he uses the examples of the minor journalists, a point I shall return to later. Second, he uses the evidence of the Evangelical texts, especially the *Mooolelo Hawai'i*, published in 1838, from information collected by the new local Evangelicals, and of course the missionary William Ellis, who first recorded the myth of the returning god Lono in 1822. But simply reiterating these data is not going to solve the methodological problems I raised. Between the English journals and *Mooolelo Hawai'i* is a fifty-year gap, during which time momentous events had taken place in Hawai'i. One must deal with the context of events, the nature of the intervening historical period, and the contexts of Hawai'ian utterances before even a tentative solution to problems of truth or authenticity can be resolved. Sahlins not only ignores such things but is lax in his interpretations in several instances. For example, when Cook was taken to the royal temple for what I identified as his "installation ceremony" (which Sahlins reads as a welcoming of the god), priests made utterances whose meanings Captain King did not comprehend. But Sahlins says, "it is said, the Kumilupo [the Hawai'ian origin myth] was chanted before him, in his honor" (N, 24). Like the previous "must have been aware," the present "it is said" is a later construction devoid of evidential value, and yet for Sahlins it is tantamount to "this is what occurred." Let me now develop these methodological criticisms of Sahlins.

Imagined Apotheoses: European Mythmaking

In Joseph Conrad's *Heart of Darkness*, Marlow opens Kurtz's testament thus: "He began with the argument that we whites, from the point of development we had arrived at, 'must necessarily appear to them [savages] in the nature of supernatural beings—we approach them with the might as of a deity,' and so on and so on."

On 13 April 1982, the *Chicago Tribune* in an interview with Marshall Sahlins reports on the cannibalism of "so-called savages": "'Europeans,' Marshall Sahlins explains, 'were thought of as gods and gods ate people. . . . The British thought the Hawai'ians were cannibals because they were less than human. The Hawai'ians thought the British were cannibals because they were *more* than human.'"

Let me begin with the crucial question of whether there is increasing evidence for my hypothesis that the apotheosis of Captain Cook was based on a previous European myth model. Fortunately, there are two important papers on "attributions of divinity" and "imagined apotheoses" by Renaissance scholar William Hamlin, the first written before Hamlin was familiar with the anthropological debate.[7] Both papers demonstrate that "the motif of Europeans perceived as gods—a common feature of Renaissance discovery narratives—appears to work differently in different kinds of ethnographic documents," and that virtually every Renaissance explorer or traveler to savage lands claimed to have divine status conferred on him by natives.[8] Let me give the reader a feel for this material. Consider Jacques Cartier on Canadian Indians who apparently thought that "God was descended and come downe from heaven to heale them." When Francis Drake bestowed goods on the Miwok Indians, of whose language he was ignorant, "they supposed us to be gods, and would not be perswaded [*sic*] to the contrary." Andre Thevet claims that when wild men first saw Christians, they "esteemed them as Prophets and honored them as Goddes." And Captain John Smith asserted that the Susquehanna Indians "with much adoe restrained from adoring us as gods," the word "adoring" neatly echoing the language used in the official narrative of Cook's voyages.[9] Hamlin's extensive documentation shows that Renaissance thinking was saturated with this myth model, both literally and as an extended trope, to the extent that "European voyagers habitually perceived, interpreted, and represented these peoples within the confines of a thought universe so densely configured that scarcely any space remained for imagining alternate realities. . . ."[10] He also shows that some educated sea captains tried to persuade natives that they were not gods, but he rightly says that these denials, like William Cowper's protestations, only affirmed the power of the underlying myth model.

This new evidence not only validates the persistence of the myth model of the civilizer as a god to savages but it also provides a European cultural context for the subtle changes in the official edition and the peculiar apotheoses of Cook going on in England. Neither Hamlin nor I say that the natives did not have certain attitudes to European navigators, only that we do not know what they were because these navigators hardly knew the local languages and had, like all others in situations of first contact, to communicate with signs. There would surely have been multiple responses to the alien presence, but Europeans eventually frame these responses in terms of their preexisting myth models.

This is what I think occurred in Hawai'i when the discourse and behavior of the Hawai'ians were assimilated into the myth model of the apotheosis. Sahlins thinks that his view of Cook as Lono returning at Makahiki and fulfilling Hawai'ian prophecies fits in with Hawai'ian thought but that mine does not. Why not? Is it so strange to believe that Hawai'ians would fit Cook into the model of one of their own chiefs as indeed occurred in many places during colonization and conquest? Why should that myth model be culture-alien? Moreover, I argue that it is perfectly conventional for Hawai'ians and others to name people in relation to important events with which they were associated, and it made Hawai'ian sense to give Cook the name of Lono because he did come at the time of the Makahiki festival (A, 96). Sahlins has not shown why that conception should be culture-alien either. Furthermore, using J. C. Beaglehole's account, I point out that while Cook was given the ceremonial honor associated with chiefs when he was seen in public in Hawai'i, he was not treated in that manner by Hawai'ians when he was in his own ship, which, according to Sahlins, was perceived as a temple (*heiau*) carrying the deity Lono from Kahiki, the mythic land beyond the horizon (N, 39; 176). Thus, a peculiar god Lono is not given "worship" in the very domain in which he is supposed to exercise his sway. Finally, outside of Lieutenant Rickman and seaman Zimmermann, I showed that virtually every one of the ships' personnel simply said that Cook was a chief for Hawai'ians.

Sahlins has a long section on "Foreign Spirits: Including Anthropologists," Europeans who were beginning to be apotheosized by Melanesians in the late nineteenth and early twentieth centuries (N, 177–89). Remember that by this late period Polynesia was no longer fertile ground for the

European mythopoeic imagination. Apparently, Sahlins believes that the multiple ways by which Melanesians dealt with whites during first contact are isomorphic with those of the Hawai'ians. We do not have to take at face value the accounts of white-Melanesian contact, including details in the interesting book by Edward Schiefflin and Robert Crittendon.[11] All of these accounts have to be deconstructed before a new appraisal can be made. But let us for a moment assume, as Sahlins does, that the conventional accounts of Melanesian-white contacts are accurate. These accounts show that the Melanesians during first contact treated the whites as returning ancestors, ghosts, cannibals, shamans, and many more, sometimes shifting ground in the same place. One would also expect similar multiple native reactions to the white presence in the Renaissance narratives reported by Hamlin. Unfortunately, all that can be recovered are those European representations that have smothered the diverse native voices that would have existed in reality. I have no objection in principle to the idea of different myth models being used by natives themselves to categorize the white intruder, but I think the reality was vastly complicated.[12] What is unfortunate about the Melanesian material is the scholarly focus on the so-called supernatural aspects of native categorizations without attention being paid to more pragmatic ones very common also in situations of contact.

In these Melanesian and other accounts, there is no idea of the white civilizer as a god coming to visit them, though this is how Sahlins represents the issue when he talks of "the Australian, Melanesian, or Micronesian *deifications* of Europeans" (N, 178, my italics). This was also the case when he speaks about cannibalism in his interview in the *Chicago Tribune*, though in reality no deification is evident. To complicate matters, in *Natives* he makes a case for cultural specificity; yet he lumps the multiple Melanesian cases under the rubric of "deification" and makes a case that when Europeans went to Melanesia, Australia, and other parts of the world, they were also deified, proving that a similar process occurred in Hawai'i. Is Sahlins not doing what I was supposed to have done, that is, constructing a "generalized native," producing the same native in different parts of the world? Further, in bringing up Melanesian "deification" he has clearly sided with the British of the opening epigraph who said that natives thought Europeans were "more than human."[13]

My answer to the larger issue involved here is that none of these accounts can be taken at face value; even the first contacts reported for Melanesia are not cases where the white explorer objectively reports the authentic voice of informants but complex dialogical situations where multiple projections, use of pidgin instead of local languages, sensitivities to language nuances and irony, mutual cultural incomprehensions and unequal power relations all culminate in what I have called "situational overdetermination" (A, 97).

Makeshift Ethnography, Shifting Traditions

It is a pleasure for me to agree with Sahlins on many issues. When he says that I am guilty of "historical fiction, makeshift ethnography," what can I do but agree with him! (N, 117) I have stated elsewhere that "social science concepts often have a fictitious character," and now I would add that ethnography is a makeshift construction of another culture, a fiction if you will, by an alien ethnographer using unfamiliar material and poor language skills and often engaged in a hopeless dialogic relationship with informants.[14] Makeshift ethnography in no way demeans our discipline; it is a tribute to human creativity that good ethnographies can be created out of such inadequacies. But it ought to make us self-conscious about our vulnerability. And the fact that we are not on very solid ground also ought to make us ethically and politically sensitive when we write about other cultures. In historical ethnography, it should alert us to several acute methodological problems when we deal with archival and documentary material written before modern ethnography even got off the ground. While making a case for forms of nomological thought, I have also mentioned elsewhere the larger foundational issues involved in makeshift ethnography: "Any ontology we use to ground the human sciences must ultimately be based on 'faith' since any ontology of even minimal significance must derive from a variety of sources, including the scholar's religious and cultural heritage; and any ontology that we employ can never be final since the very historicity of our being prevents that."[15]

In *Natives*, Sahlins says that I have expunged Hawai'ian voices from their own history, albeit histories written by missionaries, navigators, and early Hawai'ian historians. I will deal with the latter category later, but Sahlins thinks that such works really gave voice to Hawai'ian ideas about themselves. Of course, I plead guilty to all of this for the very good reason that I doubt that these texts accurately reflect any such voice. At best they re-present Hawai'ian voices in terms of European thought processes. I find it rather disconcerting that Sahlins simply ignores the complicated nature of text writing by missionaries and navigators that has been subject to such intense debate recently. The waters of poststructuralist, hermeneutical, and postcolonial criticism flow by him as he holds imperturbably to his position that these texts accurately describe Hawai'ian culture and voices. I am not suggesting that we ignore these texts; one must make do with what we have as we construct our makeshift ethnographies.

Let me begin my critique by stating that cultures consist of many "traditions" that are being constructed, reconstructed, and reified and culminate in a process that, following Hans-Georg Gadamer, involves the fusion of the horizon of the text with the horizon of the interpreter. While Gadamer approves of the process, I think that we should resist such fusion when we study other cultures, even though it is almost impossible to escape the effect of our "prejudices," to use Gadamer's language once again. Putting it in more radical terms, one cannot escape the politics, ethics, and quandaries of representation even as we try to describe the Other. None of these issues captures Sahlins's attention; there is little methodological doubt regarding the texts he uses or his own capacity to read these texts and accurately describe the Hawai'ian voices enshrined therein. In *Natives*, he piles more and more material of the same kind from more and more navigators and missionaries without once meeting the criticism that I made of his earlier work; namely, *there is not a single instance of his questioning the agendas, motivations, or social contexts underlying the writing of these texts.* In a crucial instance, he even denies such motivations as, for example, the distinction between the unofficial journals and the official account of the last voyage, when Cook's voice was taken over by John Douglas, the canon of Windsor. Sahlins finds it strange that Douglas's voice should reflect the voices of the English public troubled by the death of the great navigator, a fine flower of the Enlightenment. So, too, with these other texts. Evangelical missionaries have their own agenda, and I showed that the text of *Mooolelo Hawai'i*, while it does contain historically useful data, is also a myth of the Evangelicals. I have never said what he attributes to me, that the Hawai'ian narratives of that text are "only the echoes of Reverend Dibble's satanic verses." Mine is closer to the work of Paul Ricoeur and Michel de Certeau, who Sahlins quotes approvingly without acknowledging their insights into historical and ethnographic writing as "fiction"— that is, makeshift ethnography.[16]

Let me mention a few of the "multiple traditions" that are relevant for understanding these texts. First, there is the apotheosis myth model existing anterior to the death of Cook. In my book, this myth model was reflected initially in the discourse of Robert Wallis's sailors who, even before they landed in Tahiti for the first time, thought those savages would think they were "Demi Gods," for reasons of power that Kurtz also emphasized (A, 123). Hamlin's work indicates the strength of these traditions, which then become a much more ubiquitous trope in English literature. Second, there is the reaction to the death of Cook, the subtle editorial emendations of Douglas and King, and the publication of the official voyages in 1784. There is no question that many Englishmen believed that Cook was apotheosized by the Hawai'ians. That this was an English projection seems reasonably clear from the painting of the apotheosis and the pantomime *Omai* (A, 129–30). At this juncture, the myth model of the apotheosis of Cook was fused with the already persistent view of him as the embodiment of the Enlightenment. It is interesting that in *Natives* Sahlins simply ignores *Omai* because it would be impossible to demonstrate that "Hawai'ian voices" were being represented there. Third, reacting to the myth model of the apotheosis is the Evangelical one constructed by Cowper who, having praised Cook in a poem as the exemplar of the Enlightenment after the second voyage, reverses his position and treats him as a Herod for taking upon himself the attributes of a divinity.[17] Cowper does not doubt for a moment that Cook took upon himself the role of a god, even though the official edition only states he was treated with "religious adoration." Because the phrase "religious adoration" has clear connotations of divinity, it is not surprising that Cowper imposed his own meaning on the text: God struck Cook dead for apostasy. Thus, we can identify the particular instance of the invention of another tradition in London in 1784: an Evangelical myth of Cook as Herod (A, 126). This tradition, it is easy to show, persisted in the thought of American and other Evangelicals who went to Hawai'i after 1820. Sahlins's favorite text, *Mooolelo Hawai'i*, compiled by the Evangelical missionary Sheldon Dibble contains "satanic verses" in one sense at least: It picks up where Cowper left off and explicitly identifies Cook as Herod and states that "god struck him dead" for the sin of apostasy.[18] Moreover, there is not the slightest reference in Cowper to Lono or to Hawaiian culture; he is simply seeing Cook in terms of the apotheosis myth model and then indignantly reacting against it in Evangelical terms. Cowper's voice is hard to imagine except as a European one. This Evangelical text was given further extension by the missionary Ellis, who reported the myth of Lono's return and the identification of Cook with this returning god. These traditions do not exist by themselves but crisscross each other when told by different people at different times.

I doubt that any European navigator could have remained uncontaminated by these traditions. The edition of Cook's voyages was in every ship, and Cook's skillful knowledge of the South Seas was eagerly read and digested. His works were translated into French and Russian, and he was idealized by Otto von Kotzebue and Adelbert von Chamisso. Put differently, the ships contained their own traditions that in turn constituted "taken-for-granted beliefs" or *doxa*, to use Pierre Bourdieu's Greek. In addition, of course, each navigator came for his own purposes: trade, prospects of imperial control, or whatever. None knew the local languages in any depth, but by the first decade of the nineteenth century there were Hawai'ians and European settlers who could serve as interpreters (and needless to say they each had their own "prejudices") (A, 146–48). In this complicated situation, many navigators during brief visits wrote about Hawai'ian customs and manners; but to think that they could express in their writing the true voices of the Hawai'ian people must surely take more than a normal dose of credulity.

An example where Sahlins and I clearly disagree regarding the nature of traditions comes from Edward Bell of Captain Vancouver's expedition. Bell mentions that every Hawai'ian could prattle about Cook's death and that "they look'd up to him as to a supernatural being, indeed call'd him the 'Orono' or great God" (A, 151; N, 87). I interpret this as Bell's own interpretation of the official edition of Cook's third voyage; or to rephrase it, Bell is being influenced by the general European tradition of imagined apotheoses and the specific case of Cook. For Sahlins, this is a clear case of "Hawai'ian voices" that Obeyesekere has stilled (N, 88). I do not think we will ever prove his or my hypothesis. However, it is worth repeating that, contrary to Sahlins, Bell does not say that Cook was a god to Hawai'ians; rather, Hawai'ians looked upon him *as to* a supernatural being, which is quite a different thing and is very much in line with the similes employed in the official edition. In other words, it is Sahlins's voice that has reread Bell as expressing a Hawai'ian voice. So with the other examples Sahlins confidently cites (N, 101–3); they repeat one or more of the many traditions that have circulated about Cook, adding and enriching them in terms of current circumstances. I would say that to take these texts out of their contexts and the traditions in which they are embedded is, to use Sahlins's own phrase, "crudely unhistorical" (N, 5).

On the Hawai'ian side, there were even more momentous and sometimes disastrous events, and once again let me repeat the crucial ones. First: there was the remarkable figure of Kamehameha I, who brought the islands under a single rule but at enormous economic cost. He not only unified the nation but his priests creatively systematized the religion, including the Makahiki (so that it became easy for Sahlins to further systematize it). Second, in the reign of his son there occurred the critical event whereby the king and his family and chiefs dramatized their formal renouncing of the old religion by the remarkable act of interdining followed by the mass destruction of the images of their gods. Sahlins himself admits that Hawai'ian religion was "crumbling toward 1819," yet, for him, one aspect remained constant throughout this turmoil and after; Cook worshiped as Lono in his relics (N, 115). Third, there was a general malaise felt everywhere, including the royal household. Fourth, the year after the destruction of the native religion, the first American mission came to the islands and implanted on them the beginnings of a different religion. While I do not think that Sahlins's image of satanic verses is helpful in this regard, it is the case that missionaries like Dibble were openly contemptuous of Hawai'ian culture and its people, and this is not in the least difficult to demonstrate. How is it possible for the missions and their recently converted students to collect data from old informants and reproduce for us the voices of the Hawai'ians of Cook's time without a complicated fusion of horizons? From the point of view of the older informants themselves, one must ask how they could have provided accurate information of the past religion, given the fact that many had voluntarily rejected that religion or had profoundly ambivalent attitudes to it, and that the past they were recollecting was the

Kamehameha reforms, not the past of Kalaniʻopuʻū, Cook's contemporary? Sure, they were Hawaiʻian voices speaking to Evangelized Hawaiʻians (who were also Hawaiʻian voices, albeit of a different sort), but these multiple Hawaiʻian voices heard through the momentous changes that occurred in Hawaiʻi cannot be accepted at face value regarding the truth of a past, a truth complicated by the methodological dilemma that even when we interview ordinary people regarding contemporary events we cannot expect to hear unequivocal truths. Such "truths" have to be constructed by us in a makeshift manner. For example, take the case of the Makahiki as Sahlins himself uncritically presents it: "The extant Hawaiʻian descriptions of the Makahiki date from the early to mid-nineteenth century, after the abolition of the traditional religion and are based on the recollections of the authors or their elders."[19]

One must minimally have at least some kind of accounting or justification for Sahlins to accept such recollected evidence at face value. Even the best native ethnographers and historians such as David Malo and S. M. Kamakau (who were Christian) cannot escape the traditions that were being invented at the time (and that they helped to reconstitute). Thus, I would say that, much as I admire these native historians, they cannot, any more than the rest of us, escape their own times and "prejudices." Their texts have to be examined critically before they can be used as the basis for general theories or histories. Kamakau developed into an ardent nationalist, and though he accepted the Evangelical version of Cook's apotheosis, he was utterly skeptical about the treatment of Cook's bones (A, 166). And Malo, Sahlins's "canonical" authority and the very first class of scholars of the Lahainaluna mission school, actually says that the name of Lono was given to Captain Cook "because of the resemblance the sails of his ship bore to the *tapa* of the god."[20]

Can one even talk about remembrance of such pasts without a theory of cultural memory or at least a sophisticated account of it in the Hawaiʻian context? When Sahlins presents such a theory, it is devastatingly inimical to his own thesis. That theory of cultural memory appears in his examination of the Melanesian data where he says that the "fateful world-historical irruption into their 'traditional' existence is for many Melanesian peoples not historically or socially marked as such" (N, 188). He adds that for colonized peoples, "it is the moment of domination and transformation, the assumption of subaltern status that is marked in historical consciousness rather than the period of early contacts that preceded it" (ibid.). If one applies this theory of cultural memory to Hawaiʻi, then the period of Western domination and political control came only with the entry of the missions, in which case both native and missionary accounts of the earlier period could not possibly contain native voices that validly describe Captain Cook's visit to Hawaii. That visit clearly preceded European political control and the relegation of Hawai'ians to subaltern status.

Aside from his inadequate theory of cultural memory, Sahlins nowhere give us positive rules whereby he can disentangle the true voices of Hawai'ians in the texts, particularly complex ones like Kamakau's, that were written over eighty years after Cook's visit and after Hawai'i itself had suffered many political, religious, and economic vicissitudes. It is not reasonable to think that Sahlins, the outsider ethnographer, can work out the central features of Hawai'ian thought and culture on the basis of these texts. Neither can I; there are no mechanical rules for doing this. The best we can do is to establish reasonable criteria for interpretation, taking into consideration the agendas and cultural contexts of these texts, through, what in an earlier book I called a "hesitant dialectic of deconstruction and reconstruction."[21] Thus, one difference between us is that while I am self-consciously engaged in makeshift ethnography, Sahlins is not.

Let me consider one source of Sahlins's belief that these texts reflect accurately the voices of Hawai'ians, focusing now on Cook's last voyage. To make the argument plausible that the sailors and navigators did get Hawai'ian ethnography and voices right, they must have known the local language or had enough linguistic competence to record what they heard accurately. While culture is not synonymous with language, there is little chance that one could have access to that culture without good linguistic skills or the help of local interpreters (who were simply not available in Hawai'i in Cook's time). Though Cook and his educated officers could have had some access to Hawai'ian lifeways in the few weeks they were there, they could not possibly have had the linguistic authority necessary for Sahlins to use them in constructing Hawai'ian thought and resurrecting their voices. Thus, there is no escaping the fact that he must deal with the language competence of the many journalists.

Once again, Sahlins has rightly portrayed me as being skeptical about these language skills, of some more than of others. Basically, he makes the point that because Cook knew some Tahitian, he would be able to deal with a cognate language such as Hawai'ian. Whether such skills are transferable or not is not as germane as the fact that in this voyage Cook's knowledge of Tahitian was in disuse because he employed Omai, the Tahitian, as an interpreter. Further, Omai was left in Tahiti. Cook certainly had linguistic talent, but Zimmermann probably rightly observed that "he had a special faculty for making himself understood by the natives through gestures; and although this faculty had been developed by constant use, nevertheless it was inborn."[22] During the first visit, Cook had to rely on Anderson, the ship's doctor who died during this trip and was not present for the crucial second visit to Hawai'i island. Nor does Sahlins tell us how

Samwell and King, the two other major journalists with their more limited experience of Tahiti (not having been on Cook's first two voyages) functioned. Further, Cook himself was humble enough to admit that in Tonga, a place he knew well, he was incapable of rendering their complex religious beliefs. So was Samwell, who, like Cook, had to converse with words and gestures in Hawai'i.[23] The situation is worse with the minor journalists, who had little motivation to learn Tahitian, and then had less than three weeks to learn Hawai'ian!

Now let me pin down a few texts from two minor journalists that Sahlins interprets without the slightest reservation. I will start with the case of the ordinary sailor Zimmermann, who, according to Sahlins, "heard it directly from the Hawai'ians" (N, 17): "They made a god of Captain Cook on the Island of O-waihi and erected an idol in his honour. They called this 'O-runa no te tuti,' 'O-runa' meaning god and 'tuti' Cook. This god was made after the pattern of the others but was adorned with white feathers instead of red, presumably because Cook being a European had a fair complexion." (N,18)[24] For Sahlins, the first Hawai'ian phrase could be glossed as "Cook is indeed Lono." I have asked a several Hawai'ian language teachers to look at Zimmermann's text, on condition of anonymity. Their opinion is that if Zimmermann had some sensitivity to Hawai'ian pronunciation, then "runa" could not mean "Lono" but "above," that is, "luna." In that case, the phrase could mean "Cook is indeed above." If Zimmermann was right that a statue was erected for Cook (which no one else refers to), then "above" could in fact be understood as referring to a godly status because statues are not erected for chiefs. But if Zimmermann represents a tradition coming down from British seafarers, then what has happened here is that an image of Lono, the god, has been identified by some of the ships' crew as that of Cook who was called Lono. Even if one takes Zimmermann at face value, "above" is a relative term and could simply mean that Cook was "exalted," which is perfectly understandable. Because Zimmermann's linguistic ability was at best minimal, his statements must be interpreted cautiously. Moreover, how well did Zimmermann remember this statement three years later? More important, statements onboard ship are sometimes formed collectively in the close and tight space of the ship. All these difficulties mean that Sahlins's confident translation that "Cook is indeed Lono" cannot be taken at face value.

Now for Zimmermann's quotation from 15 February, the day after Cook was killed: "[The Hawai'ians] showed us a piece of white cloth as a countersign of peace but mocked at ours and answered as follows: 'O-runa no te tuti Heri te moi a popo Here mai' which means: 'The god Cook is not dead but sleeps in the woods and will come tomorrow.'" (N,18)[25] This in Sahlins's retranslation means, "Cook is indeed Lono, he is going to sleep, tomorrow he will come," which of course once again convinces us that Cook is "indeed Lono," and, further, according to Sahlins's theory, he is going to "come again," resurrected as a god (N, 18). But there is more trouble with the translation. First, the idea that Hawai'ians were giving factual information about Cook-Lono and his return is not consonant with what Zimmermann noted; namely, the Hawai'ians were *mocking* the English, something that Zimmermann could hardly have missed because others also noted it, including their "insolence" in, for example, showing their backsides to the British. To compound matters even further, Tewsley, the first translator of this text, says: "Nothing can be made of this with safety. It is a Hawai'ian sentence heard by a European and written down as nearly as he could remember the sound he thought he heard, and his translation is what he thought the words meant." The translator adds that "tuti" clearly meant "Cook" and that the rest of the sentence "might be equivalent to the colloquial Maori *haere ki te moe, apopo haere mai*—[Cook] has gone to sleep; tomorrow he will come."[26] In the context of Cook's death and the mockery of the Hawai'ians, one can read "tomorrow he will come" as an ironic reference. The Hawai'ians were going to bring in some useless flesh the next day "6 or 8 pounds without any bone in it"—this being a bit of a ghastly joke, because the bones, and not flesh, were necessary for the Hawai'ian treatment of Cook's remains.[27]

My anonymous Hawai'ian language teachers gave translations differing from both Sahlins's and Tewsley's renderings. They saw two possible meanings: "*O-runa no te tuti* ["tuti" being Cook] has gone to sleep. Come back tomorrow"; and "*O-runa no te tuti* has gone to sleep. He'll come back here tomorrow." They agreed that it was important that the Hawai'ians were making fun of the British. Taunting was a common practice of warriors. "In that case, the statement would be a joke, making fun of both the exalted Cook and of his men." It therefore seems that the two events—the Hawai'ian utterance in Zimmermann's text and the bringing in of Cook's flesh the next day—are parodically interrelated and have nothing to do with the resurrection of Cook. In any case, contrary to Sahlins, a resurrection of Cook a day or two after he was killed does not make any Hawai'ian sense.

There are further problems with Zimmermann. It is clear from both statements that Hawai'ians not only called Cook "Lono," they also rendered his English name as "tuti," which was how he was called everywhere in Polynesia. This indicates that even if, as Sahlins thinks, he was the god Lono to the Hawai'ians, he was also plain Cook to them. Let us, however, assume that Sahlins is right in everything he says about these two texts. Nevertheless, the Hawai'ian words were rendered in a specific way by Zimmermann, bringing them into the horizon of his own prejudices. Thus, the

term Lono means "god" and an idol is erected in God Cook's honor, something the major journalists never noted. In the second statement, he refers
to "the God Cook." This unwitting "fusion of horizons" comes out even
more clearly in Zimmermann's third important statement: "the death of
our quartermaster [William Watman] destroyed their previous belief in
our immortality, and, this belief being lost, their reverence for us was
gone."[28] This can be interpreted to mean that Hawai'ians thought that not
only was Cook a god but so was the rest of the crew, which is Sahlins's
interpretation even though the evidence is clear that ordinary crew members were not accorded any form of ceremonial "worship" and in some
instances were beaten and humiliated. Moreover, Zimmermann says that
Watman's death removed the reverence the Hawai'ians had for the English, whereas Sahlins does not accept this, firmly believing that Cook and
crew continued to be treated as deities. If Sahlins can say that Zimmermann was right in the first two instances, what is the rule by which he says
that he was wrong in the third? In my view, Zimmermann is a victim of his
own shipboard traditions, and he is bringing himself, the crew, and Cook
into the line of beliefs that Hamlin has called the "imagined apotheoses" of
sea voyagers. Now consider these three statements as a totality: the first
statement may fit Sahlins's hypothesis; the second and third flout it. By
contrast, Zimmermann's three statements do not contradict my hypothesis
of imagined apotheoses. Finally, one must ask why Sahlins takes these two
statements at face value when he, following Beaglehole, admits that Zimmermann's slim volume "is of little value" and contains "lower-deck im-
pressions of Cook," perhaps formed collectively by ordinary seamen (N, 17).

The second case is that of Rickman's conversation with the chief of
Ni'ihau, who "pointing to the sun, seemed to suppose that we should visit
that luminary in our course, and that the thunder and lightning of our
guns, and that which came from the heavens were both derived from the
same source."[29] Sahlins is right that I thought Rickman's account was a
fabrication or, to use Beaglehole's words, "a fanciful and ridiculously exaggerated production."[30] Rickman did not have his logs for use in his published account of 1781; comparison with his logs shows that he got dates
and times wildly wrong. Moreover, his logs make no reference to this important episode; on the contrary, the logs mention that the crew was subjected to "every mark of uncivility and buffoonery," which was also confirmed by King (A, 72).

I did argue that neither Rickman nor John Ledyard, who made similar
statements, had the language skills to engage in this kind of cosmological
conversation. But now I would go beyond my earlier argument and assert
that the belief about Europeans coming from some other planet is also a
Western myth of the long run, sometimes articulated with the idea of the

civilizer as a god and sometimes existing on its own. In ethnography itself, it is reflected in some of the authorities Sahlins cites, such as the explorer Nikolai Nikolaevich Mikloucho-Maclay who was reputed to have come from the moon; of Ronald Berndt's description of Eastern New Guinea Highland folk who thought Europeans were "red in colouring because they had been close to the sun; they had control of the lightning"; or those old men from the Chimbu country who believed that whites "were lightning beings from the sky" (N, 180–84). In respect to Rickman's fantasies, Sahlins has already told us that "thunder and lightning are modes of Lono." This must be strictly Hawai'ian thinking in accordance with his formula, "different cultures; different rationalities." Yet this formula cannot hold good, because even without Lono around, other cultures seem to come up with the same planetary trope of whites coming from lightning, the sun, or the moon: thus, "different cultures; same rationalities." My guess is that this trope also is a running theme in *European* popular thought and a source of bricolage for the nineteenth-century pseudo-science of solar mythology that Max Müller and others developed. It is nowadays reflected in modern science fiction and film about interplanetary travel, particularly those about white heroes bringing civilization from another planet.

Obviously, Melanesians had their own conceptions of whites as ancestors, cannibals, and "spirits" of sorts. They also had ideas about planets, but these indigenous conceptions have been fused into European preconceptions. Sahlins will be thrilled to know that Richard Hakluyt's *Principal Navigations* mentions Fernando Alacron, who, during an expedition to the west coast of Mexico in 1540, made the same point, proving no doubt for Sahlins that, as far as European planetary descent was concerned, cultural difference did not matter:

> I shewed to them Wheate and Beanes, and other seedes, to see whether they had any of those kinds: but they shewed mee that they had no knowledge of them, and wondred at all of them, *and by signes I came to understand that the thing which they most esteemed and reverenced was the Sunne: and I signified unto them that I came from the Sunne.* Whereat they marveiled, and then they began to behold me from the toppe to the toe.[31]

But before Alcaron, there were others. Thus, Antonio Pigafetta, who wrote about Magellan's voyage, tells us that off the coast of southern Argentina they "espyed a man of the stature of a giante, who came to the haven dauncing and syngynge. . . . When he sawe the capitayne with certeyne of his coompany abowte him, he was greatly amased and made signes holdynge uppe his hande to heauen, signifyinge therby that owre men came from thense."[32] It therefore seems to me that this kind of trope was a

European myth model of the long run, perhaps developed by sailors journeying on the high seas for long periods of desolate time.

I want, however, to introduce an important qualification with respect to the vicissitudes of both the apotheosis model and the planetary one as they circulated between islands and beaches, especially when contact between Europeans and natives have become an established reality: In the context of unequal power relations, these European ideas can be accepted by native populations, which was true of Hawai'i also much later. Rickman's case, however, was one of first contact, and he is simply projecting the solar myth model onto his fictionalized discourse with Hawai'ians, perhaps lifted from Hakluyt's volumes, which were widely read by educated sailors.

But the New Guinea examples could be much more problematic: If indeed the planetary myth model was circulating among islands and beaches, then it is possible that natives would also be familiar with it and might simply use it as a way of relating to Europeans. Often, conventions of politeness, flattery, patronage, or the need to engage in preliminary formal conversations would make for this kind of usage of the Western myth model. Thus, when the Russian explorer Maclay, as well as Berndt, refers to the lunar and solar myths that natives held about Europeans, it might well be due to the circulation of ideas after first contact or indeed circulating *ahead* of actual first contact, particularly in New Guinea in the late nineteenth and early twentieth centuries. One might add that the acceptance of European self-conceptions by native populations is a phenomenon well known during long-term colonial contact and domination.[33]

I have labeled Zimmermann and Rickman "minor journalists." What about the strengths and weaknesses of the major journalists, especially Cook, King, and Samwell? They were after all British; they came from a tradition that extolled empiricism and common sense. Hence, a neat paradox in Sahlins's thinking. He is contemptuous of the English empiricist tradition (to which I am also presumably addicted), yet he relies for virtually all of his understanding of what went on during this period on those very representatives of this denigrated tradition. By contrast, I rely on these journalists' strengths: descriptions of what they saw and their common-sense understandings of Hawai'ian culture. But they were not objective ethnographic reporters, if such a beast exists. They were vulnerable to the politics of their voyages and their home country; they were also victims of the taken-for-granted assumptions or doxa of their shipboard traditions. Sahlins now admits that the *major* journalists had no awareness that Hawai'ians treated Cook as a god, "not having fathomed what 'the Orono' meant to the Hawai'ians" (N, 21). Yet he goes out of his way to show that two *minor* journalists did make the connection, even though they had little or no knowledge of the language. How can he explain this anomaly?

Mythopraxis

Mythopraxis is the central term in Sahlins's work; it is the practice of the myth, a form of savage thought. Unhappily, Sahlins does not tell us what is meant by "myth" in native terms or why one narrative or myth is more significant than another. In the present case, there are two critical myths: the Makahiki as the time when the god Lono is present; and the prophecy, recorded much later by the missionary Ellis. Sahlins's Cook arrived at the Makahiki and fulfilled both aspects of the myth, such that virtually every significant event that occurred fit the mythic pattern. Sahlins says that my notion of practical rationality is a Western empiricist theory foisted on natives. My question is how Sahlins's theory not a Western one. Take the key words: "myth" is itself a term from the Western lexicon, used un-critically to incorporate all sorts of stories and traditions in Hawai'i. Then there is "praxis," also a well-known word, especially in Marxist thought but now employed in an overtly un-Marxist manner. Thus, mythopraxis is as much a Western imposition on the Hawai'ians as my notion of practical rationality. I am not opposed to such a strategy; I only object to Sahlins's not recognizing its Eurocentric character.

My second criticism is of his belief that through mythopraxis he can read the texts relatively unproblematically. If people have myths and we know what they are, then we have a key to their thoughts. That natives think mythically has been the bane of the Western representation of the savage, and I agree that it is not only Lucien Lévy-Bruhl but also Lévi-Strauss who uses similar assumptions. This is not to say that Lévi-Strauss or Lévy-Bruhl are not great thinkers, only that there are flaws in their thought, as with all of us, particularly in respect of those conceptions of the savage inherited from previous traditions. To be critical of these thinkers is not to be dismissive of them because I doubt whether any thinker in the human sciences can produce an epistemology that is beyond criticism. So with Sahlins: I find mythopraxis continues to present a pejorative view of non-Western mentalities, a shift that was already anticipated in his impor-tant book, *Culture and Practical Reason*.

In his *How "Natives" Think* he simply reaffirms mythopraxis by reiterat-ing what he said earlier, providing extra details and relentlessly adding more examples. I shall not deal with the Makahiki here because he does not give us new information. But take the crucial case of what I consider Cook's installation ceremony, which Sahlins thinks is the welcome given to the god Lono, alias Cook, by the Lono priests. King gives a good factual account of what transpired, but he admitted his incapacity to understand priestly utterances. These blank spaces have been filled in by later folklor-ists and antiquarians. In similar fashion, Sahlins juxtaposes King's account of the rituals at Hikiau with "the well-known received texts on the *hāna-*

ipū" (N, 56). This *hānaipū* ceremony, he says, was repeated many times for other British officers, particularly Captain Clerke. If this is another case of mythopraxis, then I find it a singularly loose one because the myths of Lono's return do not deal with his coming home with a whole lot of subsidiary deities!

Let me first deal with the similarities between the accounts. In both instances, Cook and the officers were "annointed" with masticated coconut; and other offerings were given to them. I find nothing unusual in Hawai'ians or other people transferring a set of ritual practices from one context to another as part of a process of creative improvisation. For example, Valerio Valeri says that there is no Hawai'ian ceremony of installation and therefore Cook was simply accorded the pregiven ritual of the *hānaipū*.[34] But no English navigator had come to Hawai'i either. Neither Sahlins nor Valeri can imagine Hawai'ians inventing a ceremony, based on existing ritual elements, to deal with the new situation where they incorporate British officers into the Hawai'ian sociopolitical order. Elements of *hānaipū* found in the rituals where Cook and Clerke were installed as chiefs before their gods are perfectly intelligible and highly plausible to me. But what is striking about the juxtaposition of the two accounts, the *hānaipū* and Cook's installation, is not the similarities but the differences and discordances.

These differences are quite remarkable. First, consider Sahlins's presentation of the *hānaipū*: "As the god was brought out of the king's house, and the eyes of the king beheld the image, they were filled with tears, and he cried for his love for the deity" (N, 56). None of this occurs anywhere in King's account. Here was Lono in person; yet none of the attendants or priests shed tears before the visible presence of the god himself or before the main image of Ku whose shrine it was. As far as the other deities were concerned, King reports that they were treated in a rather disrespectful way. Nor is there the slightest indication that priests gave Cook-Lono exaggerated respect within this temple.

Second, the *hānaipū* ritual recorded by Sahlins makes no reference to several key events mentioned by King. Cook was in fact made to prostrate himself before the Hawai'ian gods, reversing the conditions that prevailed outside the temple premises. So it is with Cook kissing the god, and however one wants to interpret Hawai'ian kissing, this is what King said.[35] Then there is the disputed event where Cook's hand is "supported" by King and the priest. To me, Cook is made to worship the Hawai'ian gods: One prays with both hands up; or, if the prayer was a long one, with one hand up; whereas Sahlins reiterates that Cook is made to imitate the Makahiki icon (N, 61). If Sahlins is correct, then this element was added to the present ritual because it is *not* part of the *hānaipū*. Sahlins objects to my interpretation, saying that Cook did not worship Lono because this is not exactly the way in which Hawai'ians worship. But if we are looking at *exact* physical coordinates, then Cook's arms being "supported" by the two men does not indicate that he was imitating the "horizontally outstretched" hand of the Makahiki icon either. The term "supported" that King uses can support either argument. Moreover, Sahlins fails to consider the local situation: Here was a reluctant Cook literally made to perform a ceremony he did not care about. Thus Cook was *made* to do certain things by the Hawai'ian priests, and in this case one of the reluctant Cook's hands was raised (whatever the level involved) by the priest and the other by his junior officer, King. In this situation, you could not possibly have had an exact replication of worship, but it did come pretty close. Moreover, all three actions must be taken collectively: Cook's prostration, his kissing the god in the Polynesian fashion familiar to him, and his raising his hands in worship. All three actions in conjunction indicate that he was not treated as the god Lono but was being brought under the aegis of that god and the other gods of the Hawai'ian pantheon. The *hānaipū* rituals and foods were offered to the Hawai'ian gods by the priests on Cook's behalf. The ritual as a totality was something more than the *hānaipū*, and Sahlins is forced to pretty much admit "that some of this ceremony was improvised for the occasion" (N, 53). He never answers the question that I have raised: What is the rationale for the improvisation? And if improvisation occurred in this crucial ritual, what is to prevent it from occurring in other contexts, particularly in situations like the unexpected arrival of Cook? What does the admission of situational improvisation do to the theory of mythopraxis?

Sahlins goes on in similar vein to produce more mythopraxical evidence. Thus, theft is also mythopraxis, though it was not so in other places in Polynesia where theft occurred (N, 70). In my thinking, the most insensitive example of mythopraxis is where Sahlins interprets the death of Cook as the grand *kāli'i* ritual. Here is Cook in a wrathful mood, according to several ships' officers, and he is going to take the king hostage. The king's chief wife tries to prevent it but Sahlins says she too is not so much interested in her husband's welfare as in acting a mythic role in a cosmic drama. In my own account of this event, I pointed that this indeed was no time for telling "stories of the death of kings." Instead of acknowledging the ironic use of the Shakespearean quotation, Sahlins insists that the queen and chiefs told Kalani'opu'ū stories just as Richard II did—an assertion for which there isn't a trace of evidence (N, 233–35; A, 178).[36] Moreover, the accounts of Cook's death that he uses have not the remotest resemblance to Sahlins's own elaborate description of the *kāli'i* ceremony (N, 29–30). Cook himself was not aware of the *kāli'i*; his motive was pretty clearly pragmatic: to take the king hostage. It is the Hawai'ians who supposedly interpreted these actions as *kāli'i*, according to Sahlins. Yet one can legitimately ask why they did not see the act of taking a hostage simply for what it was, as other Polynesians did in similar circumstances. I show that in two other places Polynesians tried to kill Cook for lesser reasons, but in Hawai'i, when their sacred king was taken hostage by armed marines, Hawai'ians, according to Sahlins, showed no emotions like anger or rage. Instead, a cosmopraxical drama was being waged, and Hawai'ians following a mythopraxical scenario killed Cook. However, *there is not a single documentary source (neither native Hawai'ian nor missionary nor later travelers) that makes even the vaguest reference to Cook's death as a ritual enactment.* Further, I show that Cook's own officers blamed their captain for directly precipitating the crisis (A, 112). Even Sahlins's favorite authority Beaglehole thought rather naively that Cook's precipitate action was due to an "imperceptible blunting of the brain that makes him, under a light searching enough, a perceptibly different man."[37] Finally, Cook's flesh and bones were distributed among the chiefs, but since in *kāli'i* no such thing occurs, it is difficult to imagine it even in Sahlins's convenient "reverse *kāli'i*." In my thinking, this is the weakest part of his argument, but he simply will not budge because that would destroy his vision of how natives think, about Captain Cook, for example.

Sahlins outdoes his European predecessors in attributing to the natives an inflexible mode of thought. Let me rephrase my argument in terms of another cognitive-cum-emotive dilemma. Hawai'ians, I think, possess like most of us—whether we are ethnographers, Sri Lankans, or European bourgeoisie—puzzlements or aporias when confronting contradictions in existential expectations. Let us assume again for argument's sake the truth of mythopraxis and review the aporias involved. The Makahiki circumambulation was on land; Cook circles around the island by sea. In the descriptions of Makahiki there is a crucial circumambulation whereby Lono walks in a clockwise direction with the right side of the god facing the area encircled as his domain. None of this could occur in Cook's going around the island by ship. The lack of fit between the Makahiki predication and Cook's circumnavigation does not apparently bother the Hawai'ians because, according to Sahlins, they do not possess the cognitive or perceptual mechanisms with which Westerners are endowed.

Or, let us say it is perfectly fine for the Hawai'ians to believe that an Englishman who did not speak Hawai'ian or look like one or dress like one could be their god Lono. But was there no puzzlement regarding the empirical lack of fit? Sahlins answer to this in *How "Natives" Think* is too simple: He says that the language of the priests was unintelligible to most Hawai'ians anyway, and therefore Cook's broken Tahitian mixed with gestures and the English he spoke with his colleagues would be mythopraxically treated by Hawai'ians (N, 121). Even if this were true for ordinary Hawai'ians, their priests would surely know that Cook's was not a priestly language. And what about the rest of the crew who also spoke a language unintelligible to Hawai'ians? Were they also priests? And if they were, how did they fit the mythopraxical schedule?

Consider yet another aporia: The god Lono brings prosperity and weal to the Hawai'ians, coming in Makahiki time with his divine crew; yet there is no puzzlement that these divine beings brought the venereal diseases that Hawai'ians were complaining about during the very time of Cook's second visit. To assert that venereal diseases were "evidence of British mana" is too easy; it is not funny either.[38]

Sahlins is especially critical of my treatment of Watman's death. I emphasized the following aporia: Watman, the English ordinary sailor, dies, and the Hawai'ians supposedly take this natural death to be the equivalent of the human sacrifice that should be performed at Makahiki time. There is no puzzlement that none of the rules associated with Hawai'ian human sacrifice were observed here; that instead of their ritual of sacrifice, there was a substitute English funeral, conducted according to very specific English rules, strikingly at variance with anything Hawai'ian. Yet for Sahlins, "Hawai'ians gave Watman's death a significance of their own [corresponding] to the customary offering of a human sacrifice" (N, 76). Not a single extant documentary source of whatever period makes this latter connection or even hints at it. Sahlins adds that there is no real reason why an ordinary seaman would not be used as a sacrificial victim, but this is double-talk because, Sahlins says earlier, for Hawai'ians Watman was not an ordinary seaman but a god. If so, in Sahlins's own terms, why was there no puzzlement that a god was being "sacrificed" when the ritual scenario does not require a divine sacrifice at this juncture?

These aporias must also be applicable to us as we look at these voyages. There were multiple interpretations of this problematic episode among the journalists, but Sahlins accepts King's version that the chiefs wanted to bury Watman at the royal shrine (N, 272). But what about Cook's motivations in allowing his friend to be buried in a heathen shrine? Moreover, consider my own puzzlement in reconciling the chiefs' alleged wishes with King's earlier statement: "Terreoboo [Kalani'opū'] had been very angry at these priests letting us have the ground above the Morai [Hikiau] for our use."[39] Sahlins is not puzzled as I am when his own authority Zimmermann mentions that the Hawai'ians were offended by the burial of Watman in the royal shrine, supporting my hypothesis that Hawai'ians boycotted the impressive ceremony that the British put up. It is not just a question of commoners not being allowed inside the temple, as Sahlins puts it, but that they were nowhere to be seen, not outside the temple nor at some distance. Finally, consider my puzzlement that all of the English journalists except Ledyard barely make reference to this important episode.

Let me deal with another feature of mythopraxis: One form of mythopraxis contradicts another expectable form. In order to maintain that the

Makahiki was going on and that Watman was the sacrificial victim, Sahlins has to drop a critical part of the sacrificial ritual where the eye of the victim is symbolically eaten. The praxis of this part of the mythical scenario is crucial if the sacrifice is to be treated seriously, but this did not and could not occur in the case of Watman's funeral. If indeed Hawai'ians could not work out these simple contradictions between expectation and experience, I would say that their actions are in fact "irrational." But, of course, they were not.

Finally, even Sahlins has to yield on an important issue that I raised in my critique; namely, that in spite of mythopraxis and the importance of the tabu system, Hawai'ians did on occasion violate Makahiki tabus. Here is Sahlins: "Concerning the trade with Hawai'ian canoes, there is good evidence that coming out to sea was ritually prohibited at this time, which is also good evidence that the December Makahiki was on—and that all the same, *with a certain inducement from the British, the Hawai'ians knew how to overcome their ritual scruples*" (N, 38, my italics). This is the crack in the mythopraxical armor because the phrase "overcome their ritual scruples" covers up an important political situation that occurred with the arrival of the British. Either a tabu on going out to sea was not in existence in this mythopraxical ritual time of Makahiki or ordinary Hawai'ians were violating tabu, the key principle of their religious life, and with impunity, in order to trade with the British. Sahlins resolves this problem by quoting the authority of the *Mooolelo Hawai'i* that "because this was Lono, the people decided the tabu could be violated" (N, 40). But if people were violating tabus, how could the integrity of Makahiki be maintained? Sahlins himself admits that women were flagrantly violating the tabu on interdining from the very start (though mostly, I suspect, on board the ships), in which case, it was an inapposite time to hold a Makahiki festival or continue one already started. Valeri makes the point that when the Makahiki is on, the king must suspend warfare; yet, says Valeri, Kalani'opo'ū flouted this important tabu by warring with Maui during this particular Makahiki.[40] This reinforces my hypothesis that the Makahiki was suspended during the period of Cook's visit.

I referred to Valeri's important observation that the great Kamehameha had to postpone the Makahiki when Vancouver arrived because the conditions were not suitable for holding this ceremony. I suggested the conditions were even worse when Cook arrived because ordinary sailors, unaware of the goings-on here, were constantly violating tabus. How could they not? Moreover, during this voyage, Cook himself violated tabus operative in the *'inasi* festival of Tonga (A, 33–34). In my imaginative reconstruction (which Sahlins scorns), I suggested that the major journalists neither mentioned the word "Makahiki," nor were they aware that an important ceremony was going on and that this was so because the Makahiki was suspended since there was no way that the integrity of the ritual could be maintained in the context of the arrival of the British. The nagging question remains: If Kamehameha later suspended the Makahiki because of the impossibility of holding it, how could Kalani'opu'ū have held this very ceremony in an even more difficult set of circumstances? If one were to reject this explanation, then another surfaces: If the British presence provoked the Hawai'ians to violate precious Makahiki tabus in respect to fishing and warfare, then what is to prevent them from violating other tabus also? According to Sahlins, Cook was killed because he came back at the ritually incorrect time, thereby violating an important Hawai'ian tabu. But then, according to Sahlins's own argument based on the authority of *Mooolelo Hawai'i*, the Hawai'ians should not be bothered about their own god violating tabus when they felt they themselves could violate tabus on the authority of that same god. Consequently, mythopraxis could not occur in this context because the Hawai'ians were not acting out their myths in the formal manner propounded by Sahlins. It is unlikely that they would have seen such things as Cook's attempt to take their king hostage during the very end of the British stay as an expression of *kāli'i* because by this time the British had violated a number of tabus. In this context, the Hawai'ian mythic thought that Sahlins has hypothesized must surely have broken down. All of this lends plausibility to my thesis that Cook did arrive at Makahiki time during the second visitation; that he was called Lono because he arrived at that time and this fitted with Hawai'ian conceptions of naming; that because the British were violating tabus from their very first visit, the integrity of Makahiki could not possibly have been maintained; that the rituals of installation helped to bring the British officers (but not ordinary seamen) within the Hawai'ian scheme of things; that the "tabu man" who went wherever Cook did was both to honor Cook and to ensure that important tabus were not violated, which had also been the situation in Tonga (A, 33–34, 89); and that once a British officer, most particularly Cook, was invested as a chief, he must indeed possess sacred powers that chiefs conventionally possessed, even though his powers were not equal to those of Kalani'opu'ū or the priest Omiah; and that Cook's bones were allocated among the chiefs in the conventional manner associated with a dead chief or someone vanquished in battle. If this latter was the case, much of the ethnography that Sahlins marshalls, particularly with respect to Cook's bones, is not at all dissonant with my hypothesis (N, 144–47). In other words, what I have presented is a plausible alternative interpretation of the events, and that is all we can do in the context of highly opaque information. This means that at the very best Sahlins's is also such a plausible interpretation, however much he claims definitiveness.

Mythopraxis and Verification: Foucault, Borges, and the Kalam

Sahlins's strategy is, as I said, to produce evidence from other cultures to validate his thesis—"different cultures, different rationalities"—and the reality of mythopraxis. Yet the unfortunate example he chose is that of "primitive classification" among the Kalam of New Guinea presented in a series of well-known papers by Ralph Bulmer—unfortunate because there are plenty of good accounts of indigenous Hawaiian classifications that exhibit striking resemblances to Western ones.[41]

Briefly stated, the Kalam, like many other peoples, have an elaborate classification of fauna and flora that seemingly flouts our current scientific modes of classification and is more in tune with what Michel Foucault, quoting Jorge Luis Borges, reports for the Chinese and which Sahlins uses to buttress his own argument. In the well-known Foucault-Borges case, there is a "certain Chinese Encyclopaedia," "in which it is written that 'animals are divided into: (a) belonging to the Emperor, (b) embalmed, (c) tame, (d) suckling pigs, (e) sirens, (f) fabulous, (g) stray dogs, (h) included in the present classification, (i) frenzied, (j) innumerable, (k) drawn with a very fine camelhair brush, (l) *et cetera*, (m) having a broken water pitcher, (n) that from a long way off look like flies" (cited in N, 162).

Foucault may be a great social theorist, but he has little understanding of Borges's topsy-turvy world where the fantastic and the real change places, where things are turned inside out, where stories exist within stories and things repeat themselves endlessly—while in the curiously Borges way they also seem unique. The only resemblance that *How "Natives" Think* has to Borges is the story within the story where Foucault takes over Borges's Chinese classification to demonstrate his view of varying epistemes and how they arise in historical contexts and Sahlins uses Foucault using Borges using the Chinese Encyclopaedia to show how different cultures have different rationalities that affect their thinking (mythopraxis), but he does so without examining the historical contexts that determine the formation of an episteme so central to Foucault's thought. Fortunately for Foucault, the Chinese case is not all that critical because he deals with the epistemic birth and continuity of Western social science. But for Sahlins, the Chinese case, like the Kalam classification, is a good example of an empirically grounded non-western mode of rationality. This "dazzling piece of textual interpretation" is, I think, questionable because it is doubtful that there is such a Chinese Encyclopaedia except in Borges's fantastic fictional imagination![42]

The empirical world could, of course, contain examples of the absurd but not as empirical classifications of the world, as Sahlins and Foucault both think. One could, however, find a parody of such a classification, a spoof, a Borges-type world deliberately constructed by a group to turn it upside down as one finds in Hindu stories within stories and so on. In reality, the Chinese possess multiple forms of classification, and these in turn can produce contested arguments and debates about such forms, and the debates in turn help create new forms. So with the Buddhists who are inveterate classifiers of psychomental states; their classifications in turn spur further debate. In other words there is no single thought process that characterizes a culture or the way people think, as the formula "different cultures, different rationalities" makes us believe.

An ethnographer can formulate Kalam classification as an ideal type or a Lévi-Straussian language game, but the belief that such a construction represents Kalam thought is mistaken. First, this case brings up the inevitable question of a generalized native culture. Thus, "the Kalam told him" and "the Kalam said" this or that to Bulmer (N, 161). Did the Kalam produce any conflict of thought and interpretation, let us say between its men and women, between big men and little, between specialists and ordinary folk? Second, does this classification mean that Kalam thinking and olfactory sensibilities are indelibly intertwined, such that while the Kalam have developed olfactory senses that help them to differentiate various kinds of animals, they cannot smell onions as you and I do? For example, Malays, Indonesians, and many Sri Lankans love durians, but for me durians smell like shit; but that does not mean that my durian-loving friends cannot differentiate durians from shit smells or that they and I cannot have similar olfactory reactions with respect to shit or onions or whatever even though we have different olfactory sensitivities regarding durians. Biology may not be destiny, but there is no way one can escape from it either. Third, the fact that the ethnographer has constructed a Kalam classificatory system is no indication that the Kalam have no parallel or opposed systems, or that ordinary people, unlike an occasional obsessive intellectual, cannot be intellectually emancipated or freed from it. And would, let us say, an imaginary native ethnographer from among the Kalam come up with the taxonomic scheme identical to Bulmer's?

The fact that an ethnographer has documented a system of classification does not speak to its ongoing social, political, or psychic significance. For example, I have in my field notes an elaborate classification of snakes, their modes of causing bites, and techniques of curing that are as impressive as the Kalam's, though less inclusive. Yet this classificatory system has meaning mostly to Sinhala physicians, and highly specialized ones at that, and no ordinary person knows or cares about it—until they get bitten by a snake and go to a physician! Yet when I write my field notes, I might, not altogether foolishly, speak of *Sinhala* snake medicine. So with the kinds of Linnean categories that the ships' botanists and zoologists engaged in during Cook's voyages: The fact that they classified fauna and flora "scientifically" did not mean that they could not see natural life in other terms, from an aesthetic perspective, for example. Nor did their categorizations throw a projective screen over everything else, which is what the mythopraxis theory and the formula "different cultures, different rationalities" compels us to conclude. I can therefore say unto the reader that, as reflective human beings, the Kalam, like the Hawai'ians and the British, are my brother and my sister.

Formalism in Mythopraxis: The Ethics of Representation

I have suggested that Sahlins's concept of mythopraxis is a continuation of a doxological belief, reified as theory, that non-western people think "mythically" and that there is a kind of inflexibility to primitive mythic thought. Sahlins blames me for using a notion of "practical rationality" that I borrow from Max Weber and also apparently from those despised British empiricists. But, insofar as mythopraxis itself is a theoretical term and not a Hawai'ian invention, that theory is also an external one imposed on historical material about Hawai'i. As theory, it explains what went on during the fateful few weeks of British presence in Hawai'i. Through this externally imposed theory (which is what theory is about), Sahlins confidently formulates the ways of Hawai'ian thought and their classical rules of thinking. He tells us that while practical rationality is a poor term, not so with mythopraxis, which can lead us to the heart of Hawai'ian lifeways. I think this is a self-delusion. With practical rationality, I don't have this problem: If indeed it is a generic human way of thinking, then there is a case to be made that Hawai'ians and British and Sri Lankans can think in similar ways, even if the theory is a Eurocentric one.

Mythopraxis is extremely formal in character. Thus, virtually every significant event that occurred in Hawai'i is an example of mythopraxis. To mention a few: the anticipation of Cook's arrival; his actual coming; his ship; the goods he brought; his welcome and worship; his entry into the royal shrine; British violation of tabus; thefts by Hawai'ians; the copulation of whites and Hawai'ians; the myth that Cook slept with a female Hawai'ian chief; a volcanic eruption caused by Cook;[43] the use of the fence for firewood; hostility between the king and priests; two houses burning at Hikiau; Watman's death; Cook's death (three forms of mythopraxis); his dismemberment; Cook's various returns; and the fate of his bones. Sahlins's employment of this formal theory expectably converts Hawai'ian thought itself into a formal system. Sahlins himself admits that "the theory is *total* in the Maussian sense";[44] but such a formal and totalistic mythopraxis cannot bring into the picture discordant voices, Hawai'ian humor and propensity to debate, or their predeliction for contentious discourses, which I have focused upon. Finally, it seems to me, in imposing upon Hawai'ians this mode of thought, Sahlins ought to face the ethics of representation.

He avoids asking himself questions such as: Are Hawai'ians given to the rigid practice of their myths without puzzling over them? Can they think pragmatically or commonsensically when dealing with politically significant events?

Let me now demonstrate the ethical and other limitations of such formal thinking through an important example that Sahlins uses in How "Natives" Think; namely, that Hawai'ian cosmological thought with its notion of spirit that pervades every living thing. I refer the reader to the section entitled, "The Multiple Forms of Hawai'ian Gods" (N, 166–77). On the purely formal level, Sahlins's description is not one I would want to dispute; only its place in the "stream of life." The chief Kalaimoku told Ellis that "all animated beings had thoughts and could deliberate and reason" and that even vegetables and coral "had sense and feeling" (N, 166). As Sahlins describes it, all of life is in some profound way interconnected, permeated by "spirit."

Similar conceptions are also found in Buddhist societies, and I have labeled this doctrine "species sentience," the doctrine that all of living existence is bound by common sentience.[45] If sentient existence implies the presence of spirit pervading life, then kings too could have it in greater measure, and this is what I think went into the anthropological construction of Polynesian mana. I doubt that the spiritual power that inheres in kings and chiefs can be glossed as "divinity," though I am open to correction on this issue. As Sahlins phrases it, such thinking has been further complicated by the idea that the spirit that pervades life is the spirit of gods such as Lono and Ku, among others. Thus, the hawk and the dog are particularizations of Ku. But soon we get into trouble in Sahlins's rendering of species sentience. For example; the pig is not only a particularization of Lono, but the pig's own manifestations follow the same logic: "certain grasses and ferns, the kukui tree, young taro leaves, certain varieties of banana, some fishes, and various other things that are the food of pigs, the oiliness of pig fat . . . remind Hawai'ians of pigs by their shape, name, mode of action, habitat," and this in turn must remind them of Lono (N. 172). Hence, Sahlins's conclusion, extrapolated from his view of Hawai'ian cosmological thought: "Relying on our own sense of reality, let alone our neurosensory equipment, we could hardly believe that someone could seriously take a sweet potato, or even an Englishman, as the manifestation of a god" (N, 169) But, says Sahlins, Hawai'ians do.

This representation of Hawai'ian cosmology meets with a jarring disjuncture. In the previous chapter, Sahlins says that for Hawai'ians and Polynesians in general "the gods are transcendent, and *no one has any idea of their nature*" (N, 120, my italics). "They are transcendent, invisible, and originate in places beyond the horizon: Kahiki or what is the same, the heavens. . . . And in his encompassing being, as distinct from worldly manisfestations, Lono is unknown and unknowable" (ibid.). What connects these two contradictory visions of Hawai'ian thought is a "transcendental apriori" that Hawai'ians allegedly possess, an abstract quality that is also manifest in their ancestor worship (N, 171).

Thus, Sahlins practices two kinds of language games as he describes Hawai'ian cosmology: one that says that animated life is bound by common sentience and that gods are concretely manifest in various forms; and a second that has subtly appropriated Hawai'ian cosmology into another form of life, strikingly European, especially reminiscent of the thinker that Sahlins refers to in his text, St. Augustine, in whose Neoplatonic "negative theology" God appears as "transcendental and unknowable." Hawai'ian religion is now converted to a *via negativa* that does not permit God's nature to be apprehended directly. Further, when the god Lono arrived in the person of Cook, the welcome that the Hawai'ians gave him amounted to an "epiphany"; and when he was in the temple, he was "anointed" and "transfigured" (N, 52). The Christological metaphors also resurface, as I show in my book, in the dismemberment of Cook and his subsequent return. I am not against a responsible use of this kind of language; I am against the suggestion that only we empiricists are guilty of fusing the horizon of native thought with the horizon of one's own.

Language use aside, consider the logical implications of the kind of cosmological thinking that Sahlins attributes to the Hawai'ians. What is it to be a "manifestation" of a god, a "realization" of a god, and a "particularization" of a god? They are all the same to Sahlins, who barely distinguishes between these terms. If I were a pious Hindu (which I am not), I might say that the world is a "manifestation" of god, his play, his jouissance or *lila*; Sai Baba or Ramakrishna or Guru Whoever is his "realization" or avatar; and his phallic icon is his "particularization." I know that Hawai'ians are not Hindus, but their formal cosmological representations are internally differentiated and seen in multiple ways in their day-to-day applications.

Now for some levity apropos sweet potatoes and Englishmen. I can sympathize with the Hawai'ian version of species sentience that sees the world as a manifestation of Hawaiian gods. But I doubt that when a Hawai'ian sees a sweet potato he or she would exclaim, "Ah, here is Lono arrived in my garden." Hawai'ians surely differentiate the god Lono of myth, the Lono of the Makahiki, the various other human and nonhuman manifestations of Lono (and of course the manifestations of the manifestations of the god) from the more immediate or more significant ones. There is a big epistemic gap between Lono as sweet potato and Lono as the god who has come in the form of Cook during Makahiki. It is a travesty of Hawai'ian (and other forms of) native knowing to think that because the sweet potato is a manifestation of Lono, Hawai'ians also must feel that Cook is simultaneously a *realization* and *particularization* of Lono and that the sweet potato and Cook are of the same ontological and ontic order. One does not need a Lockean empiricist to tell you this; ordinary citizens living in such societies are empiricist enough to make these discriminations. Further, consider the implications of Sahlins's doctrine of Hawai'ian transcendent and unknowable gods. If Lono is unknowable and unknown in the Augustianian sense, then of course *anyone* can be a manifestation of Lono, not only James Cook but all those other Englishmen in their own ways. I admit Sahlins's is a neat theory: It permits him to say that not only Cook but all those who arrived, including the unwashed from the lower decks, were forms of Lono because for Hawai'ians these beings cannot be empirically differentiated since gods are "unknowable and unknown." This kind of theorizing, if I may reformulate a Hawai'ian proverb, is that of a person "with his head on the ground and his testicles in the air" (N, 169).

Let me by switch back to seriousness in a further ethical critique of Sahlins. I have great respect for the doctrine of "species sentience" and its Hawai'ian, Amerindian, Buddhist, and Hindu forms. For me, it is not just a cosmology out there but one that permits us to cross-examine the Western epistemological divorce of man from nature. In such cosmologies, the distinction between nature and culture, dear to structuralism and European thought in general, is obliterated. Sentient existence is interconnected; implied in such a doctrine is the argument that the wanton destruction of nature is wrong. Thus, when Northwest Coast Indians kill an animal, they put a part of the body back into the water and implore it to return, to be literally reborn to replenish the seas. Yet the fact that animals are kin does not mean that they should not be killed; otherwise, human existence in such societies would be impossible. Natives do recognize the aporia of killing an animal who shares a kinship with you. Though these epistemologies are not without contradiction in their practice, they can teach us a lesson regarding the respect due to nonhuman forms of sentient existence. But while Sahlins can give a formal description of a similar doctrine among the Hawai'ians and appreciate the esthetic elegance of that cosmology, he has contempt for those who would use those cosmologies to interrogate contemporary capitalist culture, as for example when he refers to unnamed scholars who see the "Cree or the Maori or the Kayapo . . . to be paragons of ecological wisdom" (N, 119).

Let me conclude this part of the discussion by trying to draw a final distinction between Sahlins's approach and my own. I do not pretend that I can present the natives' point of view, as Sahlins does confidently through his specific mode of analysis.[46] Further, Sahlins and several other critics have imputed to me the idea that I, as a native Sri Lankan, claim to have privileged access to Hawai'ian culture. I have never once asserted or implied this, though, being a native from a colonized nation, I might have insights into the lifeways of other colonized peoples. On the contrary, in

The Work of Culture I show that the natives' point of view is a fiction, an ethnographic device to present the other culture, an ideal type if you wish. Even when natives write, there can be no natives' point of view because those native voices are multiple and often disparate and cannot be separated from their own thought and the history of colonization and the influence of Enlightenment ideologies on the modern world. Sahlins's and Valeri's "canonical" native thinkers are a figment of the ethnographic imagination; the very imposition of the word "canonical" illustrates the prejudice involved. There is no "native point of view"; yet it is impossible to write an ethnography without such rhetoric as "how Hawai'ians think" or "Sri Lankan thinking" or "according to my informants."[47] This rhetorical strategy can be deadly if reified as reality. Such a reification is exemplified in Valeri's account of Hawai'ian "sacrifice": Valeri has reconstituted early Hawai'ian kingship and sacrifice on the basis of later texts, and he confidently formulates how Hawai'ians think "according to the classical rules," to use Sahlins's phrase (N, 37). I find it utterly presumptuous that ethnographers should tell native peoples how they think or formulate their "classical rules" for them without an iota of skepticism or tentativeness. My guess is that this kind of appropriation and arrogance, which refuses to acknowledge the invented nature of ethnography, has made it a "pariah discipline" in the eyes of native Hawai'ian intellectuals, in spite of ethnographers' enormous contributions to the knowledge of small-scale societies and "subaltern" peoples hitherto debarred from history.

If there is no single native point of view, or if there are multiple forms of thought, belief, and knowing in a single culture, then the important epistemic reorientation that I now want to suggest might make sense. Whether we are using "practical rationality" or mythopraxis or whatever, we are imposing Western epistemological concepts on the other culture. There ought to be ways to disentangle ourselves from this dilemma. For example, why not shift our strategies and test the insights of alternative epistemologies from other cultures on our understandings of Western cultural forms and perhaps the ethnographies we construct? Though difficult to achieve, such a strategy might help question those epistemologies we have inherited from the Enlightenment, perhaps even reversing some of our time-honoured presuppositions or even creating new forms of social theory apposite to a time when cultural and other boundaries have become permeable. For example, I think that the Buddhist notions of the absence of "self," its convention-bound and fluctuating character, or the Buddhist theory of "conditioned genesis," which stipulates that the world is permeated with causality, might be creatively rephrased to problematize Western notions of selfhood and causal understanding. Or, one can attempt what Sahlins dismisses contemptuously, namely, use ideas from the culture of the Cree or the Maori and so forth to interrogate with a sense of ethical responsibility the contemporary ravaging of world ecology. Thus, instead of saying "different cultures, different epistemologies," I would encourage *cross-epistemological thinking*, whereby ethnographers can experimentally use other epistemologies to interrogate European society and its forms of thought. If it is good for us to understand other cultures in terms of Western epistemologies, it might be a salutary move to occasionally reverse our strategies. Neither strategy is ever going to get us the natives' point of view except as an artifice, a fiction, or an ideal type. But there is nothing wrong with that.

Laws of Thought, Inference, and Hawai'ian Mythopraxis

Sahlins spends considerable effort on showing the various logical fallacies that underlie my arguments. Let me deal with my alleged failure to conform to the "laws of thought" through an example critical to my hypothesis of the apotheosis. Apparently, I have a "habitual reliance on the logical fallacy of converting an absence of evidence into the evidence of an absence" (N, 4). This fallacy is elaborated at length as "double-bind question begging." "It consists of two propositions. First, the absence of a European mention that Cook = Lono, means that for Hawai'ians Cook was not Lono. And second, the presence of a Hawai'ian mention of Cook = Lono is an indication of the European myth to that effect" (N, 20). The second can easily be shown to be Sahlins's position not mine, because I repeatedly show that the Hawai'ian mention of Cook = Lono meant exactly that for Hawai'ians, that such naming procedures were very much Hawai'ian, and that there are dozens of Hawaiian chiefs with the appellation Lono in Hawai'ian history. It is Sahlins who infers that Cook was the *god* Lono from Hawai'ians *calling* him Lono. I will admit that I occasionally flout the first part of the logical equation, but while it might be a "logical fallacy" in Sahlins's sense, it is not a fallacy for those of us who, following Ludwig Wittgenstein, believe that such "fallacies" are "language games" that must be seen *in use* as part of "the stream of life." I can make the case that such logical procedures can be sometimes fallacious and sometimes not, depending on the contexts of use and utterance, both of which Sahlins seems to ignore in his own work.

Let me place this so-called logical fallacy in the larger context, beginning with an event on the afternoon of 30 November 1778, when a chief of Hawai'i island along with his warriors coming from northeastern Maui approached the *Discovery* and, according to the master Thomas Edgar, "Ask'd for our Arrona or Chief," Arrona of course being "O Lono" (N, 36). Edgar's naive report shows, according to Sahlins, that "the Hawai'i islanders knew Captain Cook as 'Lono' before they set eyes on him, and that his visit coincided with the (December) Makahiki festival." Edgar had to be naive because he translated "Arrona" as "chief." This event is crucial to Sahlins's interpretation because he refers to Edgar's statement three times in his book.[48] Sahlins's hypothesis of Hawai'ians knowing Captain Cook as Lono refers strictly to the natives of the *island of Hawai'i* eleven months after his first visitation to the island of Kaua'i. Hence the paradox: while Cook was immediately called Lono when he made his *second* visit to Hawai'i island, and, beginning with Edgar, every journalist noted it, *none noted it in his visit to Kaua'i in January 1778 when Cook first came to the Hawai'ian islands, also during Makahiki.* "Two years running," Sahlins says, "Cook had made his advent during the Makahiki . . . in the classic Frazerian mode of the dying god."[49] The absence of any reference to Lono during the first visit, I suggested in a later paper, indicated that Cook was not called Lono during that first visit.[50] Sahlins also admits this in his book *Historical Metaphors* but qualifies it by saying that Cook "was certainly treated as a divine appearance" while Captain Clerke "was a divine being from Kahiki."[51] How is it that Hawai'ians could not figure out that Cook was their god Lono during first contact? In *How "Natives" Think*, Sahlins resolves this dilemma by virtually ignoring this crucial first visit and instead reviewing "the documentary evidence that he was greeted in *Hawai'i island* as a personification of the New Year god Lono" during the second visit (N, 20, my italics). It is to overcome the embarrassingly illogical nature of this argument that Sahlins invokes the laws of thought.

The major journalists constituted a group of people who by Sahlins's own judgment come from a British empiricist tradition. None of them was a trained ethnographer in the modern sense, though Cook has some good descriptions of what he saw, including a splendid account of a human sacrifice in Tahiti just before his arrival in Hawai'i. By Sahlins's own account, King was a good journalist, recording complex genealogies. The whole point of the three voyages of Cook, from the scientific angle, was the classification of fauna and flora and of course human lifeways. Thus, if Cook came at Makahiki time during the first visit and people knew he was their god Lono and he was referred to and addressed by that term, why is it that not one of the ships' journalists recorded this fact? On this first visit also, Cook was accorded prostrations but no one ever said "O Lono." By contrast, when Cook returned for the second time eleven months later, according to Edgar, a chief wanted to know even before they landed who their "Arrona" was. For Sahlins, this is "proof" that Cook was called "Lono" before he arrived in Hawai'i. In my view, the absence of reference to Lono in the first visit indicates that Cook was not called by that that name at that time, and further that name was applied in accordance with Hawai'ian naming procedures during the second visit when Cook did arrive during Makahiki time. Moreover, there is not a trace of evidence in the ships' journals that any kind of festival was going on during this first visit to Kaua'i, but on the logic of mythopraxis Sahlins has to invent one.

My so-called logical fallacy has other embarassments in store for Sahlins that I have already stated in the main text. Briefly, not a single journalist knew that a festival was occurring, *even during the second visit*. Nor does anyone mention the word "Makahiki" even though some journalists, especially Samwell, were especially good with names of person, places, and events (A, 58). This poses no puzzlement or aporia to Sahlins because it can be justified according to his laws of inference, but not according to mine. Hence, I can unabashedly reinstate the conclusion I made in the book, that it is strange that while the ships' journalists knew that Cook was called Lono during the second visit and that "Lono" meant "chief," they could not, in spite of constant probing, make the inference that this Lono was a Hawai'ian god returning at Makahiki according to prophecy. As a matter of fact, I wonder how Sahlins can make that inference because he says elsewhere that "by all evidence, it appears that an explicit myth of the annual return of Lono from Kahiki . . . developed in the latter eighteenth to early nineteenth century."[52] That statement was very likely a later rationalization of Cook's visit, but these puzzles hardly trouble him.

A second example of my flouting the laws of logic: "It is the elementary rule of logical argument that the truth or falsity of an idea pertains to its intellectual substance, not to the character or disposition of its proponent" (N, 42). I have similar criticisms for Sahlins regarding this convention of logic. First, Sahlins flouts his dictum in respect to my book when he analyzes my dispositions and character and relates it to the substance of my argument (N, 193). More important, Sahlins does not provide a rule whereby one can take a text and decide what in it is true or false. This is particularly so with the mission texts, which contain statements that are patently pejorative and Eurocentrically mythological. I think there are cases where the character and disposition of the person are relevant for understanding a complex text, such as an obvious case like Judge Schreber's or a not-so-obvious case like Max Weber's or a recent and more subtle analysis where Ray Monk shows that some of Wittgenstein's later ideas on psychology and aesthetics were influenced by his mysticism and highly individualistic Christian faith.[53] But here's the rub: I did not analyze the "character and disposition" of Evangelicals such as Dibble and Hiram Bingham but pointed out their "prejudices" or prejudgments and the prejudices of their native students, which is a very different thing.

Contrary to Sahlins's assertion, there is a strong tradition from Weber to contemporary hermeneutics that deals with the impact of our values, prejudices, and prejudgments on our scholarly work, with Weber arguing for the recognition of our prejudgments and then using our methodologies to control them. Gadamer makes the case that prejudices are not necessarily bad, that they result in the fusion of the horizon of the text with the author's historical and cultural situation. Thus, for example, we know that every production of *Hamlet* has been affected by the times in which it was produced. In ethnography, it is the foolhardy person who does not believe that our discipline itself originated in the background of a colonialist enterprise. There is no text that is not tied to a historical context, and if Sahlins has a technique for disaggregating the truth and falsity of texts from the prejudices of the time and the historical situation of text writers, he should let the world of scholarship know that instead of simply affirming a spurious logical principle that few believe in nowadays.

There are further complications with Sahlins's logic. He has a peculiar propensity to take the works of past writers—missionaries, native intellectuals, navigators—as true, whereas he dismisses the thought of contemporary native Hawai'ian intellectuals who question not only his work but, unhappily, the validity of the discipline of ethnography itself, owing to their anger at the way Hawai'ian ethnography has been written. The writers of the past are silent witnesses who cannot be interrogated easily. The voices of contemporary Hawai'ian intellectuals will not go away. Sahlins is comfortable with a historical ethnography that does not engage in a debate with him. He does not give equal consideration to those native Hawai'ian intellectuals who make the texts talk back to him in a discordant language.[54] It is this unease of Sahlins that I shall now deal with, using some of his own language to characterize his thinking.

Two Forms of Practical Rationality

Sahlins's unease with my book is manifest in various ways. Initially, let me deal with the manner in which he represents my idea of "practical rationality" in *How "Natives" Think* in order to demonstrate that there are two versions of it, his and mine. I used that term in the first place to counter the idea that savage thought is cosmologically or mythopraxically bound or that native thought is overdetermined by their sign systems (while none of this applies to Europe). However much Sahlins wants to deny this, I think it is the case that social thought has implicitly incorporated some of these visions of the native into the very structure of the human sciences. Anyone familiar with my work knows my indebtedness to Freud, even though I blame him for his nineteenth-century prejudice equating savage thought with that of children. As for Lévi-Strauss, let me quote what Sahlins thinks I say about him: "Obeyesekere pretends that Lévi-Strauss's 'science of the concrete' is of the same character as Lévy-Bruhl's 'prelogical mentality.' He writes: 'Even those who explicitly try to counter the idea of the savage mind end up, as Lévi-Strauss does, with categorical distinctions not too far removed from the older models'" (N, 152). The reader who had not read my text closely would naturally think that this statement of mine refers to Lévi-Strauss's "science of the concrete"; but in fact it refers to his categorical distinctions between "hot" and "cold" societies, which is strictly parallel with similar distinctions made by others, including Todorov, Freud, and Lévy-Bruhl, that is in effect a distinction between ways of thinking between the West and the rest (A, 15). Does Sahlins want to deny that Lévi-Strauss made these distinctions? The trouble with "science of the concrete" is just what it says: characterizing non-Western thought as "bricolage" brings it down to the level of creativity of the European artisan. This is not to disparage Lévi-Strauss's contribution to the science of the concrete but to show its limitations and, if I may now add, his refusal to consider "savages" capable of possessing or learning, let us say, a "science of the abstract." To be liberated from these doxa is not to reject the thought of social theorists in their entirety but rather to move social theory away from some of the vitiating assumptions that underlie it, or, as I put it, to reject this "human scientist's myth of the Other" (A, 16). To expose these assumptions is in principle no different a task than exposing similar methodological ones, though I do think that the idea of the cosmologically bound savage additionally entails serious ethical and epistemological implications that I have already discussed. Sahlins is not entirely scrupulous in politicizing this critique as a rejection by a naive non-Western intellectual of Western thought in general, with the exception of British empiricism, which of course he despises.

My notion of "practical rationality" had therefore a practical purpose; to blur the distinction between civilized and savage, the West and its Other, to counter the assumption that non-Western peoples are "dividuals" and that they are, regardless of context, incapable of improvisation, mythopractically tied as they are to signs. For me, practical rationality helps us create a space "if one is to talk of the other culture in human terms" and, in the case of Polynesians, seeing them "like me in some sense" (A, 21). I still unrepentently hold it as essential for my conception of ethnography as a *human* science. I admit that I borrow the term "practical rationality" from Weber but explicitly state that I want to divest it of is "utilitarian aura" emphasizing reflective thinking—that is, "the ability to make reasoned judgments" or "weighing of the issues involved in any problematic situation" which in turn entails "argument, debate, and contentious discourse resulting in a formation of judgments whether consensually validated or not" (A, 20, 21). It seems to me that Sahlins turns this to his advantage by insisting that practical rationality is coterminous with "utility" (N, 8–9).

The central feature of my definition of practical rationality is that it pertains to a "mode of thinking" and not to a "mode of thought" or belief. That is, reflexive thought processes and the weighing of anticipated consequences can exist in virtually any realm of belief, though it most obviously obtains in the field of utility. I make a point to emphasize that this propensity, though based on common neurobiological and cognitive processes, is not culturally uniform. Thus, one must be emancipated from two erroneous assumptions; namely, that common biology must necessarily produce common culture and the reverse mythopraxical assumption that culture is so supreme that it overrides common perceptual and cognitive mechanisms completely (A, 20–22). In other words, practical rationality provides spaces for considering both cultural commonalities and differences. I might, however, agree with Sahlins and other critics that "practical rationality" might not be the best term for describing what I want to say. But, to use my favorite Buddhist metaphor, methodologies are a "raft for crossing the river but not for getting a hold of"—that is, one should not be attached to them.[55] What is important are the ideas that underlie the concept, and here Sahlins deliberately misrepresents me.

He says that a universal practical rationality means that "all 'natives' are alike"; thus, "they one and all enjoy a healthy, pragmatic, flexible, rational and instrumental relation to the empirical realities" or even "know things as they truly are" (N, 5). "Indeed, it is a physiological capacity of the species. . . . It follows that on the basis of a common humanity and a shared sense of reality, Obeyesekere has the possibility of immediately understanding Hawai'ians, without regard for any cultural peculiarities or presuppositions" (N, 5–6). Again, I am supposed to have said that "Hawai'ians alone have systematically practiced a universal rationality—that had nothing to do with their own particular system of the universe" (N, 119). Contrary to acknowledging that my notion of practical rationality is derived from Weber and justified in terms of our contemporary knowledge of neurophysiology, Sahlins goes on to push the idea that it is based on British empiricism and Lockean-type sensationalism. "Hawai'ians are the expert practioners of Western intellectual virtues, such as the ability to accurately negotiate the dualism of received belief and objective reality" (ibid.). Not satisfied with this, he has me transcend Lockean epistemology in attributing to Hawai'ians the "highest Western bourgeois values," which are once again a product of a "pan-human practical rationality . . . *independent of any specific cultural or historical knowledge*" (N, 150, Sahlins's italics). His is not only a theoretical misrepresentation, but it can be easily disproved in the body of my text.

Though my book is not about Polynesia but about Europe, Polynesian societies do intersect with Cook's travels and Hawai'i is especially significant in this regard. I do not subsume Hawai'ian culture into a common human one. (Sahlins surely ought to know that no ethnographer believes nowadays in any such thing.) The critical installation ceremony that I deal with is peculiarly Hawai'ian, but I do emphasize that it expresses a

Hawai'ian capacity for creative improvisation that other native peoples also possess—so are Hawai'ian notions of mana and tabu. I think, as Sahlins does, that some of these cultural ideas are broadly Polynesian but that others, such as the deification of dead ancestors, are much more widespread in the cross-cultural record, and in that sense Hawai'ian culture intersects with many others, including Sri Lankan. I make a distinction between different kinds of Hawai'ian rhetorical strategies, some closer to pragmatic thinking than others. Thus, I show that during first contact in Kaua'i the chief Ka'eokulani asked perfectly commonsensical questions of the ships' officers regarding English "customs and manners"; but Kamakau's priestly informants, at least seventy years later, represented that same chief's voice in the dense, metaphoric, and allusive language of priestly discourse, leading me to propose a distinction between two types of discursive traditions in Hawai'i, that of counselors and that of priests (A, 171). If my book was an account of Hawai'ian culture rather than the way Europe intersected with it, I should have approached my account of it in quite a different way.

Practical rationality has a role akin to that of the "unconscious" in my previous book, *The Work of Culture*. The fact that, according to my thinking, unconscious thought processes are universal does not mean that the unconscious is structured in an identical manner cross-culturally or that the cultural forms embodying such processes are necessarily universal. For example, I show that while the word "guilt" does not appear in the Sinhala lexicon, that emotion is nevertheless recognizable among Sinhala-Buddhists; the cultural forms that embody that emotion are quite different in the two religions, Buddhism and Christianity.[56] Once again, the existence of a common emotion does not necessarily indicate the existence of a common culture, though on occasion "family resemblances" within and across cultures may be identified. As for "healthy, pragmatic" natives who "know things as they really ares," that is hardly the position of a Freudian who has written extensively subverting those very notions!

For Sahlins, any notion of a universal human nature or common cultural or social processes are anathema, even though he himself in his Marxist phase did subscribe to similar ideas; and, strangely enough, his present hero Lévi-Strauss bases his science of the concrete explicitly on an assumption of a common neurobiological capacity among all human beings. This assumption does not lead Lévi-Strauss to formulate a universalized human being, nor does it provide him with ready access to another culture. For Sahlins, an assumption of a common human nature is "anti-anthropology," thereby excluding the many cognitive and psychoanalytic ethnographers and the many physical and medical anthropologists who have been influenced by both culture and biology (N, 151). Unhappily, all of these have been banished from anthropology by Sahlins, thanks to Obeyesekere's book.

Nevertheless, Sahlins does address an important section of the discipline that has developed the ideal of cultural and ethical relativism as the charter myth for a special kind of ethnography that plays on difference and the uniqueness of cultures and is hostile to any form of "essentialism." In *The Work of Culture* I deal extensively with the problem of reconciling the necessary assumption of a common human nature with the need to recognize both difference and similarity. This, I suggest, calls for rejecting the older positivism and the now fashionable relativism by reformulating ethnography in terms of the Wittgensteinian idea of "family resemblance" in "forms of life" within and across cultures.[57] This, needless to say, is not the only solution to this troubling issue, but it is one I particularly use to criticize the tradition of cultural relativism in ethnography. I want to add that many relativists influenced by postmodern thought are not Sahlins-type relativists at all. They eschew his doctrine of "different cultures, different rationalities" and instead see multiple and varying forms of thought within a single culture.

Nevertheless, the ethnographic tradition of relativism poses an enormous paradox. There is virtually no one, from Franz Boas onward, who really believes that natives are biologically different from Europeans. But this universalist assumption cannot be brought directly into our writing nowadays because it essentializes human beings, and "essentialism" is a dirty word. Instead, we have moved in the reverse direction and have celebrated *difference*; thus, each culture is different, and we have proclaimed a doctrine of cultural relativism to rationalize that difference. If the older positivists thought that one could erect *universal* institutions on the basis of a universal human nature, we have made a case for cultural *particularism* on the same basis. Thus, reversing the positivist position, we think common human nature produces different cultures. Some also assume that while cross-cultural differences exist, intracultural differences are miniscule; this is especially thought true of isolated, small-scale societies and "islands of history." This kind of assumption has led anthropologists to formulate uniform modes of thought or belief ("the classical rules") of small-scale societies, instead of positing multiple rationalities, even contradictory ones, within each culture. Further, given our common neurobiological nature, the possibility exists that different cultures might also share similarities, both substantive and structural—a viewpoint developed at length in *The Work of Culture*.[58]

Cultural relativism is, I think, the charter myth of American cultural anthropology, a naive credo even if idealistically motivated. It is not surprising, therefore, that ethnographers often forget that cultural relativism has had a long run in European thought. For present purposes, let me refer to Michel de Montaigne's humanist expression of that propensity in his paper "On Cannibalism," written around 1580. Cannibalism is the other side of the myth model of the apotheosis: The savage as cannibal and the European as a god to savages are two sides of the coin, and both are related to "civilization, imperialism and conquest." Both "prejudices" are neatly and ironically juxtaposed by Shakespeare in *The Tempest* in the relation between Caliban (the word itself comes from "cannibal") and the drunken European sailors (whom Caliban mistakes for gods). The cannibal myth in turn is probably a refraction of another powerful myth model, one which has its genesis in the European medieval notions of the wild man that began to be foisted on the savage and the native during and after the voyages of discovery. "Cannibalism" is the savage propensity, often innate, to eat human flesh as Westerners do meat, and it often culminates in "cannibal feasts." Like the myth of the apotheosis, this myth model is often confused with the existence of forms of anthropophagy, including sacrificial consubstantiality, that are found in the cross cultural record. I am suggesting that *both* cultural relativism and the myth model of cannibalism reflect an European attitude to the Other in terms of difference, the one by humanistically motivated thinkers, the other a pernicious popular attitude reflected in a multitude of persons and texts. These two trends can sometimes effect an unholy alliance. For example, in the interests of difference and relativism, ethnographers have literalized cannibal narratives such as sailors' yarns that have not been critically examined.[59]

The doctrine of cultural relativism isolates the other as a species and enhances our predilections toward exoticizing other cultures. This does not mean that an ethnographer should not document practices that are different from his or hers. That is the ethnographer's duty; but he or she should make them intelligible in terms of mechanisms that are common to all human beings; or see their refractions in Western cultures, or see forms of life elsewhere that show family resemblances to them. The hermeneutical principle of making the familiar strange and the strange familiar would be another way of dealing with this issue. It is no paradox, I think, to make the claim that cultural differences can coexist with family resemblances and structural similarities. It is cultural relativism that inhibits this recognition.

Looking at European culture from this perspective is, I think, a salutary move because it helps to blur the distinctions between the West and the rest that has bedeviled the human sciences. In my thinking, by no means original, Westerners are also mythmakers. I can now add another strand to my earlier argument regarding Enlightenment rationality. Such a self-conception is also a myth, and Cook represents the mythic ideal of Enlightenment rationality, which was powerfully entrenched in eighteenth century culture and was invoked to give scientific legitimacy to the voyages of discovery. This book shows the dark side of these voyages by depicting

Cook as a Kurtz-type character and by emphasizing the imperialist agenda that underlies that idealized self-conception. This is not to deny the Prospero persona in Cook and the value of the scientific rationality of the period. To do full justice to these latter themes, one has to deal with all three voyages as a totality, and admittedly this is missing here.

I can only refer the reader to *The Work of Culture*, which deals with the cross-cultural theory of myth formation at length. Briefly stated, I argue there that while humans everywhere, by virtue of their psychoneurological constitution, have the identical potential to create symbolic forms (of which "myth" is but one expression), the actual use of that potential in existent cultures is highly variable, with Indians and other South Asians given to extreme symbolic elaboration and demystified cultures like European ones given to much less elaborate work of symbolic creation. I did, however, qualify this somewhat here: If one does not define myth too narrowly, then myths, and particularly myth models, are much more widespread in European cultures than I had previously acknowledged (A, 10). But that is not how Sahlins represents my position. He says that I think that "Westerners presumably have been incapable of freeing themselves from the myths of their own superiority," forcing upon me a view of the generalized Westerner. I do say, however, that Europeans have their myths of the Other, and they cannot easily free themselves from them, whether the myth of the apotheosis or that of prelogical mentality. To be subject to the doxological assumptions of one's culture does not imply that people, Europeans or others, are incapable of freeing themselves from pernicious myths. Indeed, I had hoped the writing of this book would assist in that liberation. And it is rather odd to attribute to me the idea that "Western scholars slavishly repeat the irrational beliefs of their ancestors" (N, 9). I do not see how Sahlins can hope to gain a "high moral ground" by misrepresenting my position any more than he could by dismissing my own serious interpretations (however troubling they may be to him), owing to his own, equally reasonable, attitude to recent orientalist and postcolonial criticism.

Yet on reflection, I now find Sahlins's work disconcerting in this regard. Sahlins is the only modern scholar I know who, without a trace of irony, uses the demeaning and anachronistic colonialist label "Sandwich Islands," as in his *Historical Metaphors*, to designate the Hawai'ian islands and the loudly touted voices of its natives. And the title of his newest book is no better: It aligns him to the thought of Lévy-Bruhl and others who wrote on that very subject. I think that his refusal to allow natives the capacity to think reflectively, to assess events in terms of practical criteria, is part of that larger doxological thought that underlies his writing.

Let me add that I am quite happy to attribute to the native the capacity to negotiate between received belief and the reality of actual experience, and it is simply wrong to assume with Sahlins that this is a Western intellectual virtue (N, 119).[60] Retranslating this idea in terms of Weber's thought, one might even say that disjunctions between expectation and experience pose "problems of meaning" that people have to resolve, whether they are natives or Other. My emphasis on the disjuncture between expectation and experience cannot be equated with the Lockean philosophical belief that what we know we experience through our senses and that truth is our sensory capacity to effect a correspondence with the external world. Part of the political problem that ethnographers face nowadays relates to their denying native peoples such capacities as I have highlighted in this book. For Sahlins, practical rationality is the European bourgeois virtue I have foisted on natives who do not possess such a capacity; for me, it is liberating to believe that both natives and Europeans are capable of thinking in similar terms even if the substance of their thought is different.

Exegesis of a Refrain: "It Is a Scandal"

Sahlins's book is without any give: as he relentlessly reaffirms the theory and practice of mythopraxis, he cannot see an iota of worth in my book. While I have referred to him as one of the most creative minds in our discipline, he cannot see anything but error in me. This uncompromising dogmatism and inflexibility is easily demonstrable in the language of revenge and the denigration of the Other, which Kerry Howe has neatly spotlighted in a recent review. To quote Howe:

> Obeyesekere's work is variously described (to give but a small alphabetical sample) as: absurd, anti-anthropological, blundering, blustering, careless, contradictory, defective, distorted, dubious, evasive, epistemic murk, falsely accusative, fictitious, highly righteous, helterskelter, implausible, misrepresentational, pidgin-anthropology, quixotic, scattershot, slanderous, scholier-than-thou, sophistically fallacious, stratified palimpsest of confusion and contradiction, symbolically violent, unaware, unhistorical, ventriloquism, willy-nilly, wrong. Then there are the dreaded (and I hope not obscene) acts of *petitio principii, suggestio falsi, suppressio veri*, and *ignoratio elenchi*.[61]

Howe has missed some choice terms, such as Sahlins's references to Obeyesekere's "kooky congeries of images," "Obeyesekere's yarn," his "spurious anthropological clichés," "pop psychology," "pop nativism," his "intellectual chutzpah," and many more. Textual violence becomes even more apparent once you see whole sentences, such as this typical piece: "For all the blustering and blundering character of Obeyesekere's work, together with the evasions and distortions of the texts, it is hard to credit oneself the self-congratulatory assertion that at least his interpretations reflect a proper respect for the evidence" (N, 192–193). The reader might also remember the University of Chicago Press blurb, withdrawn after my protests, that states that I am guilty of "wholesale fabrications of Hawai'ian ethnography." Because such language use is not necessary in conducting an argument, one must seek Sahlins's motivation elsewhere. I think that these demeaning references have their parallels in his labeling of Hawai'i as the Sandwich Islands; his contempt of those who would use epistemologies from other cultures; and his astonishingly pejorative reference to his own colleagues in Pacific history and ethnography who have had the temerity to review my book favorably. "It is rather a scandal how many reviewers have been gulled into praising Obeyesekere's scholarship" (N, 118). Much of my argument is dependant on Te Rangi Hiroa, also known by his Anglo name as Peter Buck. In Sahlins's *Islands of History*, this Maori scholar is generously referred to by his Polynesian name; because I have used his ideas, Sahlins now demotes him by using his other name, consistently referring to him as "Sir Peter," a not-so-subtle dig at Te Rangi Hiroa's colonialist credentials.[62] It is perhaps in reference to the "violence in the text" that Howe says that Sahlins acts very much like Cook with his "stampings in the Deck in the paroxysms of passion . . . tipping a heiva."[63] I think Sahlins's verbal violence against me is in the style of his previous intolerance with those who disagree with him.

To show this aspect of Sahlins's work, let me refer to his role in a controversy in the *New York Review of Books* of March 1979, with William Arens who tried to "deconstruct" the anthropological category of "cannibalism" and depict it as a "man eating myth" both among natives and anthropologists. "It is a scandal," Sahlins said, that a major university press was going to publish Arens's book, because the truth of cannibalism is based on "unimpeachable evidence" and to deny it is tantamount to denying the Holocaust, imputing to Arens a dark insensitivity bordering on anti-Semitism.[64] With this kind of authoritarian imposition ("stonewalling") by a major thinker, it is no wonder that the deconstructive analysis of "cannibalism" was stalled till very recently.[65] This, I think, is a scandal!

The same political and ethical insensitivity is reflected in his references to me everywhere in his text and especially so in his discussion of the death of my friend Wijedasa and the deadly political violence in my native country. Most readers saw the point of my story correctly; namely, that the violence that Cook initiated pales into insignificance in relation to the violent times we now live in. The personal loss of Wijedasa illustrates a human tragedy that could strike anyone anywhere, whenever political violence is unleashed, whether it is Cook's Polynesia or Sri Lanka or in the

West Bank or in New York City. And yet how does Sahlins see this? "I could not even guess at the deeper motivation for making Cook and me somehow responsible for the tragedy of Obeyesekere's friend. It seems an odd way to end the violence by thus wildly displacing it" (N, 193). If this is his understanding of violence, the psychodynamics of motivation, and of human tragedy, it is no wonder that neither motivational understanding nor the understanding of violence nor the tragic politics of confrontation between an emergent imperialist power and a complex culture with Stone Age technologies ever appear in his work except as "mythopolitics" or as the "politics of the Makahiki," forms of mythopraxis (N, 70, 79, 81).

It is not difficult to see the strongly authoritarian nature of the writing in *How "Natives" Think*. Virtually every page is about me, and the narcissistic hurt felt by Sahlins begins in the very first sentence, where he says, "Gananath Obeyesekere . . . attacked me and Captain Cook as agents (in our different ways) of Western violence and imperialism" (N, ix). Then there is his overwhelming preoccupation with Hawai'ian history and culture rather than "European mythmaking in the Pacific," the theme of my book. For example, there is not a single reference to Cook's violent behavior in Tahiti or in Eimeo or in Hawai'i. On the European side, there is not one reference to the crucial enactment of *Omai*, which clearly illustrated that the mythmaking process was going on in London in the very year the official journals were published. Sahlins's authoritarianism appears in his language use, which rarely has any equivocation, doubt, or qualification. The answers are clear, and he is right all the time. Yet his close colleague, fellow Polynesianist Valerio Valeri, says that "probably, there was nothing preordained about Cook's identity" and that the "performance of rituals [at Hikiau] was an attempt to orient and fix this identity in a direction favorable to the Hawai'ians."[66] Valeri provides a plausible alternative interpretation of why the Hawai'ians gave Cook the appelation Lono: "Indeed, it is possible that the populace's identification of the unexpected visitor, Cook, with *a Lono type of divine chief* was also a veiled form of protest against Kalani'opu'ū's (and Kahekeli's—the king of Maui) disastrous war."[67] Valeri, in effect, totally destroys his colleague's central thesis. John Charlot, the meticulous scholar whom Sahlins (rightly) praises, doubts whether living chiefs were seen as gods or *akua* in Kalani'opu'ū's period.[68]

Appendix-citis

Sahlins appends no less than seventeen appendixes to his book, and the disease of citing so many appendixes is infectious. I must confess that I have contracted it myself. However, in order to spare the reader the boredom of reading seventeen separate appendixes, I will put them all in one section, using the opportunity to respond to some specific criticisms of my work.

DID THE BRITISH COME FROM HEAVEN (KAHIKI)?

For Sahlins, the British were from Kahiki, "invisible and celestial realms beyond the horizon."[69] Cook and his accompanying divinities could not come from any other place. Yet we know that British navigators had to inform native peoples about their nation, their venture, and their sovereign, and not one Polynesian group found it difficult to grasp these ideas—except, of course, Sahlins's Hawai'ians, who could not make this out because of their mythopraxical orientations. Yet how can he reconcile the chief of Kaua'i who, just like other Polynesian peoples, asked the British about their manners and customs, king and god during their very first contact in January 1778, according to King? During the fateful return visit, in Sahlins's own account, the Hawai'ians thought that the British were going to settle down in their land—strange fear for a mythopraxical people to have about their returning god and his divine attendants (N, 140).

Sahlins's thesis of Kahiki (Tahiti), the land beyond the horizon from which Cook came, has recently been given a severe blow by Ben Finney and his colleagues at the University of Hawai'i who have shown, in a serious navigational experiment, that Hawai'ians might well have had continuing contacts with other Polynesian islands. The work of Finney and his collaborators demystifies the ethnographic exoticization of Polynesian peoples and shows Hawai'ians in particular as experienced navigators using traditional techniques and know-how to navigate the surrounding islands with considerable "practical rationality" (even though this term is mine, not Finney's).[70] Finney et al. make the point that Kahiki can in fact be a real place for Hawai'ians;[71] which gives substance to Malo's restatement of old legends describing the back and forth movements from Tahiti to Hawai'i.[72] All this casts further suspicion on Sahlins's thesis of the god Cook coming from heavenly Kahiki bringing a cargo of goods during Makahiki; or that Hawai'ians were incapable of figuring out from the information supplied by the British that the new arrivals were from a land known as "Britanee." What is worse is that Sahlins's Hawai'ians, even after thoroughgoing contact with European navigators and employment in ships that sailed as far as New Zealand, the Philippines, Australia, and even China, still continued to think of Britain as Kahiki or heaven and Cook as a god and continued to venerate his relics. It is this imputation to Hawai'ians and others of a lack of discrimination and reflective thought and the inability to strategically weigh options and alternatives that I have tried to meet with my imperfect term "practical rationality."

ON DE-SAHLINIZATION

HAWAI'IAN POLITICS: KALANI'OPU'Ū AND COOK

I had suggested in an admitedly imaginative reconstruction that Kalani'opu'ū might have sought Cook's help in his war with Maui. I had pointed out that this happened everywhere Cook went. On the way home, after Cook's death, Maui chiefs sought Captain Clerke's assistance in their local wars. The next official British visit occurred with Vancouver, from whom Kamehameha, the reigning king, sought aid. Because Kalani'opu'ū was engaged in a difficult war with Maui, I suggested that it was unlikely he was an exception to the general rule and that much of what transpired at that time would make sense in terms of this hypothesis. Sahlins says there is a serious contradiction here because if Kalani'opu'ū was Cook's ally, why should he want Cook to leave at the beginning of February? (N, 139) While I said that Kalani'opu'ū might have sought Cook's help, I also said that Cook would have refused it, as generally he did. And, moreover, there could be a multitude of other reasons for the Hawai'ians to want Cook to leave. I suggested that the main reason for the Hawai'ians' relief at the British departure was, among other things, related to their problems with food, which brings me to my next topic.

INVENTION OF A HAWAI'IAN FOOD SURPLUS

Sahlins accuses me of the "invention of Hawai'ian food scarcity" because I pointed out that, according to King, the Hawai'ians thought that the British had come from a land where food was scarce, and now that they had their fill, they were glad to see them go because "to feed the British for an extended period of time meant starving themselves" (A, 88, see also 63). Sahlins comes in with a brilliant thesis that the Kona area was richly irrigated and cultivated with "breadfruit, taro, sugar cane, bananas, sweet potato, and paper mulberry" and that therefore there was no problem of food scarcity (N, 141).

The logic of Sahlins's analysis leaves me unrepentant. It requires considerable "intellectual chutzpah" to "gull" Pacific historians and ethnographers with this thesis of plenty. In the first place, simply saying that an area is fertile and had plenty of food is inadequate because even in modern agriculture a drought or some such disaster could reduce the food supply. Therefore, the Hawai'ian "voices" expressed through King in 1778–1779 cannot be ignored, unless of course Sahlins can show through his favorite computer-simulation techniques that there were excellent weather conditions that year. Second, if the land was held by chiefs and if Malo is correct that "all they [ordinary folk] produced from the soil belonged to the chiefs," then commoners probably obtained only a small portion of the surplus. Therefore, the siphoning of the food to the ships would indeed cause a "dent" in the supply available to the ordinary person.[73] Third, agricultural surplus is not the only issue: While the British consumed a lot of agricultural produce, it was pork that was truly desirable for protein-starved deities. Additionally, the ships were packed with salted pork during the first visit in order to face the winter in the Arctic during the hopeless search for a Northwest Passage. It is Sahlins who says that all of this had no effect on the food supply. Midshipman Gilbert, his source, says that breadfruit, taro, and other foods—especially sugar cane—were "all in greater plenty than we had ever met before," a relativist statement that tells us neither about pork nor the effect on ordinary people of this seemingly endless supply of food that chiefs and priests ordered for the British (N, 143). Fourth, Sahlins misses the significance of key information that he himself supplies from midshipman Gilbert and Lieutenant Burney; namely, Hawai'ian fears that the British were going to settle down on their island (N, 139–140). These fears were expressed forcibly when the British returned as a result of the damage to their foremast, but it is hard to believe that the chiefs were not aware of it a few days earlier when King made his observation about Hawai'ian food anxiety. Thus the fears of colonization not only had a political meaning for chiefs (which Sahlins ignores), but it also had an economic one. Fifth, Sahlins's own canonical authority, Kamakau, mentions two famines in this same region of surplus. A few months after Cook's ships left Hawai'i "trouble came in the form of a famine in Kona" when Kalani'opu'ū was eighty[74]. His successor Kamehameha later caused considerable disruption in movements of labor when he ordered people to cut sandalwood, so that there was another famine in Kona and "people were forced to eat herbs and tree ferns."[75] David Malo has two lists of undesirable foods and ways of processing them "in a time of famine."[76] Hawai'ian islanders were familiar with the consequences of disruptions in their socioeconomic lives, even though many lived in proximity to an agriculturally rich area. Hence, my new arguments can further support my earlier statement: "People who, under the threat of constant warfare, were aware of the reality of food shortage must surely have been concerned over the demands made by chiefs to provide as many provisions as possible for the foreigners" (A, 88).

"WOMEN'S JOY": WHEN VILLAGES BURN?

Sahlins's diagrees with my critique of his hypothesis that Hawai'ian women on board the ships enjoyed the sight of their villages being burned and their kinfolk killed. This is again to bring Western common sense into the picture. I show that in Samwell's account only one woman said "matai" (good) which as a form of expression could mean almost anything. Sahlins disputes this with two counterarguments. First, he maintains that King's account in the official edition is correct regarding what he calls "women's joy" seeing their village burn, but he does not tell us why King did not mention this important event in the unofficial edition of his text, from which presumably he derived his information for the official one. It does not seem illogical for me to make the inference that because Douglas and King, as the official editors, were given all the ships' documents and were expected to use them, they simply took the account from Samwell and gave it their own slant. Indeed, Beaglehole says that King used Samwell's work almost exclusively for his account of the return home following Cook's death.[77] If Sahlins does not like my commensensical interpretation that the delight of these women seems utterly unlikely, what alternative motivational explanation can he give? Second, for Sahlins, the fact that women continued to have sexual intercourse with European sailors despite ongoing hostilities is proof that these same women would enjoy the death of their relatives and the burning of their houses. Surely, Sahlins cannot be that blind: Some women who had already established liaisons with the sailors simply continued to do so. Malo says that "prostitution" was also well recognized in Hawai'i; if one qualifies that unfortunate term to mean that Hawai'ian women enjoyed sex that some could combine with business, then visits to ships were expectable.[78] Sahlins refers to another source, "Anonymous of Mitchell [Library] to Mrs. Strachen," who mentions women on board the ship the day Cook was killed: "They seemed to be little affected by anything they had seen and yet it is possible but that many of them must have lost their Relations" (N, 245). It is only Anonymous who mentions that the "ships were at this time *full of women*" (ibid., my italics), whereas the more reliable Samwell, writing about that same day, says that "notwithstanding we were at open war with these people we had *a few girls on both Ships* all this day."[79] Even if Anonymous's account is true, it only means there were classes of women who continued to have liaisons with the sailors, presumably for a variety of motives. But the crux of the issue is this: How can Sahlins possibly establish a *qualitative* connection between the two acts? What pleasure or profit could women possibly have had in seeing their houses and the royal temple itself going up in flames?[80]

Anonymous's statement, however, does tell us how the British read signs of Hawai'ian emotions. Why so? The British were certainly capable of identifying Hawai'ian expressive reactions such as rage, bawdy humor, and "insolence" that resonated with their own but were grossly incapable of understanding those that did not. Thus, Cook constantly reiterated that even when chiefs were punished and humiliated, they remained "our constant friends." Once again, Cook thought that the high chief in Tonga who constantly maintained a solemn demeanor was an "idiot."[81] On 8 April 1774, Cook reached the Marquesas, and the confrontation resulted in violence. On Cook's orders, the crew fired at natives in their canoes and killed one of them with "the third Shott," while two others jumped overboard and then jumped back into their canoe. One man, thought Cook, "seem'd to laugh at what happened," while the other, a youth, had "a serias and dejected countinance," being the son of the dead man. While Cook could correctly read the "dejection" of the youth, he did not comprehend the "laugh" of the other.[82]

FIREWOOD

I think it fair that Sahlins contests my account of the "desecration" of the temple because for him the British only did what the Hawai'ians would do mythopraxically anyway—that is, ritually dismantle the temple. Sahlins is right that this depends on whether we accept Ledyard's graphic and detailed account as an invention or not and disregard King's. I did accept Ledyard's version and also suggested political motives for King ignoring this event; alternatively, I tried to reconcile King's account with Ledyard's (which is the position I now take). But Sahlins says that we cannot "disregard King and Zimmermann's reports that the transaction has been satisfactorily negotiated" (N, 269). This may be true with King but not Zimmermann, who reports Hawai'ian "dissatisfaction" on their return (after the loss of the foremast) for two reasons; the removal of the temple fence and the burial of William Watman in the temple.[83] Zimmerman adds that the "removal of the poles had caused a great deal of indignation although it was not given expression, on account of their king having given his sanction to the action; nevertheless, *it was easy to read it in their faces*" (my italics). By "not given expression," I take it that Zimmermann meant there was no Hawai'ian retaliatory action against the British. Zimmermann does give the conventional shipboard account, which says that a payment of hatchets was made; this Ledyard does not deny but instead graphically describes its larger context. The clinching argument in favor of my hypothesis is the Hawai'ian voice that Sahlins has conveniently forgotten. Fourteen years later, the high priest of this very temple told Lieutenant Puget of Vancouver's expedition that Cook was killed owing to the "depradations being committed on its fence."[84] Why is it that Sahlins ignores a Hawai'ian voice expressed so soon after the event but takes at face value missionary texts such as the *Mooolelo Hawai'i*, written much later in highly changed circumstances?

Sahlins tries to discredit Ledyard by insisting that the priest Keli'ikea, who was present during this episode, continued to be a favorite of the British and helped them. But Ledyard's account is a lot more complex because, in addition to Keli'ikea, "some other chiefs" were present, and it was these chiefs who were "dismayed." Cook twice offered the hatchets to these chiefs, and they refused them both times. Then Cook put in an extra hatchet and gave it to Keli'ikea, who "turned pale" but actually took the hatchets. In a bizarre sense, the transaction was "satisfactorily negotiated" (A, 116–17). Yet there is a complex scenario here, and Keli'ikea's is but one character in it. Moreover, Keli'ikea helping the British does not mean that he did not share the sentiments of the other chiefs. All along he acted like an astute diplomat and tactitian, as other politicians did later. In my narrative, Keli'ikea was instrumental in allaying tempers on both sides during those fateful last days. Sahlins seems to think that if Keli'ikea was good to the English, it must mean that he was hostile to the king—a structural argument based on the absolute opposition between the Lono priests and the king and his chiefs, by virtue of which the Lono priests must have been friendly to the English.[85] Such a situation is unlikely for Hawai'i or elsewhere; Sahlins's own sacred Lono priest Omiah was thoroughly hostile to the English.[86]

Sahlins admits that the British saw the phenomenon of burning the fence and carrying away the images of the gods as "desecration" or "sacrilege." If so, one cannot avoid the question of Cook's own motivations. What made Cook commit what, even in European eyes, seemed a sacrilege? The scarcity of wood is a poor explanation because Zimmermann says that, though scarce wood was obtainable from the mountains; further, Beaglehole thought that Cook should have sought "permission to fell trees nearby."[87]

I agree with Sahlins that there was a continuing debate in Hawai'i regarding the desecration of the fence. The major exponent of the view that it was not a desecration is Thomas Thrum in his paper "The Paehumu of Heiaus Non-Sacred." Briefly, Thrum argues that the wooden images outside the *heiau* were not restricted for use "even as fuel" and "on some occasions these wooden images were burned as firewood by the people." But he can give only one such example and that at the close of a sacrificial service by a king "in provision for his war with Kaua'i" (A, 221–47). I would now add the following to my previous critique. First, it is essential for Sahlins's hypothesis that the fence be ritually dismantled at Makahiki. Yet Malo, the only Hawai'ian scholar to describe clearly the process, makes no reference whatever to the dismantling of the fence. Instead, he mentions "the entire dismantling of the Makahiki idols, leaving nothing but the bare images; after which they and all their appurtenances were bundled up and deposited in the *luakini*"—not exactly conforming with British practice.[88] Valeri, in his important study of Hawai'ian sacrifice, reiterates Malo, which means that the dismantling of the fence as ritual is simply Sahlins's mythopraxical imagination at work.[89] Moreover, if the fence was ritually dismantled every year, then a new fence has to be erected for the next Makahiki. Yet the existence of the heads of Maui chiefs stuck on it from previous wars shows that it had been there for some time. The heads, of course, could be replaced on a new fence every year, but Sahlins, unlike me, accepts King's official version, which says that it was a "decrepit fence," which had to have been there for some time. Second, if it is correct that in Hawai'ian religion the world is permeated with spirit (species sentience) and that many objects are infused with the essence of deities, then it is hard to believe that the images of the gods and the fence itself were not "sacred," even though the Hawai'ian concept of the "sacred" is not a European one. The fact that on occasion the deities represented in their images can be treated irreverently does not mean that they were not sacred beings.[90] And it is because they were sacred that god images were stored at a royal shrine. Obviously, images and shrines can be demolished or burned on rare occasions, as Thrum says, but they do require proper ritual procedures that the sailors, however divine, were incapable of performing. Finally, if King's account is true, Ledyard is lying; if Ledyard lies not, then King's account is either false or, more likely, incomplete. Sahlins, however, cannot account for Ledyard's lying or King's truthfulness or incompleteness, which takes us now to our next topic.

THE POLITICS OF REPORTAGE

Many books begin with an author's assurance of order. One slipped into their waters with a silent paddle.
I begin my work at the time when Servius Galba was Consul. . . .
The histories of Tiberius, Caligula, Claudius and Nero, while they
were a power, were falsified through terror and after their death
were written under a fresh hatred.
So Tacitus begins his annals.[91]

Right through Sahlins's book, he accuses me of being downright unfair and wrong in attributing to the major journalists any attempt to alter, subtly or otherwise, for political reasons, accounts of the events that occurred on islands and on board ships. This is especially true of King: Sahlins innocently writes that "King's private journal is indeed all innocence" (N, 267). This might mean that his "public" journal was not; but no, that too, in spite of the important changes and additions King and Douglas made in the official edition of 1784, in which phrases such as "religious adoration" were introduced. There *are* differences between the official and unofficial versions, and they cannot be swept under the carpet. Sahlins treats eighteenth-century editors with the kind of scrupulousness that we nowadays associate (sometimes erroneously) with contemporary scholarship. Characteristically, he does not tell us how he justifies the absence of a political stance among officers of the admiralty engaged in sensitive imperial missions. The journals that the major journalists wrote on board ship were not "private" documents in Sahlins's sense; everyone knew that they had to be given over to the admiralty, and it was from these and the ships' logs that official or authorized versions were written. What was offensive to public morality and the integrity of His Majesty's government had to be carefully vetted and sometimes excluded, owing to the public nature of these so-called private journals. I have shown that Captain Clerke wrote a politically correct and acceptable account of the death of Cook in his "private journal," exonerating officers such as Williamson and Rickman, ignoring their ineptitude or downright irresponsibility (A, 111–13).

For their official edition of 1784, Douglas wrote volumes 1 and 2, and King dealt with the main events on the island of Hawai'i in volume 3. Contrary to Sahlins, Beaglehole states that, while the volumes "have strong roots in Cook," Douglas "was also capable of invention."[92] King was so inexperienced that he also sought Douglas's help, relying on him to deal with "any thing in it you disapprove, or any alterations you think may be made for the better."[93] Here is one of Douglas's inventions when he describes the early English navigators as argonauts: "Even the hulks of the ships that carried them, though not converted into constellations in the Heavens, used to be honoured and visited as *sacred reliques upon earth*."[94] This is not Cook's voice; it is Douglas patriotically employing the apotheosis and planetary tropes, and it is the same voice that made the subtle yet significant changes that I spoke of earlier.

The politics of reportage is most visible when it comes to gratuitous or excessive violence against native peoples because that seems to violate British public morality and the instructions given by Lord Morton of the Royal Society during the very first voyage. Let me deal with Cook's second voyage (1772–1775), in which Cook blossomed into a major journalist in his own right and one, incidentally, that provided opportunities for the expression of his Prospero persona. Nevertheless, violence did occur, and let us hear John Marra, who relates an event in Tahiti not recorded in Cook's journal.

Marra's account of 9 May 1774 begins with the man who stole a water cask, and "it was judged necessary to punish him as a terror to others." He was therefore tied up and severely whipped in the presence of the chiefs and a "great concourse of the natives . . . who looked with an evil eye upon those concerned in what they called a cruel punishment." Undeterred by this example, others continued to steal and were punished similarly. About this time, says Marra, one of the sentinels fell asleep and lost his musket. Cook wanted to punish the sentinel in the presence of the chiefs, but they fled in their canoes.

> The Captain, who himself commanded in the pursuit, made signals for them to bring to, to which they paid no regard: at length he gave orders to fire; but as none of them were hurt by that order they rowed

on. The fire was renewed, and the bullets flying thick about their boats, they at length thought it proper to yield. When they were taken on board, they were shewn the sentinel in irons, and were given to understand that he was again to be punished if his musket was not returned, and that he would in the end be killed for not killing the man in attempting to steal and to carry it away.

This threat of cruel and unusual punishment was so effective that the chiefs wept, but Cook was not mollified and he threatened them with what he actually carried out in Eimeo during the third voyage and threatened Hawai'ians with again just before his death. "The Captain declared with a severe tone of voice, that he would set fire to every boat on the island, and would not leave them a single vessel to go out to fish with."[95] Obviously, the musket was returned.

Let us see how Cook presents these kinds of events in his own journal entry for 10 May 1774. Cook notes pragmatically that when a chief is "matou'd" (a marvelous Anglicization of a Tahitian word to indicate fear of Cook), people also flee and provisions are not available. Tahitians know that the ship depends on provisions and therefore chiefs have to be mollified eventually. They, however, do not seem to realize that "all their War Canoes . . . and even the fruit they refuse to supply us are intirely in our power." But, he adds, he had no occasion to practice any of this except "detaining some of their Canoes for awhile." Otherwise his treatment of them has been "equitable and mild," and the fact that "they were the first aggressors had very little influence on my conduct." "Three things made them our fast friends, Their own good natured and benevolent disposition, gentle treatment on our part and the dread of our fire Arms."[96]

The "minor journalists" such as Marra, Rickman, Gilbert, and Ledyard wrote without reference to their logs (if they had any) which were with the admiralty. They did not face the constraints of the major journalists. Yet while they were inept in their knowlege of the local languages, they did possess several strengths. They could sometimes be trusted to report what they actually saw in Hawai'i and what went on on board ship. For example, if one can take Rickman's account of life on the *Discovery* seriously, then it is not only Cook who comes out with threats of death and devastation but also the playful ("waggish") Captain Clerke in his own inimitable style.

The scene is set in Eimeo during the third voyage, after Cook had inflicted massive destruction on the people of Eimeo on account of a lost goat. Says Rickman:

Two young natives of quality, being found on board our ship, were made prisoners, and told they were to be put to death, if the goat should not be restored within a certain period of time. The youths protested their own innocence, and disclaimed all knowledge of the guilty persons; notwithstanding which, every preparation was apparently made for putting them both to death. Large ropes were carried upon the main deck, and made fast fore and aft; axes, chains, and instruments of torture were placed upon the quarter deck in the sight of the young men, whose terrors were increased by the information of Omai, who gave them to understand that, by all these solemn preparations, their doom was finally determined.[97]

We know Clerke had a fondness for practical jokes, and the two young men were not killed after all; but it is unlikely that the Tahitian youths appreciated the humor. Nor is it likely that events like this would be reported in Clerke's log or journal. However, even in these instances, one must ask whether there were motivations among the minor journalists for bearing false witness.

How do some troubling accounts manage to get included in the major journals? I had suggested that Cook's account of the destruction of Eimeo went into his journal because by this time he had lost control of himself, something noted by his own crew (A, 38). I think King's condemnation of Cook was something felt genuinely by him, but it could also help protect him if an official inquiry was held in London. We have a clear example of this from the second voyage. On one occasion, the philosopher Reinhold Foster wanted his son George to include in his journal a troubling encounter with Tahitians because he felt that if an official inquiry was held, the journal account could be treated as evidence and George could "testify the same upon oath."[98] In other instances, actions that seem to us morally dubious were included in the journals because the author did not think it mattered very much to his reading public or because of his own personal insensitivity. A good example is Samwell's account of the visit to the Nootka on their return trip to Hawai'i after the futile quest for the Northwest Passage. An inveterate womanizer, Samwell wrote on 28 April 1778:

The Women were dirtier and more loathsome and despicable looking Figures than the Men, they were never cloathed in Skins or adorned with ornaments of any kind. Their Hair full of filth hung over their faces in clots, in short a woman could not present herself to us under a more disagreeable form than these did, however we had the Courage and perseverance to attempt the refining of this ore, among which it must be confessed we sometimes found some Jewels that rewarded our trouble, Namely two sparkling black Eyes accompanied with a beautiful Face, and when such was our fortune we never regretted the time and trouble it had cost us in digging through loads of red Oaker, Soot and other Dirt to get at them.[99]

Perhaps Samwell, insensitive to the implications of what he was saying, felt that his peers in England would appreciate his sense of humor.

COOK'S RESURRECTION AND RETURN

Sahlins persists in thinking that the many questions about the reappearance of Cook implied that he was the god Lono and that he was certainly coming back. I am convinced that, given Sahlins's Augustinian predilections, this is also a Christological conception unwittingly foisted on the Hawai'ians, easy to do given that Cook is the good Christlike figure killed and dismembered in a ritual enactment and whose relics are worshiped by natives. As far as I know, the myth of Lono recorded by Ellis says only that Cook will come back in his physical form; Ellis makes no reference to time, date, or place of arrival. If indeed Cook was Lono and he had already come, then he had fulfilled Hawai'ian prophecies because there is no indigenous myth that says that he should come back once again (or again and again). If so, the conception of Cook coming back must be demystified and seen in its full complexity.

The trouble with Sahlins is that he presents only a single discourse regarding the "return" of Cook and that is his Christological one, even though there is no consensus: he would come the next day, in two months, in three, in a short time, and so forth. What I tried to do was to show that this "return," like the other discourses I have sketched, is ambiguous and could mean many things and ought not to be fit into the straitjacket of a single interpretation. Thus, Cook could return as an avenging ghost, also a perfectly acceptable Hawai'ian explanation. Again, Kamakau's priestly informants recollected much later that "our 'aumakua [ancestral spirit] has returned," which is quite different from saying "Lono has returned."[100] There could be many other forms of the "return," some of which I have sketched in my book. I have already shown that the Melanesians cited by Sahlins also have multiple notions of the European as someone "returned" and it is wrong to subsume those complexities under the single rubric of "deification" or under that ghastly term "supernaturalism." To clinch matters, let me give a further illustrative example from Sri Lankan Buddhism.

When someone I know dies, I can, given my belief in reincarnation, say that he has "returned" in the form of my child or someone else's child; others could say that he is a *preta*, a greedy ancestral spirit, who has "returned" to haunt the house he has lived in owing to his excessive attachment to it; for others, he could be a demon who has "returned" to possess the living and cause demonic illness; or he might "return" as a benevolent being, a *devata*; in the rare case, if someone thought he was a powerful chief, he could "return" as a deity who has to be propitiated. And all these persons might agree that his "return" could be the product of his karma, entailing the possibility of a generalized consensual understanding beneath specific differences. Ethnographers familiar with other cosmologies could easily cite similar examples. Different people with varying attitudes to the dead person can spell "return" differently and yet on another level maintain common understandings. So with the Hawai'ians; Cook had as powerful an impact on the local culture as he did on the European. Inasmuch as European culture interpreted his death variously, so did the Hawai'ian. It would not do to fit words like "return," with their rich ambiguities in the local culture, to a single denotation. Sahlins does not even bother to tell us the multiple ways in which Hawai'ians represented the English word "return" in their own lexicon.

COOK'S BONES

Sahlins has a whole section entitled "The Invention of Cook's Postmortem (Only) Deification." Once again, I am happy to accept his criticism that I have invented Cook's postmortem deification, given my assumption that "culture" is something invented by ethnographers on the basis of whatever evidence is at hand. I am willing to admit that, owing to the opacity of the ethnographic data, my invention might well be wrong. But Sahlins's "true account" of what transpired is much worse than my invented one. I show that after Cook's death Hawai'ians treated the English with mockery and insolence, hardly the treatment accorded a dead god. But for Sahlins, these actions also indicate mythopraxis. His proof comes from an anonymous account that says that a Hawai'ian made "signs of insolence and contempt," mimetically showing how he cut up Captain Cook and separated his body parts and also "challenged us on shore" (N, 146). One can reasonably ask whether the context of mockery indicating Hawai'ian triumph over an enemy indicates that they were treating Cook as a dead god. Anonymous, I think, correctly interprets the Hawai'ian mimetic actions as challenging the British and as an example of "insolence." Other accounts describe the Hawai'ians showing their backsides to the British; yet others describe them brandishing Cook's hat and sword. Such behavior is fully consonant with general Polynesian practice. For example, the Maori also made similar triumphant gestures when they killed the Frenchman Marion du Fresne in July 1772, a year before Cook's second visit to New Zealand.[101] For Sahlins, these are not parodic actions but prove that Cook was treated as a sacrificial victim because the body parts of such a victim are divided among chiefs. Kalani'opu'ū himself is "said to have offered him [Cook] as a sacrifice," even though his source, James King, makes no such reference (N, 147). Sahlins believes that Cook was the god Lono even unto death. If so, how can the god Lono be treated as a *human* sacrificial victim? There is also no precedence in Hawai'i for a *divine* sacrificial victim; unless superimposed on all of this is Sir James Frazer's dying god, who is indeed a "sacrificial victim."[102] Has not the supposedly unique Hawai'ian thought then been assimilated into Frazer's? What we have here is a confused melange of conflicting arguments. In fact, Sahlins's skeletal argument fits my thesis better than his because I say that Cook was treated as a human adversary killed in battle and that his bones were divided among chiefs to share his mana, which is quite in keeping with Polynesian custom in general.

I am afraid that in these concluding remarks I have come perilously close to the trivia that Sahlins deals with in his seventeen appendixes, and the mere thought of practicing another form of "stereotypic reproduction" makes me stop.

APPENDIX I

$$\mathcal{R}\mathcal{B}$$

The Destruction of Hikiau and the Death of William Watman

A key question that I plan to deal with in my later work pertains to the catalyst that spurred Cook to destroy the temple. My own guess is that the provocation was William Watman, who lay dying. Watman, according to Beaglehole's reckoning, was a forty-four-year-old ordinary seaman.[1] But all ships' accounts refer to him as an old man, and Law thinks he was sixty.[2] Clearly, irrespective of actual age, he was subjectively perceived as an old man by the crew. Watman had served Cook in the previous voyage and seemed to have a special relationship with him. When Cook retired after the second voyage, he obtained for Watman, as he did for himself, a sinecure at Greenwich Hospital.[3] This action is quite inexplicable unless Cook was especially attached to Watman. Cook got on well with older people, who appeared to him as father figures. Thus he had a special affection for John Walker of Whitby, his former employer and benefactor; and on the second voyage he called old Ri, the chief of Huahine, a father. Watman, a similar figure, suffered a stroke, the culmination of a long illness, only a few days before the destruction of the shrine.

The death of Watman, according to the various journal entries, seemed to have produced a debate regarding how he would have wished to be buried. We know what actually transpired: Watman was buried in Hikiau, the temple of Kū, the very place that Cook was ceremonially received. However one looks at it, the action seems very bizarre—burying a British seaman in a heathen shrine. A year before in Kaua'i, when an ordinary seaman died, Cook ordered a sea funeral.[4] Why the change now? There are two broad versions in the ship's accounts of the decision to bury Watman in Hikiau. The first comes from shipboard gossip: Rickman says that Watman wanted to be buried "according to his own desire in the Morai [temple] belonging to the King."[5] It seems utterly improbable that Watman desired to be buried in a heathen shrine. More reasonable would be a wish to be buried on shore. King's unofficial journal says that "the chiefs knowing of his death expressed a desire that he might be bury'd on shore, which he was accordingly upon the Morai."[6] The official journal neatly converts this into a request by King Kalani'opu'u himself.[7] The latter version is implicitly contradicted by King, because neither Kalani'opu'u nor any

251

chiefs were present at the funeral, something quite unbelievable if the site was chosen by them. Only the priests were there on "sufferance."[8] If so, here is a real breach of courtesy on the part of the British, for if the chiefs and king requested the burial at Hikiau, and Cook agreed, it seems strange that only the priests would be tolerated there. This hardly sounds like a funeral conducted at the request of the Hawaiians.

Polynesians were sensitive to hierarchy and status and made clear distinctions between officers and ordinary seamen—distinctions emblematically expressed on the ship itself by the uniforms worn. Hikiau was tabu to ordinary Hawaiians, and it is not likely that the chiefs would have agreed to the burial of an ordinary seaman there. There is also no way that they would have known about Cook's special relationship with Watman, because this was a private, not public, friendship. By contrast, the relation between Cook and Lieutenant King was publicly visible, such that the Hawaiians referred to King as Cook's own "son" (probably in the classificatory sense). Finally, even if the improbable occurred, and Watman was buried at the King's request, why did Cook agree to have his friend buried in a heathen shrine? It seems as if the journals have to justify an unusual act, the burial of an English seaman "at the feet of an Image on the Pile of stones called O-hekeaw [Hikiau]."[9]

None of the ships' officers seemed to know what actually transpired, because Cook's own notes and logs are not available. Ledyard, I think, echoed the common puzzlement: The priests "anticipated Cook's request by making him an offer of a place in the morai which Cook promised him [Watman] should be done."[10] Ledyard reconciles the various accounts, that is, Watman's wish to be buried on shore, the fact that he was buried in Hikiau, and that this burial was Cook's own wish, but anticipated by the priests themselves.

Let me now once again analyze the rationale for Cook's irrational action. Watman was an old man, a friend and father figure for Cook, sufficiently important to Cook that he wanted his company in his planned retirement at Greenwich Hospital after the second voyage. Watman probably wanted to be buried on shore, and Cook probably felt he had to give him a proper royal funeral. Where should he be buried? The Polynesian shrines were labeled "burial grounds" in the ships' journals, and Hikiau was the "royal burying ground." It was here that Cook himself was ceremonially received. Watman must be buried alongside Hawaiian royalty. But in a place where human sacrifices were offered and idols worshipped? Here Cook's ambivalence regarding his own ritual reception must have surfaced. Thus, the palings with their sacrificial heads and the semicircle of images had to be removed and burned. This action simultaneously annulled the significance of Cook prostrating and kissing the heathen god and, at the same time, cleared the ground of idolatrous objects, so that Watman could be buried

among royalty and according to Christian rites. I think it was also a deliberate act of defiance, a deliberate violation of Hawaiian sacred values. Neither the king nor chiefs were there, and only "Kao and his brethren were
suffered to be present."[11]

Ledyard gives a description of the impressive funeral ceremony.

> As the circumstances of this mans death was an event that would be
> much noticed by the natives as well as the manner in which we should
> dispose of the corps, it was determined to render the whole matter as
> magnificent and respectable as the situation of the affair would permit,
> the body was therefore inclosed in a coffin covered with colors and
> borne by the bargemen, who walked in the centre. Cook and his
> officers with some of the people followed two and two according to
> their rank. In the front at an advanced distance preceeding a guard of
> marines marching to the tune of a fife that played the funeral march,
> and with their arms reverted, when we had asscended the Morai and
> reached the grave opened their ranks and performed the usual evolu-
> tions on those occasions; Cook and his officers read prayers, and Ki-
> kinny [Keli'ikea] and his [people] squat down upon their hams be-
> fore them paying great attention, and were ostensibly much affected.
> When we began to cover the remains, Kikinny seized a small pig he
> had under his arm by his hinder legs, and beating its head against the
> stones hove into the grave, and would have done the same with one or
> two more hogs they had with them had not Cook interposed."[12]

It seems strange that extensive journal writers like Samwell neither describe this event nor give us the native responses. The reason for this silence
is clear from Ledyard's account. There was something amiss: The grand
funerary show was to a largely empty audience, for he tells us that "when
the Pinnace landed with Watman's body we expected the curiosity of the
natives would have been excited to come in crowds to see it and observe our
conduct upon the occasion—but it was quite otherwise, the people all shut
themselves up in their houses, and nobody was seen but for two or three
men who attended Kikinny."[13] It is not that the priests were "suffer'd to be
present"; even Samwell and King make no reference to anyone else being
present! One can reasonably interpret this Hawaiian boycott as a reaction
to the pollution of the royal *heiau* by the burial of a commoner. Furthermore, if the destruction of the shrine occurred the previous day, as the
evidence suggests, then the refusal of the Hawaiians to witness this grand
show is not surprising. The priests were the only ones present and their
ritual actions on this occasion had nothing to do with honoring Watman
but were attempts to counter the effects of pollution or the violation of the
temple taboos. Thus, Keli'ikea killed a pig and placed it in the grave, spoil-
ing the Christian part of the ritual, so that Cook had to stop him. But this

was a temporary interruption, because according to both King and Ledyard the Hawaiians went on performing similar rituals for several consecutive nights. Ledyard observed these performances but did not understand them. He also says that at the funeral itself the priests paid "great attention" and were "ostensibly much affected." Those visible but ambiguous signs of emotion might well indicate their fears and concern regarding the violation of the sanctity of the shrine.

APPENDIX II

——————————— 🔳 ———————————

Kāliʻi and the Divinity of Kings

In Kāliʻi, according to Sahlins, the opposition between Kū and Lono is simultaneously an opposition between Kalaniʻopuʻu and Cook. Underlying Sahlins's analysis is his central premise: In Hawaiian culture chiefs were in fact "divine," that is, they were imbued with the essence of a god (*akua*) or they were "incarnations" of gods. Recently, however, Charlot has questioned this premise and shown quite clearly that the use of *akua* for chiefs is virtually nonexistent in the earlier literature.[1] However, one can argue that the lack of explicit reference does not negate an implicit recognition.[2] I have also shown that in Cook's installation ritual priests told Lieutenant King that the *akua* "resided in us."[3] If so, the installation ritual itself is to effect such a residence. One does not know how reliable King is for this kind of information, but it is not improbable that some kind of divinity did inhere in their most sacred chiefs, probably based on a notion of "godly blood" (*waiakua*). But this means that proper descent was absolutely essential, and it is likely that brother-sister marriage preserved "godly blood." Thus Kamehameha, even though a king, was of insufficiently high rank to be called anything but human (*kanaka*).[4] What is almost certain is that Hawaiians did not possess "divine kings" in the Frazerian sense. Such a conception was perhaps applicable to Fiji but my reading of Maori, Marquesan, Tahitian, and Samoan ethnography does not warrant the assumption of an unambiguous divinity of kings. The "sacredness" of chiefs is primarily based on pan-Polynesian conceptions of *mana* and *tabu*, rather than of divinity.

The extension of the term *akua* to chiefs and others also does not necessarily imply divinity. In Sri Lanka, for example, chiefs can be addressed on occasion as "deyiyo" (god), even though everyone knows that chiefs are *not* gods. Such metaphors are very common and in the Sri Lankan case capitalize on the idea of *power* that inheres in deities. Another situation can provoke a different extension of a divine attribute: Thus children are affectionately labeled as *deyiya*, a variation of *deyiyo* or *deviyo*. On occasion this term can be extended to greet the long-absent ethnographer! So it is with the Polynesian extension of *akua* to foreigners. Hawaiians used this term to label Tahitians because they (Tahitians) were opposed to normal Hawaiians (*kanaka*).[5] This oppositional use of the term for whites was very common all over Polynesia and should not be misconstrued as implying that Polynesians thought foreigners were gods. Such oppositional use was perhaps reinforced by the whites' willingness to accept the label. Greg Dening in a personal communication tells me that this extension of *atua/akua* for whites was very common among the Marquesans, but it should not be translated as "god." Thus, it is possible that Hawaiians had some notion of divinity inherent in chiefs of high descent; but the presence or absence of *akua* as a term of address or reference does not constitute evidence for the existence of such a conception.

It is therefore doubtful whether the ritual of Kāliʻi could be seen as a grand conflict between the king (as the god Kū) and those who ritually oppose him (Lono). The most reliable account of Kāliʻi, by Kamakau of Kaʻawaloa, a court chanter of Kamehameha I, does not warrant this interpretation:

> The king came in from the sea, and when he was near the lower side of the temple towards the sea he saw a great number of people with the deity. A very large number of men ran in front of the image, holding spears in their hands. One of them had several spears in his hands which he intended to throw at one of the men who landed with the king from the canoe. The king and his companion landed, and when the man who held the several spears saw them he ran forward quickly and threw a spear at the king's companion. He parried it with something that he held in his hand, leaping upwards. The people there shouted at the man's skill. The man then touched the king with the second spear thus freeing him from restrictions. Then there was a general sham fight among the people.[6]

The following account was written by Lisianskii in 1804. He tends to literalize the ritual:

> With several craft or, sometimes, in a single craft he then sets out from the shore and is so steered as to touch the shore again as the sun rises. One of the strongest and most skillful warriors is appointed to meet the king as he lands. This warrior follows the king's craft, moving along the shore then, as soon as the craft touches and the king has thrown off his cloak, hurls a spear at his sovereign from a distance not more than thirty paces. The king must either catch the spear or be killed—for in all this, they say, there is no jesting. Seizing the spear, the king turns it around so that the blunt end is uppermost and, holding it under his arm, continues on his way into the *geiava* [*heiau*] or principal temple of the gods. Sham battle breaks out suddenly and everywhere. . . .[7]

From Corney's account it seems as if Kamehameha himself warded off three spears thrown at him during Kāli'i.[8] It is likely that there was no single invariant form of Kāli'i. Like other Hawaiian rituals, the ritual of Kāli'i has space for improvisation and innovation. However, none of the accounts suggest that this ritual is a combat between Lono and Kū, though clearly there is a ritual attack on the king. There is also no substantive or structural similarity between the Kāli'i ritual and the death of Cook.

NOTES

―――――――――― ❧❧ ――――――――――

In this manuscript I use two sets of Cook's journals, the first being the official edition edited by the Reverend John Douglas in 1784. Volumes 1 and 2 of this edition are Douglas's revisions of Cook's own journals. Volume 3 is the journal by Lieutenant King and pertains to the last days in Hawai'i. King wrote this in collaboration with John Douglas. This edition is abbreviated as Cook (D) 1, 2, or 3.

Cook's journals of all three voyages have been recently edited by J. C. Beaglehole for the Hakluyt Society. I abbreviate these as Cook (B). The voyage of the *Endeavor* is Cook (B) 1; the voyage of the *Resolution* and *Adventure* is Cook (B) 2; the last voyage, that of the *Resolution* and *Discovery* (2 vols.), is Cook (B) 3a and 3b. These two volumes also contain the journals of Samwell and King and excerpts from other journalists.

PREFACE

1. Quoted by Rodney Needham, ed., *Imagination and Proof, Selected Essays of A. M. Hocart* (Tucson: The University of Arizona Press, 1987), p. 1.

I

1. Ralph S. Kuykendall, *The Hawaiian Kingdom 1778–1854: Foundation and Transformation* (Honolulu: University of Hawaii Press, 1938), p. 16.
2. J. C. Beaglehole, *The Life of Captain James Cook* (London: The Hakluyt Society, 1974); Lynne Withey, *Voyages of Discovery: Captain Cook and the Exploration of the Pacific* (Berkeley and Los Angeles: University of California Press, 1989).
3. J. C. Beaglehole, "On the Character of Captain James Cook," *The Geographical Journal* 122, 4 (1956), p. 428.
4. Douglas L. Oliver, *The Pacific Islands*, 3d ed. (Honolulu: University of Hawaii Press, 1989), p. 45.
5. R. A. Skelton, *Captain James Cook: After Two Hundred Years* (London: The Hakluyt Society, 1969), p. 30.
6. Paul Carter, *The Road to Botany Bay: An Exploration of Landscape and History* (Chicago: University of Chicago Press, 1989), especially chs. 1–3, pp. 1–98.
7. For the scientific significance of the transit of Venus, see Sir Richard Wooley, "The Significance of the Transit of Venus," in G. M. Badger, ed., *Captain Cook, Navigator and Scientist* (London: C. Hurst, 1970), pp. 118–35.
8. Cook (B) 1, p. 171.
9. Johann Reinhold Forster, *Observations Made during a Voyage round the World . . .* (London, 1778).
10. "British Cannibals: Contemplation of an Event in the Death and Resurrection

of James Cook, Explorer," in *Identities*, special issue, *Critical Inquiry* (June 1992), ed. Henry Louis Gates, Jr., and Anthony Appiah.

11. Actually the events in Hawai'i must be placed in a still larger context of all of Cook's voyages. This more complex task I postpone for my future work.

12. Marshall Sahlins has two major books on this subject: *Historical Metaphors and Mythical Realities: Structure in the Early History of the Sandwich Islands Kingdom* (Ann Arbor: University of Michigan Press, 1981); and *Islands of History* (Chicago: University of Chicago Press, 1985). His other articles on this subject will be referred to in the course of this volume.

13. Frederic Spotts, ed., *Letters of Leonard Woolf* (London: Weidenfeld and Nicolson, 1989), p. 131.

14. J. P. Lewis, ed., "Journal of a Tour to Candia in the Year 1796," *Journal of the Royal Asiatic Society*, Ceylon Branch, vol. 26, no. 70 (1917), p. 95.

15. Claude Lévi-Strauss, "The Structural Study of Myth," in *Structural Anthropology* (New York: Basic Books, 1963).

16. Tzvetan Todorov, *The Conquest of America: The Question of the Other*, trans. Richard Howard (New York: Harper Torchbooks, 1987), p. 253.

17. Clifford Geertz, "Religion as a Cultural System," in *The Interpretation of Cultures* (New York: Basic Books, 1973), p. 93.

18. Carter, *Road to Botany Bay*.

19. James Douglas, Earl of Morton, "Hints Offered to the Consideration of Captain Cooke, Mr. Bankes, Doctor Solander, and the Other Gentlemen Who Go upon the Expedition on Board the *Endeavour*," reprinted in Cook (B) 1, pp. 514–19. Morton urges the gentlemen to first shoot birds or animals to show people the power of firearms and says that "natives are more easily gained by mild, than by rough treatment." The reason for these "hints" is also clear: In recent expeditions "Natives have been wantonly killed without any just provocation."

The British officers on Cook's voyages felt that theirs were practices of a more humane age. In fact, however, Morton's hints were essentially no different from the Ordinances of Phillip II of Spain in 1573: (See Tzvetan Todorov, *Conquest of America*, pp. 173–75). "Discoveries are not to be called conquests. Since we wish them to be carried out peacefully and charitably, we do not want the use of the term 'conquest' to offer any excuse for the employment of force or the causing of injury to the Indians. . . . They are to seek friendship with them through trade and barter . . . in no way they are to be harmed, for all we seek is their welfare and their conversion."

20. Cook (B) 2, p. 435.

21. Ibid., p. 435; see also p. 437.

22. John Hawkesworth, *An Account of the Voyages Undertaken by His Present Majesty for Making Discoveries in the Southern Hemisphere . . .* , 3 vols. (London, 1773), p. xvii.

23. *Diary and Letters of Madame D'Arblay Vol. 1, 1778–1781* (London: Macmillan and Company, 1904), p. 318.

24. This is found in Trevenen's notes scribbled on volumes 2 and 3 of the Douglas edition and available in the appendix of the *Penrose Memoirs of James Trevenen* in the National Maritime Museum in Greenwich. "No anecdote relative to Capt. Cook can be uninteresting to a Briton, although it might not be right to

expose the rougher part of his character, if the world were not already aware that this great man was of a hasty and somewhat tyrannical disposition to his inferior officers and crew, and that mankind knew themselves at least so well, as not to expect perfection from a fellow mortal," p. 6.

25. Greg Dening, *The Bounty: An Ethnographic History* (Melbourne: University of Melbourne History Department Monograph Series #1, 1988). Here are Dening's statistics: "Cook flogged 20, 26 and 37 percent respectively on his three voyages. Vancouver flogged 45 percent of his men. Bligh on the *Bounty* flogged 13 and on the *Providence*, 8 percent, the least number of men punished on any ship that came into the Pacific," p. 22. One might add that Vancouver not only had the larger number but he also had the most intense floggings, so that he consistently violated the Admiralty norm of 12 lashes.

26. Michael E. Hoare, ed., *The Resolution Journal of Johann Reinhold Forster 1772–1775*, vol. 2 (London: The Hakluyt Society, 1982), p. 365.

27. This account is reprinted in the appendix to U. Tewsley, trans., *Zimmermann's Third Voyage of Captain Cook 1776–1780* (Wellington, 1926), pp. 48–49.

28. Ibid., p. 49.

29. Michael E. Hoare, ed., *The Resolution Journal*. Unfortunately the Forsters had a bad press, not only in Wales's intemperate contemporary attack, but also among modern biographers such as Beaglehole. (See William Wales, *Remarks on Mr. Forster's Account of Captain Cook's Last Voyage* [London, 1778].) Here is a historian, James A. Williamson, writing about Forster in 1952: "Like so many Germans, he carried with him through life the callow puppyishness which the youth of other peoples shed as they grow up." (James A. Williamson, *Cook and the Opening of the Pacific* [New York: Macmillan, 1948], p. 160.) Other critics of Cook have also been dismissed or overlooked. Ledyard, an American from Connecticut, was corporal of the marines and was a strong critic of Cook's behavior in Hawai'i. (James Kenneth Munford, ed., *John Ledyard's Journal of Captain Cook's Last Voyage*, Corvallis: Oregon State University Press, 1963.) But Cook scholarship rarely refers to him, except disparagingly as "unreliable" and as a "plagiarist." The fact is that every journal of Cook's voyages was unreliable by modern standards and practically everyone "plagiarized" each other, in the logs they kept on board ship and in the journals they wrote much later.

One of the most interesting accounts of Cook's irrational violence was written by George Gilbert, whose father served Cook in the second voyage. A naive seventeen-year-old midshipman, Gilbert idealized Cook and was appalled at the violence he saw unleashed. The journal was meant to be published but it was not; instead it lay in the family until it was given to the British Museum in 1912. (George Gilbert, *Captain Cook's Final Voyage . . .* , ed. Christine Holmes [Honolulu: University of Hawaii Press, 1982], p. 1.) Modern writers, including Beaglehole and Sahlins, refer to it but not to its disturbing contents. The manuscript was published only in 1982; but it still is barely used by scholars, as if there is a silent conspiracy to stifle work that provides harsh criticism of Cook. One of the few modern writers who was critical of both Cook and the Pacific voyages of exploration was Alan Moorehead, but scholars do not bother with this "journalistic" work. (Alan Moorehead, *The Fatal Impact: An Account of the Invasion of the South Pacific 1767–1840* [London: 1966].) Others are critical of his thesis and its title: *The Fatal Impact*. It is unfortunate that the debate provoked by the theme of the "fatal impact"—a metaphor of the sort that every scholar uses—has resulted in submerging Moorehead's important ethical concerns.

30. Lucien Lévy-Bruhl, *How Natives Think*, trans. Lilian A. Clare (Princeton: Princeton University Press, 1985).

31. Claude Lévi-Strauss, *The Savage Mind* (Chicago: University of Chicago Press, 1966), p. 234.

32. For a brilliant critique of a recent manifestation of the idea that savage equals child, see Richard Shweder, "On Savages and Other Children," *American Anthropologist* 84 (1982), pp. 354–66.

33. Todorov, *Conquest of America*.

34. Ibid., p. 62.

35. Ibid., p. 87.

36. Ibid., p. 67.

37. McKim Marriott has spent practically his entire scholarly life justifying this thesis. I think the root error is the conflation of "individualism," a specific type of social movement or condition associated with the development of Western capitalism with "individual," "individuality" or "ego-identity." This is the trap of language. A person who lives in a society that values collective responsibility can still have a sense of his own self-separatedness and individuality. His sense of himself as an individual is, however, partially constituted out of his communal values. Such an introjection of communal culture does not mean that he is a "dividual" or merely a unit in a collectivity.

38. Todorov, *Conquest of America*, p. 68.

39. Ibid., p. 67.

40. Ibid., p. 88.

41. Ibid. I do not think that this statement of Bernal Diaz can be taken as proof of Aztec "cannibalism," i.e., indiscriminate anthropophagy. The Spaniards, like some modern scholars, thought that the Aztecs ate human flesh as a food substitute. The Spaniards constantly expressed their fear and revulsion for human sacrifice and cannibalism, and the Aztecs exploited this by taunting them and saying that if they were captured they would be sacrificed and eaten. In the scenario quoted by Todorov, they ate the Spaniards with tomatoes and pepper or put them in their wild beast houses (or pretended to perform these actions by miming them) as a technique of humiliating and frightening the Spaniards. One cannot infer from this scenario that the Aztecs were "cannibals"; rather, they put their ritual cannibalism to new uses in the context of their conflict with Cortés and his men.

42. Ibid., p. III.

43. Ibid., p. 104.

44. At the time of writing this, I had not seen the important essay by Inga Clendinnen, "'Fierce and Unnatural Cruelty': Cortés and the Conquest of Mexico," *Representations* 33 (Winter 1991), pp. 65–100. She has an excellent critique of Cortés and refers to many examples of improvisations by Indians.

45. My ideas of the "world's messiness" are influenced by my colleague James Boon. See his *Affinities and Extremes* (Chicago: University of Chicago Press, 1990), especially chs. 3 and 4.

46. Ibid., p. 49.
47. Ibid., pp. 88–89.
48. Weber used "rationality" in several senses, but two meanings are especially significant. First, "rationality" is the systematic thinker's mastery over the world by means of his use of increasingly sophisticated concepts. This form of "rationality" can exist in many cultures. In the West rational systematization of thought was articulated to a "pragmatic rationality" where goals are achieved through technically efficient means, culminating in modern capitalism. Weber believed that this latter process was unique to the West. I take the position that "practical rationality," if not the systematization of conceptual thought, must exist in most, if not all, societies, admittedly in varying degrees of importance. For a brief look at Weber's views, see his "Social Psychology of the World Religions," in Hans Gerth and C. Wright Mills, eds., *From Max Weber* (New York: Oxford University Press, 1976), p. 293; Guenther Roth and Wolfgang Schluchter, *Max Weber's Theory of History* (Berkeley and Los Angeles: University of California Press, 1979); and see especially his definition in Guenther Roth and Claus Wittich, eds., *Economy and Society*, vol. 1 (New York: Bedminster Press, 1968), p. 26: "Action is instrumentally rational (*zweckrational*) when the end, the means and the secondary results are all rationally taken into account and weighed."
49. The extraordinary complex system of fish ponds (aquaculture) that the Hawaiians developed could not have functioned without managerial skills and practical rationality. For a discussion and overview, see Diana M. Clifford, *Lokoi'ao Hawai'i. Ancient Hawaiian Fishponds and Their Changing Role in Society*, Senior Thesis, Princeton University, 1991.
50. Clifford Geertz, "Common Sense as a Cultural System," in Clifford Geertz, *Local Knowledge* (New York: Basic Books, 1983), pp. 73–93.
51. Ibid, p. 80.
52. For example Bryan Wilson, ed., *Rationality* (Oxford: Blackwell, 1970), and the more recent Martin Hollis and Steven Lukes, eds., *Relativism and Rationality* (Cambridge, Mass.: M.I.T. Press, 1984); and of course the fairly extensive literature on African thought.

II

1. J. C. Beaglehole, *The Life of Captain James Cook* (London: The Hakluyt Society, 1974), p. 475.
2. Ibid., p. 141.
3. Ibid.
4. For those who have missed my irony here, let me state that I refer to Banfield's term "amoral familism" in Edward C. Banfield, *The Moral Basis of a Backward Society* (Glencoe, Ill.: The Free Press, 1952). However, one can as easily use the term "moral familism" to embrace the very same phenomenon by looking at it from a different perspective. I am not being entirely facetious in my parody of Banfield, because I think his term illustrates the notorious problem in social science, where concepts employed by the scholar can be given an opposite meaning by looking at the phenomenon from a different ethical angle.

5. Beaglehole, *Life*, pp. 472–75.

6. Ibid., p. 464.

7. For details of this intrigue, see Michael E. Hoare's introduction to the *Resolution Journal of Johann Reinhold Forster, 1772–1775*, 4 vols. (London: The Hakluyt Society, 1982, pp. 59–76); and his *The Tactless Philosopher: Johann Reinhold Forster (1729–98)* (Melbourne: Hawthorn Press, 1976). It should also be remembered that George Forster, the son, was an ethnographer in his own right and the book, though based on his father's journals, contains much of George's own insights and speculations.

8. Beaglehole, "Introduction," in Cook (B) 2, p. xxxi.

9. Ibid.

10. Cook's major modern biographers, Beaglehole and Withey, do not refer to this prize. Others mention it, among them Zimmermann: "For this [discovery of the passage] a prize of £10,000 had been offered" plus "a further sum of £5,000 if we reached the 5th degree from the Pole." (U. Tewsley, trans., *Zimmermann's Third Voyage of Captain Cook 1776–1780* [Wellington, 1926], p. 11).

11. Apologies to John Masefield. Bligh reported that Mai had acquired a monkey, but I suspect this creature was purchased from later European visitors.

12. "Israelites" is Beaglehole's term in *Life*, p. 510.

13. Cook (B) 3a, p. 23.

14. Ibid., p. 48, n. 1.

15. Ibid., p. 52.

16. Ibid., p. 53.

17. Ibid., p. 69.

18. Ibid.

19. Cook (B) 3b, p. 996.

20. Ibid., p. 999.

21. Cook (B) 3a, p. 77, n. 1.

22. Ibid., p. 77, n. 1.

23. Ibid., p. 100.

24. Ibid., p. 101.

25. Ibid.

26. Ibid.

27. Cook (B) 3a, p. 101, n. 4.

28. Beaglehole, *Life*, p. 134; Lynne Withey, *Voyages of Discovery: Captain Cook and the Exploration of the Pacific* (Berkeley and Los Angeles: University of California Press, 1989), p. 48; Richard Hough, *The Last Voyage of Captain James Cook* (New York: William Morrow, 1979). The Hough reference appears as a caption to the picture of Clerke following p. 48.

29. Cook (B) 3a, p. 101.

30. Ibid., p. 108, n. 3.

31. Ibid., p. 102.

32. John Martin, *An Account of the Natives of the Tonga Islands . . . Communications of Mr. William Mariner*, vol. 2 (London, 1817), pp. 64–65.

33. Cook (B) 3a, p. 132, n. 1.

34. Thomas Edgar, *The Edgar Journal of Captain Cook's Third Voyage 1776–1778*, Adm. 55/21, Public Records Office ms., London.

35. See pp. 36, 70, and footnote 62, p. 214.
36. Edgar, *Journal.*
37. Cook (B) 3a, p. 133.
38. Ibid.
39. Ibid.
40. Ibid.
41. Cook (B) 3b, p. 1029; George Gilbert, *Captain Cook's Final Voyage, The Journal of Midshipman George Gilbert,* ed. Christine Holmes (Honolulu: University of Hawaii Press, 1982), pp. 33–34.
42. Ibid., p. 36.
43. Cook (B) 3a, p. 175.
44. See especially Cook (B) 2, pp. 246–67, 269.
45. Cook (B) 3a, pp. 123–24, n. 4.
46. Beaglehole, *Life,* p. 543.
47. Cook (B) 3a, p. 151.
48. For example, on the previous trip in Tonga, Cook went to what he thought was "a place of worship." "I had no intention to offend either them or their gods, [and] did not so much as touch them," see Cook (B) 2, p. 251.
49. Cook (B) 3a, p. 169.
50. There is a wonderful account of the delaying tactics employed by Cook's interpreter Hitihiti during the second voyage. See especially Cook (B) 2, pp. 393–97.
51. Cook (B) 3a, p. 197.
52. Cook (B) 3b, p. 1344.
53. Ibid., p. 974.
54. Cook (B) 3a, p. 224.
55. Cook (B) 2, pp. 386–88.
56. Cook (B) 3a, p. 197.
57. Ibid., pp. 197–98.
58. Ibid., p. 198.
59. Ibid., see also n. 6 for Beaglehole's identification of this shrine.
60. Ibid., p. 206.
61. Ibid., p. 214.
62. Ibid.
63. Ibid., p. 227.
64. Ibid.
65. Ibid.
66. Ibid., p. 228, n. 1.
67. Ibid., p. 228.
68. Ibid., p. 229.
69. Ibid., p. 228, n. 1.
70. Ibid., p. 229.
71. Ibid., pp. 229–30.
72. Ibid., p. 230, my italics.
73. Ibid.
74. Ibid., p. 231.
75. Ibid.
76. Ibid., pp. 231–32.

77. Ibid., p. 232.
78. Cook (B) 3b, p. 1069.
79. Cook (B) 3a, p. 232, n. 1.
80. Gilbert, *Journal*, p. 46.
81. Cook (B) 3b, p. 1383, my italics. I do not know whether the following account by Rickman is reliable, but it is worth noting: "Add to this, that two young natives of quality, being found on board our ship, were made prisoners, and told they were to be put to death, if the goat should not be restored within a certain time. The youths protested their own innocence, and disclaimed all knowledge of the guilty persons; notwithstanding which, every preparation was apparently made for putting them both to death. Large ropes were carried upon the main deck, and made fast fore and aft; axes, chains, and instruments of torture were placed upon the quarter deck in the sight of the young men, whose terrors were increased by the information of Omai, who gave them to understand that, by all these solemn preparations, their doom was finally determined." (John Rickman, *Journal of Captain Cook's Last Voyage to the Pacific Ocean* [London, 1781; rpt. Readex Microprint, 1966], pp. 166–67.)
82. Cook (B) 3b, p. 1069; see also Cook (B) 3a, p. 231, no. 5. It is interesting to note that, according to Gilbert, when they landed in Eimeo, "we found provision of all kinds . . . very scarce"; but Ledyard, who does not mention the violence, says that in Eimeo they "procured a considerable addition to our stock." We now know that this addition came from plunder! Gilbert, *Journal*, p. 46; James Kenneth Munford, ed., *John Ledyard's Journal of Captain Cook's Last Voyage* (Corvallis: Oregon State University Press, 1963), p. 58.
83. Rickman, *Journal*, pp. 171–72. Rickman writes about this episode: "The example made of the first Indian thief, by exposing him to the ridicule of his countrymen, had a better effect than a thousand lashings, which were forgotten almost as soon as inflicted; whereas the laughable figure the fellow made with one ear off, and half the hair of his head shaved, was a perpetual punishment, which it was not in his power to conceal. By this reasonable severity and the vigilance of the officers . . . we continued unmolested for several days."
84. Ibid. The tradition of cutting off of ears of natives seems to be an old one in Europe. See Tzvetan Todorov, *The Conquest of America: The Question of the Other*, trans. Richard Howard (New York: Harper Torchbooks, 1987), p. 40, where Columbus cuts off the nose and ears of an Indian "thief." Todorov says that these punishments were the same in Spain.
85. Cook (B) 3a, p. 234.
86. Ibid., p. 236.
87. Cook (D) 2, p. 100.
88. Cook (B) 3a, p. 237.
89. Ibid., p. 238, n. 2.
90. Ibid., p. 237.
91. This was noted by Bayly; see Cook (B) 3, p. 243, n. 2.
92. Cook (B) 3a, p. 244.
93. Ibid., p. 248.
94. For an account of the relationship in the previous voyage, see Cook (B) 2, pp. 224–31.

95. Cook (B) 3b, p. 1318.
96. Cook (B) 3a, pp. 249–50.
97. Ibid., p. 265. "It is no more than what I did when I first visited the Friendly Islands yet I afterwards found it did not succeed and I am much afraid this will always be the case . . . " (pp. 265–66).
98. Cook (B) 3b, p. 1348.
99. Cook (B) 3a, p. 267.
100. Cook (B) 3b, p. 1349.
101. Cook (B) 3a, p. 269.
102. Cook (B) 3b, p. 1349.
103. Cook (B) 3a, p. 269.
104. Ibid., p. 274, n. 4.
105. Ibid., p. 239. The reason that Cook gives for his action is equally bizarre. "His armour consi[s]ted of a Musket, bayonet and cartouch box; a Fowling piece, two pair of pistols and two or three swords and cutlasses. And I left him about twenty pound of powder, a few Musket Cartridges, Musket and pistol balls; these made him quite happy which was my only view for giving him them . . . " (p. 239).
106. Ibid., p. 278. See also Beaglehole, p. 278, note 2.
107. Cook (B) 3b, p. 1421; see also Beaglehole, *Life*, p. 603.
108. Rupert T. Gould, "Bligh's Notes on Cook's Last Voyage," *The Mariner's Mirror* 14 (October 1928), p. 377: "Here is a gross mistake for Anderson's and the East end of Clerk's Island is one and the same land"; Beaglehole, *Life*, p. 628.
109. Hough, *The Last Voyage*, p. 248.
110. Beaglehole, *Life*, pp. 619–20.
111. Cook (B) 3b, pp. 1453–54; Beaglehole in Cook (B) 3a, pp. 419–20, n. 2, has a good summary of various opinions regarding this matter.
112. Hough, *The Last Voyage*, p. 249.
113. James Trevenen, *Penrose Memoirs of James Trevenen*, Greenwich Maritime Museum ms.
114. Cook to the Secretary of the Admiralty, 20 October 1778, reprinted in Cook (B) 3b, p. 1532.
115. Cook (B) 3a, p. 474.
116. Ibid., p. 475.
117. Cook (B) 3b, p. 1534.
118. Beaglehole, *Life*, p. 646.
119. Cook (B) 3a, p. 475, n. 2.
120. Beaglehole, *Life*, pp. 640–41.
121. Cook (B) 3a, p. 504.
122. Ibid., p. 479.
123. Ibid.
124. Ibid., pp. 479–80, n. 4.
125. Beaglehole, *Life*, p. 641.
126. Cook (B) 3a, p. 479–80, n. 4.
127. The discourse on love is parallel to the discourse on guilt experienced as a consequence of introducing venereal diseases and is far too complex a subject for me to deal with in this volume. I plan to write an extended discussion of it in my larger book on Cook.

128. Cook (B) 3a, pp. 479–80, n. 4.

129. Beaglehole, *Life*, p. 503.

130. Cook (B) 3a, pp. 502–3; for a discussion of these estimates see David E. Stannard, *Before the Horror: The Population of Hawaii on the Eve of Western Contact* (Honolulu: University of Hawaii Press, 1989), pp. 13–21.

131. Kennedy, Sahlins and others think that those numbers provide further evidence that Cook was thought to be Lono; hence the extreme enthusiasm of the Hawaiians. But surely this is sheer prejudice since we know that, after Cook's death, on their way back home, the crew were confronted with similar numbers in Kaua'i. Samwell's entry for 1 March 1779 is, "There could be no less than ten or twelve thousand Indians" on shore, who "could have easily destroyed the handful of Men we had there," Cook (B) 3b, p. 1223. Moreover, when Vancouver arrived in Kealakekua Bay in February 1793, there were "between four to five thousand on or in the water" in addition to vast crowds on shore. See George Vancouver, *The Voyage of George Vancouver, 1791–1795*, vol. 3, ed. W. Kaye Lamb (London: The Hakluyt Society, 1984), p. 811.

132. Cook (D) 3, p. 3.

133. This is James Burney in Cook (B) 3a, p. 504, n. 5.

134. Ibid., p. 514, n. 6.

135. Cook (B) 3a, pp. 510–11. For the kinship ties between Kao, Koah, Keli'ikea, and others, see my discussion on p. 93. The ship's officers were only partly aware of these ties.

136. Cook (D) 3, p. 16.

137. Ibid.; see also Cook (B) 3a, p. 511.

138. Cook (D) 3, pp. 16, 17.

139. Cook (B) 3a, p. 512.

140. Cook (D) 3, p. 18.

141. See John Charlot, "The Feather Skirt of Nahi'ena'ena" in *Journal of the Polynesian Society* (forthcoming), note 85, where he shows that Kamehameha gave his cloak to Vancouver to be given to the King of England. "The point of Kamehameha's action is therefore that he is peerless in Hawai'i and recognizes only the King of England as equal to him. . . . These considerations might apply to Kalani'opu'u's similar presentation of a cloak to Cook; that is, he may be treating him as a chief rather than a god."

142. Cook (D) 3, pp. 17–18.

143. Ibid., p. 18.

144. Ibid., p. 19.

III

1. John Papa I'i, *Fragments of Hawaiian History*, trans. Mary K. Pukui (Honolulu: Bishop Museum Press, 1983), pp. 60, 75–77; Kamakau of Ka'awaloa (Kelou Kamakau), "Concerning Ancient Religious Ceremonies," in Abraham Fornander, *Fornander Collection of Hawaiian Antiquities and Folklore*, Memoirs of the Bernice Pauahi Bishop Museum (Honolulu: Bishop Museum Press, 1919), vol. 6, part 1, pp. 2–45.

2. William Ellis, *Polynesian Researches, during a Residence of Nearly Eight Years in the Society and Sandwich Islands*, vol. 4 (London, 1831); William Ellis (Missionary), *Narrative of a Tour through Hawaii* (London, 1928); S. M. Kamakau, *Ruling Chiefs of Hawaii* (Honolulu: The Kamehameha Schools Press, 1961); S. M. Kamakau, *Ka Poʻe Kahiko, the People of Old*, trans. Mary K. Pukui, ed. Dorothy B. Barrère (Honolulu: Bishop Museum Press, 1964). It is likely that Kamakau's work was based on Sheldon Dibble's compilation, *Mooolelo Hawaii* (ed. Dorothy Kahananui), to be discussed in Part VI of this book.

3. Gavin Kennedy, *The Death of Captain Cook* (London: Duckworth, 1978).

4. Ibid., p. 22.

5. Ibid., p. 23.

6. Ibid. See also Hiram Bingham, *A Residence of Twenty-One Years in the Sandwich Islands . . .* , 3d ed. (New York, 1855), p. 32.

7. Kennedy, *Captain Cook*, pp. 23–24.

8. Ibid., p. 24.

9. Ibid., pp. 25–28. Kennedy's measurements of the *heiau* are inaccurate. Those dimensions apply to the fence perhaps.

10. Ibid., p. 28.

11. Marshall Sahlins, *Historical Metaphors and Mythical Realities: Structure and Early History in the Sandwich Islands Kingdom* (Ann Arbor: University of Michigan Press, 1981), p. 11.

12. Ibid.

13. Ibid.

14. Ibid., p. 17.

15. Ibid.

16. Ibid., p. 19.

17. Ibid.

18. Ibid.

19. Ibid., p. 20.

20. Ibid., p. 21.

21. Ibid.

22. Marshall Sahlins, *Islands of History* (Chicago: University of Chicago Press, 1985), p. 105.

23. Sahlins, *Historical Metaphors*, p. 22.

24. Ibid., p. 24.

25. Ibid.

26. Sahlins, *Islands of History*, p. 137.

27. Ibid., pp. 4–5.

28. Sahlins, *Historical Metaphors*, p. 24.

29. Sahlins, *Islands of History*, p. 146.

30. Sahlins, *Historical Metaphors*, pp. 3–8.

31. Ibid., p. 22.

32. Valerio Valeri, *Kingship and Sacrifice: Ritual and Society in Ancient Hawaii* (Chicago: University of Chicago Press, 1985), pp. 225–26. Valeri's argument has been subjected to serious criticism by John Charlot. See his review in *Pacific Studies* 10, 2, pp. 107–47, and Valeri's reply, pp. 148–214.

33. S. M. Kamakau, *Ka Poʻe Kahiko, the People of Old*, trans. Mary K. Pukui, ed.

Dorothy B. Barrère (Honolulu: Bishop Museum Press, 1964), pp. 19–20; and Valeri, *Kingship*, p. 198, where he clearly shows that the Western part of the island followed a different calendar. Sahlins himself says in *Historical Metaphors*, p. 18: "The extant Hawaiian descriptions of the Makahiki date from the early to mid-nineteenth century, after the abolition of the traditional religion, and are based on recollections of the authors or their elders." See also Valeri, *Kingship*, p. 230, and my discussion on pp. 98–101 of this book.

34. Valeri, *Kingship*, p. 229.
35. Sahlins, *Islands of History*, p. 147.
36. Sahlins, *Historical Metaphors*, p. 74, n. 8.
37. Charlot, review of Valeri, pp. 128–29.
38. Cook (B) 3a, p. 525.
39. Marshall Sahlins, "The Apotheosis of Captain Cook," in *Between Belief and Transgression: Structuralist Essays in Religion, History, and Myth*, ed. Michael Izard and Pierre Smith (Chicago: University of Chicago Press, 1982), p. 86.
40. Cook (B) 3a, p. 508.
41. Cook (D) 3, p. 26.
42. Valeri, *Kingship*, p. 209.
43. Ibid., pp. 206–7; Martha Beckwith, *Hawaiian Mythology* (New Haven: Yale University Press, 1940), pp. 34–35.
44. These oppositions are recognized by Sahlins himself in his study of Fiji, yet he does not apply them to Hawai'i. See Marshall Sahlins, *Culture and Practical Reason* (Chicago: University of Chicago Press, 1974), pp. 39–45.
45. Cook (B) 3a, p. 498.
46. Ibid, p. 576.
47. Ibid., p. 586.
48. Valeri, *Kingship*, p. 214.
49. Ibid., p. 12; Cook (D) 3, p. 7.
50. A. R. Radcliffe-Brown, *Structure and Function in Primitive Society* (New York: The Free Press, 1965), p. 3.
51. Sahlins, *Historical Metaphors*, p. 51. In order to avoid double indentation, I have placed indented passages in Sahlins in quotation marks.
    Sahlins misreads this text. The official edition follows the convention of that time by using similar typesetting for *s* and *f*. Thus, Sahlins reads "fight" for "sight"; hence this "fight" is what the women admired!
52. This is Cook (B) 3a.
53. Cook (B) 3b, p. 1213.
54. J. C. Beaglehole, "Introduction," in Cook (B) 3a, p. clviii. Some rough estimates could be made regarding the number of women on board the *Discovery* (Samwell's ship) from 14 January (the day of Cook's death) to 20 January, the period of acute tension and conflict between Hawaiians and Englishmen. Samwell, an inveterate womanizer, tended to record the presence of women on board. He was impressed by the fact that, though they were at war, the British were willing to have women on board and the latter did in fact come. The numbers, however, were few. The following references to women on board are from Samwell (Cook [B] 3b); William Ellis (surgeon), *An Authentic Narrative of a Voyage . . . Performed by Captain Cook and Captain Clerke . . .* , vol. 2 (London,

1782; rpt. New York: Da Capo Press, 1969); and Thomas Edgar, excerpts in Rupert T. Gould, "Some Unpublished Accounts of Cook's Death," *Mariner's Mirror* 14 (1928), pp. 301–19.

14 February
Samwell: "Notwithstanding we were at open war with these people we had a few girls on board" (p. 1204).
Ellis and Edgar: No reference.
(Comment: Cook was killed on the fourteenth morning and it can be presumed that before that there were many men and women, including the king's son, on board. What is implied in Samwell's note is that the ships were empty of Hawaiians except for a "few girls.")

15 February
Samwell: No reference.
Ellis: "About twelve [midnight], three girls from the Morai side of the bay, swam on board, and soon after a canoe, in which were two Indians, came alongside, but were desired to return. . . . *The girls remained on board*" (pp. 115–16, my italics).
Edgar: He refers to the same incident and says that the two men "came in search of the Girls" (p. 313).
(Comment: It is clear that these three girls came surreptitiously and the two men were probably concerned about their safety.)

16 February
No reference in Edgar, Ellis, or Samwell.

17 February
Samwell: "We had two or three Girls on board all this Day, one of them . . . maitai. . . ."
Ellis and Edgar: No reference.
(Comment: It is likely that Samwell is referring to the three women who came midnight Friday and stayed on. There was good reason for them not to go back to their village. There is no reference to women in Edgar and Ellis because they have already mentioned these three women.)

18 February
Samwell: "About eight o' clock at night . . . two or three Canoes came loaded [with breadfruit] and one with Girls which were admitted to the Ship, tho' we are at open war with their Countrymen" (p. 1215).
Ellis and Edgar: No reference.
(Comment: It is not clear whether these girls stayed on or not; it is clear that the ships only admitted women on board.)

19 February
Trading has resumed and both Samwell and Edgar say that "several girls" came on board (Samwell, p. 1216; Edgar, p. 314).

The only reasonable conclusion one can draw is that there were very few women on board during this period, and some of them visited surreptitiously. It is almost certain that during the period 15–18 February there were only three girls on board the *Discovery*.
55. M. M. Bakhtin, *Speech Genres and Other Late Essays* (Austin: University of Texas Press, 1986), p. 85.

56. Even this statement of the one woman is understandable in the history and context of utterance. A few days previously, the ships had a display of rockets and fireworks for the benefit of the Hawaiians. Journal writers noted the Hawaiian reactions of awe, pleasure, and astonishment. Some inevitably would have said "mai tai." Now in the context of burning houses, it is not surprising if the earlier expression was reactivated. In any case it seems obvious that the Hawaiian "mai tai," like the English "very fine," can have all sorts of intonative subtleties.

57. Sahlins, *Historical Metaphors*, pp. 17–18.

58. J. C. Beaglehole, "Textual Introduction," in Cook (B) 3a, p. cxcix.

59. Cook (D) 2, p. 195.

60. Cook (B) 3a, p. 265.

61. Ibid., p. 272, my italics.

62. This happened in Eimeo or Moorea; see p. 36. In the second voyage Marra makes reference to seamen who "without ceremony cut down their trees," John Marra, *Journal of the Resolutions Voyage* . . . (London, 1775), p. 45.

63. Cook (B) 3a, p. 264.

64. Ibid.

65. Ibid.

66. Ibid., p. 272, n. 1; Bayly, *Log* Adm 55/20, Public records Office, Bayly's log entry for 19 January says this of the Kaua'i people: "These people appeared to be very numerous but the best disposed of any we were among being very honest in both their dealings or otherwise."

67. Cook (B) 3b, p. 1322.

68. Ibid., p. 1082.

69. Cook (B) 3a, p. 483.

70. Ibid., p. 474, n. 2.

71. Sahlins, *Historical Metaphors*, p. 16.

72. John Rickman, *Journal of Captain Cook's Last Voyage to the Pacific Ocean* (London, 1781; rpt. Readex Microprint, 1966).

73. I have compared Rickman's journal with the log he kept on board ship that is now available in the Public Records Office, London. There are some places where the log and journal tally, but at other times the journal widely deviates from the log.

74. John Rickman, *Log*, Adm 51/4529/46 PRO, entry for 1 March 1779.

75. Cook (B) 3a, p. 587.

76. Cook (D) 3, p. 90.

77. Rickman, *Journal*, p. 330.

78. Ibid., p. 332. It is possible that Rickman confuses this Noo-oh-a of Ni'ihau with one of their informants, Nu'a of Hawai'i, who was probably killed by the British on 14 February 1779 and in any case could not possibly have been around on 1 March 1779 on Ni'ihau or Kaua'i! Ledyard makes a similar observation around 25 January regarding the Hawaiian perception of the astronomical preoccupations of the officers: "But after all the only conclusion they made was that as we had so much to do with the sun and the rest of the planets whose motions we were constantly watching by day and night, and which we had informed them we were guided by on the ocean, we must either have come from thence, or in

some other way particularly connected with those objects, and to strengthen this inference they observed that the colour of our skins partook of the red from the sun, and the white from the moon and stars . . . " (James Kenneth Munford, ed., *John Ledyard's Journal of Captain Cook's Last Voyage* [Corvallis: Oregon State University Press, 1963], pp. 112–13). The context makes Ledyard's account much more plausible than Rickman's, but it is unlikely that Ledyard could undertake any complex conversation in Hawaiian either. This account seems to be a combination of information, hearsay, and gossip on board ship. Ledyard borrowed freely from Rickman, and it is likely that Rickman got some of his information personally from Ledyard. But if Ledyard's context of observation is plausible, Rickman's is totally improbable.

79. Rickman, *Journal*, p. 331.
80. Sahlins, *Historical Metaphors*, p. 16.
81. Cook (B) 3b, p. 1223.
82. Tom Dutton, "Successful Intercourse Was Had with the Natives: Aspects of European Contact Methods in the Pacific," in *A World of Language: Papers Presented to Professor S. A. Wurm on his 65th Birthday*, ed. Donald C. Laycock and Werner Winter (Canberra: Department of Linguistics Research School of Pacific Studies, Australian National University, 1987), pp. 153–71.
83. Rickman is not only a bad journalist; even his logs are occasionally wildly wrong. For example, he notes in his log that William Watman died on 17 January 1779 when we know from other sources that it was 1 February. Even more careless, this particular entry is found with other February entries while there is another (probably correct) entry for 17 January. Some of his journal accounts are also patently wrong, as for example when he says Chief Oree [Ri] of Huahine had died, when he was only indisposed [pp. 168–69].
84. George Little, *Life on the Ocean; or, Twenty Years at Sea . . .* (Boston, 1846), 12th ed.
85. Little, *Life*, p. 132; Marshall Sahlins, "Captain Cook in Hawaii," *Journal of the Polynesian Society* 98, 4 (December 1989), p. 381.
86. Little, *Life*, pp. 87, 132, my italics.

IV

1. Cited in Marshall Sahlins, "The Apotheosis of Captain Cook," in *Between Belief and Transgression: Structuralist Essays in Religion, History and Myth* ed. Michael Izard and Pierre Smith (Chicago: University of Chicago Press, 1982), p. 85, n. 9.
2. I am inclined to think that the representation of Lono's boats was exactly that and no more. It was developed by Kamehameha after he converted Lono into his guardian deity and the main god of the new Hawaiian kingdom.
3. See Ralph S. Kuykendall, *The Hawaiian Kingdom 1778–1854: Foundation and Transformation* (Honolulu: University of Hawaii Press, 1938), pp. 29–60.
4. David Malo, *Hawaiian Antiquities*, trans. Nathaniel B. Emerson (Honolulu: Bishop Museum Press, 1898), pp. 142, 143.
5. Ibid., p. 145.

6. Sahlins, *Apotheosis*, pp. 97–98. Sahlins erroneously assumes that Lono virtually displaced Kū, but there is evidence that Kū continued to be an important deity for Kamehameha.

7. Te Rangi Hiroa (Sir Peter Buck), "Cook's Discovery of the Hawaiian Islands," in *Report of the Director for 1944, Bishop Museum Bulletin 186* (Honolulu, 1945), pp. 26–27. For a recent discussion of Hawaiian conceptions of gods and chiefs, see John Charlot, *The Hawaiian Poetry of Religion and Politics* (Honolulu: University of Hawaii Press, 1985), published by The Institute for Polynesian Studies, Monograph Series no. 5, p. 3 and his appendix, "The Use of Akua for Living Chiefs," pp. 31–35.

8. For details see pp. 82–87, 90–91, 93–95, 110–14, 124–30 of this book.

9. Cook (D) 3, p. 69; Cook (B) 3a, p. 509.

10. Cook (B) 3a, p. 509.

11. Cook (B) 3b, pp. 1161–65.

12. Cook (B) 3a, p. 510.

13. Ibid., p. 513.

14. Cook (B) 3b, p. 1159.

15. Cook (B) 3b, pp. 1161–62.

16. Ibid., p. 1164.

17. Cook (D) 3, pp. 159–60.

18. Cook (B) 3b, p. 1184.

19. James Kenneth Munford, ed., *John Ledyard's Journal of Captain Cook's Last Voyage* (Corvallis: Oregon State University Press, 1963), p. 111.

20. Ibid., p. 130.

21. Ibid., pp. 129–30.

22. Martha Beckwith, *Hawaiian Mythology* (New Haven: Yale University Press, 1940), p. 81.

23. Munford, ed., *John Ledyard's Journal*, p. 37.

24. Cook (B) 3a, p. 269.

25. Beaglehole in Cook (B) 3a, p. cxliv, n. 1.

26. Cook (B) 2, p. 62: "But if I had followed the advice of all our pretended friends, I might have extirpated the whole race, for the people of each Hamlet or village applyed by turns to me to distroy the other. . . . "

27. Cook (B) 2, pp. 386–88.

28. This was the motivation of Tupaia as well as Mai. It was also the motivation of Maori warriors in the early nineteenth century.

29. Beaglehole, "Textual Introduction," in Cook (B) 3a, p. clxxv. According to Beaglehole's investigations, Cook's logs survived the voyage itself but soon disappeared. My own suspicious mind assumes that these logs (and also other Cook papers) contained so much damaging evidence of Cook's violence that they were deliberately "lost" by the Admiralty. Shredding of damaging evidence is an old custom.

30. Abraham Fornander, *An Account of the Polynesian Races . . .* , 3 vols. in 1 (1878–80; rpt. Rutland, and Tokyo: Charles Tuttle, 1980). This account is understandably similar to S. M. Kamakau, *Ruling Chiefs of Hawaii* (Honolulu: The Kamehameha Schools Press, 1961), pp. 78–91. In my quotations from Fornander, I have removed the underlining of proper names.

31. Fornander, *Account*, vol. 2, pp. 146–79.

32. Ibid., p. 151.

33. Ibid., p. 152.

34. Ibid., p. 173, n. 1.

35. Ibid., p. 152.

36. Ibid., p. 152.

37. Ibid., p. 25.

38. Ibid., p. 152.

39. Ibid., pp. 152–53.

40. Ibid., p. 153.

41. Ibid.

42. Ibid., p. 155.

43. Ibid., p. 156. Kamakau in *Ruling Chiefs*, p. 89, adds that it was a "feigned friendship" on Kalaniʻopuʻu's part.

44. Ibid., p. 156.

45. Ibid., p. 157.

46. Ibid.

47. Marshall Sahlins, "Captain Cook in Hawaii," *Journal of the Polynesian Society* 98, 4 (December 1989), p. 410.

48. Cook (B) 3b, p. 1160; John Rickman, *Journal of Captain Cook's Last Voyage to the Pacific Ocean* (London, 1781), rpt. Readex Microprint, 1966, p. 298.

49. Cook (B) 3a, p. 499.

50. Beckwith, *Hawaiian Mythology*, p. 11. For the complexity of the Hawaiian pantheon, see the discussion by John Charlot, "Valerio Valeri, *Kingship and Sacrifice: Ritual and Society in Ancient Hawaii*" [Review], *Pacific Studies* 10, 2 (1987), especially pp. 124–25.

51. Ibid., p. 26.

52. Samwell called it *O-he-kee-aw* in Cook (B) 3b, p. 1159, King's *O'heekeeow* in Cook (B) 3a, p. 508.

53. Cook (B) 3a, p. 504.

54. Cook (B) 3b, p. 1159.

55. Cook (B) 3a, p. 505, my italics.

56. Cook (D) 3, p. 6; see also Cook (B) 3a, p. 505.

57. Sahlins, "Apotheosis," p. 84.

58. Cook (B) 3a, p. 505.

59. Valerio Valeri, *Kingship and Sacrifice: Ritual and Society in Ancient Hawaii* (Chicago: University of Chicago Press, 1985), p. 15.

60. Cook (D) 3, p. 7.

61. It might well be that this ritual was creatively "invented" or put together from other rituals, precisely for this unusual and unexpected occasion.

62. Cook (B) 3b, p. 1374.

63. Cook (B) 3a, pp. 505–6.

64. Ibid., p. 506.

65. Malo, *Hawaiian Antiquities*, p. 81.

66. Marshall Sahlins, *Historical Metaphors and Mythical Realities: Structure and Early History of the Sandwich Islands Kingdom* (Ann Arbor: University of Michigan Press, 1981), p. 21. Sahlins does seem to realize the distinction between "mas-

ticated coconut" and "coconut oil." In *Historical Metaphors* Sahlins's Cook is anointed with oil, but in *Islands of History* (Chicago: University of Chicago Press, 1985), he is anointed with masticated coconut (p. 121). I think the confusion comes from Malo's account of Makahiki.

67. Cook (D) 3, p. 159.
68. Cook (B) 3b, pp. 1161–62.
69. Cook (B) 3a, pp. 596, 597.
70. Lynne Withey, *Voyages of Discovery: Captain Cook and the Exploration of the Pacific* (Berkeley and Los Angeles: University of California Press, 1989), p. 381. It is Ledyard who noted this on the very first day in Hawai'i (January 17). "Cook in the mean time improving the awful respect he saw paid him among the natives, permitted himself to be carried upon the shoulders of his bargemen from the boat to the summit of the beach" (Munford, *Ledyard's Journal*, p. 105).
71. Cook (B) 3b, p. 1168.
72. Ibid., p. 1193.
73. Rickman, *Journal*, p. 319.
74. Ibid., p. 322.
75. Cook (B) 3a, p. 578.
76. This was clearly evident in Tonga and elsewhere; see p. 29, 63, 139.
77. David Samwell, *Captain Cook and Hawaii* (San Francisco: David Magee, 1957), p. 6. Samwell writes: "There appeared no change in the disposition or behavior of the inhabitants. I saw nothing that would induce me to think that they were displeased with our return, or jealous of the intention of our second visit. On the contrary, that abundant good nature which had always characterized them, seemed still to glow in every bosom, and to animate every countenance." In the same volume Samwell continues: "I never saw sufficient reason to induce me to believe that there was anything of design or a pre-concerted plan on their part on their side, or that they purposely sought to quarrel with us" (p. 24).
78. Cook (B) 3a, p. 535.
79. Cook (D) 3, p. 68.
80. Ibid., p. 78.
81. Ibid.
82. Ibid., p. 80.
83. Ibid.
84. Malo, *Hawaiian Antiquities*, pp. 104–106.
85. Katherine Luomala, "Polynesian Religious Foundations of Hawaiian Concepts Regarding Wellness and Illness," in *Healing and Restoring: Health and Medicine in the World's Religious Traditions*, ed. Lawrence E. Sullivan (New York: Macmillan, 1989), p. 320.
86. Beckwith, *Hawaiian Mythology*, p. 4.
87. Cook (B) 3a, p. 542. This is Clerke's phrase.
88. Malo, *Hawaiian Antiquities*, p. 106, my italics.
89. Cook (D) 3, p. 159; see also Cook (B) 3a, p. 514.
90. George Vancouver, *The Voyage of George Vancouver, 1791–1795*, vol. 3, ed. W. Kaye Lamb (London: The Hakluyt Society, 1984), p. 1148.
91. Louis de Freycinet, *Hawaii in 1819: A Narrative Account by Louis Claude de*

Saulses de Freycinet, chs. 27, 28, trans. Ella L. Wiswell (Honolulu: Bishop Museum, Department of Anthropology, Pacific Records No. 26, 1978), p. 1.

92. Cook (B) 3a, p. 514.

93. Nevertheless, an alternate genealogy of Omiah as the brother of Pailiki is possible, in which Kao had two sons, Omiah and Pailiki, and a daughter married to Koah. But this alternative genealogy, I think, is not plausible.

94. Cook (B) 3b, pp. 1161–62.

95. Cook (D) 3, p. 159. Sahlins along with practically all other scholars thinks that Samwell's reference to a character partaking of divinity is to the god Lono. Needless to say, their myopia is simply due to the presupposition that Cook was a god. See Sahlins, "Captain Cook in Hawaii," pp. 402–3.

96. Cook (D) 3, p. 5, footnote.

97. John Law, British Library ms. 37327, entry for 2 February 1779. The handwriting is not very clear. I have copied the word *mented* from this manuscript but I am not sure whether it is correct. I have glossed it as "guided."

98. Cook (D) 3, p. 165. According to this account, Omiah was offended at his wife's attention to the foreigners and indeed publicly assaulted her. King says that this "was the only instance of anything like jealousy among them."

99. Steen Bergendorff, Ulla Hasager, and Peter Henriques, "Mythopraxis and History: On the Interpretation of the Makahiki," *Journal of the Polynesian Society* 97, pp. 391–408.

100. Sahlins, "Captain Cook in Hawaii."

101. Beaglehole in Cook (B) 3a, pp. 514–15, n. 6.

102. Mary Kawena Pukui, E. W. Haertig, and Catherine A. Lee, *Nānā I Ke Kumu*, vol. 1 (Honolulu: Hui Hanai, 1972), p. 96.

103. Fornander, *An Account of the Polynesian Races*, pp. 18–19.

104. S. M. Kamakau, *Ka Po'e Kahiko, the People of Old*, trans. Mary K. Pukui, ed. Dorothy B. Barrère (Honolulu: Bishop Museum Press, 1964), pp. 19–20.

105. Sahlins, "Captain Cook in Hawaii," p. 405.

106. Peter Corney, *Voyages in the Northern Pacific* ... (Honolulu: Thomas G. Thrum, 1896), p. 102.

107. Ibid., p. 103. According to Valerio Valeri's scholarly account, Kāli'i occurs on the sixteenth day of Makali'i, and it is not held at the beginning of Makahiki as Corney thinks. Though Valeri tends to formalize the divergent accounts of Makahiki into a single system, he is probably right that Makahiki formally commences much earlier. But even so, Corney's and Campbell's accounts suggest a shortened Makahiki. My own interpretation is that the priestly Makahiki calendar (or calendars) constitutes an "ideal calendar" in contrast to a more popular one. Probably ordinary people perceived the Makahiki as effectively beginning with Kāli'i. It is also likely that much of the pre-Kāli'i activities of Makahiki were innovations of Kamehameha's reign, and consequently ordinary people continued to believe in an earlier calendar where the festival effectively commences with Kāli'i. Right now there are no answers to these problems.

108. Archibald Campbell, *A Voyage round the World from 1806 to 1812 ... with an Account of the ... Sandwich Islands* (Honolulu: University of Hawaii Press, 1967), p. 129. Kotzebue makes a similar point in 1824: "one of their biggest festivals

which starts in the first half of November and continues for twenty one days"
(Otto Von Kotzebue, *A New Voyage round the World in the Years 1823–1826*, vol.
2 (New York: Da Capo Press, 1967 [1830]), pp. 210–11.

109. Vancouver, *The Voyage of George Vancouver*, p. 1141, n. 1.

110. Ibid., p. 1171; see also Beckwith, *Hawaiian Mythology*, p. 40.

111. Valeri, *Kingship*, p. 230.

112. Sahlins, "Captain Cook in Hawaii," p. 408–9.

113. Ibid., p. 408.

114. Sahlins, *Historical Metaphors*, p. 22.

V

1. Cook (B) 3b, p. 1190.
2. Ibid.
3. Ibid., p. 1191.
4. Cook (B) 3a, p. 528.
5. Cook (D) 3, p. 36.
6. Ibid., p. 37.
7. Ibid.
8. Cook (B) 3a, p. 525.
9. Cook (D) 3, p. 38.
10. Cook (B) 3b, p. 1191.
11. Ibid.
12. Cook (B) 3a, p. 532.
13. Ibid., p. 529.
14. This happened in Malekula and later in Tanna in the New Hebrides. It is
Forster who recorded these events. See Michael E. Hoare, ed., *The Resolution
Journal of Johann Reinhold Forster 1772–1775* (London: The Hakluyt Society,
1982), vol. 3, pp. 566 and 587–88.
15. Cook (B) 3a, pp. 529–30.
16. Beaglehole in Cook (B) 3a, p. 529, n. 1.
17. Ibid.
18. Ibid., p. 530.
19. Ibid.
20. Ibid.
21. Cook (B) 3b, p. 1192.
22. Ibid., pp. 1191–93.
23. Cook (B) 3a, p. 533.
24. Cook (D) 3, pp. 41–42.
25. Ibid., p. 42.
26. Ibid.
27. Cook (B) 3b, p. 1194, my italics.
28. Cook (B) 3a, p. 534.
29. Ibid., pp. 536–37, n. 2.
30. William Ellis (surgeon), *An Authentic Narrative of a Voyage ... Performed by
Captain Cook and Captain Clerke ...*, vol. 2 (London, 1782; rpt. New York: Da
Capo Press, 1969), p. 108.

31. J. C. Beaglehole, *The Life of Captain James Cook* (London: The Hakluyt Society, 1974), p. 668.

32. Cook (B) 3a, p. 530.

33. Samwell, *Captain Cook and Hawaii* (1796; rpt. San Francisco: David Magee, 1957), p. 12.

34. Phillips cited in Cook (B) 3a, pp. 534–35.

35. Cook (D) 3, p. 44.

36. Phillips in Cook (B) 3a, pp. 535–36.

37. Bligh's comments were directed at the purported heroic actions of Phillips. "A most infamous li[e] for I took down in writing all that happened here before I slept and particularly the Lieutenants opinion, who told me that as soon as the Musquets were discharged they ran to the Boats, having no time to reload, and was stabed in the back when unable to make any resistance." Rupert T. Gould, "Bligh's Notes on Cook's Last Voyage," *The Mariner's Mirror*, 14 (October 1928), p. 381. Even King says that "Mr. Phillips called the Marines to fire, which *some* obey'd." Ibid., p. 556, my italics.

38. See Gavin Kennedy, *The Death of Captain Cook* (London: Duckworth, 1978), pp. 82–83, for a summary of Bligh's views and Williamson's conduct.

39. Cited in Beaglehole, "Textual Introduction," in Cook (B) 3a, p. clxxvi, n. 1.

40. Cook (B) 3a, pp. 538–39.

41. Cook (D) 3, pp. 45–46. It is this heroism that Bligh was contemptuous of. See footnote 37.

42. King (D) 3, p. 45.

43. Ibid., pp. 45–46.

44. Ibid., p. 46.

45. Ibid., p. 49.

46. Peter Puget, *Log*, Adm 55/17, Public Records Office, London, entry for 26 February 1793. See also the shorter extract in George Vancouver, *The Voyage of George Vancouver, 1791–1795*, 4 vols., ed. W. Kaye Lamb (London: The Hakluyt Society, 1984), p. 831, n. 1. Puget's interview is one of the few occasions in which the native speaks. Yet Sahlins discounts the Hawaiian voice and says that the priest's statement is true of the events of 1793 (Vancouver's visit) and not of 1779 (Cook's death). For him this is a later Hawaiian rationalization. Yet he takes the statement of missionaries and Christian converts, recorded between forty to eighty years after Cook's death, as expressive of the actualities of 1779!

47. See John F. G. Stokes, "Origin of the Condemnation of Captain Cook in Hawaii," *Hawaiian Historical Society 39th Annual Report* (Honolulu, 1930), pp. 68–104; Thomas G. Thrum, "The Paehumu of Heiaus Non-Sacred," *Hawaiian Historical Society 35th Annual Report* (Honolulu, 1926), pp. 56–57; Beaglehole in Cook (B) 3a, p. 516, n. 3, and Beaglehole's *Life*, pp. 655–56. Most of the debate is based on Thrum's brief paper. I quote the relevant section: "These wooden images set up outside the heiau were not restricted (kapu) from use even as fuel. *On some occasions* these wooden images were burned as firewood by the people" (my italics). But the *only* example Thrum gives of these "occasions" is the case of "Ka-we-lo at his embarking for war on Kauai, at his consecrating the heiau of Pu-ehu at Wai-a-nae. At the close of the sacrificial service he commanded that the wood of the paehumu, the fence wood, and also the images of the heiau be

taken for firewood, in provision for his war in Kauai." This action performed at
the close of a "sacrificial service" could hardly serve as an example of people using
the fence and the images for firewood!

48. Cook (D) 3, pp. 25–26.

49. Cook (B) 3a, p. 516.

50. James Kenneth Munford, ed., *John Ledyard's Journal of Captain Cook's Last
Voyage* (Corvallis: Oregon State University Press), 1963.

51. For a criticism of Ledyard, see Beaglehole in Cook (B) 3a, p. ccix; with reference to the Banks expedition, see Patrick O'Brian, *Joseph Banks, a Life* (London:
Collins Harvill, 1988), pp. 230–31.

52. Munford, ed., *Ledyard's Journal*, pp. 90–100.

53. Ibid., p. 102.

54. Ibid., pp. 136–37.

55. James Trevenen, *Penrose Memoirs of James Trevenen*, Greenwich Maritime Museum ms.

56. Munford, ed., *Ledyard's Journal*, p. 137.

57. John Law, *Log*, entry for 1 February 1779. My italics.

58. Thomas Edgar, *The Edgar Journal of Captain Cook's Third Voyage 1776–1778*,
Adm. 55/21, Public Records Office ms., London, entry for 1 February 1779.

59. U. Tewsley, ed., *Zimmermann's Third Voyage of Captain Cook 1776–1780* (Wellington, 1926), p. 37.

60. George Vancouver, *The Voyage of George Vancouver 1791–1795*, ed. W. Kaye
Lamb, vol. 3, p. 817.

VI

1. Cook (B) 3a, p. 596.

2. J. C. Beaglehole, *The Life of Captain James Cook* (London: The Hakluyt Society,
1974), p. 580.

3. Ibid., p. 652.

4. Cook (D) 3, p. 69.

5. Ibid., p. 9.

6. Ibid., pp. 6, 5.

7. Cook (B) 3b, p. 1216.

8. Ibid., p. 1201.

9. James Trevenen, *Penrose Memoirs of James Trevenen*, Greenwich Maritime Museum ms.

10. Cited in Sir Joseph Carruthers, *Captain James Cook, R.N.: One Hundred and
Fifty Years After* (New York: Dutton and Company, 1930), p. 125.

11. Cook (B) 3b, p. 1200.

12. U. Tewsley, ed., *Zimmermann's Third Voyage of Captain Cook 1776–1780* (Wellington, 1926), p. 43.

13. The best known of these stories is the romantic love affair between an English
sailor and a Maori lady, Ghowannahe. John Rickman, *Journal of Captain Cook's
Last Voyage to the Pacific Ocean* (London, 1781), rpt. Readex Microprint, 1966, pp.
59–67.

14. Ibid., p. 305. Rickman's Hawaiian was rendered by John Charlot as *he atua nui*,
"a big god." It is likely that Hawaiians told Rickman that Lono was "a big god,"

and Rickman typically completed the equation: Cook = Lono = the big god. It should be noted that Rickman is simply recording gossip; and his account of these ceremonies has the times and places all wrong.

15. Ibid., p. 306.
16. U. Tewsley, ed., *Zimmermann's Third Voyage*, p. 36.
17. Ibid., p. 37.
18. George Robertson, *The Discovery of Tahiti* (London: The Hakluyt Society, 1948), p. 156, my italics.
19. Tzvetan Todorov, *The Conquest of America: The Question of the Other*, trans. Richard Howard (New York: Harper Torchbooks, 1987), p. 117.
20. Cook (D) 3, p. 5.
21. Ibid., p. 15.
22. Cook (B) 3a, p. 510. The only place in the unofficial journal that comes close to the idea of "religious adoration" is p. 564, where Cook is paid "almost divine honour."
23. Trevenen, *Penrose Memoirs*, ms.
24. William Cowper, *The Works of William Cowper: His Life, Letters, and Poems*, ed. Rev. T. S. Grimshawe (Boston, 1854), pp. 201–2. Two years before this date in June–July 1781, Cowper, on hearing of Cook's death, wrote a eulogy expressing the Enlightenment idea of Cook, the civilizer. In this poem, *Charity*, the good Cook is contrasted with Cortés, the evil conquistador.

> When Cook—lamented, and with tears as just
> As ever mingled with heroic dust—
> Steer'd Britain's oak into a world unknown,
> And in his country's glory sought his own,
> Wherever he found man to nature true,
> The rights of man were sacred in his view:
> He soothed with gifts, and greeted with a smile,
> The simple native of the new-found isle;
> He spurn'd the wretch that slighted or withstood
> The tender argument of kindred blood;
> Nor would endure that any should control
> His freeborn brethren of the southern pole.
> But, though some nobler minds a law respect,
> That none shall with impunity neglect,
> In baser souls unnumber'd evils meet,
> To thwart its influence, and its end defeat.
> *While Cook is loved for savage lives he saved;*
> *See Cortez odious for a world enslaved!*
>
> (Ibid., p. 546, my italics)

25. A. Kippis, *A Narrative of the Voyages . . . Performed by Captain James Cook . . .* (Boston, 1830), p. 173.
26. Ibid.
27. Ibid., pp. 174–75.
28. Ibid., p. 174.
29. It is worth quoting the full title of this text:

> A short account of the new Pantomime called OMAI or a Trip round the World; performed at the Theatre-Royal in Covent Garden with the Recitatives, Airs,

Duetts, Trios and Chorusses; and a Description of the PROCESSION. The Pantomime and the whole of the Scenery, designed and invented by Mr. LOUTHERBOURG. The Words written by Mr. O'KEEFFE; and the Music composed by Mr. Shields. London for T. CADELL in the Strand [MDCCLXXXV].

For other accounts of this pantomime, see R. Joppien, "Philippe Jacques de Loutherbourg's pantomime 'Omai, or, A Trip round the World' and the Artists of Cook's Voyages," *Captain Cook and the South Pacific* (London: British Museum Yearbook 3, 1979); and Greg Dening, "Possessing Tahiti," *Archaeology and Physical Anthropology in Oceania* 21 (1986), pp. 103–18.

30. According to Clarke, *Omai* was "one of the six most successful stage shows in the entire century" and even the king commanded it to be shown often (Thomas Blake Clarke, *Omai, First Polynesian Ambassador to England* [Honolulu: University of Hawaii Press, 1969 [1940]], pp. 87, 92). A fine collection of the playbills of this production is available in the Huntington Library.

31. The preceding quotations are from *Omai, or a trip round the world . . .* , p. 23. Italics in the original.

32. Ibid.

33. Ibid., p. 24.

34. Ibid., p. 23.

35. Robin Fisher and Hugh Johnston, eds., *Captain James Cook and His Times* (Seattle: University of Washington Press, 1979), pp. 159–85.

36. Bernard Smith, "Cook's Posthumous Reputation," in Fisher and Johnston, eds., *Captain Cook*, p. 159.

37. Ibid., p. 161.

38. Ibid., p. 160.

39. Ibid., p. 175.

40. Ibid., p. 178.

41. Ibid., p. 179.

42. Ibid., p. 189.

43. J. C. Beaglehole, "On the Character of Captain James Cook," *The Geographical Journal* 122, 4 (1956), p. 425.

44. Alan Frost, "New Geographical Perspectives and the Emergence of the Romantic Imagination," in Fisher and Johnston, eds., *Captain James Cook*, p. 45.

45. For an exposition of this thesis, see Sir James Watt, "Medical Aspects and Consequences of Cook's Voyages," in Fisher and Johnston, eds., *Captain James Cook*, pp. 129–57. This bizarre thesis says that Cook suffered from "a parasitic infection of the intestine, probably of the lower ileum," with the following symptoms: "prolonged ill health, fatigue, loss of appetite, stubborn constipation, loss of weight, digestive disturbances, loss of interest and initiative; irritability, depression, loss of concentration and memory, and change of personality" (p. 155). Worms must have had a particular partiality for Cook, since none of the other officers seemed to have suffered from these symptoms, especially from a "change of personality."

46. David Mackay, "The New Zealand Legacy of James Cook," paper delivered at *The New Zealand Universities Graduates Association*, 1990, 17 pp., typescript, p. 1.

47. Ibid., p. 15.

48. Ibid., p. 16.
49. Ibid., pp. 15–16.
50. Ibid., p. 17.
51. Ibid., p. 13.
52. Ibid., p. 17.
53. Keith Sinclair, *History of New Zealand* (London: Penguin, 1969), pp. 32–33.
54. J. C. Beaglehole, *The Discovery of New Zealand* (London: Oxford University Press, 1961), p. 88. Beaglehole has reprinted Te Horeta's account as Appendix B, pp. 88–93.
55. Ibid., p. 89.
56. Ibid., p. 93.
57. Ibid., p. 91.
58. Robert McNab, *From Tasman to Marsden* (Dunedin, 1914), p. 176.
59. Lynne Withey, *Voyages of Discovery: Captain Cook and the Exploration of the Pacific* (Berkeley and Los Angeles: University of California Press, 1989), p. 213.
60. Harrison M. Wright, *New Zealand, 1769–1840: Early Years of Western Contact* (Cambridge: Harvard University Press, 1959), p. 7. Sahlins says that Cook was known among the Maori as Rongo-Tuute (i.e., Lono-Cook), and he thinks that this is an independent Maori invention. My own guess is that this is simply a later Maori translation of the Hawaiian. Greg Dening in *Islands and Beaches* (Honolulu: University of Hawaii Press, 1980), p. 16, attributes a similar reaction to the Marquesans. However, in a personal communication he tells me that the Marquesans labeled all foreigners *akua* but it is inappropriate to translate this as "god" in the Western sense. I think that when one tracks down these references to their original sources, they will turn out to be as empty as Te Horeta's account.
61. Mackay, "The New Zealand Legacy," p. 1.
62. Once one blurs the distinction between biography, history, and myth, it is easy to show that the Western imagination is full of myths. Cook myths flourish in New Zealand and Australia as ancestral myths of origin. For modern myth-makers Cook cannot have a dark side, for that is not what a founding ancestor of a modern nation should be. He ought to be a god to Hawaiians and a noble founder of a modern nation for whites. Biography, then, can as easily move into hagiography and myth, beautifully illustrated in another debate initiated by Sir Joseph Carruthers, Prime Minister of New South Wales between 1904–1908, who wrote a book to defend Cook's defamation by missionaries. In the foreword W. M. Hughes, a former prime minister of Australia, says that Cook was "the real founder of Australia" and that Cook's memory has been "besmirched by narrow minded men." Carruthers laments that nowadays (in 1930) young people "have not a sufficient veneration" for Cook. There has been "a slackness in the spirit of veneration" and one cannot afford that (p. x). The place in Australia where Cook first landed is "sacred soil to the people of Australia and to the people of the race which produced such a man as Captain Cook" (p. x). One cannot permit "calumny to overcome the reputation of so great and good a man as Captain Cook. In my humble judgement he stands foremost amongst men of the Anglo-Saxon race as an Empire Builder" (p. 5). Thus, the aim of his book, he says, is to correct the false belief that the last few weeks in Hawai'i "belied his unbroken record for humane and honourable dealing with the native races" (p.

6). His death "was due to an unfortunate misunderstanding, the responsibility of which lay more with the Hawaiians than with Cook" (p. 7). Samwell thought that the venereal was not introduced by the British; the Hawaiians always had it. Now we have the notion that the prime responsibility for the "unfortunate misunderstanding" that led to Cook's death lies with the Hawaiians. See Sir Joseph Carruthers, *Captain James Cook, R.N.*

63. Marshall Sahlins, *Historical Metaphors and Mythical Realities: Structure in the Early History of the Sandwich Islands Kingdom* (Ann Arbor: University of Michigan Press, 1981), p. 24.

64. Ibid.

65. Cook (D) 3, p. 69.

66. Cook (D) 2, pp. 208–9, 214.

67. Martha Beckwith, *Hawaiian Mythology* (New Haven: Yale University Press, 1940), pp. 340–43.

68. Cook (B) 3b, p. 1217.

69. Beckwith, *Hawaiian Mythology*, p. 164.

70. Peter Corney, *Voyages in the Northern Pacific* ... (Honolulu: Thomas G. Thrum, 1896), p. 103. Corney has a vivid example of such a visitation. A Hawaiian (servant of Don Marin, also known as Mr. Manning) "was one night awoke by some person calling him by name, and telling him to attend to what he said; he looked up, and was much terrified on beholding the pale form of the late King Pereoranee (Peleioholani) before him. . . . " (p. 115). This man's European employer had also been so much socialized into Hawaiian belief that he had similar confrontations with spirits (p. 116). Note also Freycinet: "It is a well established fact that the souls of the dead appear to the living and communicate with them in dreams." Louis de Freycinet, *Hawaii in 1819: A Narrative Account by Louis Claude de Saulses de Freycinet*, trans. Ella L. Wiswell (Honolulu: Bishop Museum, Department of Anthropology, Pacific Records No. 26, 1978), p. xx.

71. Beckwith, *Hawaiian Mythology*, p. 164.

72. Ibid., p. 2.

73. S. M. Kamakau, *Ka Po'e Kahiko, the People of Old*, trans. Mary K. Pukui, ed. Dorothy B. Barrère (Honolulu: Bishop Museum Press, 1964), p. 28.

74. Beckwith, *Hawaiian Mythology*, p. 2.

75. John Meares, *Voyages Made in the Years 1788 and 1789* ... (London, 1790; rpt. New York: Da Capo Press, 1967), p. 9.

76. See Gould, "Bligh's Notes on Cook's Last Voyage," *The Mariner's Mirror* 14 (October 1928), p. 383: "A strange absurdity [They] only feared when another Chief of equa[l] power to C. Cook ... should be sent from Brittania or Beretanee as they p[ro]nounced it, that they would be kill'd by [the] Number of Men he [would] bring with him."

77. James Colnett, *The Journal of James Colnett* (Toronto: The Champlain Society, 1940), p. 220.

78. S. M. Kamakau, *Ka Po'e Kahiko*, p. 54.

79. Archibald Campbell, *A Voyage round the World from 1806 to 1812* ... *with an Account of the* ... *Sandwich Islands* (Honolulu: University of Hawaii Press, 1967), p. 120.

80. See John Charlot, *The Hawaiian Poetry of Religion and Politics* (Honolulu:

University of Hawaii Press, 1985), published by The Institute for Polynesian Studies, Monograph Series no. 5, p. 67, n. 91. The text is found in Abraham Fornander, *Fornander Collection of Hawaiian Antiquities and Folklore*, vols. 4–6 (Honolulu: Memoirs of the Bernice Pauahi Bishop Museum, Bishop Museum Press, 1920), vol. 6, part 3, pp. 435–38. The text, however, is not absolutely clear on this point.

81. Otto Von Kotzebue, *A Voyage of Discovery into the South Sea and Beering's Straits*, 3 vols. (1821; rpt. New York: Da Capo Press, 1967; *A New Voyage round the World in the Years 1823–1826*, 2 vols. (1830; rpt. New York: Da Capo Press, 1967).

82. Kotzebue, *A Voyage*, vol. 3, p. 239.

83. Kotzebue, *A New Voyage*, vol. 2, p. 180.

84. Adelbert von Chamisso, *A Voyage around the World in the Romanzov Exploring Expedition . . . 1815–1818*, trans. and ed. Henry Kratz (Honolulu: University of Hawaii Press, 1986 [1836]), p. 306. Actually, this observation was published in Chamisso's appendix to the Russian edition of Kotzebue's voyages published in 1821 in a piece entitled "Notes and Opinions." It is added by the translator Henry Kratz to Chamisso's *A Voyage around the World . . .* , pp. 241–317. It is very explicitly an attempt to correct or qualify Kotzebue's statements. I am indebted to Professor Kratz, who rechecked this translation for me. Kratz thinks Chamisso meant "They honored him as if he were a god" (personal communication).

85. Ibid., p. 310, my italics.

86. V. M. Golovnin, *Around the World on the KAMCHATKA 1817–1819*, trans. with introduction and notes by Ella Lury Wiswell (Honolulu: The Hawaiian Historical Society and University of Hawaii Press, 1979 [1822]).

87. Kotzebue, *A New Voyage*, vol. 2, p. 179.

88. Ibid., p. 179.

89. Ibid., p. 184.

90. John Martin, *An Account of the Natives of the Tonga Islands . . . Communications of Mr. William Mariner* (London, 1817), vol. 2, p. 67.

91. Gilbert F. Mathison, *Narrative of a Visit to Brazil, Chile, Peru and the Sandwich Islands . . .* (London, 1825), p. 431.

92. Puget, *Log*, Adm 55/17, Public Records Office, London.

93. Cited in Marshall Sahlins, "Captain Cook in Hawaii," *Journal of the Polynesian Society* 98, 4 (December 1989), p. 381.

94. Freycinet, *Hawaii in 1819*, p. 73.

95. See especially ibid., pp. 67, 68–69, 76, 78.

96. These are James Hunnewell, Jacques Arago, George Mortimer, and John B. Whitman.

97. Maria Graham, comp., *Voyage of the H.M.S. Blonde to the Sandwich Islands in the Years 1824–25* (London: John Murray, 1826), p. 123.

98. Ibid., p. 196.

99. Andrew Bloxam, *Diary of Andrew Bloxam Naturalist of the "Blonde"* (Honolulu: Bishop Museum Special Publication No. 10, 1925), p. 49.

100. Ralph S. Kuykendall, *The Hawaiian Kingdom 1778–1854: Foundation and Transformation* (Honolulu: University of Hawaii Press, 1938), p. 23.

101. Ibid., pp. 23, 25.

102. Urey Lisiansky, *A Voyage round the World in the Years 1803, 4, 5 and 6* (London, 1814), pp. 113, 133.

103. Kuykendall, *The Hawaiian Kingdom*, pp. 39–60.

104. Glynn Barratt, *The Russian Discovery of Hawaii* (Honolulu: Editions Limited, 1987), p. 106.

105. Ibid.

106. Ibid., p. 111.

107. Ibid., p. 113.

108. Campbell, *A Voyage*, p. 119.

109. Ibid., p. 148.

110. Marshall Sahlins, *Islands of History* (Chicago: University of Chicago Press, 1985), p. 9.

111. Marshall Sahlins, "The Apotheosis of Captain Cook," in *Between Belief and Transgression: Structuralist Essays in Religion, History and Myth*, ed. Michael Izard and Pierre Smith (Chicago: University of Chicago Press, 1982), p. 96.

112. Peter Puget, British Museum Library ms; Add. 17546.

113. Kamakau, *Ka Po'e Kahiko*, p. 109.

114. Kotzebue, *A Voyage*, vol. 1, p. 312.

115. Barratt, *The Russian Discovery*, p. 105.

116. Kamakau, *Ka Po'e Kahiko*, p. 7.

117. Sahlins, "Apotheosis," p. 97.

118. Kamakau, *Ka Po'e Kahiko*, p. 7.

119. Mathison, *Narrative*, pp. 431–32.

120. Thomas Manby, "Journal of Vancouver's Voyage to the Pacific Ocean (1791–1793)," *The Honolulu Mercury* 1, 2 (July 1929), p. 44.

121. Ibid.

122. Edward Bell, "Log of the Chatham," *The Honolulu Mercury* 1, 6 (November 1929), p. 80. Sahlins in "Captain Cook in Hawaii" (p. 378) produces proof of Cook's divinity by omitting the crucial "to" in Bell's sentence: "They look'd upon him as [to] a supernatural being."

123. Robert Dampier, *To the Sandwich Islands on H.M.S. Blonde*, ed. Pauline King Joerger (Honolulu: University of Hawaii Press, 1971), p. 65.

124. Maria Graham, comp., *Voyage of the H.M.S. Blonde*, p. 111.

125. W. D. Westervelt, *Hawaiian Historical Legends* (New York: Fleming H. Revell Company, 1926).

126. Ibid., pp. 108–9.

VII

1. Dorothy M. Kahananui, ed., *Ka Mooolelo Hawaii, Hawaiian Language Reader Based on Sheldon Dibble, Ka Mooolelo Hawaii* (Honolulu: University of Hawaii Press, 1984).

2. Malo was born in 1795, John Papa I'i in 1800, and Kamakau in 1815. Malo's father was connected with Kamehameha's court and army. Kamakau, among the Hawaiian scholars, was the youngest and the most Christianized. According to N. B. Emerson, Malo got his information from Auwai, an old chief of Kamehameha I's time. As a result of his conversion, he turned against his old culture,

including traditional song and dance. He called it the pit from which he was dragged. See Nathaniel B. Emerson, introduction to David Malo, *Hawaiian Antiquities*, 2d ed., trans. Nathaniel B. Emerson (Honolulu: Bishop Museum Press, 1951), pp. 6–7.

3. David Malo, *Hawaiian Antiquities*, p. 145.

4. Cowper's works were well-known in the United States. "In 1790, nearly a hundred newspapers were printed in the United States. They carried local news and advertisements and excerpts from the works of William Cowper and Goldsmith and Cook's *Voyages*"; Richard A. Van Orman, *The Explorers* (Albuquerque: University of New Mexico Press, 1984), p. 63.

5. For a recent account of this momentous event, see S. Lee Seaton, "The Hawaiian *Kapu* Abolition of 1819," *American Ethnologist* 1, 1 (1974), pp. 193–206.

6. Glynn Barratt, *The Russian Discovery of Hawaii* (Honolulu: Editions Limited, 1987), p. 70.

7. Ralph S. Kuykendall, *The Hawaiian Kingdom 1778–1854: Foundation and Transformation* (Honolulu: University of Hawaii Press, 1938), pp. 65–70.

8. Ibid., p. 68. This account reported by Kuykendall is probably mythicized. Other accounts say that the king was in a drunken state when he effected this "reform." For a brief overview, see Dorothy B. Barrère, *Kamehameha in Kona: Two Documentary Studies*, Pacific Anthropological Records No. 23 (Honolulu: Bishop Museum, Department of Anthropology, 1975), pp. 33–34.

9. Louis de Freycinet, *Hawaii in 1819: A Narrative Account by Louis Claude de Saulses de Freycinet*, trans. Ella L. Wiswell (Honolulu: Bishop Museum, Department of Anthropology, Pacific Records No. 26, 1978), p. 28.

10. Gilbert F. Mathison, *Narrative of a Visit to Brazil, Chile, Peru and the Sandwich Islands* . . . (London, 1825). "The royal beast lay sprawling on the ground in a state of total drunkenness and insensibility" (pp. 364–65). The table "groaned under the weight of bottles of wine, and almost every known spirituous liquor" (p. 367). In reference to the old religion: "They now entertain sentiments as strong the other way, and despise the very idols which till lately they adored: the mere mention of them appears ridiculous, and scarcely a vestige remains to satisfy the curiosity of strangers" (pp. 430–31). Reference to the destruction of the tabu system: "The images were committed to the flames; and so complete was the work of destruction, that, in the course of a few months, neither sacrifices nor religious observances of any sort were kept, and even thought of, by the inhabitants" (p. 447). Kava seems to have been discontinued and instead: "Drunkenness is a far more universal and dangerous propensity; all classes indulging, more or less, to excess in the use of spirituous liquors, from the king himself downwards: the consumption therefore is enormous" (p. 469).

11. William Ellis, *Journal of William Ellis. A Narrative of a Tour through Owhyhee* . . . (Rutland and Tokyo: Charles Tuttle, 1979); *Polynesian Researches, during a Residence of Nearly Eight Years in the Society and Sandwich Islands*, vol. 4 (London, 1831).

12. Ellis, *Journal*, p. 83.

13. It is also possible that Ellis was familiar with myths of Rono [i.e., Lono] developed elsewhere in Polynesia and incorporated the Hawaiian into the larger Polynesian version.

14. Ellis, *Polynesian Researches*, pp. 134–35.
15. Note that the ship's officers were clear that it was not Lono but Kū who was covered in (probably red) cloth.
16. Ellis, *Journal*, p. 84; see also *Polynesian Researches*, pp. 132–33.
17. James Jackson Jarves, *History of the Hawaiian or Sandwich Islands* ... (Boston, 1843).
18. John F. G. Stokes, "Origin of the Condemnation of Captain Cook in Hawaii," *Hawaiian Historical Society 39th Annual Report*, 1930, p. 93.
19. Ibid., p. 94.
20. Sheldon Dibble, *A History of the Sandwich Islands* (Honolulu: Thomas G. Thrum, 1909), p. 134.
21. Ibid., p. 19.
22. Stokes, *Origin*, p. 96.
23. Ibid., pp. 96–97.
24. Kahanui, ed., *Mooolelo*, pp. 194–95.
25. Ibid., p. 194.
26. Ibid., p. 195.
27. Ibid.
28. Ibid., pp. 194–95.
29. Ibid., p. 230.
30. Ibid.
31. Ibid., p. 231.
32. Ibid., p. 173.
33. Ibid., p. 174.
34. Hiram Bingham, *A Residence of Twenty-One Years in the Sandwich Islands* ... , 3d ed. (New York, 1855), p. 35.
35. Cook (B) 2, p. 274.
36. Cook (B) 3a, p. 200.
37. Abraham Fornander, *An Account of the Polynesian Races* ... , 3 vols. in 1 (1878–80; rpt. Rutland, Vermont, and Tokyo: Charles Tuttle, 1980), vol. 2, p. 163.
38. Dorothy B. Barrère, "Foreword," in S. M. Kamakau, *Ka Po'e Kahiko, the People of Old*, trans. Mary K. Pukui, ed. Dorothy B. Barrère (Honolulu: Bishop Museum Press, 1964), p. viii.
39. S. M. Kamakau, *Ruling Chiefs of Hawaii* (Honolulu: The Kamehameha Schools Press, 1961), p. 98.
40. Kamakau, *Ka Po'e Kahiko*, p. 59.
41. Kamakau, *Ruling Chiefs*, p. 100.
42. Ibid., pp. 99–100.
43. Ibid., p. 100.
44. Ibid., pp. 103–4.
45. N. B. Emerson, *The Long Voyages of the Ancient Hawaiians*, Hawaiian Historical Society Papers No. 5, pp. 5–13; Ellis, *Polynesian Researches*, p. 437.
46. Martha Beckwith, *Hawaiian Mythology* (New Haven: Yale University Press, 1940), p. 384.
47. Ibid., p. 46.
48. Cook (B) 3a, p. 625.
49. Cook (D) 3, p. 131. The first arrivals after Cook were Portlock in the *King*

George and Dixon in the *Queen Charlotte* in 1786. Beresford, the author of Dixon's journal, wrote about Tiara, a chief of Kaua'i. "He asked many questions about the vessel: In what manner we steered her? How we managed the sail? etc. He admired the compass very much, and seemed to comprehend, that it was our guide to various parts of the world: he was particularly anxious to know which part of the compass pointed towards Pritane [Brittanee]. . . . So far from being asked merely to satisfy an idle curiosity . . . they [his questions] maintained an eager desire of information, and entirely shewed that the questioner was possessed of strong natural abilities," in George Dixon, *A Voyage round the World . . . Performed in 1785, 1786, 1787 and 1788* (London, 1789), pp. 121–22.

50. Kamakau, *Ruling Chiefs*, pp. 94–95.

51. Ibid., p. 96.

52. Ibid., p. 95.

53. Ibid., p. 101.

54. Gananath Obeyesekere, *The Work of Culture: Symbolic Transformation in Psychoanalysis and Anthropology* (Chicago: University of Chicago Press, 1990), pp. 130–36.

55. Dibble, *A History*, pp. 22–23.

56. Ibid., pp. 23–24. It is fascinating to see how false information of this sort can be incorporated into a tradition. Here is Varigny who was in Hawai'i during 1855–1868 writing about a Hawaiian informant telling him that Cook's people "were eating and drinking blood, and after eating of the flesh they tossed into the water a thick green skin (the ships came from Monterey and the sailors were probably on the deck eating watermelons)." Charles de Varigny, *Fourteen Years in the Sandwich Islands, 1855–1868* (Honolulu: University of Hawaii Press, 1981), p. 15.

57. Dibble, *A History*, p. 33.

58. Ibid., p. 86.

59. *Rājāvaliya, The Rājāvaliya or A Historical Narrative of Sinhalese Kings*, ed. B. Gunasékara (Colombo: Government Press, 1900), p. 63. For a good discussion of the Sri Lankan reaction to the arrival of the Portuguese, see Michael Roberts, "A Tale of Resistance: The Story of the Arrival of the Portuguese in Sri Lanka," *Ethnos* 55, 1–2, pp. 69–82.

60. See p. 135 of this volume.

61. George Forster, *A Voyage round the World in His Brittanic Majesty's Sloop, Resolution . . .* , vol. 2 (London, 1777), pp. 68–69.

62. Marshall Sahlins, "The Apotheosis of Captain Cook," in Michael Izard and Pierre Smith, eds., *Between Belief and Transgression: Structuralist Essays in Religion, History and Myth* (Chicago: University of Chicago Press, 1982), p. 94.

63. Ibid.

64. M. M. Bakhtin, "The Problem of Speech Genres," in M. M. Bakhtin, *Speech Genres and Other Late Essays* (Austin: University of Texas Press, 1986), pp. 76–94; and John R. Searle, *Expression and Meaning: Studies in the Theory of Speech Acts* (Cambridge: Cambridge University Press, 1985), pp. 77–78.

65. Cook (B) 3b, p. 1186.

66. George Robertson, *The Discovery of Tahiti* (London: The Hakluyt Society, 1948), p. 159.

67. Cook (B) 3a, p. 507.
68. Forster, *A Voyage round the World*, p. 315.
69. Cook (B) 1, pp. 291–94. For details see Gordon R. Lewthwaite, "The Puzzle of Tupaia's Map," *New Zealand Geographer* 26 (1976), pp. 1–19.
70. Lynne Withey, *Voyages of Discovery: Captain Cook and the Exploration of the Pacific* (Berkeley and Los Angeles: University of California Press, 1989), p. 222; see also Forster, *A Voyage round the World*, p. 302.
71. Withey, *Voyages of Discovery*, p. 246.

VIII

1. Marshall Sahlins, "Captain James Cook; or the Dying God," in *Islands of History* (Chicago: University of Chicago Press, 1985), p. 106.
2. Cook (B) 3a, p. 536.
3. Cook (B) 3b, p. 1195.
4. Cook (D) 3, p. 43.
5. Sahlins, "The Dying God," pp. 106–7, my italics.
6. Ibid., p. 107.
7. Cook (B) 3a, p. 535, my italics.
8. Sahlins, "The Dying God," p. 109.
9. Ibid., p. 129.
10. Ibid.
11. Valerio Valeri, *Kingship and Sacrifice: Ritual and Society in Ancient Hawaii* (Chicago: University of Chicago Press, 1985), p. 211.
12. Bligh says: "The Marines fire[d] and ran which occasioned al[l] that followed for had the[y] fixed their bayonets and not have run, so frighte[ned] as they were, they migh[t] have drove all before t[hem]." Again: "I took down in writing all that happened here before I slept . . . as soon as the Musquets were discharged they ran into the Boats, having no time to reload, and was stabed in the back when unable to make any resistance" (Rupert T. Gould, "Bligh's Notes on Cook's Last Voyage," *The Mariner's Mirror* 14 [October 1928], pp. 280, 281).
13. Sahlins, "The Apotheosis of Captain Cook." in *Between Belief and Transgression: Structuralist Essays in Religion, History and Myth*, ed. Michael Izard and Pierre Smith (Chicago: University of Chicago Press, 1982), p. 85, n. 9.
14. The relevant part of this chant reads:

> Born was Laʻilaʻi a woman
> Born was Kiʻi a man
> Born was Kāne a god
> Born was Kanaloa the hot striking Octopus . . .

Martha Beckwith, *The Kumulipo, a Hawaiian Creation Chant* (Honolulu: The University of Hawaii Press, 1972), pp. 97–98. Nowhere in the *Kumulipo* is there any reference to an original triad in Sahlins's sense.
15. Cook (B) 3a, p. 535.
16. Cook (D) 3, p. 44.
17. Cook (B) 3b, p. 1196.
18. Sahlins, "The Dying God," p. 129.
19. Marshall Sahlins, *Historical Metaphors and Mythical Realities: Structure in the*

Early History of the Sandwich Islands Kingdom (Ann Arbor: University of Michigan Press, 1981), pp. 23–24, my italics.

20. Valeri, *Kingship and Sacrifice*, pp. 211–12.

21. Ibid., p. 226.

22. Sahlins, "The Dying God," p. 129.

23. Ibid., p. 129.

24. Ibid., p. 108.

25. Ibid., p. 129.

26. Ibid., p. xiii.

27. Ibid., p. 130.

28. Bernard Smith, *European Vision and the South Pacific* (New Haven and London: Yale University Press, 1985), pp. 113–14.

29. Ibid., p. 114.

30. R. Joppien and B. Smith, *The Art of Captain Cook's Voyages, The Voyage of the Resolution and Discovery 1776–1786*, part 1 (New Haven and London: Yale University Press, 1988), p. 12.

31. Ibid., p. 127.

32. Ibid.

33. Trevenen, *Penrose Memoirs*, Greenwich Maritime Museum ms.

34. Cook (B) 3a, p. 624. Omiah's motivation is jealousy and/or the sense of public humiliation seeing his wife in the company of an English officer. In his official account, King refers to what occurred before the episode of beating: "At one of the entertainments of boxing, Omeah was observed to rise from his place two or three times, and go up to his wife with strong marks of displeasure, ordering her, as it appeared to us from his manner, to withdraw" (Cook [D], p. 165). Clearly she was in the company of the same officer and far from withdrawing, she walked arm in arm with him after the show.

35. Puget, British Museum Library ms. Add. 17546.

36. Ibid.

37. Edward Bell, "Log of the Chatham," *The Honolulu Mercury* 1, 6 (November 1929), p. 86, my italics. For a list of other candidates claiming the honor of killing Cook, see Beaglehole, n. 3, in Cook (B) 3a, p. 557. Perhaps the most bizarre account is from a "native chant" recorded by Charles de Varigny, *Fourteen Years in the Sandwich Islands 1855–1868* (Honolulu: University of Hawaii Press, 1981), pp. 15–16, where a chief, Kalaimano, killed Cook. He was actually wielding a bow!

38. Archibald Campbell, *A Voyage round the World from 1806 to 1812 . . . with an Account of the . . . Sandwich Islands* (Honolulu: University of Hawaii Press, 1967), p. 101.

39. Peter Corney, *Voyages in the Northern Pacific . . .* (Honolulu: Thomas G. Thrum, 1896), p. 86.

40. Dorothy B. Barrère, *Kamehameha in Kona: Two Documentary Studies*, Pacific Anthropological Records No. 23 (Honolulu: Bishop Museum, Department of Anthropology, 1975), pp. 25–26.

41. Cook (B) 3a, p. 554.

42. Cook (D) 3, p. 56.

43. Ibid., pp. 64–65. The phrase "sign of Defiance" is from Cook (B) 3a, p. 561.

44. Trevenen, *Penrose Memoirs*, Greenwich Maritime Museum ms.

45. Cook (B) 3a, p. 545.
46. Cook (B) 3b, p. 1210.
47. Cook (B) 3a, p. 545.
48. Cook (B) 3a, p. 562, n. 2.
49. Ibid.
50. Ibid. This is Trevenen's statement quoted by Beaglehole from the *Penrose Memoirs*.
51. Ibid.
52. Ibid.
53. The first quote is from Samwell in Cook (B) 3b, p. 1213, and the second is from the Trevenen ms. and in Cook (B) 3a, p. 562, n. 1.
54. Cook (B) 3a, p. 563.
55. Cook (B) 3b, p. 1211.
56. Cook (D) 3, pp. 76–77.
57. Cook (B) 3a, p. 563, n. 1. "The two heads were thrown overboard in his sight, least he should suppose us Cannibals."
58. See Didier Anzieu, *Freud's Self-Analysis* (London: Hogarth Press, 1986), pp. 112–13; and Bruno Bettleheim, *Symbolic Wounds: Puberty Rites and the Envious Male* (New York: Collier Books, 1971), pp. 24–32.
59. Rupert T. Gould, "Some Unpublished Accounts of Cook's Death," *The Mariner's Mirror* 14 (1928), p. 312.
60. Cook (B) 3b, p. 1207.
61. Gould, "Some Unpublished Accounts," p. 312, n. 1.
62. This is described in the journal of Lieutenant Roux in Robert McNab, *Historical Records of New Zealand*, vol. 2 (Wellington: Government Printer, 1914), p. 423: "A chief was now wearing it [Marion's velvet waistcoat], and held in his hands the dead man's gun, which was silver-mounted, and which the savage held up so that it could be seen. Others of the savages imitated his example, exhibiting the uniforms of the two officers whom they had murdered with our commander." See also Du Clesmeur's journal in McNab, *Historical Records*, p. 465.
63. Sahlins, "The Dying God," pp. 133–34.
64. Ibid., p. 131.
65. Cook (D) 3, p. 66.
66. According to King's informants 17 people, 5 of them important chiefs, were killed in the fray at Ka'awaloa; later 8 people, among them 3 of note, were killed near the observatory (Cook [B] 3a, p. 561). Clerke had the following estimates for the whole period: 4 chiefs killed and 6 wounded, and 25 ordinary people killed and 15 wounded (Cook [B] 3a, p. 547).
67. The anthropological reader will know that I refer to the seminal paper by Victor Turner, "Betwixt and Between: The Liminal Period in *Rites de Passage*," in his *The Forest of Symbols* (Ithaca: Cornell University Press, 1967), pp. 93–111.

Afterword

1. In this afterword I shall employ the same notational system as in the main work, except that the references to *How "Natives" Think* and this volume shall be referred to as "N" and "A," respectively.

2. "Ritual murder" is Sahlins's term; see, for example, p. 238. It is a contradiction because the classic killing of the king or god is "ritual," never murder. Sometimes an enactment takes place, while at others there is a sacrificial-type killing. In neither case does this constitute "murder."

3. See Gananath Obeyesekere, "Reweaving the Argument: A Response to Parker," *Oceania* 65 (1995), pp. 265–73. For Henry James, see especially chapter 23 of *The Bostonians*. See also Herman Melville, *Mardi*, chaps. 53–55.

4. Cook (B) 3a, p. 269.

5. Cook (B) 3b, pp. 1161–62. See also A, pp. 86–87; N, pp. 129, 134.

6. Cook (D) 3, p. 5, n.; N, p. 134.

7. William Hamlin, "Attributions of Divinity in Renaissance Ethnography and Romance; or, Making a Religion of Wonder," *Journal of Medieval and Renaissance Studies* 24 (1992), pp. 415–47; "Imagined Apotheoses: Drake, Harriot, and Raleigh in the Americas" *Journal of the History of Ideas* 57 (1996), pp. 405–28.

8. Hamlin, "Attributions of Divinity," p. 418.

9. Ibid., pp. 430–31, n. 36.

10. Ibid., p. 424.

11. Edward L. Schiefflin and Robert Crittendon, *Like People You See in a Dream*, (Stanford: Stanford University Press, 1991).

12. In Melanesia itself, an obvious case would be where an ethnographer or a white adminstrator or missionary enters into a cargo-cult situation where all sorts of projective mechanisms around the expected Messiah are released and get focused on the alien presence.

13. Sahlins has personal reports from Melanesianists in the field who reported cases of cultural projections without analyzing them in detail. The most interesting case is that of Maria Lepowsky, who told Sahlins that she was treated as a "supernatural being," something that made her "politically uncomfortable." I doubt Melanesians made a distinction between nature and supernature. Further, one wonders where ethnographic integrity lies when a scholar elides important information in her published work owing to "political discomfort" (N, pp. 188–89).

14. Gananath Obeyesekere, *The Work of Culture: Symbolic Transformation in Psychoanalysis and Anthropology* (Chicago: University of Chicago Press, 1990), p. 94.

15. Ibid., p. 105.

16. Paul Ricoeur, *Time and Narrative*, 3 vols. (Chicago: University of Chicago Press, 1984, 1985, 1988); for a succinct account of history as "fiction," see "The Narrative Function," in *Hermeneutics and the Human Sciences*, John B. Thompson, ed. (Cambridge: Cambridge University Press, 1981), pp. 274–96; Michel de Certeau, *Heterologies: Discourse on the Other*, trans. Brian Massumi. Theory and History of Literature, vol. 17 (Minneapolis: University of Minnesota Press, 1986), especially the essay "The Freudian Novel: History and Literature," pp. 17–34.

17. See A, 281, n. 24, for the text of Cowper's marvelous paean of praise of Cook.

18. Dorothy M. Kahananui, ed., *Ka Mooolelo Hawai'i* (Honolulu: University of Hawai'i Press, 1984), p. 173.

19. Marshall Sahlins, *Historical Metaphors and Mythical Realities: Structure in the Early History of the Sandwich Islands Kingdom* (Ann Arbor: University of Michigan Press, 1981) p. 18.

20. David Malo, *Hawai'ian Antiquities*, 2d ed., trans. Nathaniel B. Emerson [1898] (Honolulu: Bishop Museum Press, 1951), p. 145.

21. Obeyesekere, *The Work of Culture*, p. 104.

22. U. Tewsley, trans., *Zimmermann's Third Voyage of Captain Cook 1776–1780* (Wellington, 1926), p. 42.

23. Cook (B) 3a, p. 179; for Samwell see A, p. 72.

24. For a slightly different translation see Tewsley, *Zimmermann's Third Voyage*, p. 36.

25. See also ibid., p. 39.

26. Ibid.

27. This is in Captain Clerke's account in Cook (B) 3a, p. 542. King's account suggests that Cook's flesh was brought the day before.

28. Tewsley, *Zimmermann's Third Voyage*, p. 37.

29. John Rickman, *Journal of Captain Cook's Last Voyage to the Pacific Ocean* (London, 1781; rpt. Readex Microprint, 1966), p. 332; N, p. 174; A, pp. 71–72.

30. Cook (B) 3a, ccv.

31. Cited in Hamlin, "Imagined Apotheoses," p. 421, my italics.

32. Ibid., p. 427.

33. These issues are dealt with at great length for Buddhist Sri Lanka by Richard Gombrich and Gananath Obeyesekere and very recently by the Sri Lankan anthropologist Sasanka Perera. See Richard Gombrich and Gananath Obeyesekere, *Buddhism Transformed: Religious Change in Sri Lanka* (Princeton: Princeton University Press, 1988); Sasanka Perera, "Sinhalas, Their Extra-Terrestrial Origins and Scholars from Gagaland," *Pravada* 4 (9) (1997), pp. 16–18.

34. Valerio Valeri, review of *The Apotheosis of Captain Cook*, *Pacific Studies* 17 (2) (1994), p. 129.

35. Cook, incidentally, was totally familiar with this mode of kissing from his extensive experiences in Polynesia.

36. The phrase that Sahlins uses from Samwell to prove that a kind of Shakespearean act was taking place is given in N, p. 234: "They [the queen and chiefs] wou'd not suffer him to go any further, *telling him that is he went on board the Ship he would be killed*" (Sahlins's italics). Telling the frightened husband/king that he would be killed if he went on board ship is for Sahlins "telling such stories of the death of kings."

37. Cook (B) 3a, cliv.

38. Sahlins, *Historical Metaphors*, p. 18.

39. Cook (B) 3a, p. 550.

40. Valeri, Review, pp. 130–31.

41. For example, see Malo, *Hawai'ian Antiquities*, especially the classification of "Domestic and Wild Animals" (chap. 13, pp. 37–41) and "The Fishes" (chap. 15, pp. 45–47).

42. None of the Chinese scholars I have talked to has been able to locate this Chinese encyclopedia. Keith Windschuttle has a highly polemical critique of the bleaker forms of postmodernism in *The Killing of History: How a Discipline is Murdered by Literary Critics and Social Theorists* (Sydney: Macleay Press, 1994). In the new edition to this work, he has a chapter entitled "The Return to Tribalism: Cultural Relativism, Structuralism and the Death of Cook," where he makes the same point that there is no such Chinese encyclopedia. Unfortunately, Windschuttle overdoes his case without recognizing that one can have responsible social theories emphasizing

nomological thought that have been both influenced by and critical of poststructuralist and postmodern thought.

43. This is another of Sahlins's bizarre interpretations. "Thus, by way of the Hawai'ian cosmic scheme, a seemingly bizarre report such as Colnett's can be understood as a coherent synthesis of history (Cook's death), seismology (two volcanic eruptions) and theology (the return of Lono). That's what I mean by 'mythopraxis'" (N, p. 92). With such definitions, virtually anything could be subsumed under mythopraxis.

44. Sahlins, *Historical Metaphors*, p. 17, italics in original.

45. In *Imagining Karma: Ethical Transformation in Amerindian, Buddhist and Greek Rebirth* (forthcoming).

46. Though the phrase "natives' point of view" is nowadays associated with Clifford Geertz, it was Bronislaw Malinowski's term originally.

47. Obeyesekere, *The Work of Culture*, pp. 218–25.

48. The trouble with Sahlins is that he takes a single word or phrase heard by a British seaman as an accurate rendering of Hawai'ian for Lono and this is true of his use of Zimmermann's and Edgar's accounts. Herb Kane's recent essay casts doubt on Edgar's rendering of "Arrono." "*Lono* (formerly *rono*) has several meanings. It can mean news or announcement and, with the prefix *ho'o* (*ho'orono*), a warning to be attentive. *Ho'orono* may have been what the British heard when Cook landed and was lead to the temple by a herald crying what sounded like *orono*, for it was the command by which commoners were warned of the approach of a chief of the highest rank, requiring them to prostrate themselves as an act of deference. . . . Commoners referring to Cook as *orono* during the circuit of the island may actually have been saying *ho'orono* to caution others of the British chief's presence." *Current Anthropology* 38 (1997), p. 266.

49. Marshall Sahlins, *Islands of History* (Chicago: University of Chicago Press, 1985), pp. 4–5.

50. Gananath Obeyesekere, "How to Write a Cook Book: Mythic and Other Realities in Anthropological Writing," *Pacific Studies*, 17 (2) (1994), p. 148.

51. Sahlins, *Historical Metaphors*, pp. 17, 34.

52. Ibid., p. 74, n. 8.

53. Judge Schreber's case is only too well known; for Max Weber, I refer to Athur Mitzman, *The Iron Cage: A Historical Interpretation of Max Weber* (New York: Grosset and Dunlap, 1971); and for Wittgenstein, Ray Monk, *Ludwig Wittgenstein: The Duty of Genius* (London: Vintage Books, 1991).

54. I refer especially to the work of Haunani Kay Trask and Lilikalā Kame'eleihiwa.

55. Obeyesekere, *The Work of Culture*, p. 89.

56. See Gananath Obeyesekere, *Medusa's Hair: An Essay in Personal Symbols and Religious Experience* (Chicago: University of Chicago Press, 1981), pp. 76–83; and lecture 3, "The Parricide in Buddhist History" in *The Work of Culture*, pp. 143–88.

57. Obeyesekere, *The Work of Culture*, pp. 89–105.

58. Ibid., pp. 101–4; for another strong antirelativist argument, see Melford E. Spiro, "Some Reflections on Cultural Determinism and Relativism with Special Reference to Emotion and Reason," in *Essays on Mind Self and Emotion*, Richard A. Shweder and Robert A. LeVine, eds. (Cambridge: Cambridge University Press, 1984), pp. 323–46; "Cultural Relativism and the Future of Anthropology," *Cultural Anthropology* 1 (1986): 259–86.

59. Gananath Obeyesekere, "Cannibal Feasts in Nineteenth-Century Fiji: Seamen's Yarns and the Ethnographic Imagination," in *Cannibalism and the Colonial World*, Francis Barker, Peter Hulme, and Margeret Iverson, eds. (Cambridge: Cambridge University Press, forthcoming).

60. I cannot see how he reconciles this assertion with his own idea of the "structure of the conjuncture" of his previous work.

61. Howe, "Review Article: The Making of Cook's Death," *The Journal of Pacific History* 31 (1) (1996), p. 116.

62. Sahlins, *Islands of History*, pp. 62, 164.

63. The phrase is James Trevenen's; cited in Howe, "The Making of Cook's Death," p. 116; see A, p. 43, for the full quotation.

64. Marshall Sahlins, "Cannibalism: An Exchange," *New York Review of Books*, March 22, 1979, 46–47.

65. For a detailed analysis of this issue, see the papers in Barker, Hulme, and Iverson, *Cannibalism and the Colonial World*.

66. Valeri, review, p. 130.

67. Ibid., p. 131.

68. John Charlot, "The Use of Akua for Living Chiefs," Appendix 1, in *The Hawai'ian Poetry of Religion and Politics*, The Institute for Polynesian Studies, Monograph Series, no. 5 (Honolulu: University of Hawai'i Press, 1985), pp. 31–35.

69. Sahlins, *Islands of History*, p. 74.

70. Ben Finney et al., *Voyage of Rediscovery: A Cultural Odyssey through Polynesia* (Berkeley and Los Angeles: University of California Press, 1994).

71. Ibid., p. 317.

72. Malo, *Hawai'ian Antiquities*, pp. 6–7.

73. Ibid., p. 61.

74. S. M. Kamakau, *Ruling Chiefs of Hawai'i*, (rev. ed.), (Honolulu: The Kamehameha Schools Press, 1992), p. 105.

75. Ibid., p. 204.

76. Malo, *Hawai'ian Antiquities*, pp. 22, 43.

77. Cook (B) 3a, p. cciii.

78. Malo, *Hawai'ian Antiquities*, pp. 65, 74.

79. Cook (B) 3b, p. 1204. Sahlins other reference is Trevenen: "Notwithstanding our state of hostility the women swam off to the ships every night" (N, 245). Unfortunately, this account was scribbled much later in 1784 on the official account of the voyage, and it does not indicate any numbers. I have given an estimate of these numbers as far as the *Discovery* is concerned in A, pp. 270–71, n. 54.

80. Regarding the burning houses, Sahlins once again engages in his outrageous mythopraxis. He ignores the burning of the temple and instead says that the British "in the attack in Kealakekua of 17 February, after Cook's death, burned the houses *between* the cliff and the temple" (N, p. 266, Sahlins's italics). Here is Samwell's observation of that day's violence in Cook (B) 3b, p. 1211: "At three o'Clock our people began to set the Town of Kerag-egooa [Kealakekua] on fire at the Corner close to the Well, and all the Houses, about 50 or 60 in number, from thence to Ohekeaw [Hikiau] were soon in a blaze; they were proceeding further but Orders were sent from the ship for them to desist. One Circumstance hurt us all very much, which was

that the House of Kaireekea [Keli'ikea] the Priest was burnt down with the rest and *all the sacred Buildings and Images about it"* (my italics). Having ignored the burning of the temple Sahlins justifies another burning in terms of mythopraxis. This is a reference to the two houses at Hikiau given over to the British for their use that were, according to both Burney and King, burned accidentally by the Hawai'ians themselves while looking for things the British might have left behind (Cook [B] 3a, p. 520). Ledyard thinks that, owing to the firewood incident, the Hawai'ians deliberately set fire to these two houses, which Sahlins thinks is "manifestly incorrect" (N, p. 266). Instead, he thinks here were Hawai'ians burning these buildings as a part of the ritual dismantling of the shrine! Needless to say, no Hawai'ian source mentions that burning buildings near Hikiau was part of the ritual dismantling during Makahiki.

81. Cook (B) 2, p. 257.
82. Ibid., pp. 365–66.
83. Tewsley, *Zimmermann's Third Voyage*, p. 37.
84. Peter Puget, *Log* Adm 55/17, Public Records Office, London, entry for 26 February 1793. For details, see A, pp. 113–14.
85. This structural opposition between Lono priests and the king and his chiefs is central to Sahlins's argument; see, for example, N, pp. 66–67, 70–72, 241–43.
86. For Omiah's hostility to the British, see A, pp. 108–9, 186, including n. 34.
87. Tewsley, *Zimmermann's Third Voyage*, p. 37; J. C. Beaglehole, *The Life of Captain James Cook* (London, The Hakluyt Society, 1974), p. 655.
88. Malo, *Hawai'ian Antiquities*, p. 151.
89. Valerio Valeri, *Kingship and Sacrifice: Ritual and Society in Ancient Hawaii* (Chicago: University of Chicago Press, 1985), pp. 224–25.
90. Sahlins says that because Hawai'ian deities were "ridiculed" on occasion, they were not "sacred," once again doing what I am supposed to have done; namely, imposing Western notions of the "sacred" on Hawai'i. Actually, even in the West it is a mistake to think that God, Jesus, and Mary were always treated with reverence—witness the many disrespectful ways in which they are treated in swear words, ditties, and so forth.
91. Michael Ondaatje, *The English Patient* (London: Picador, 1993), p. 93, author's italics.
92. Cook (B) 3a, pp. cci (my italics).
93. Ibid., p. cciii.
94. Ibid., p. cci.
95. John Marra, *Journal of the Resolutions' Voyage in 1772, 1773, 1774, and 1775* (London, 1775), pp. 183–86.
96. Cook (B) 2, p. 398.
97. Rickman, *Cook's Last Voyage*, pp. 166–67.
98. Michael E. Hoare, ed., *The Resolution Journal of Johann Reinhold Forster 1772–1775*, vol. 2 (London: The Hakluyt Society, 1982), p. 364.
99. Cook (B) 3b, p. 1100.
100. Sahlins, *Historical Metaphors*, p. 7.
101. Having ambushed and killed many Frenchmen, the Maoris taunted the French from a distance, exultantly wearing Marion's velvet waistcost, holding his gun, and displaying his silver pistols while others wore the uniforms of the officers they had

killed. See Robert McNab, *Historical Records of New Zealand*, vol. 2 (Wellington: Government Printer, 1914), p. 423.

102. Sahlins, "Captain James Cook; The Dying God" in *Islands of History*, pp. 104–35.

APPENDIX I

1. Cook (B) 3b, p. 1464.
2. This is from John Law's logs at the Public Records Office, London.
3. Cook (B) 2, pp. 217, 220, 231.
4. This was not recorded by Cook, but midshipman Martin noted it. See Cook (B) 3a, p. 274, n. 4.
5. John Rickman, *Journal of Captain Cook's Last Voyage to the Pacific* (London, 1781), p. 307, rpt. Readex Microprint, 1966.
6. Cook (B) 3a, p. 517.
7. Cook (D) 3, p. 24.
8. Cook (B) 3a, p. 517.
9. Cook (B), 3b, p. 1172.
10. James Kenneth Munford, ed., *John Ledyard's Journal of Captain Cook's Last Voyage* (Corvallis: Oregon State University Press, 1963), p. 124.
11. Cook (B) 3a, p. 517.
12. Munford, ed., *Ledyard's Journal*, p. 124.
13. Ibid.

APPENDIX II

1. John Charlot, "The Use of Akua for Living Chiefs," in his *The Hawaiian Poetry of Religion and Politics* The Institute for Polynesian Studies, Monograph Series no. 5 (Honolulu: University of Hawaii Press, 1985), pp. 31–35.
2. See the recent paper by Valerio Valeri, "Diarchy and History in Hawaii and Tonga," in *Culture and History in the Pacific*, edited by Jukka Sikala (Helsinki: The Finnish Anthropological Society, 1990), pp. 45–79.
3. See p. 86 of this book.
4. Charlot, "The Use of *Akua*," p. 31.
5. Ibid., p. 5.
6. Na Kamakau o Kaawaloa, "Concerning Ancient Religious Ceremonies," in Abraham Fornander, *Fornander Collection of Hawaiian Antiquities and Folklore*, Memoirs of the Bernice Pauahi Bishop Museum (Honolulu: Bishop Museum Press, 1919), vol. 6, part 1, pp. 42–44.
7. Glynn Barratt, *The Russian Discovery of Hawaii* (Honolulu: Editions Limited, 1987), p. 41.
8. Peter Corney, *Voyages in the Northern Pacific . . .* (Honolulu: Thomas G. Thrum, 1896), p. 101.

BIBLIOGRAPHY

—————————————— ✲✲ ——————————————

Anzieu, Didier. *Freud's Self-Analysis*. London: Hogarth Press, 1986.

Bakhtin, M. M. *Speech Genres and Other Late Essays*. Austin: University of Texas Press, 1986.

Banfield, Edward C. *The Moral Basis of a Backward Society*. Glencoe, Ill.: The Free Press, 1952.

Barratt, Glynn. *The Russian Discovery of Hawaii*. Honolulu: Editions Limited, 1987.

Barrère, Dorothy B. *Kamehameha in Kona: Two Documentary Studies*. Pacific Anthropological Records No. 23. Honolulu: Bishop Museum, Department of Anthropology, 1975.

Bayly, William. *Log* Adm 55/20. Public Records Office, London.

Beaglehole, J. C. "On the Character of Captain James Cook." *The Geographical Journal* 122, 4 (1956), pp. 417–29.

Beaglehole, J. C. *The Discovery of New Zealand*. London: Oxford University Press, 1961.

Beaglehole, J. C. *The Life of Captain James Cook*. London: The Hakluyt Society, 1974.

Beckwith, Martha. *Hawaiian Mythology*. New Haven: Yale University Press, 1940.

Beckwith, Martha. *The Kumulipo, a Hawaiian Creation Chant*, Honolulu: University of Hawaii Press, 1972.

Bell, Edward. "Log of the Chatham." *The Honolulu Mercury* 1, 6 (November 1929), pp. 76–90.

Bergendorff, Steen, Ulla Hasager, and Peter Henriques. "Mythopraxis and History: On the Interpretation of the Makahiki." *Journal of the Polynesian Society* 97, pp. 391–408.

Bettleheim, Bruno. *Symbolic Wounds: Puberty Rites and the Envious Male*. New York: Collier Books, 1971.

Bingham, Hiram. *A Residence of Twenty-One Years in the Sandwich Islands* ... 3d edition. New York, 1855.

Bloxam, Andrew. *Diary of Andrew Bloxam Naturalist of the "Blonde."* Honolulu: Bishop Museum Special Publication No. 10, 1925.

Boon, James. *Affinities and Extremes*. Chicago: University of Chicago Press, 1990.

Buck, Sir Peter (Te Rangi Hiroa). "Cook's Discovery of the Hawaiian Islands." In *Report of the Director for 1944, Bishop Museum Bulletin 186*. Honolulu, 1945.

Burney, Fanny. *Diary and Letters of Madame D'Arblay Vol. 1, 1778–1781*. London: Macmillan and Company, 1904.

Campbell, Archibald. *A Voyage round the World from 1806 to 1812 ... with an Account of the ... Sandwich Islands*. Honolulu: University of Hawaii Press, 1967.

Carruthers, Joseph. *Captain James Cook, R.N.: One Hundred and Fifty Years After*. New York: Dutton and Company, 1930.

Carter, Paul. *The Road to Botany Bay: An Exploration of Landscape and History*. Chicago: University of Chicago Press, 1989.

Chamisso, Adelbert von. *A Voyage around the World in the Romanzov Exploring Expedition ... 1815–1818*. Translated and edited by Henry Kratz. Honolulu: University of Hawaii Press, 1986 [1836].

Charlot, John. *The Hawaiian Poetry of Religion and Politics*. The Institute for Polynesian Studies, Monograph Series no. 5. Honolulu: University of Hawaii Press, 1985.

Charlot, John. "Valerio Valeri, *Kingship and Sacrifice: Ritual and Society in Ancient Hawaii*" [Review]. *Pacific Studies* 10, 2 (1987), pp. 107–47.

Charlot, John. "The Feather Skirt of Nahi'ena'ena." In *Journal of the Polynesian Society*. Forthcoming.

Clarke, Thomas Blake. *Omai, First Polynesian Ambassador to England*. 1940, Rpt. Honolulu: University of Hawaii Press, 1969.

Clendinnen, Inga. "'Fierce and Unnatural Cruelty': Cortés and the Conquest of Mexico." *Representations* 33 (Winter 1991), pp. 65–100.

Clifford, Diana M. *Lokoi'ao Hawai'i. Ancient Hawaiian Fishponds and Their Changing Role in Society*. Senior Thesis, Princeton University, 1991.

Colnett, James. *The Journal of James Colnett*. Toronto: The Champlain Society, 1940.

Cook, James. *The Journals of Captain James Cook. The Voyage of the* Endeavor. Edited by J. C. Beaglehole. London: The Hakluyt Society, 1968. I abbreviate this as Cook (B) 1.

Cook, James. *The Journals of Captain James Cook. The Voyage of the* Resolution *and* Adventure. Edited by J. C. Beaglehole. London: The Hakluyt Society, 1969. I abbreviate this as Cook (B) 2.

Cook, James. *The Journal of Captain James Cook. The voyage of the* Resolution *and* Discovery. Edited by J. C. Beaglehole. 2 vols. London: The Hakluyt Society, 1967. I abbreviate these as Cook (B) 3a and 3b. These two volumes also contain the journals of Samwell and King and excerpts from other journalists.

Cook, James. *A Voyage to the Pacific Ocean. Undertaken by the Command of His Majesty*. Edited by John Douglas, vols. 1 and 2. 1784. This edition is abbreviated as Cook (D) 1 or 2.

Corney, Peter. *Voyages in the Northern Pacific* ... Honolulu: Thomas G. Thrum, 1896.

Cowper, William. *The Works of William Cowper: His Life, Letters, and Poems*. Edited by Rev. T. S. Grimshawe. Boston, 1854.

Dampier, Robert. *To the Sandwich Islands on H.M.S. Blonde*. Edited by Pauline King Joerger. Honolulu: The University of Hawaii Press, 1971.

Dening, Greg. *Islands and Beaches*. Honolulu: University of Hawaii Press, 1980.

Dening, Greg. "Possessing Tahiti." *Archaeology and Physical Anthropology in Oceania* 21, (1986), pp. 103–118.

Dening, Greg. *The Bounty: An Ethnographic History*. Melbourne: University of Melbourne History Department Monograph Series #1, 1988.

Dibble, Sheldon. *A History of the Sandwich Islands.* Honolulu: Thomas G. Thrum, 1909.

Dixon, George. *A Voyage round the World . . . Performed in 1785, 1786, 1787 and 1788* (London, 1789).

Douglas, James (Lord Morton). "Hints Offered to the Consideration of Captain Cooke, Mr. Bankes, Doctor Solander, and the Other Gentlemen Who Go upon the Expedition on Board the *Endeavour.*" In Cook, *The Journals of Captain James Cook. The Voyage of the* Endeavor. Edited by J. C. Beaglehole. London: The Hakluyt Society, 1968, pp. 514–19.

Dutton, Tom. "Successful Intercourse Was Had with the Natives: Aspects of European Contact Methods in the Pacific." In *A World of Language: Papers Presented to Professor S. A. Wurm on his 65th Birthday,* edited by Donald C. Laycock and Werner Winter. Canberra: Department of Linguistics, Research School of Pacific Studies, Australian National University, 1987, pp. 153–71.

Edgar, Thomas. *The Edgar Journal of Captain Cook's Third Voyage 1776–1778.* Adm. 55/21. Public Records Office ms., London.

Ellis, William. *An Authentic Narrative of a Voyage . . . Performed by Captain Cook and Captain Clerke . . . ,* vol. 2. (London, 1782; rpt. New York: Da Capo Press, 1969).

Ellis, William. *Polynesian Researches, during a Residence of Nearly Eight Years in the Society and Sandwich Islands,* vol. 4. London, 1831.

Ellis, William. *Narrative of a Tour through Hawaii.* London, 1928.

Ellis, William. *Journal of William Ellis. A Narrative of a Tour through Owhyhee. . . .* Rutland and Tokyo: Charles Tuttle, 1979.

Emerson, N. B. *The Long Voyages of the Ancient Hawaiians.* Hawaiian Historical Society Papers No. 5.

Fisher, Robin, and Hugh Johnston, eds. *Captain James Cook and His Times.* Seattle: University of Washington Press, 1979.

Fornander, Abraham. *An Account of the Polynesian Races . . . ,* 3 vols. in 1. 1878–80. Rpt. Rutland, Vermont, and Tokyo: Charles Tuttle, 1980.

Fornander, Abraham. *Fornander Collection of Hawaiian Antiquities and Folklore.* Memoirs of the Bernice Pauahi Bishop Museum, vols. 4–6. Honolulu: Bishop Museum Press, 1920, vol. 6, part 3.

Forster, George. *A Voyage round the World in his Brittanic Majesty's Sloop, Resolution . . . ,* 2 vols. London, 1777.

Forster, Johann Reinhold. *Observations Made during a Voyage round the World. . . .* London, 1778.

Freycinet, Louis de. *Hawaii in 1819: A Narrative Account by Louis Claude de Saulses de Freycinet,* chs. 27, 28. Translated by Ella L. Wiswell. Honolulu: Bishop Museum, Department of Anthropology, Pacific Records No. 26, 1978.

Geertz, Clifford. "Religion as a Cultural System." In his *The Interpretation of Cultures.* New York: Basic Books, 1973, pp. 87–125.

Geertz, Clifford. "Common Sense as a Cultural System." In his *Local Knowledge.* New York: Basic Books, 1983, pp. 73–93.

Gilbert, George. *Captain Cook's Final Voyage. The Journal of Midshipman George*

Gilbert. Edited by Christine Holmes. Honolulu: University of Hawaii Press, 1982.

Golovnin, V. M. *Around the World on the KAMCHATKA 1817–1819.* Translated with introduction and notes by Ella Lury Wiswell. Honolulu: The Hawaiian Historical Society and University of Hawaii Press, 1979 [1822].

Gould, Rupert T. "Bligh's Notes on Cook's Last Voyage." *The Mariner's Mirror* 14 (October 1928), pp. 371–85.

Gould, Rupert T. "Some Unpublished Accounts of Cook's Death," *The Mariner's Mirror* 14 (1928), pp. 301–19.

Graham, Maria, comp. *Voyage of the H.M.S. Blonde to the Sandwich Islands in the Years 1824–25.* London: John Murray, 1826.

Guṇasékara, B., ed. *Rājāvaliya. The Rājāvaliya or A Historical Narrative of Sinhalese Kings.* Colombo: Government Press, 1900.

Hawkesworth, John. *An Account of the Voyages Undertaken by His Present Majesty for Making Discoveries in the Southern Hemisphere. . . .* 3 vols. London, 1773.

Hoare, Michael E. *The Tactless Philosopher: Johann Reinhold Forster (1729–98).* Melbourne: Hawthorn Press, 1976.

Hoare, Michael E., ed. *The Resolution Journal of Johann Reinhold Forster 1772–1775,* 4 vols. London: The Hakluyt Society, 1982.

Hollis, Martin, and Steven Lukes, eds. *Relativism and Rationality.* Cambridge, Mass.: M.I.T. Press, 1984.

Hough, Richard. *The Last Voyage of Captain James Cook.* New York: William Morrow, 1979.

I'i, John Papa. *Fragments of Hawaiian History.* Translated by Mary K. Pukui. Honolulu: Bishop Museum Press, 1983.

Jarves, James Jackson. *History of the Hawaiian or Sandwich Islands. . . .* Boston, 1843.

Joppien, R. "Philippe Jacques de Loutherbourg's Pantomime 'Omai, or, A Trip round the World' and the Artists of Cook's Voyages." In *Captain Cook and the South Pacific.* London: British Museum Yearbook 3, 1979, pp. 81–136.

Joppien, R., and B. Smith. *The Art of Captain Cook's Voyages. The Voyage of the Resolution and Discovery 1776–1786,* part 1. New Haven and London: Yale University Press, 1988.

Kahananui, Dorothy M., ed. *Ka Mooolelo Hawaii, Hawaiian Language Reader Based on Sheldon Dibble, Ka Mooolelo Hawaii.* Honolulu: University of Hawaii Press, 1984.

Kamakau, S. M. *Ruling Chiefs of Hawaii.* Honolulu: The Kamehameha Schools Press, 1961.

Kamakau, S. M. *Ka Po'e Kahiko, the People of Old.* Translated by Mary K. Pukui. Edited by Dorothy B. Barrère. Honolulu: Bishop Museum Press, 1964.

Kamakau of Ka'awaloa (Kelou Kamakau). "Concerning Ancient Religious Ceremonies." In Abraham Fornander, *Fornander Collection of Hawaiian Antiquities and Folklore.* Memoirs of the Bernice Pauahi Bishop Museum, vol. 6, part 1. Honolulu: Bishop Museum Press, 1919, pp. 2–45.

Kennedy, Gavin. *The Death of Captain Cook.* London: Duckworth, 1978.

King, James, and John Douglas, eds. *A Voyage to the Pacific Ocean.* vol. 3. London, 1784. This edition is abbreviated as Cook (D) 3.

BIBLIOGRAPHY

Kippis, A. *A Narrative of the Voyages ... Performed by Captain James Cook. . . .* Boston, 1830.

Kotzebue, Otto Von. *A New Voyage round the World in the Years 1823–1826*, 2 vols. 1830, Rrt. New York: Da Capo Press, 1967.

Kotzebue, Otto Von. *A Voyage of Discovery into the South Sea and Beering's Straits*, 3 vols. 1821. Rpt. New York: Da Capo Press, 1967.

Kuykendall, Ralph S. *The Hawaiian Kingdom 1778–1854: Foundation and Transformation.* Honolulu: University of Hawaii Press, 1938.

Law, John. British Library ms. 37327. Entry for 2 February 1779.

Lévi-Strauss, Claude. "The Structural Study of Myth." In *Structural Anthropology.* New York: Basic Books, 1963.

Lévi-Strauss, Claude. *The Savage Mind.* Chicago: University of Chicago Press, 1966.

Lévy-Bruhl, Lucien. *How Natives Think.* Translated by Lilian A. Clare. Princeton: Princeton University Press, 1985.

Lewis, J. P. "Journal of a Tour to Candia in the Year 1796." *Journal of the Royal Asiatic Society*, Ceylon Branch, vol. 26, no. 70 (1917), pp. 49–100, 113–33, 115–55, 172–237.

Lewthwaite, Gordon R. "The Puzzle of Tupaia's Map." *New Zealand Geographer* 26 (1976), pp. 1–19.

Lisiansky, Urey. *A Voyage round the World in the Years 1803, 4, 5 and 6.* London, 1814.

Little, George. *Life on the Ocean; or, Twenty Years at Sea. . . .* 12th ed. Boston, 1846.

Luomala, Katherine. "Polynesian Religious Foundations of Hawaiian Concepts Regarding Wellness and Illness." In *Healing and Restoring: Health and Medicine in the World's Religious Traditions*, edited by Lawrence E. Sullivan. New York: Macmillan, 1989, pp. 287–326.

Mackay, David. "The New Zealand Legacy of James Cook." Paper delivered at *The New Zealand Universities Graduates Association*, 1990, 17 pp. Typescript.

Malo, David. *Hawaiian Antiquities*, 2d edition. Translated by Nathaniel B. Emerson. Honolulu: Bishop Museum Press, 1951.

Manby, Thomas. "Journal of Vancouver's Voyage to the Pacific Ocean (1791–1793)." *The Honolulu Mercury* 1, 2 (July 1929), pp. 33–45.

Marra, John. *Journal of the Resolutions Voyage. . . .* London, 1775.

Martin, John. *An Account of the Natives of the Tonga Islands . . . Communications of Mr. William Mariner*, vol. 2. London, 1817.

Mathison, Gilbert F. *Narrative of a Visit to Brazil, Chile, Peru and the Sandwich Islands. . . .* London, 1825.

McNab, Robert. *From Tasman to Marsden.* Dunedin, 1914.

McNab, Robert. *Historical Records of New Zealand*, vol. 2. Wellington: Government Printer, 1914.

Meares, John. *Voyages Made in the Years 1788 and 1789. . . .* London, 1790; rpt. New York: Da Capo Press, 1967.

Moorehead, Alan. *The Fatal Impact: An Account of the Invasion of the South Pacific 1767–1840.* London, Hamish Hamilton, 1966.

Munford, James Kenneth, ed. *John Ledyard's Journal of Captain Cook's Last Voyage.* Corvallis: Oregon State University Press, 1963.

Needham, Rodney, ed. *Imagination and Proof, Selected Essays of A. M. Hocart.* Tucson: The University of Arizona Press, 1987.

Obeyesekere, Gananath. *The Work of Culture: Symbolic Transformation in Psychoanalysis and Anthropology.* Chicago: University of Chicago Press, 1990.

Obeyesekere, Gananath. "British Cannibals: Contemplation of an Event in the Death and Resurrection of James Cook, Explorer." In *Identities,* special issue of *Critical Inquiry* (June 1992), ed. Henry Louis Gates, Jr., and Anthony Appiah.

O'Brian, Patrick. *Joseph Banks, a Life.* London: Collins Harvill, 1988.

Oliver, Douglas L. *The Pacific Islands.* 3d ed. Honolulu: University of Hawaii Press, 1989.

Puget, Peter. British Museum Library ms. Add. 17546.

Puget, Peter. *Log* Adm 55/17. Public Records Office, London. Entry for 26 February 1793.

Pukui, Mary Kawena, E. W. Haertig, and Catherine A. Lee. *Nānā I Ke Kumu,* vol. 1. Honolulu: Hui Hanai, 1972.

Radcliffe-Brown, A. R. *Structure and Function in Primitive Society.* New York: The Free Press, 1965.

Rickman, John. *Journal of Captain Cook's Last Voyage to the Pacific Ocean.* London, 1781; rpt. Readex Microprint, 1966.

Rickman, John. *Log* Adm 51/4529/46 Public Records Office, London.

Roberts, Michael. "A Tale of Resistance: The Story of the Arrival of the Portuguese in Sri Lanka." *Ethnos* 55, 1–2, pp. 69–82.

Robertson, George. *The Discovery of Tahiti.* London: The Hakluyt Society, 1948.

Roth, Guenther, and Claus Wittich, eds. *Max Weber, Economy and Society,* vol. 1. New York: Bedminster Press, 1968.

Roth, Guenther, and Wolfgang Schluchter. *Max Weber's Theory of History.* Berkeley and Los Angeles: University of California Press, 1979.

Sahlins, Marshall. "The Apotheosis of Captain Cook." In *Between Belief and Transgression: Structuralist Essays in Religion, History and Myth,* edited by Michael Izard and Pierre Smith. Chicago: University of Chicago Press, 1982.

Sahlins, Marshall. "Captain Cook in Hawaii." *Journal of the Polynesian Society* 98, 4 (December 1989), pp. 371–423.

Sahlins, Marshall. *Culture and Practical Reason.* Chicago: University of Chicago Press, 1974.

Sahlins, Marshall. *Historical Metaphors and Mythical Realities: Structure in the Early History of the Sandwich Islands Kingdom.* Ann Arbor: University of Michigan Press, 1981.

Sahlins, Marshall. *Islands of History.* Chicago: University of Chicago Press, 1985.

Samwell, David. *Captain Cook and Hawaii.* 1976. Rpt. San Francisco: David Magee, 1957.

Searle, John R. *Expression and Meaning: Studies in the Theory of Speech Acts.* Cambridge: Cambridge University Press, 1985.

Seaton, S. Lee. "The Hawaiian *Kapu* Abolition of 1819." *American Ethnologist* 1, 1 (1974), pp. 193–206.

A Short Account of the New Pantomime Called OMAI. . . . London: T. CADELL in the Strand, 1785.

Shweder, Richard. "On Savages and Other Children." *American Anthropologist* 84 (1982), pp. 354–66.

Sinclair, Keith. *History of New Zealand.* London: Penguin, 1969.

Skelton, R. A. *Captain James Cook: After Two Hundred Years.* London: The Hakluyt Society, 1969.

Smith, Bernard. *European Vision and the South Pacific.* New Haven and London: Yale University Press, 1985.

Spotts, Frederic, ed. *Letters of Leonard Woolf.* London: Weidenfeld and Nicolson, 1989.

Stannard, David E. *Before the Horror: The Population of Hawaii on the Eve of Western Contact.* Honolulu: University of Hawaii Press, 1989.

Stokes, John F. G. "Origin of the Condemnation of Captain Cook in Hawaii." *Hawaiian Historical Society 39th Annual Report* (Honolulu, 1930), pp. 68–104.

Tewsley, U., trans., *Zimmermann's Third Voyage of Captain Cook 1776–1780.* Wellington, 1926.

Thrum, Thomas G. "The Paehumu of Heiaus Non-Sacred." *Hawaiian Historical Society 35th Annual Report* (Honolulu, 1926), pp. 56–57.

Todorov, Tzvetan. *The Conquest of America: The Question of the Other.* Translated by Richard Howard. New York: Harper Torchbooks, 1987.

Trevenen, James. *Penrose Memoirs of James Trevenen.* Greenwich Maritime Museum ms.

Turner, Victor. "Betwixt and Between: The Liminal Period in *Rites de Passage.*" In *The Forest of Symbols.* Ithaca: Cornell University Press, 1967.

Valeri, Valerio. *Kingship and Sacrifice: Ritual and Society in Ancient Hawaii.* Chicago: University of Chicago Press, 1985.

Valeri, Valerio. "Diarchy and History in Hawaii and Tonga." In *Culture and History in the Pacific,* edited by Jukka Siikala. Helsinki: The Finnish Anthropological Society, 1990, pp. 45–79.

Vancouver, George. *The Voyage of George Vancouver, 1791–1795.* Edited by W. Kaye Lamb. 4 vols. London: The Hakluyt Society, 1984.

Van Orman, Richard A. *The Explorers.* Albuquerque: University of New Mexico Press, 1984.

Varigny, Charles de. *Fourteen Years in the Sandwich Islands 1855–1868.* Honolulu: University of Hawaii Press, 1981.

Wales, William. *Remarks on Mr. Forster's Account of Captain Cook's Last Voyage.* London, 1777.

Weber, Max. "Social Psychology of the World Religions." In *From Max Weber,* edited by Hans Gerth and C. Wright Mills. New York: Oxford University Press, 1976.

Westervelt, W. D. *Hawaiian Historical Legends.* New York: Fleming H. Revell Company, 1926.

Williamson, James A. *Cook and the Opening of the Pacific.* New York: Macmillan, 1948.

Wilson, Bryan, ed. *Rationality.* Oxford: Blackwell, 1970.

Withey, Lynne. *Voyages of Discovery: Captain Cook and the Exploration of the Pacific.* Berkeley and Los Angeles: University of California Press, 1989.

BIBLIOGRAPHY

Wooley, Richard. "The Significance of the Transit of Venus." In *Captain Cook, Navigator and Scientist*, edited by G. M. Badger. London: C. Hurst, 1970.

Wright, Harrison M. *New Zealand. 1769–1840: Early Years of Western Contact*, Cambridge: Harvard University Press, 1959.

INDEX

❦❧

Akua (god), 140, 141, 143, 255–56, 283n.60
Alcohol addiction, 157
American settlers, 147
Anderson, William (ship surgeon), 29, 34, 35, 66–67; death of, 43
Anthropology. *See* Ethnography
Apotheosis: of Columbus, 8, 123, 143; of Cortés, 8, 123–4, 130
Apotheosis of Captain Cook, The (painting), 129–30, 131f.
Apotheosis of Cook. *See* Cook, James Captain; Cook-Lono myth; European myths; Kāli'i rite; Makahiki festival
Aztecs, 8, 16–19, 262n.41

Bakhtin, M. M., 19, 68, 175
Banfield, Edward C., 263n.4
Banks, Joseph Sir (naturalist), 5, 14, 15
Barrère, Dorothy B., 74, 158, 163, 181
Bayly, William (astronomer), 30, 51, 71, 86, 272n.66
Beaglehole, J. C., 3, 9, 25, 108, 122, 133, 154; on Cook, 23, 25, 42, 44, 50, 96, 133
Beckwith, Martha, 77, 82, 140
Bell, Edward (ship clerk), 151
Berkh, V. N., 149
Bettleheim, Bruno, 189
Billy Pitt. *See* Kalaimoku
Bingham, Hiram (missionary), 51, 143, 144, 152, 161–62
Biography, 3, 10, 60, 283–84n.62. *See also* Myth; Myth models
Bligh, William (Master), 50, 112, 279n.37, 284n.76, 290n.12
Bloxman, Andrew (naturalist), 146
Bones of Cook. *See under* Death of Cook
Boon, James, xv, 262n.45
Borabora (island), 39
Boswell, James, 23
Braudel, Fernand, 55

Buck, Peter Sir. *See* Te Rangi Hiroa
Buddha, Gautama, 11, 91, 140
Byron, John Captain, 151–52

Cannnibalism, 17–18, 138–39, 262n.45, 289n.41
Canoes, 158, 273n.2; Lono's triangular, 51, 53, 62f.
Captain Cook and His Times (Smith), 131–32
Carter, Paul, 12
Ceremonial prostration, 8–9, 32, 41, 64, 75, 76, 94, 120–21
Chamisso, Adelbert von, 142–43, 285n.84
Charlot, John, xv, 61, 141, 268n.141
Chiefs: apparel of, 84, 288n.15; ceremonial respect toward, 9, 32, 41, 76; flogging of, 29–30; and installation rites, 76, 84, 87–88, 121; named for deities, 76–77, 85, 96–97; relations with Cook, 27, 29, 32–34, 35–36, 47, 81–82, 88, 102, 107–11, 178–83. *See also under individual names*
Christianity, 96, 139, 145, 148, 181, 187; Lahainaluna seminary, 154, 157, 162, 164; missionaries, 144, 155, 161
Circumnavigation, of Hawaiian islands, 43, 45, 64, 78
Civilization, paradox of, 13–14
Clendinnen, Inga, 262n.44
Clerke, Charles Captain, 26, 29, 106, 110, 118, 120; actions following Cook's death, 112, 187–89; character of, 29; relations with natives, 76, 87–88, 167. See also *Discovery*
Clifford, Diana, 263n.49
Colnett, James, 140–41
Columbus, Christopher, apotheosis of, 8, 123, 143
Conflicts: European-Hawaiian, 105–6, 111–12, 156; European-Polynesian, 6, 13, 27, 29–31
Conquest of America, The (Todorov), 16–18

INDEX

Ka-maka-helei, Chiefess (Hawaiian), 165–66

Kamakau of Ka'awaloa (Kelou Kamakau), 49, 198

Kamakau, S. M., 50, 59, 98, 168, 171, 198; Christianity of, 154, 163–64; on Cook, 163–70; on Hawaiian religion, 140–41, 149–50

Kamehameha I, King of Hawai'i, 19–20, 47, 74–75, 95, 98, 102, 198; death of, 143; and Lono cult, 95, 148–51; reforms of, 95, 98–99, 148–49, 154, 157, 160

Kamehameha II. See Liholiho

Kamehamehanui, Chief (Maui), 78–79

Kanaloa, Hawaiian deity, 82, 170, 290n.14

Kāne, Hawaiian deity, 82, 170, 290n.14

Kaneena, Chief (Hawai'i), 167

Kaneikapolei, wife of Kalani'opu'u, 110, 178, 181

Kao (chief priest), 46–47, 79, 92, 93f., 116; genealogy of, 92–93, 277n.93

Kapu. See Tabu

Kapu moe, 75, 76, 126. See also Ceremonial prostration

Kar'na'cub'ra. See Kaneikapolei

Kaua'i, 40–41, 43, 71–72, 79, 95, 98

Kealakekua Bay: final return to, 102–3; landing and ceremony at, xiii, 49–51, 80, 172, 289n.56; Lono priests at, 51, 92; tabu on, 88, 102

Keli'ikea (priest), 46, 51, 83–84, 92, 93f., 117, 189, 195

Kennedy, Gavin, 50–52

Kikinny. See Keli'ikea

King, James Lieutenant, 14, 27, 44, 45–46, 47, 65, 76, 104f., 113, 115–16, 121, 194; criticism of Cook, 38, 44; on death of Cook, 137–38, 144; distinction between official and unofficial journal, 124–25; on Hawaiians' perception of Europeans, 63–64, 76; official edition of journals, 68, 69, 92–93, 102–3, 113, 115–16, 125–26; on Omiah, 92, 94, 108–9; witnessing of temple rite, 51, 83–86

Kings: and divinity, 9, 52, 54, 86, 91, 197–99; exchange of names by chiefs and, 47, 84, 88, 210n.141. See also under individual names

Kippis, A., 124, 127, 128, 277n.93

Koah, priest, 46, 51, 65, 82–84, 102; genealogy, 92–93

Kotzebue, Otto von, 142–44

Kratz, Henry, 285n.84

Kū, 52–53, 57, 64, 82; decline of cult, 149; identification of Cook with, 65, 169; -ka'ili-moku, 79, 149; rites and images of, 53–54, 82–84, 86, 193; subservience of Cook to, 64, 84–86, 95, 119

Kuali'i, priestly order, 149. See also Lono, rites of

Kumulipo (ed. Beckwith), 181, 290n.14

Kurtz persona, 11–13, 23, 28, 45, 189

Kuykendall, Ralph S., 3, 156

Lahainaluna seminary, 154, 157, 162, 164

Language: games, 121, 155; native discourse, 155, 166, 173–75; of ship journalists, 120–22, 124–26; sign communication, 72–73; use of tropes, 173–75

Law, John (ship surgeon), 94, 118, 188, 277n.97

Ledyard, John Corporal, 67, 76, 77, 116–18, 194–96, 272n.78

Lévi-Strauss, Claude, 11, 15, 18, 19

Lévy-Bruhl, Lucien, 15

Lewin, Lord, Admiral of the Fleet, 133

Life of Captain James Cook (Beaglehole), 3, 133

Liholiho, King of Hawai'i, 141, 143, 145, 155–57, 287n.8; abolition of tabu by, 156–57, 287n.10

Lisianski, Iurii, 146, 147, 156, 198

Little, George, 73, 144

Lono: Hawaiian deity, 3, 20, 46, 76, 143; as Hawaiian name, 76–77, 85, 96–97, 149, 293n.1; -ika'ouali'i (Lononuiakea), 149; myth and iconography of, 50–51, 56, 58, 61, 62f., 86, 150–51; native beliefs about, 82, 94–95; priests of, 52, 149; rise of cult, 149–51; rites of, 74, 83, 86–87, 149; Sahlins on, 52–54; symbolic death of, 58; temple of, 86–87; as wandering god, 150

Lono-Cook. See Cook-Lono myth

Lono-i-ka-makahiki, Chief, 90, 96, 149, 154, 157, 170

Lono Kaeho, ancient chief of Kahiki, 96–97

Lono-Omiah. See Omiah (Pailiki)

Lono-Tuute. See Cook, James Captain

Loutherbourg, Jacques de, 129

Luakini. See Temple Hikiau

Luomala, Katherine, 190